A MOTLEY WISDOM

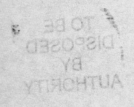

A Motley Wisdom

The Best of G. K. Chesterton

chosen and introduced by

NIGEL FORDE

Hodder & Stoughton
LONDON SYDNEY AUCKLAND

British Library Cataloguing in Publication Data
A record for this book is available from the British Library

ISBN 0 340 61228 2

Printed and bound in Great Britain by
Cox and Wyman Ltd, Reading, Berks

Hodder and Stoughton Ltd
A Division of Hodder Headline PLC
338 Euston Road
London NW1 3BH

For
Murray and Julie
who have the true Chestertonian virtues
of wit, wisdom and hospitality

Contents

Preface

IT IS NOT difficult to discover who steers the fashions and moulds the cast of the modern mind; who governs and shapes our imaginations and ambitions; and who it is that, on departure, leaves the unfillable gap. When film stars die there is the equivalent of a funeral with full military honours. An era is said to have passed; a great good has been taken from us. Contemporaries pay tribute, the work is evaluated and re-evaluated, a retrospective season of their films is mounted on television and sometimes dominates the schedules for week after week. It is a natural, and indeed praiseworthy, celebration of their talents.

But when a writer dies the consequences are often very different. A ten-minute obituary may be given on a late-night arts show – even an hour for a very great writer. But the books are not re-issued. If you are busy on the day, you might go for weeks without realizing that X is dead. The works are allowed to fade as quickly as the memory.

It happens to all writers. There is resurrection, of course, for the long dead who have attained the status of Classics: Milton, Jane Austen, Wordsworth, Hardy and, indeed, dozens of figures much less impressive who have been granted a kind of specious authority and importance by the mere passage of time. Worth, which should be measured by the scales, is measured by the clock. For few writers have managed to sustain an unblemished reputation if they were popular in the first half of this century. When did you last read – or even read *about* – Huxley, de la Mare, Henry Williamson, Nesbit, Powys, Charles Williams, Edwin Muir or Christopher Fry? Familiar in our mouths, perhaps, as household words, but literally and metaphorically a closed book to all but a few. All have their particular and unique excellences; and I dare predict that future critics will give them a new lease of life and we shall be condemned for neglecting them.

So let it be with G. K. Chesterton. In trawling the bookshops for his works I have heard many a variation on the remark that Chesterton seems to be undergoing something of a revival. I hope that is true; and, if it is, I hope this anthology of Chesterton's writings will add momentum to it. For it is the responsibility of a new generation to winnow the massive harvest of the past and find in it nourishment for the future. And it is not a light responsibility. We may never have had even such a massive figure as J. S. Bach had it not been for another composer, Mendelssohn, and, although I am not discovering GKC in the same way as Mendelssohn discovered Bach, my aim is to copy his method. He did not criticize, appraise, make judgments or apologies: he simply revealed. He played Bach and let the audience judge. I will not be able to avoid making some kind of appraisal for I am not offering whole books and what is omitted may sometimes need explanation. But the purpose of this volume is to let Chesterton speak for himself.

There are two problems with such a method. The first is that success will breed frustration. If Chesterton succeeds in interesting the reader in his mind or his matter, then that reader will want to get hold of the originals for which this book is only a kind of trailer. Scarcely any Chesterton is in print.

There have been some relatively recent Penguin editions of fiction such as *The Man Who was Thursday*, *The Club of Queer Trades*, *The Napoleon of Notting Hill* and some of the Father Brown stories; other books are virtually impossible to find. The Ignatius Press in New York has a plan to publish the complete works and, indeed, a start has already been made, but it is going to be a necessarily long process (see the list of Chesterton's works on p. 388) and it may well be hampered by changes in the laws of copyright. For the moment, Chesterton has to be run to earth in second-hand and antiquarian bookshops; a process not without its delights for the leisured and easier for the traveller, but not sure in its results. Still not all is gloom; Chesterton was a very popular writer in his time and his books were issued in great numbers and some frequently reprinted, so there *are* some around and, unless you want first editions in mint condition, they are not likely to be even as expensive as a new paperback.

The second problem is a literary one. The world that GKC knew has gone, and many of its good habits – as well as its bad – have gone with it. It was a world where any educated person was allowed a say and was listened to with respect. The expert – the man or woman of *training* rather than of education, the person who knows everything about something rather than something about everything, the person of deliberately limited vision or even, dare it be said, tunnel vision – had not yet appeared. It was an age of argument, discussion, debate which was carried on by professional and lay people alike. They argued about the things that mattered to them; they accepted one another's challenges and argued on, for even when deeply held personal beliefs were at stake – perhaps particularly then – personal attacks were avoided, with the result that respect for a worthy antagonist could easily mature into friendship.

Today there could well be truth in the retort 'You do not (or cannot) know what you are talking about.' Then, it would have been merely an insult. Men such as Chesterton's friend H. G. Wells could fully comprehend the whole of scientific knowledge and its implications; and, indeed, contribute to it albeit in a way we might find difficult to admire today. Physics, astronomy, biology, chemistry, even theology are no longer part of the educated person's mental wardrobe unless that person is a scientist or theologian. I do not expect to understand an article in *Nature* or *New Scientist*: Chesterton would have done. For him everything connected, everything spilled over into everything else.

Thus, when he wrote he grabbed illustrations from every discipline available to his intellect. They may not be so readily available to ours. He develops complex arguments over several chapters and though he is immensely witty and entertaining he writes in a gently-paced, spacious manner. Of course, one man's 'gently-paced and spacious' is another man's 'slow and long-winded' and it must be conceded that it is not necessarily an easy style for those of us brought up to believe that we have no right to trespass on another person's area of expertise, nor for those of us who have been numbed into shallow opinions by endless talking heads, or bullied into thinking in simplistic black-and-white by that nefarious innovation the soundbite. Such a style may take some getting used to, but it calls only for patience, not for hard work or application.

Because each chapter is so dependent on the previous chapters and the arguments are so carefully and logically assembled, it is tempting to edit Chesterton too closely and try to produce a précis of a whole book in his own words, keeping all one's favourite passages and all the brilliant asides. But this would be to ruin him. All his ideas would be retained but at the expense of the writing. And Chesterton would be the first to say that his ideas were interesting only to those who had forgotten them or had come to take them so much for granted that they could no longer see them for what they are. The man's distinctive flavour is in his mind and in the style that mind evolved. The two are inseparable and cannot be communicated by a digest.

I have allowed him to speak at length. At the beginning of the different sections each extract is placed in context if it needs to be and, where possible, by using Chesterton's own comments on his writing. Essays, poems and short stories are printed in full. Extracts from longer works are usually whole chapters but if these have been edited I have made it clear.

If there are any loose ends, tantalizing references or cliff-hanging endings, I hope these will be seen not as blemishes but as invitations to go on and savour the wit and ingenuity of the original. I have included something from every genre in which he wrote except the work for the stage. He had no conspicuous success in the theatre, despite the encouragement of his friend George Bernard Shaw, who perhaps always enjoyed ideas rather than the flesh that drama must always clothe them with, and none of the plays seemed susceptible of being read with enjoyment in anything but its complete form.

For those who are interested in the life rather than – or as well as – the works, there are two books which ought to be read, apart from Chesterton's own *Autobiography*. One is *Gilbert Keith Chesterton* by Maisie Ward, published in 1944 by Sheed and Ward. Maisie Ward knew Chesterton personally and this is a long, detailed and fascinating study of his life. It now has a rival in the shape of a much more compact but excellent biography by Michael Coren: *Gilbert, The Man Who Was G. K. Chesterton*, published in 1989 by Jonathan Cape. It is the sort of biography he would very much have approved of: written by a man who understands and loves his subject, but steadfastly refuses to view him through rose-tinted spectacles. I owe a great deal to both of them where I touch on the life of Chesterton.

This book is dedicated to all who have suffered unjust neglect – those who have not yet been allowed an introduction to one of the most fascinating, genial, positive, patient, direct, consistent, radical and entertaining thinkers of the century.

Nigel Forde
York, 1994

Acknowledgments

ALL DIRECT quotations have been acknowledged within the text and it will be seen that I owe a huge debt to Chesterton's two finest biographers, Maisie Ward – *Gilbert Keith Chesterton*, Sheed and Ward 1944; and Michael Coren – *Gilbert: The Man Who Was Chesterton*, Jonathan Cape 1989. Marie Smith in her collection of Chesterton's *Nonsense and Light Verse*, Methuen 1987, and *The Spirit of Christmas*, Xanadu 1984 provided the texts of two poems not included in Chesterton's *Collected Poems*; they are *A Curse in Free Verse* and *Gloria In Profundis*.

My thanks are due to HarperCollins Publishers Ltd for permission to use material from *The Screwtape Letters* by C. S. Lewis.

I must thank my wife, Hilary, for her cold eye and her warm photocopier; and David White for the provision of books otherwise unobtainable.

For most of the information about world events and contemporary literature in the Chesterton Chronology, I have gone to Martin Gray's invaluable reference book *A Chronology of English Literature* (Longman/York Press 1989).

Introduction

CHESTERTON was a large man; large in every sense of the word. There are innumerable testimonies to his largeness of heart and they do not come only from his close friends. He may have given no quarter in debate nor in his polemical writings, attacking what he perceived as woolly thinking, stupidity or plain error, but those attacks were entirely without personal malice. He hated the sin but loved the sinner; and it is said that he never made an enemy in his life.

He was large in his interests. Nothing was too small, nothing too vast to capture his imagination and his insatiable curiosity. At one moment he could be considering the sweep of human history or the influence of Chaucer on the Renaissance; the next he could be meditating, in the light of the same eternity, on a tram ticket found in his pocket or on the peculiar quality of the colour grey.

He was large in his appetites. Life, he believed, was to be enjoyed and lived to the full with all the faculties that humans possess. He spent his life in obedience to that principle, reading, writing, talking, listening and laughing. One thing he did not neglect was eating and drinking which he did rapidly, somewhat inelegantly and with great enjoyment. 'Gilbert's symbol of hospitality,' wrote his sister-in-law, Ada Chesterton, 'was sausages and beer.' Quantities of both were available on convivial evenings in the Chesterton flat; but Gilbert also had a childlike addiction to puddings and cakes and sticky buns. What did not go down the Chesterton gullet went down the shirt-front or the waistcoat where it joined sundry ink splashes and smears on his creased and crumpled suit. Michael Coren recalls a typical incident:

> On one afternoon he was served two poached eggs in a teashop. As gesticulation was an essential part of his conversation, it did not take long before his wild movements

knocked the plate from the table and into his lap. His friends noticed the accident, but Gilbert did not; and proceeded to order another helping, informing the giggling waitress that he had misplaced the first.[1]

Owing to his gargantuan appetite and an indifference to exercise which bordered on aversion, Chesterton was extremely large in girth. Fortunately he was also very tall; even by the age of twenty-one he was more than six feet two, and his beer drinking turned him into what George Bernard Shaw affectionately but accurately called 'a large abounding gigantically cherubic person who . . . seems to be growing larger as you look at him'.

Give this cherub a moustache and pince-nez, dress him in a suit and cloak, add a large hat and a swordstick, and there stands Gilbert Keith Chesterton.

There is a story which, if it is apocryphal and it almost certainly is, was at least invented by someone who understood Chesterton's quickness of wit, if not Shaw's. At a party, it is said, George Bernard Shaw, who in complete contrast to Chesterton was as thin as a sliver of wind, prodded Chesterton in his massive belly and enquired 'Well, GK, and what are you going to call it?' Unperturbed, Chesterton replied 'If it is a boy I shall call it John; if it is a girl I shall call it Mary; and if it is wind, which I think it is, I shall call it George Bernard Shaw.' Chesterton did not in the least mind jokes about his shape. He made many himself, and was delighted when he was on one occasion introduced as 'Mr. Chesterton who has been looking round in America.'

Chesterton himself is the best person to describe how his life began.

Bowing down in blind credulity, as is my custom, before mere authority and the tradition of the elders, superstitiously swallowing a story I could not test at the time by experiment of private judgment, I am firmly of the opinion that I was born on the 29th of May, 1874, on Campden Hill, Kensington; and baptised according to the formularies of the Church of England in the little church of St. George opposite the large Waterworks Tower that dominated that ridge. I do not allege any significance in the relation of the two buildings; and I indignantly deny that the church was chosen because it needed the whole water-power of West London to turn me into a Christian.[2]

As a child he was not the precocious talent that might seem to be indicated by the intellect we encounter as an adult. He spoke little before the age of three and apparently did not read until he was eight. But perhaps he had better things to do: when his brother, Cecil, was born, Gilbert greeted the new arrival with 'Now I shall always have an audience.'

After his prep. school, Colet Court, he went across the road to St. Paul's School where his height, his untidiness and his legendary absence of mind made him the butt of a thousand schoolboy jokes and – perhaps worse – schoolmasters' jokes. Yet he seems not to have been miserable. The image one gets of Chesterton at this age is that of a large puppy: limbs too big and slightly uncontrolled; immensely enthusiastic; completely true to himself but a different species from all those around him; lacking in malice but possessing an awkwardness that breeds laughter and a playfulness that might have resulted in someone being hurt. Luckily it did not seem to. The teasing was certainly there, but it never turned into bullying; instead it became a kind of affection and any odd or eccentric behaviour was greeted with 'Oh, it's only Chesterton.'

In his *Autobiography*, Chesterton refers to this period in a chapter entitled 'How to be a Dunce' which reflects not only his natural modesty but the fact that he was not considered to be academically distinguished at school. His reports include the following remarks:

Wildly inaccurate about everything; never thinks for two consecutive minutes to judge by his work. A great blunderer with much intelligence. Means well. Can get up any work, but originates nothing.

We know now that Chesterton suffered from myopia and much of his apparent stupidity and vagueness was due simply to his not being able to see properly. But even while these remarks were being made about him, he was filling notebook after notebook with illustrations, perceptions, remarkable insights and ideas which his brain had been breeding during that enforced solitude. Many of these were the starting points on a journey which was to end in the biography of Charles Dickens, or *Orthodoxy* or *The Everlasting Man*.

Several important friendships started at St. Paul's; the greatest of these began as a playground fight. Neither of the combatants can remember what started it, but both agree on how it ended. One of them quoted a line from Macaulay, the other continued the quotation and a lifelong alliance was formed between Gilbert Chesterton and Edmund Clerihew Bentley. To this day the verse form which bears his middle name – the clerihew – is as popular as the limerick and, at its best, just as difficult. It consists of a kind of critical biography in four short lines:

> John Stuart Mill
> By a mighty effort of will
> Overcame his natural bonhomie
> And wrote 'Principles of Political Economy'.

From this friendship, shared with another boy, Lucian Oldershaw, grew the Junior Debating Club, Chairman GKC, which in turn led to a magazine, *The Debater*, in which Chesterton's first poems were published as well as his first attempts at literary criticism. The word 'attempts' suggests a lack of complete success, but is it really so obvious that this characterization of the poet Shelley is by a 'great blunderer' of eighteen rather than a bright Oxford don?

> He was not a bad man; he was not a good man; he was not an ordinary man; he was a sincere philanthropist and Republican; yet he was often as lonely and ill-tempered as a misanthrope; he had far purer feelings towards women than either Burns or Byron, yet he was a far worse husband than they: he was one of those men whose faults and failures seem due, not to the presence of tempting passions or threatening disasters, so much as to a mysterious inner weakness, a certain helplessness in the hands of circumstance.[3]

Though the punctuation may leave something to be desired, we can see in that passage the sort of mind that could reveal truths about Dickens or Aquinas, Browning or Chaucer, that had eluded the experts. He went on to win the Milton prize for poetry with a poem on the subject of St. Francis Xavier[4] and the High Master of St. Paul's overturned all previous judgments on Chesterton when he confided to Mrs. Chesterton: 'Six foot of genius. Cherish him, Mrs. Chesterton, cherish him.'

Gilbert's education continued not as one might have expected at one of the two older universities, but at Calderon's Art College in St. John's Wood, London. Most of his friends had gone to Oxford or Cambridge; Chesterton, it seems, chose to fulfil his father's dreams of becoming a professional artist. From Calderon's he went on to University College, London, to study Fine Art – a course which included the study of English, Latin and French. He soon gave up Latin, though he was to love it for the rest of his life, and thus missed an opportunity for what would certainly have been an interesting and fruitful friendship with the Professor of Latin – the poet A. E. Housman who was, during those years, at work on the poems that were to become *A Shropshire Lad*.

The Slade School was at this time a department of University College, and just beginning to acquire the reputation it was later to enjoy. Here Chesterton studied the Fine Art section of his course, and here it was decided that he was unteachable and was asked to leave after only a year. He had, as always, firm ideas, not necessarily fashionable ones, and was probably a thorn in the flesh of his professor, Frederick Brown. Aestheticism and a pose of world-weariness, agnostic materialism and the cult of the individual were the order of the day: everything that is summed up in the French phrase *fin de siècle* and everything that Chesterton despised. He left with notebooks crammed with jottings, ideas, seed-thoughts, like so many characters in search of an author. And Chesterton too was in search of himself; a self which he first discovered in journalism.

He began by reviewing for *Academy* and, after a change of editor, joined the publishing house of Redway for a month or two. Then he settled for over six years with the firm T. Fisher Unwin in Paternoster Row. He claims to have read over ten thousand books during those six years, which works out at roughly five per day every day. It would seem to have been something of an exaggeration except for the fact that, when challenged, he could recall the plot and characters of any book the challenger liked to name.

It was during this period that he came in contact with the Blogg family of Bedford Park, an area which appears in his novel *The Man Who Was Thursday*, thinly disguised under the name of Saffron Park. The Bloggs were members of a debating circle which included Chesterton's old friends E. C. Bentley and Lucian Oldershaw. Chesterton joined the circle, which was known as the I.D.K. When a stranger asked what the letters stood for, he or she was told, accurately but misleadingly, 'I don't know.'

Gilbert fell deeply and immediately in love with the eldest Blogg daughter, Frances. His love, happily, was returned, but it was a long time before they admitted it to each other or to their friends and families. Both mothers were a problem. After their engagement was announced, Gilbert wrote to Frances:

> Your mother would certainly have worried if you had been engaged to the Archangel Michael (who, indeed, is bearing his disappointment very well): how much more when you are engaged to an aimless, tactless, reckless, unbrushed, strange-hatted, opinionated scarecrow who has suddenly walked into the vacant place. I could have prophesied her unrest: wait and she will calm down all right, dear. God comfort her: I dare not . . .[5]

And perhaps, on a wage of twenty-five shillings a week, *could* not.

Photographs point up the physical differences between the massive Gilbert and his delicate, petite wife. A letter of 1899 – one of the daily ones from Gilbert to Frances – delightfully indicates others:

> . . . I always think of the Kosmos first and the Ego after-wards. I admit, however, that you are not engaged to the Kosmos: dear me! What a time the Kosmos would have! All

its Comets would have their hair brushed every morning. The Whirlwind would be adjured not to walk about when it was talking. The Oceans would be warmed with hot-water pipes. Not even the lowest forms of life would escape the crusade of tidiness: you would walk round and round the jellyfish, looking for a place to put in shirt-links.

By 1900, when Chesterton was twenty-six, he was reviewing regularly for two magazines, the *Speaker* and the *Bookman*; he was also encouraged to submit articles of his own on any subject he fancied. In this year, too, his first books were published. They were both books of poems: *Greybeards at Play* and *The Wild Knight and Other Poems*. His much-admired articles and brilliant reviews, his witty and memorable speeches and now his books had, along with his eccentric character, turned Chesterton into something of a celebrity, particularly in London. He considered that he was now earning enough to marry, which he did on 28th June 1901, in Kensington Parish Church.

Unpredictably, he was on time for the service. Predictably, he was without a tie. When he knelt, the price of his shoes was advertised to the entire congregation; and when they left for the honeymoon they missed the train (which had already been loaded with their luggage) because Gilbert stopped at a dairy bar for a glass of milk with his wife; and then at a gunsmith's to buy a revolver and some bullets.

Their first home, which they had searched out while staying with friends after the honeymoon, was Overstrand Mansions in Battersea where they rented a flat for £80 a year. A frequent visitor was the French-born writer Hilaire Belloc whom Chesterton had met several months before at a small cafe in Soho. The friendship was instant, and the meeting is memorably described in Chesterton's *Autobiography* in a passage which ends:

It was from that dingy little Soho cafe that there emerged the quadruped, the twiformed monster Mr. Shaw has nicknamed the Chesterbelloc.

Chesterton's ideas about God, philosophy and literature can all be traced back to the explorations he was making in his student days and with which he packed his notebooks; but Belloc's particular influence can be seen in the awakening of social and political thought, and in the relationship between those ideas and religious belief. Much of this – by no means all – remains as dead wood for us today: it has not outlasted its topicality. It was obviously an important part of his character for those who read his journalism or heard him speak. But we value Chesterton now much more for the religious, critical and fictional works, where social comment is adumbrated or appears in asides.

We are not surprised that Chesterton should enjoy the friendship of Belloc; Belloc was what the young Chesterton wanted to be, and he found in him a mentor and a soul-mate and a fervent apologist for the Roman Catholic Church and the faith that Chesterton was to embrace as his own. Much more surprising is the relationship he had with George Bernard Shaw and the novelist and historian H. G. Wells whose opinions and beliefs differed so markedly from those of Chesterton.

In the latter part of the twentieth century we seem to have lost a whole dimension of the concept of friendship, and this can cause us confusion when we find it retained by Chesterton. It seems natural for us to seek out as friends those who think as we do, or vote as we do, or believe what we believe; what C. S. Lewis called 'folks like us'. Their candidature for friendship is based much more often on their career than on their character; as if the wage-packet hired the mind and the thoughts as well as the time. A true, deep friendship between a cellist and a footballer, a painter and a marketing manager seems unlikely; one between an atheist and a Christian, even more so. What can be the attraction, we wonder.

The simple answer is, of course, that Chesterton liked both George Bernard Shaw and Wells. He admired their intellects and enjoyed with them a lifetime of teasing and arguing. He was not frightened of friends who would constantly challenge his deepest convictions, which is one reason for them remaining so sharp and focused and lively. It was quite a triumvirate. There was no enquiring mind at the time that did not find itself in some way affected by the influence of one of these three. That seems a particularly remarkable thing to us in the age of television where we constantly meet that strange creature which is just the opposite of mind, which is everything *but* mind: the personality.

This view of friendship is supported by Chesterton himself. In *Orthodoxy* he wrote: 'A man's friend likes him, but leaves him as he is.' No wonder Chesterton's friendship was considered an unalloyed pleasure.

After his marriage to Frances, the story of Chesterton's life becomes the story of his mental life. There was action and adventure, but it was cerebral even when it included foreign travel. It is a chronicle of developing ideas, of articles and public debates, of book after book after book.

Even Chesterton's massive frame, however, was capable of taxis rather than merely of tropism. The couple left Battersea in 1909 and rented a small house called 'Overroads' in 'a sort of village' – Beaconsfield. In the year following he published five books: *The Ball and the Cross*, *What's Wrong with the World*, *William Blake*, *Alarms and Discursions*, and *Five Types*. During the next year, three more came out – four if *A Chesterton Calendar* is included. The move was obviously one which suited him even if his friends complained that he had put himself out of reach of London. Scarcely a complaint that would be made of Beaconsfield today, and scarcely fair even then.

But nine books in two years, along with a massive amount of journalism for many different periodicals, plus his lectures and debates, took their toll of Chesterton's health as they would have done with a man much leaner and fitter. At the end of 1913 he collapsed and was unconscious for ten weeks; so close to death that Frances was seriously considering the last rites for him. Even though his Christian beliefs had been maturing over the years, he was not yet a convert to Roman Catholicism, and Frances desperately needed guidance. She wrote:

> I do pray to God He will restore him to himself that we may know. I feel in His Mercy He will, even if death is the end of it – or the beginning shall I say?[6]

Chesterton did recover by the following Easter and, despite

warnings that he must cut down on his work as much as on the intake of food and alcohol, plunged back into writing.

His brother Cecil was editor of the magazine *New Witness*. When he was sent to the western front in 1916, Gilbert felt duty bound to take over the editorship alongside all his other commitments. It was, of course, a huge task and not one in which he was experienced. It involved not only the usual challenge of finishing contributions in time for a deadline – editorials this time, though not unlike the essays he was writing for other journals – but also administration, diplomatic mediation and a personal subsidy of about £50 a week towards the costs of running the magazine. This despite generous gifts from Sir Thomas Beecham among many others.

Gilbert, as may be imagined, was totally unfit for military service being, as he was, totally unfit. A society lady asked him why he wasn't 'out at the front'. 'If you go round to my side, Madam,' replied Chesterton, 'you will see that I am.'

When the war came to an end in 1918, *New Witness* rejoiced that 'The Prussian Devil' was defeated. But Gilbert had suffered his own defeat: Cecil had died. Gilbert was shocked beyond belief. His grief for Cecil and the pain he felt at that bereavement could never be overcome.

Gilbert and Frances had hardly moved into their new house – 'Top Meadow', which they had had built for themselves next to 'Overroads' – when another blow fell. Gilbert's father, Edward Chesterton, died. While it is impossible to point to one or even two events as being the cause of a third, it would certainly seem that the deaths of the two relations who were closest to Gilbert were the final straws that broke the 'secular' man and led to his conversion and acceptance into the Roman Catholic Church. The journey to this point had begun years earlier and milestones along the road can be seen in all his writings from the notebooks onwards. It may be significant, it may just be neatly symbolic, that the move to a new physical home should parallel his arrival in a new spiritual home. He would remain in both for the rest of his life.

New Witness had swallowed all the money that could be poured into it and still had starved to death. Instead of breathing a sigh of relief – as his wife did – Chesterton took a deep breath and began a new publication which came to be known as *GK's Weekly*. It struggled, but Chesterton persevered and its future beame assured when it became the mouthpiece of a political philosophy known as Distributism. Chesterton wrote a pamphlet on the subject with K. L. Kendrick, Secretary of the Birmingham branch of the Distributist League. Kendrick describes the philosophy thus:

> There are three economic theories struggling for supremacy in the modern world. They are Capitalism – the doctrine that property is best concentrated in large masses in the hands of a few people; Socialism – the doctrine that property is best owned and controlled by the state; and Distributism – the doctrine that property is best divided up among the largest number of people. Broadly speaking, we may say that Distributism means every man his own master (as far as possible); Socialism means nobody his own master, but the State master of all; Capitalism means a select few their own masters and the rest of us their servants.

The most important event of 1926 was the arrival in Chesterton's life of Dorothy Collins. Chesterton had always been absentminded. What impinged on his creative imagination was always more important than any low tricks the physical world might play. He would have described it as presence of mind on the things that mattered; but it caused him complications. Once he failed to turn up for a board meeting of *GK's Weekly*. It had recently changed its address.

> On calling a taxi at Marylebone he realised that he could not give the address, so he told the driver to take him to Fleet Street. There, as his memory still refused to help, he stopped the taxi outside a tea-shop, left it there while he was inside, and ordering a cup of tea began to turn out all his pockets in the hope of finding a letter or a proof bearing the address. Then, as no clue could be found, he told the driver to take him to a bookstall that stocked the paper. At the first and second he drew blanks, but at the third bought a copy of his own paper and thus discovered the address.[7]

But Dorothy Collins was to change all that. The man who had once sent the poignantly bewildered telegram 'Am in Market Harborough. Where ought I to be?' was now being superbly organized and given direction. She was exactly what Gilbert (and Frances) needed: a combination of secretary, accountant, diary-keeper, amanuensis, chauffeuse, and trustworthy companion.

To his perhaps already rather overstrung bow was added another string in these final years: that of broadcasting. He was an extraordinary success from the moment of his first broadcast in the autumn of 1932. A letter from Broadcasting House tells how 'The building rings with your praises!' and 'You bring us something rare to the microphone.' The letter does not specify what that something is, but it may have been an unexpected spontaneity, since he was invited to submit more manuscripts and told: 'We should like you to make variations as these occur to you as you speak at the microphone.' They trusted him and the public loved him.

Biographers have said of Chesterton, as they have said of Wells, that he had a high, squeaky voice. But, unless the archive records of the BBC lie, this would appear to be something of an exaggeration. Those who say it, may have been misled by their knowledge of the man's enormous bulk. From such a frame one might legitimately expect a basso profundo; instead we hear a light tenor. Any radio listener who had not seen him – if such a person existed – would not have thought the voice unusual. But the mountain labours and if anything less than the expected mammoth comes forth it is liable to be seen as a mouse. A rich, deep voice it may not have been; it may not have been an appropriate voice; but it was not the infantile squeak that some would have us believe.

By 1936 he was beginning to overtire himself again, and his friends were anxious. He began to fall asleep during his work. He had bronchitis and the spring that year was bleak and unfriendly. His heart was weak: he was slipping away.

At one point, awaking to full consciousness for a moment, he declared: 'The issue is now quite clear. It is between light and darkness and everyone must choose his side.' Those were almost the last words he was to speak. He died quietly on the morning of 14th June 1936. Tributes flowed in: from friends, of course, such as Wells, Shaw, Belloc and Maurice Baring; from Ronald Knox, J. M. Barrie, Hugh Kingsmill and Eric Gill the artist and sculptor; also from the Pope and from scores of ordinary people who had never met Chesterton but who had fallen under the spell of his writings or his broadcasts. At his funeral a policeman on the gate remarked 'Most of the lads are on duty, else they would all have been here.'

Walter de la Mare contributed four lines for his memorial card:

> Knight of the Holy Ghost, he goes his way,
> Wisdom his motley, Truth his loving jest;
> The mills of Satan keep his lance in play,
> Pity and innocence his heart at rest.

They are not great lines compared with the best of de la Mare, but they do point to an important aspect of Chesterton: the idea that Truth can be communicated in a jest; that there is a level of seriousness that can be reached and explored only by those whose mode is humour. Not mockery, not flippancy, but humour. Humour bypasses many of the defences we put up against accepting ideas that are new or that call into question the attitudes that we have adopted already. A joke, a play on words, a startling piece of wit is not an argument, it is a revelation; it disarms us for a moment. Our prejudices can be carefully marshalled during an argument but, unless we are too stupid to see it, a joke suddenly pierces solemnity with sincerity. Chesterton teaches us – and how we need to be taught – that we must beware of judging an author as 'light' simply because he has a light touch. He makes the point very clearly in *Heretics*:

> Mr. McCabe thinks that I am not serious but only funny, because Mr. McCabe thinks that funny is the opposite of serious. Funny is the opposite of not funny, and of nothing else. The question of whether a man expresses himself in a grotesque or laughable phraseology, or in a stately and restrained phraseology, is not a question of motive or of moral state, it is a question of instinctive language and

self-expression. Whether a man chooses to tell the truth in long sentences or short jokes is a problem analogous to whether he chooses to tell the truth in French or German. Whether a man preaches his gospel grotesquely or gravely is merely like the question of whether he preaches it in prose or verse. The question of whether Swift was funny in his irony is quite another sort of question to the question of whether Swift was serious in his pessimism . . . The truth is, as I have said, that in this sense the two qualities of fun and seriousness have nothing to do with each other, they are no more comparable than black and triangular. Mr. Bernard Shaw is funny and sincere. Mr. George Robey is funny and not sincere. Mr. McCabe is sincere and not funny. The average Cabinet Minister is not sincere and not funny.[8]

The really remarkable and glorious things of our physical life are spoiled by too much self-awareness; love, for instance, music, or good wine. Analysis of them tends to appear pretentious, silly or just beside the point. It can describe the describable aspects, but the really important part is that which is unique and indescribable. Let us not, then, delve too deeply into the unfunny business of what constitutes the funny. It is enough to say that nearly all humour is based upon the difference between what we expect and what we get; the gap between the ideal and the actual. Religion, taken seriously, is a wonderful source of laughter and humour, since it is continually emphasizing that difference. It is the unbeliever who imagines religion must always be something solemn, dutiful and dull. The believer sees it as a cause for joy and laughter.

In nearly every worthwhile activity that can be mentioned, it is the outsider who sees the hardships, the difficulties, the disciplines; the insider has a very different view. One sees a barrier, the other sees a freedom. The non-poet looks at the sonnet or the ottava rima with a kind of horror: restrictions, disciplines, straitjackets! The poet sees the same problems as a source of power and inspiration. Scales and arpeggios and back-breaking practice are nothing to the pianist who can play a Mozart concerto. Latin verbs and innumerable declensions may look terribly serious, but they lead to Catullus and Ovid.

The outsider always seems to get hold of the wrong end of the stick: the trees are very visible, but the wood is beyond his comprehension. 'How *do* you learn all those lines?' gasps the audience member to the actor; and it is very hard to make reply because it is not something the actor will have thought about. Learning lines is not only no problem, it is the very means by which he or she can have the freedom to act. A tool, not a stumbling block. The acting, like the concerto, the poem or the reading of a foreign language, is the marvellous end that renders the means quite insignificant.

So the unbelieving outsider, trying to understand, will use grim solemn words such as *dogma* or even *religion* with its etymological echo of binding and tying down, and look askance at a joke or a paradox. *Religion* is a prison of a concept when set against the light breath of the insider's word *faith*. That breath, that illuminating lightness, is apparent in all Chesterton's most serious writing as it is in his most fanciful and whimsical squibs. It is his mode of perception:

> Seriousness is not a virtue. It would be a heresy, but a much more sensible heresy, to say that seriousness is a vice. It is really a natural trend or lapse into taking oneself gravely, because it is the easiest thing to do. It is much easier to write a good *Times* leading article than a good joke in *Punch*. For solemnity flows out of men naturally; but laughter is a leap. It is easy to be heavy: hard to be light. Satan fell by the force of gravity.[9]

That last image sums up perfectly what people mean – even those who do not admire Chesterton as a poet – when they say that Chesterton was primarily a writer of poetry. For that sentence, 'Satan fell by the force of gravity', condenses all the previous lines and sums up everything he has been saying. It could stand by itself, but then it would be too oblique for prose; so he puts it last, and it is as if light, coming through a prism in all its variety of colours, were suddenly focused in a single, sparkling point. It surprises, it delights; and because it does so it remains in the memory.

He does the same thing in his fiction. In *Manalive*, Innocent Smith deals us a remarkable and memorable image:

> With our weak spirits we should grow old in eternity if we were not kept young by death. Providence has cut immortality into lengths for us, as nurses cut the bread and butter into fingers.

There is another hallmark of Chesterton's style which is not unconnected with this capacity for memorable imagery. Time and time again, a pun, an antithesis or a paradox is used in his writing rather as a stepping-stone is used to cross a river. Move from one to the other, remember each of them, and you are left with a pathway through the argument whatever turbulent waters have flowed between.

Because we do remember them so clearly, we take away the impression of a man who thinks in paradoxes. What he is really doing, however, is untwisting them to reveal that they are not paradoxes at all except to those who do not think logically; or he is using them to point out that the truth is very often the exact opposite to what we have supposed; or in order to make a kind of wild conceit that by its extraordinary nature can point to the very heart of his thesis.

Epigrams, they have been called. They are actually the reverse of epigrams. They do not clinch the argument and tie up the ends; they tend rather to open up another area of discussion, to unloose the ends and free a whole new train of thought. Here are a few taken out of context. They seem to me to be more like essay titles than conclusions:

> The morality of a great writer is not the morality he teaches, but the morality he takes for granted.[10]

> It is always the humble man who talks too much; the proud man watches himself too closely.[11]

> There is a great deal of difference between the eager man who wants to read a book, and the tired man who wants a book to read.[12]

Despair does not lie in being weary of suffering, but in being weary of joy.[13]

Truth, of course, must of necessity be stranger than fiction, for we have made fiction to suit ourselves.[14]

Those who dislike Chesterton dismiss him too easily; those who love him are sometimes in danger of turning him into some sort of saint. It is true that Chesterton himself said of the saint that he is: 'a medicine because he is an antidote . . . He will generally be found restoring the world to sanity by exaggerating whatever the world neglects.'[15] And that is a very fair summary of Chesterton's own methods. That is not to say that he was infallible.

His great virtue was enthusiasm and, while that quality needs to be restored to us, he had the faults of the enthusiast too. Inaccuracy was one of them. He seldom bothered to check his facts – dates or quotations. His publishers feared that his book on Browning was so inaccurate, so full of errors and misremembered quotations, that it was going to disgrace them. When he was nearly halfway through his biography of Aquinas, he stopped and remarked to his secretary that he thought it was about time he read some Aquinas. Even in his fiction there are signs that the narrative was moving faster than the intellect that should have been controlling it. So, in The Man Who Was Thursday, it is implied that a channel-crossing takes only the time that has elapsed during a single conversation – and the conversation takes about five minutes. Likewise, the seasons in the same book seem to rearrange themselves according to Chesterton's convenience rather than some slavish adherence to the calendar.

Does it matter? Kingsley Amis reluctantly defends the time-shifts in The Man Who Was Thursday by pointing out that Chesterton called it not a novel but A Nightmare and so may be allowed a dreamlike quality. It is perfectly possible to write a great deal about Aquinas and his times before moving on to specific commentary on the works, so we must not be misled into believing that the Aquinas anecdote proves an unscholarly attitude. Factual inaccuracies seem harder to defend especially since, in the case of Browning or Dickens, they are so easy to check or emend.

But how many of us would bother to check quotations which had become second nature to us? Those quotations, whether from Shakespeare, Wordsworth, Betjeman or *Monty Python's Flying Circus*, that we have grown up with are now so much part of our cerebral furniture that we would no more think of verifying them than we would think of checking how to spell 'spider' or 'upholstery'.

This, I suggest, was Chesterton's only mistake: that he was as familiar with a hundred writers as we are with four or five. It does not mean that he is not ultimately trustworthy. Correct those quotations in *Browning* and it makes not one iota of difference to his argument; it does not depend upon such details. He sees the whole picture and talks about it in its wholeness. This is his gift, and this is what we have lost in the age of the expert. We are so intent on the single brushstroke, the exact tint here, the tiny crack there, that we cannot view the whole canvas, let alone the wall it hangs on. Both approaches are valid, but we must beware of criticizing the one for not being the other, and of thinking that the methods must be the same in each case.

The advantage of Chesterton's method is that you need bring only your own mind to his arguments. You can do without the *Dictionary of National Biography*, Brewer's *Dictionary of Phrase and Fable* and tables of logarithms. He is doing something bigger and more difficult than lapidary work, he is characterizing a whole opus, a complete achievement and its distinctive flavour. Chesterton inhabits literature like a sportive whale, and we cannot fully admire the magnificence of the whale if we are forever complaining that it makes unsightly splashes on the bathroom floor.

Chesterton was a positive man. So positive that it is easy to take exception to him, especially in an age which sets such a high value on cynicism and despair. There is, of course, plenty of reason for cynicism and despair and Chesterton was no stranger to those reasons. There is a great deal of truth in the familiar sigh: 'There are no easy answers.' But this should not blind us to the fact that one plus one still equals two, however simple the equation seems. There are few sights more dispiriting than the man who refuses the right answer simply because it is an obvious one. It may be that Chesterton's sword sometimes cuts too easily through the Gordian

Knot, but we should not therefore say that string will never yield to steel.

Quot homines, tot sententiae, says the old Latin tag which I have not checked but which I still take to mean 'There are as many opinions as there are people'. And as far as opinions about Chesterton go, that is certainly true. He wrote too much; he should have written more. We can only admire him as a philosopher; philosophy was not his strength. He was in essence a poet; his verse is weak and unimportant. He was really a journalist; if *only* he had not been a journalist. His religious writings alone are valuable; he is fine until he gets on his religious hobby-horse. He was not a fiction writer; the Father Brown stories will live for ever. All these things have been said of Chesterton. I have merely reduced them to simple statements. Now here is a passage from *Orthodoxy*:

> Suppose we heard an unknown man spoken of by many men. Suppose we were puzzled to hear that some men said he was too tall and some too short; some objected to his fatness, some lamented his leanness; some thought him too dark, and some too fair. One explanation (as has already been admitted) would be that he might be an odd shape. But there is another explanation. He might be the right shape.

Perhaps after all Chesterton is not so deformed as some have made him out.

As to Chesterton's cleverness, which is a quality much in demand by the twentieth century, he at least would have approved of the final judgment being pronounced by a small boy who had been to one of Chesterton's parties in Beaconsfield:

> I dunno about clever, but you should see him catch buns in his mouf.

FATHER BROWN

NOTHING of Chesterton's work has been quite so enduring as the Father Brown detective stories. It is said that he walked into his agent's office one day and asked if there was anything special that publishers were looking for. He was told that there was nothing in his line, but that *The Saturday Evening Post* was wanting detective stories. Chesterton mused for a moment and then sat down and wrote the first of the Father Brown stories.

Why did he choose a detective as unusual and as unlikely as Father Brown? Chesterton answers that question in his *Autobiography*:

> When a writer invents a character for the purposes of fiction, especially of light or fanciful fiction, he fits him out with all sorts of features meant to be effective in the setting and against that background. He may have taken, and probably has taken, a hint from a human being. But he will not hesitate to alter the human being, especially in externals, because he is not thinking of a portrait but of a picture. In Father Brown it was the chief feature to be featureless. The point of him was to appear pointless; and one might say that his conspicuous quality was not being conspicuous. His commonplace exterior was meant to contrast with his unsuspected vigilance and intelligence; and that being so, of course, I made his appearance shabby and shapeless, his face round and expressionless, his manners clumsy, and so on. At the same time I did take some of his inner intellectual qualities from my friend, Father John O'Connor of Bradford, who has not, as a matter of fact, any of these external qualities.[16]

Father O'Connor was the man who was to be the means of

Chesterton's entering the Roman Catholic Church. He and
Chesterton met in Keighley, Yorkshire, after a lecture. What
struck Chesterton, as their acquaintance deepened, was the depth
to which this genial, delicate and dexterous man understood the
worst horrors and perversions of the human psyche. He knew about
sin in a real, practical and unsentimental way. And there sprang up
in Chesterton's mind the idea of 'constructing a comedy in which
a priest should appear to know nothing and in fact know more
about crime than the criminals'.[17] It was a very successful idea.
The only thing that Chesterton had to learn was the attractiveness
of villainy. His arch-villain, Flambeau, was so popular that he had
to repent and join Father Brown on the side of the angels, so that
he could remain in the books. His knowledge of the criminal mind
from the inside in specific cases is of use to Father Brown in several
stories.

The extraordinary thing about Father Brown is that his methods
are not scientific or merely logical, like those of Holmes or Lord
Peter Wimsey, but spiritual. In *The Secret of Father Brown* – the
first story in the collection of the same name – the method is
explained by the priest himself to his friend, Grandison Chace.
Father Brown has been accused of having some kind of sixth sense
or magical ability. He refutes the idea:

'The secret is,' he said; and then stopped as if unable to go
on. Then he began again and said:
   'You see, it was I who killed all those people.'
   'What?' repeated the other in a small voice out of a vast
silence.
   'You see, I had murdered them all myself,' explained
Father Brown patiently. 'So, of course, I knew how it
was done.'
   Grandison Chace had risen to his great height like a man
lifted to the ceiling by a sort of slow explosion. Staring down
at the other he repeated his incredulous question.
   'I had planned out each of the crimes very carefully,' went
on Father Brown. 'I had thought out exactly how a thing
like that could be done, and in what style or state of mind
a man could really do it. And when I was quite sure that I

felt exactly like the murderer myself, of course I knew who
he was.'. . .

'Science is a grand thing when you can get it; in its real
sense one of the grandest words in the world. But what
do these men mean, nine times out of ten, when they use
it nowadays? When they say detection is a science? When
they say criminology is a science? They mean getting *outside*
a man and studying him as if he were a giant insect; in what
they would call a dry impartial light; in what I should call a
dead and dehumanised light. They mean getting a long way
off him, as if he were a distant prehistoric monster; staring
at the shape of his "criminal skull" as if it were a sort of
eerie growth like the horn of a rhinoceros's nose. When
the scientist talks about a type, he never means himself,
but always his neighbour; probably his poorer neighbour. I
don't deny the dry light may sometimes do good; though in
one sense it's the very reverse of science. So far from being
knowledge, it's actually suppression of what we know. It's
treating a friend as a stranger, and pretending that something
familiar is really remote and mysterious. It's like saying that a
man has a proboscis between the eyes, or that he falls down
in a fit of insensibility once every twenty-four hours. Well,
what you call "the secret" is exactly the opposite. I don't try
to get outside the man. I try to get inside the murderer . . .
Indeed it's much more than that, don't you see? I *am* inside
a man. I am always inside a man, moving his arms and legs;
but I wait till I know I am inside a murderer, thinking his
thoughts, wrestling with his passions; till I have bent myself
into the posture of his hunched and peering hatred; till I
see the world with his bloodshot and squinting eyes, looking
between the blinkers of his half-witted concentration; looking
up the perspective of a straight road to a pool of blood. Till I
am really a murderer.'

The Innocence of Father Brown (1911) and *The Wisdom of Father
Brown* (1914) are easily the best collections. There are good
stories in the other volumes, but Chesterton's enthusiasm was

waning after twenty-four stories. There is an appetite, not entirely blameworthy, on the part of publishers and public alike for what they know and love rather than for something new and untried. Not an attitude of mind that would have appealed to Chesterton. He had, however, little choice but to fulfil the demand for more of Father Brown; it earned him enough money to be able to spend time in less lucrative activities. Many writers have this 'Robin Hood' attitude to their work, allowing the rich to pay them for what they would rather not do in order to subsidize the important work for which there is little money available. Robert Graves said: 'Prose books are the show dogs I breed and sell to support my cat.' For 'cat' read 'poetry'.

Chesterton was not a Roman Catholic at the time when he started writing the Father Brown stories. A Catholic priest was chosen, not just because he could be based on Father O'Connor, but because his strength, his knowledge of the sinful mind comes from hours of listening to confessions. A Catholic priest is far more likely to understand the true and terrifying nature of sin than a priest from any other denomination. Temptation is not adequately described as longing for 'a second piece of blackcurrant pie'; the truth is much less palatable and much more readily available to Father Brown.

Different though Chesterton's 'little Suffolk Dumpling from East Anglia' was from his rival detectives, the stories conform to logic and possibility as much as those of his colleagues. Holmes, on occasion, makes some rash deductions. Not illogical ones, but ones which ignore other possibilities. As Chesterton was president of the Detection Club, formed by Anthony Berkeley in 1930, he had to abide by some very sensible but very amusing rules. They are expressed in the marvellous initiation ceremony:

Ruler: Do you promise that your detectives shall well and truly detect the crimes presented to them using those wits which it may please you to bestow upon them and not placing reliance on nor making use of Divine Revelation, Feminine Intuition, Mumbo Jumbo, Jiggery-Pokery, Coincidence or Act of God?
Candidate: I do.

Ruler: Do you solemnly swear never to conceal a vital clue from the reader?

Candidate: I do.

Ruler: Do you promise to observe a seemly moderation in the use of Gangs, Conspiracies, Death-Rays, Ghosts, Hypnotism, Trap-Doors, Chinamen, Super-Criminals and Lunatics; and utterly and forever to forswear Mysterious Poisons unknown to Science?

Candidate: I do.

Ruler: Will you honour the King's English?

Candidate: I will.

The Blue Cross is the first of the Father Brown stories and, some consider, the finest. It has some wonderful insights and a chase in the grand manner, as well as some intriguing paradoxes. Since it is the first, everything the reader needs to know about Father Brown is contained within the story.

By the time we come to *The Invisible Man*, Flambeau has become an ally. One may object to this particular story that it is not logical; but it is logical in terms of human behaviour and perceptions, and that is what Chesterton was about in these far-fetched tales. The truth it tells of human nature demands a little inaccuracy in the telling. The inaccuracy, it will be observed, is not born of Chesterton's mind but of those of his characters.

The Blue Cross

Between the silver ribbon of morning and the green glittering ribbon of sea, the boat touched Harwich and let loose a swarm of folk like flies, among whom the man we must follow was by no means conspicuous – nor wished to be. There was nothing notable about him, except a slight contrast between the holiday gaiety of his clothes and the official gravity of his face. His clothes included a slight, pale grey jacket, a white waistcoat, and a silver straw hat with a grey-blue ribbon. His lean face was dark by contrast, and ended in a curt black beard that looked Spanish and suggested an Elizabethan ruff. He was smoking a cigarette with the seriousness of an idler. There was nothing about him to indicate the fact that the grey jacket covered a loaded revolver, that the white waistcoat covered a police card, or that the straw hat covered one of the most powerful intellects in Europe. For this was Valentin himself, the head of the Paris police and the most famous investigator of the world; and he was coming from Brussels to London to make the greatest arrest of the century.

Flambeau was in England. The police of three countries had tracked the great criminal at last from Ghent to Brussels, from Brussels to the Hook of Holland; and it was conjectured that he would take some advantage of the unfamiliarity and confusion of the Eucharistic Congress, then taking place in London. Probably he would travel as some minor clerk or secretary connected with it; but, of course, Valentin could not be certain; nobody could be certain about Flambeau.

It is many years now since this colossus of crime suddenly ceased keeping the world in a turmoil; and when he ceased, as they said after the death of Roland, there was a great quiet upon the earth. But in his best days (I mean, of course, his worst) Flambeau was a figure as statuesque and international as the Kaiser. Almost every morning the daily paper announced that he had escaped the consequences of one extraordinary crime by committing another. He was a Gascon of gigantic stature and bodily daring; and the wildest tales were told of his outbursts of athletic humour; how he turned the *juge d'instruction* upside down and stood him on his head, 'to clear his mind'; how he ran down the Rue de Rivoli with a policeman under each arm. It is due to him to say that his fantastic physical strength was generally employed in such bloodless though undignified scenes; his real crimes were chiefly those of ingenious and wholesale robbery. But each of his thefts was almost a new sin, and would make a story by itself. It was he who ran the great Tyrolean Dairy Company in London, with no dairies, no cows, no carts, no milk, but with some thousand subscribers. These he served by the simple operation of moving the little milk-cans outside people's doors to the doors of his own customers. It was he who had kept up an unaccountable and close correspondence with a young lady whose whole letter-bag was intercepted, by the extraordinary trick of photographing his messages infinitesimally small upon the slides of a microscope. A sweeping simplicity, however, marked many of his experiments. It is said he once repainted all the numbers in a street in the dead of night merely to divert one traveller into a trap. It is quite certain that he invented a portable pillar-box, which he put up at corners in quiet suburbs on the chance of strangers dropping postal orders into it. Lastly he was known to be a startling acrobat; despite his huge figure, he could leap like a grasshopper and melt into the treetops like a monkey. Hence the great Valentin, when he set out to find Flambeau, was perfectly well aware that his adventures would not end when he had found him.

But how was he to find him? On this the great Valentin's ideas were still in process of settlement.

There was one thing which Flambeau, with all his dexterity of disguise, could not cover, and that was his singular height. If Valentin's quick eye had caught a tall apple-woman, a tall grenadier, or even a tolerably tall duchess, he might have arrested them on the spot. But all along his train there was nobody that could be a disguised Flambeau, any more than a cat could be a disguised giraffe. About the people on the boat he had already satisfied himself; and the people picked up at Harwich or on the journey limited themselves with certainty to six. There was a short railway official travelling up to the terminus, three fairly short market-gardeners picked up two stations afterwards, one very short widow lady going up from a small Essex town, and a very short Roman Catholic priest going up from a small Essex village.

When it came to the last case, Valentin gave it up and almost laughed. The little priest was so much the essence of those Eastern flats: he had a face as round and dull as a Norfolk dumpling; he had eyes as empty as the North Sea; he had several brown-paper parcels which he was quite incapable of collecting. The Eucharistic Congress had doubtless sucked out of their local stagnation many such creatures, blind and helpless, like moles disinterred. Valentin was a sceptic in the severe style of France, and could have no love for priests. But he could have pity for them, and this one might have provoked pity in anybody. He had a large, shabby umbrella, which constantly fell on the floor. He did not seem to know which was the right end of his return ticket. He explained with a moon-calf simplicity to everybody in the carriage that he had to be careful, because he had something made of real silver 'with blue stones' in one of his brown-paper parcels. His quaint blending of Essex flatness with saintly simplicity continuously amused the Frenchman till the priest arrived (somehow) at Stratford with all his parcels, and came back for his umbrella. When he did the last, Valentin even had the good nature to warn him not to take care of the silver by telling everybody about it. But to whomever he talked, Valentin kept his eye open for someone else; he looked out steadily for anyone, rich or poor, male or female, who was well up to six feet; for Flambeau was four inches above it.

He alighted at Liverpool Street, however, quite conscientiously secure that he had not missed the criminal so far. He then went to Scotland Yard to regularize his position and arrange for help in case of need; he then lit another cigarette and went for a long stroll in the streets of London. As he was walking in the streets and squares beyond Victoria, he paused suddenly and stood. It was a quaint, quiet square, very typical of London, full of an accidental stillness. The tall, flat houses round looked at once prosperous and uninhabited; the square of shrubbery in the centre looked as deserted as a green Pacific islet. One of the four sides was much higher than the rest, like a dais; and the line of this side was broken by one of London's admirable accidents – a restaurant that looked as if it had strayed from Soho. It was an unreasonably attractive object, with dwarf plants in pots and long, striped blinds of lemon yellow and white. It stood specially high above the street, and in the usual patchwork way of London, a flight of steps from the street ran up to meet the front door almost as a fire-escape might run up to a first-floor window. Valentin stood and smoked in front of the yellow-white blinds and considered them long.

The most incredible thing about miracles is that they happen. A few clouds in heaven do come together into the staring shape of one human eye. A tree does stand up in the landscape of a doubtful journey in the exact and elaborate shape of a note of interrogation. I have seen both these things myself within the last few days. Nelson does die in the instant of victory; and a man named Williams does quite accidentally murder a man named Williamson; it sounds like a sort of infanticide. In short, there is in life an element of elfin coincidence which people reckoning on the prosaic may perpetually miss. As it has been well expressed in the paradox of Poe, wisdom should reckon on the unforeseen.

Aristide Valentin was unfathomably French; and the French intelligence is intelligence specially and solely. He was not 'a thinking machine'; for that is a brainless phrase of modern fatalism and materialism. A machine only *is* a machine because it cannot think. But he was a thinking man, and a plain man at the same time. All his wonderful successes, that looked like conjuring, had been gained by plodding logic, by clear and commonplace French thought. The French electrify the world not by starting any paradox, they electrify it by carrying out a truism. They carry a truism so far – as in the French Revolution. But exactly because Valentin understood reason, he understood the limits of reason. Only a man who knows nothing of motors talks of motoring without petrol; only a man who knows nothing of reason talks of reasoning without strong, undisputed first principles. Here he had no strong first principles. Flambeau had been missed at Harwich; and if he was in London at all, he might be anything from a tall tramp on Wimbledon Common to a tall toastmaster at the Hôtel Métropole. In such a naked state of nescience, Valentin had a view and a method of his own.

In such cases he reckoned on the unforeseen. In such cases, when he could not follow the train of the reasonable, he coldly and carefully followed the train of the unreasonable. Instead of going to the right places – banks, police-stations, rendezvous – he systematically went to the wrong places; knocked at every empty house, turned down every *cul de sac*, went up every lane blocked with rubbish, went round every crescent that led him uselessly out of the way. He defended this crazy course quite logically. He said that if one had a clue this was the worst way; but if one had no clue at all it was the best, because there was just the chance that any oddity that caught the eye of the pursuer might be the same that had caught the eye of the pursued. Somewhere a man must begin, and it had better be just where another man might stop. Something about that flight of steps up to the shop, something about the quietude and quaintness of the restaurant, roused all the detective's rare romantic fancy and made him resolve to strike at random. He went up the steps, and sitting down by the window, asked for a cup of black coffee.

It was half-way through the morning, and he had not breakfasted; the slight litter of other breakfasts stood about on the table to remind him of his hunger; and adding a poached egg to his order, he proceeded musingly to shake some white sugar into his coffee, thinking all the time about Flambeau. He remembered how Flambeau had escaped, once by a pair of nail scissors, and once by a house on fire; once by having to pay for an unstamped letter, and once by getting people to look through a telescope at a comet that might destroy the world. He thought his detective brain as good as the criminal's, which was true. But he fully realized the disadvantage. 'The criminal is the creative artist; the detective only the critic,' he said with a sour smile, and lifted his coffee cup to his lips slowly, and put it down very quickly. He had put salt in it.

He looked at the vessel from which the silvery powder had come; it was certainly a sugar-basin; as unmistakably meant for sugar as a champagne-bottle for champagne. He wondered why they should keep salt in it. He looked to see if there were any more orthodox vessels. Yes, there were two salt-cellars quite full. Perhaps there was some speciality in the condiment in the salt-cellars. He tasted it; it was sugar. Then he looked round at the restaurant with a refreshed air of interest, to see if there were any other traces of that singular artistic taste which puts the sugar in the salt-cellars and the salt in the sugar-basin. Except for an odd splash of some dark fluid on one of the white-papered walls, the whole place appeared neat, cheerful and ordinary. He rang the bell for the waiter.

When that official hurried up, fuzzy-haired and somewhat blear-eyed at that early hour, the detective (who was not without an appreciation of the simpler forms of humour) asked him to taste the sugar and see if it was up to the high reputation of the hotel. The result was that the waiter yawned suddenly and woke up.

'Do you play this delicate joke on your customers every morning?' inquired Valentin. 'Does changing the salt and sugar never pall on you as a jest?'

The waiter, when this irony grew clearer, stammeringly assured him that the establishment had certainly no such intention; it must be a most curious mistake. He picked up the sugar-basin and looked at it; he picked up the salt-cellar and looked at that, his face growing more and more bewildered. At last he abruptly excused himself, and hurrying away, returned in a few seconds with the proprietor. The proprietor also examined the sugar-basin and then the salt-cellar; the proprietor also looked bewildered.

Suddenly the waiter seemed to grow inarticulate with a rush of words.

'I zink,' he stuttered eagerly, 'I zink it is those two clergymen.'

'What two clergymen?'

'The two clergymen,' said the waiter, 'that threw soup at the wall.'

'Threw soup at the wall?' repeated Valentin, feeling sure this must be some Italian metaphor.

'Yes, yes,' said the attendant excitedly, and pointing at the dark splash on the white paper; 'threw it over there on the wall.'

Valentin looked his query at the proprietor, who came to his rescue with fuller reports.

'Yes, sir,' he said, 'it's quite true, though I don't suppose it has anything to do with the sugar and salt. Two clergymen came in and drank soup here very early, as soon as the shutters were taken down. They were both very quiet, respectable people; one of them paid the bill and went out; the other, who seemed a slower coach altogether, was some minutes longer getting his things together. But he went at last. Only, the instant before he stepped into the street he deliberately picked up his cup, which he had only half

emptied, and threw the soup slap on the wall. I was in the back
room myself, and so was the waiter; so I could only rush out in
time to find the wall splashed and the shop empty. It didn't do
any particular damage, but it was confounded cheek; and I tried
to catch the men in the street. They were too far off though; I only
noticed they went round the corner into Carstairs Street.'

The detective was on his feet, hat settled and stick in hand. He
had already decided that in the universal darkness of his mind he
could only follow the first odd finger that pointed; and this finger
was odd enough. Paying his bill and clashing the glass doors behind
him, he was soon swinging round into the other street.

It was fortunate that even in such fevered moments his eye
was cool and quick. Something in a shop-front went by him
like a mere flash; yet he went back to look at it. The shop
was a popular greengrocer and fruiterer's, an array of goods
set out in the open air and plainly ticketed with their names
and prices. In the two most prominent compartments were two
heaps, of oranges and of nuts respectively. On the heap of nuts
lay a scrap of cardboard, on which was written in bold, blue chalk,
'Best tangerine oranges, two a penny.' On the oranges was the
equally clear and exact description, 'Finest Brazil nuts, 4d. a lb.' M.
Valentin looked at these two placards and fancied he had met this
highly subtle form of humour before, and that somewhat recently.
He drew the attention of the red-faced fruiterer, who was looking
rather sullenly up and down the street, to this inaccuracy in his
advertisements. The fruiterer said nothing, but sharply put each
card into its proper place. The detective, leaning elegantly on his
walking-cane, continued to scrutinize the shop. At last he said:
'Pray excuse my apparent irrelevance, my good sir, but I should
like to ask you a question in experimental psychology and the
association of ideas.'

The red-faced shopman regarded him with an eye of menace;
but he continued gaily, swinging his cane. 'Why,' he pursued, 'why
are two tickets wrongly placed in a greengrocer's shop like a shovel
hat that has come to London for a holiday? Or, in case I do not
make myself clear, what is the mystical association which connects
the idea of nuts marked as oranges with the idea of two clergymen,
one tall and the other short?'

The eyes of the tradesman stood out of his head like a snail's; he really seemed for an instant likely to fling himself upon the stranger. At last he stammered angrily: 'I don't know what you 'ave to do with it, but if you're one of their friends, you can tell 'em from me that I'll knock their silly 'eads off, parsons or no parsons, if they upset my apples again.'

'Indeed?' asked the detective, with great sympathy. 'Did they upset your apples?'

'One of 'em did,' said the heated shopman; 'rolled 'em all over the street. I'd 'ave caught the fool but for havin' to pick 'em up.'

'Which way did these parsons go?' asked Valentin.

'Up that second road on the left-hand side, and then across the square,' said the other promptly.

'Thanks,' said Valentin, and vanished like a fairy. On the other side of the second square he found a policeman, and said: 'This is urgent, constable; have you seen two clergymen in shovel hats?'

The policeman began to chuckle heavily. 'I 'ave, sir; and if you arst me, one of 'em was drunk. He stood in the middle of the road that bewildered that — '

'Which way did they go?' snapped Valentin.

'They took one of them yellow buses over there,' answered the man; 'them that go to Hampstead.'

Valentin produced his official card and said very rapidly: 'Call up two of your men to come with me in pursuit,' and crossed the road with such contagious energy that the ponderous policeman was moved to almost agile obedience. In a minute and a half the French detective was joined on the opposite pavement by an inspector and a man in plain clothes.

'Well, sir,' began the former, with smiling importance, 'and what may — ?'

Valentin pointed suddenly with his cane. 'I'll tell you on the top of that omnibus,' he said, and was darting and dodging across the tangle of the traffic. When all three sank panting on the top seats of the yellow vehicle, the inspector said: 'We could go four times as quick in a taxi.'

'Quite true,' replied their leader placidly, 'if we only had an idea of where we were going.'

'Well, where *are* you going?' asked the other, staring.

Valentin smoked frowningly for a few seconds; then, removing his cigarette, he said: 'If you *know* what a man's doing, get in front of him; but if you want to guess what he's doing, keep behind him. Stray when he strays; stop when he stops; travel as slowly as he. Then you may see what he saw and may act as he acted. All we can do is to keep our eyes skinned for a queer thing.'

'What sort of a queer thing do you mean?' asked the inspector.

'Any sort of queer thing,' answered Valentin, and relapsed into obstinate silence.

The yellow omnibus crawled up the northern roads for what seemed like hours on end; the great detective would not explain further, and perhaps his assistants felt a silent and growing doubt of his errand. Perhaps, also, they felt a silent and growing desire for lunch, for the hours crept long past the normal luncheon hour, and the long roads of the North London suburbs seemed to shoot out into length after length like an infernal telescope. It was one of those journeys on which a man perpetually feels that now at last he must have come to the end of the universe, and then finds he has only come to the beginning of Tufnell Park. London died away in draggled taverns and dreary scrubs, and then was unaccountably born again in blazing high streets and blatant hotels. It was like passing through thirteen separate vulgar cities all just touching each other. But though the winter twilight was already threatening the road ahead of them, the Parisian detective still sat silent and watchful, eyeing the frontage of the streets that slid by on either side. By the time they had left Camden Town behind, the policemen were nearly asleep; at least, they gave something like a jump as Valentin leapt erect, struck a hand on each man's shoulder, and shouted to the driver to stop.

They tumbled down the steps into the road without realizing why they had been dislodged; when they looked round for enlightenment they found Valentin triumphantly pointing his finger towards a window on the left side of the road. It was a large window, forming part of the long façade of a gilt and palatial public-house; it was the part reserved for respectable dining, and labelled 'Restaurant.' This window, like all the rest along the frontage of the hotel, was of frosted and figured glass, but in the middle of it was a big, black smash, like a star in the ice.

'Our cue at last,' cried Valentin, waving his stick; 'the place with the broken window.'

'What window? What cue?' asked his principal assistant. 'Why, what proof is there that this has anything to do with them?'

Valentin almost broke his bamboo stick with rage.

'Proof!' he cried. 'Good God! the man is looking for proof! Why, of course, the chances are twenty to one that it has *nothing* to do with them. But what else can we do? Don't you see we must either follow one wild possibility or else go home to bed?' He banged his way into the restaurant, followed by his companions, and they were soon seated at a late luncheon at a little table, and looking at the star of smashed glass from the inside. Not that it was very informative to them even then.

'Got your window broken, I see,' said Valentin to the waiter, as he paid his bill.

'Yes, sir,' answered the attendant, bending busily over the change, to which Valentin silently added an enormous tip. The waiter straightened himself with mild but unmistakable animation.

'Ah, yes, sir,' he said. 'Very odd thing, that, sir.'

'Indeed? Tell us about it,' said the detective with careless curiosity.

'Well, two gents in black came in,' said the waiter; 'two of those foreign parsons that are running about. They had a cheap and quiet little lunch, and one of them paid for it and went out. The other was just going out to join him when I looked at my change again and found he'd paid me more than three times too much. "Here," I says to the chap who was nearly out of the door, "you've paid too much." "Oh," he says, very cool, "have we?" "Yes," I says, and picks up the bill to show him. Well, that was a knock-out.'

'What do you mean?' asked his interlocutor.

'Well, I'd have sworn on seven Bibles that I'd put 4s. on that bill. But now I saw I'd put 14s., as plain as paint.'

'Well?' cried Valentin, moving slowly, but with burning eyes, 'and then?'

'The parson at the door he says, all serene, "Sorry to confuse your accounts, but it'll pay for the window." "What window?" I says. "The one I'm going to break," he says, and smashed that blessed pane with his umbrella.'

All the inquirers made an exclamation; and the inspector said under his breath: 'Are we after escaped lunatics?' The waiter went on with some relish for the ridiculous story:

'I was so knocked silly for a second, I couldn't do anything. The man marched out of the place and joined his friend just round the corner. Then they went so quick up Bullock Street that I couldn't catch them, though I ran round the bars to do it.'

'Bullock Street,' said the detective, and shot up that thoroughfare as quickly as the strange couple he pursued.

Their journey now took them through bare brick ways like tunnels; streets with few lights and even with few windows; streets that seemed built out of the blank backs of everything and everywhere. Dusk was deepening, and it was not easy even for the London policemen to guess in what exact direction they were treading. The inspector, however, was pretty certain that they would eventually strike some part of Hampstead Heath. Abruptly one bulging and gas-lit window broke the blue twilight like a bull's-eye lantern; and Valentin stopped an instant before a little garish sweetstuff shop. After an instant's hesitation he went in; he stood amid the gaudy colours of the confectionery with entire gravity and bought thirteen chocolate cigars with a certain care. He was clearly preparing an opening; but he did not need one.

An angular, elderly young woman in the shop had regarded his elegant appearance with a merely automatic inquiry; but when she saw the door behind him blocked with the blue uniform of the inspector, her eyes seemed to wake up.

'Oh,' she said, 'if you've come about that parcel, I've sent it off already.'

'Parcel!' repeated Valentin; and it was his turn to look inquiring.

'I mean the parcel the gentleman left – the clergyman gentleman.'

'For goodness' sake,' said Valentin, leaning forward with his first real confession of eagerness, 'for Heaven's sake tell us what happened exactly.'

'Well,' said the woman, a little doubtfully, 'the clergymen came in about half an hour ago and bought some peppermints and talked a bit, and then went off towards the Heath. But a second after, one of them runs back into the shop and says, "Have I left a parcel?" Well, I looked everywhere and couldn't see one; so he says, "Never mind; but if it should turn up, please post it to this address," and he left me the address and a shilling for my trouble. And sure enough, though I thought I'd looked everywhere, I found he'd left a brown-paper parcel, so I posted it to the place he said. I can't remember the address now; it was somewhere in Westminster. But as the thing seemed so important, I thought perhaps the police had come about it.'

'So they have,' said Valentin shortly. 'Is Hampstead Heath near here?'

'Straight on for fifteen minutes,' said the woman, 'and you'll come right out on the open.' Valentin sprang out of the shop and began to run. The other detectives followed him at a reluctant trot.

The street they threaded was so narrow and shut in by shadows that when they came out unexpectedly into the void common and vast sky they were startled to find the evening still so light and clear. A perfect dome of peacock-green sank into gold amid the blackening trees and the dark violet distances. The glowing green tint was just deep enough to pick out in points of crystal one or two stars. All that was left of the daylight lay in a golden glitter across the edge of Hampstead and that popular hollow which is called the Vale of Health. The holiday makers who roam this region had not wholly dispersed: a few couples sat shapelessly on benches; and here and there a distant girl still shrieked in one of the swings. The glory of heaven deepened and darkened around the sublime vulgarity of man; and standing on the slope and looking across the valley, Valentin beheld the thing which he sought.

Among the black and breaking groups in that distance was one especially black which did not break – a group of two figures clerically clad. Though they seemed as small as insects, Valentin could see that one of them was much smaller than the other. Though the other had a student's stoop and an inconspicuous manner, he could see that the man was well over six feet high. He shut his teeth and went forward, whirling his stick impatiently. By the time he had substantially diminished the distance and magnified the two black figures as in a vast microscope, he had perceived something else; something which startled him, and yet which he had somehow expected. Whoever was the tall priest, there could be no doubt about the identity of the short one. It was his friend of the Harwich train, the stumpy little *curé* of Essex whom he had warned about his brown-paper parcels.

Now, so far as this went, everything fitted in finally and rationally enough. Valentin had learned by his inquiries that morning that a Father Brown from Essex was bringing up a silver cross with sapphires, a relic of considerable value, to show some of the foreign priests at the congress. This undoubtedly was the 'silver with blue stones'; and Father Brown undoubtedly was the little greenhorn in the train. Now there was nothing wonderful about the fact that what Valentin had found out Flambeau had also found out; Flambeau found out everything. Also there was nothing wonderful in the fact that when Flambeau heard of a sapphire cross he should try to steal it; that was the most natural thing in all natural history. And most certainly there was nothing wonderful about the fact that Flambeau should have it all his own way with such a silly sheep as the man with the umbrella and the parcels. He was the sort of man whom anybody could lead on a string to the North Pole; it was not surprising that an actor like Flambeau, dressed as another priest, could lead him to Hampstead Heath. So far the crime seemed clear enough; and while the detective pitied the priest for his helplessness, he almost despised Flambeau for condescending to so gullible a victim. But when Valentin thought of all that had happened in between, of all that had led him to his triumph, he racked his brains for the smallest rhyme or reason in it. What had the stealing of a blue-and-silver cross from a priest from Essex to do with chucking soup at wallpaper? What had it to do with calling nuts oranges, or with paying for windows first and breaking them afterwards? He had come to the end of his chase; yet somehow he had missed the middle of it. When he failed (which was seldom), he had usually grasped the clue, but nevertheless missed the criminal. Here he had grasped the criminal, but still he could not grasp the clue.

The two figures that they followed were crawling like black flies across the huge green contour of a hill. They were evidently sunk in conversation, and perhaps did not notice where they were going; but they were certainly going to the wilder and more silent heights of the Heath. As their pursuers gained on them, the latter had to use the undignified attitudes of the deer-stalker, to crouch behind clumps of trees and even to crawl prostrate in deep grass. By these ungainly ingenuities the hunters even came close enough to the quarry to hear the murmur of the discussion, but no word could be distinguished except the word 'reason' recurring frequently in a high and almost childish voice. Once, over an abrupt dip of land and a dense tangle of thickets, the detectives actually lost the two figures they were following. They did not find the trail again for an agonizing ten minutes, and then it led round the brow of a great dome of hill overlooking an amphitheatre of rich and desolate sunset scenery. Under a tree in this commanding yet neglected spot was an old ramshackle wooden seat. On this seat sat the two priests still in serious speech together. The gorgeous green and gold still clung to the darkening horizon; but the dome above was turning slowly from peacock-green to peacock-blue, and the stars detached themselves more and more like solid jewels. Mutely motioning to his followers, Valentin contrived to creep up behind the big branching tree, and, standing there in deathly silence, heard the words of the strange priests for the first time.

After he had listened for a minute and a half, he was gripped by a devilish doubt. Perhaps he had dragged the two English policemen to the wastes of a nocturnal heath on an errand no saner than seeking figs on thistles. For the two priests were talking exactly like priests, piously, with learning and leisure, about the most aerial enigmas of theology. The little Essex priest spoke the more simply, with his round face turned to the strengthening stars; the other talked with his head bowed, as if he were not even worthy to look at them. But no more innocently clerical conversation could have been heard in any white Italian cloister or black Spanish cathedral.

The first he heard was the tail of one of Father Brown's sentences, which ended: '. . . what they really meant in the Middle Ages by the heavens being incorruptible.'

The taller priest nodded his bowed head and said:

'Ah, yes, these modern infidels appeal to their reason; but who can look at those millions of worlds and not feel that there may well be wonderful universes above us where reason is utterly unreasonable?'

'No,' said the other priest; 'reason is always reasonable, even in the last limbo, in the lost borderland of things. I know that people charge the Church with lowering reason, but it is just the other way. Alone on earth, the Church makes reason really supreme. Alone on earth, the Church affirms that God Himself is bound by reason.'

The other priest raised his austere face to the spangled sky and said:

'Yet who knows if in that infinite universe — ?'

'Only infinite physically,' said the little priest, turning sharply in his seat, 'not infinite in the sense of escaping from the laws of truth.'

Valentin behind his tree was tearing his finger-nails with silent fury. He seemed almost to hear the sniggers of the English detectives whom he had brought so far on a fantastic guess only to listen to the metaphysical gossip of two mild old parsons. In his impatience he lost the equally elaborate answer of the tall cleric, and when he listened again it was again Father Brown who was speaking:

'Reason and justice grip the remotest and the loneliest star. Look at those stars. Don't they look as if they were single diamonds and sapphires? Well, you can imagine any mad botany or geology you please. Think of forests of adamant with leaves of brilliants. Think the moon is a blue moon, a single elephantine sapphire. But don't fancy that all that frantic astronomy would make the smallest difference to the reason and justice of conduct. On plains of opal, under cliffs cut out of pearl, you would still find a notice-board, "Thou shalt not steal."'

Valentin was just in the act of rising from his rigid and crouching attitude and creeping away as softly as might be, felled by the one great folly of his life. But something in the very silence of the tall priest made him stop until the latter spoke. When at last he did speak, he said simply, his head bowed and his hands on his knees:

'Well, I still think that other worlds may perhaps rise higher than our reason. The mystery of heaven is unfathomable, and I for one can only bow my head.'

Then, with brow yet bent and without changing by the faintest shade his attitude or voice, he added:

'Just hand over that sapphire cross of yours, will you? We're all alone here, and I could pull you to pieces like a straw doll.'

The utterly unaltered voice and attitude added a strange violence to that shocking change of speech. But the guarder of the relic only seemed to turn his head by the smallest section of the compass. He seemed still to have a somewhat foolish face turned to the stars. Perhaps he had not understood. Or, perhaps, he had understood and sat rigid with terror.

'Yes,' said the tall priest, in the same low voice and in the same still posture, 'Yes, I am Flambeau.'

Then, after a pause, he said:

'Come, will you give me that cross?'

'No,' said the other, and the monosyllable had an odd sound.

Flambeau suddenly flung off all his pontifical pretensions. The great robber leaned back in his seat and laughed low but long.

'No,' he cried; 'you won't give it me, you proud prelate. You won't give it me, you little celibate simpleton. Shall I tell you why you won't give it me? Because I've got it already in my own breast-pocket.'

The small man from Essex turned what seemed to be a dazed face in the dusk, and said, with the timid eagerness of 'The Private Secretary':

'Are – are you sure?'

Flambeau yelled with delight.

'Really, you're as good as a three-act farce,' he cried. 'Yes, you turnip, I am quite sure. I had the sense to make a duplicate of the right parcel, and now, my friend, you've got the duplicate, and I've got the jewels. An old dodge, Father Brown – a very old dodge.'

'Yes,' said Father Brown, and passed his hand through his hair with the same strange vagueness of manner. 'Yes, I've heard of it before.'

The colossus of crime leaned over to the little rustic priest with a sort of sudden interest.

'*You* have heard of it?' he asked. 'Where have *you* heard of it?'

'Well, I mustn't tell you his name, of course,' said the little man simply. 'He was a penitent, you know. He had lived prosperously for about twenty years entirely on duplicate brown-paper parcels. And so, you see, when I began to suspect you, I thought of this poor chap's way of doing it at once.'

'Began to suspect me?' repeated the outlaw with increased intensity. 'Did you really have the gumption to suspect me just because I brought you up to this bare part of the heath?'

'No, no,' said Brown with an air of apology. 'You see, I suspected you when we first met. It's that little bulge up the sleeve where you people have the spiked bracelet.'

'How in Tartarus,' cried Flambeau, 'did you ever hear of the spiked bracelet?'

'Oh, one's little flock, you know!' said Father Brown, arching his eyebrows rather blankly. 'When I was a curate in Hartlepool, there were three of them with spiked bracelets. So, as I suspected you from the first, don't you see, I made sure that the cross should go safe, anyhow. I'm afraid I watched you, you know. So at last I saw you change the parcels. Then, don't you see, I changed them back again. And then I left the right one behind.'

'Left it behind?' repeated Flambeau, and for the first time there was another note in his voice beside his triumph.

'Well, it was like this,' said the little priest, speaking in the same unaffected way. 'I went back to that sweet-shop and asked if I'd left a parcel, and gave them a particular address if it turned up. Well, I knew I hadn't; but when I went away again I did. So, instead of running after me with that valuable parcel, they have sent it flying to a friend of mine in Westminster.' Then he added rather sadly: 'I learnt that, too, from a poor fellow in Hartlepool. He used to do it with handbags he stole at railway stations, but he's in a monastery now. Oh, one gets to know, you know,' he added, rubbing his head again with the same sort of desperate apology. 'We can't help being priests. People come and tell us these things.'

Flambeau tore a brown-paper parcel out of his inner pocket and rent it in pieces. There was nothing but paper and sticks of lead inside it. He sprang to his feet with a gigantic gesture, and cried:

'I don't believe you. I don't believe a bumpkin like you could manage all that. I believe you've still got the stuff on you, and if you don't give it up – why, we're all alone, and I'll take it by force!'

'No,' said Father Brown simply, and stood up also; 'you won't take it by force. First, because I really haven't still got it. And, second, because we are not alone.'

Flambeau stopped in his stride forward.

'Behind that tree,' said Father Brown, pointing, 'are two strong policemen and the greatest detective alive. How did they come here, do you ask? Why, I brought them, of course! How did I do it? Why, I'll tell you if you like! Lord bless you, we have to know twenty such things when we work among the criminal classes! Well, I wasn't sure you were a thief, and it would never do to make a scandal against one of our own clergy. So I just tested you to see if anything would make you show yourself. A man generally makes a small scene if he finds salt in his coffee; if he doesn't, he has some reason for keeping quiet. I changed the salt and sugar, and *you* kept quiet. A man generally objects if his bill is three times too big. If he pays it, he has some motive for passing unnoticed. I altered your bill, and *you* paid it.'

The world seemed waiting for Flambeau to leap like a tiger. But he was held back as by a spell; he was stunned with the utmost curiosity.

'Well,' went on Father Brown, with lumbering lucidity, 'as you wouldn't leave any tracks for the police, of course somebody had to. At every place we went to, I took care to do something that would get us talked about for the rest of the day. I didn't do much harm – a splashed wall, spilt apples, a broken window; but I saved the cross, as the cross will always be saved. It is at Westminster by now. I rather wonder you didn't stop it with the Donkey's Whistle.'

'With the what?' asked Flambeau.

'I'm glad you've never heard of it,' said the priest, making a face. 'It's a foul thing. I'm sure you're too good a man for a Whistler. I couldn't have countered it even with the Spots myself; I'm not strong enough in the legs.'

'What on earth are you talking about?' asked the other.

'Well, I did think you'd know the Spots,' said Father Brown, agreeably surprised. 'Oh, you can't have gone so very wrong yet!'

'How in blazes do you know all these horrors?' cried Flambeau.

The shadow of a smile crossed the round, simple face of his clerical opponent.

'Oh, by being a celibate simpleton, I suppose,' he said. 'Has it never struck you that a man who does next to nothing but hear men's real sins is not likely to be wholly unaware of human evil? But, as a matter of fact, another part of my trade, too, made me sure you weren't a priest.'

'What?' asked the thief, almost gaping.

'You attacked reason,' said Father Brown. 'It's bad theology.'

And even as he turned away to collect his property, the three policemen came out from under the twilight trees. Flambeau was an artist and a sportsman. He stepped back and swept Valentin a great bow.

'Do not bow to me, *mon ami*,' said Valentin, with silver clearness. 'Let us both bow to our master.'

And they both stood an instant uncovered, while the little Essex priest blinked about for his umbrella.

The Invisible Man

In the cool blue twilight of two steep streets in Camden Town, the shop at the corner, a confectioner's, glowed like the butt of a cigar. One should rather say, perhaps, like the butt of a firework, for the light was of many colours and some complexity, broken up by many mirrors and dancing on many gilt and gaily-coloured cakes and sweetmeats. Against this one fiery glass were glued the noses of many gutter-snipes, for the chocolates were all wrapped in those red and gold and green metallic colours which are almost better than chocolate itself; and the huge white wedding-cake in the window was somehow at once remote and satisfying, just as if the whole North Pole were good to eat. Such rainbow provocations could naturally collect the youth of the neighbourhood up to the ages of ten or twelve. But this corner was also attractive to youth at a later stage; and a young man, not less than twenty-four, was staring into the same shop window. To him, also, the shop was of fiery charm, but this attraction was not wholly to be explained by chocolates; which, however, he was far from despising.

He was a tall, burly, red-haired young man, with a resolute face but a listless manner. He carried under his arm a flat, grey portfolio of black-and-white sketches which he had sold with more or less success to publishers ever since his uncle (who was an admiral) had disinherited him for Socialism, because of a lecture which he had delivered against that economic theory. His name was John Turnbull Angus.

Entering at last, he walked through the confectioner's shop into the back room, which was a sort of pastry-cook restaurant, merely raising his hat to the young lady who was serving there. She was a dark, elegant, alert girl in black, with a high colour and very quick, dark eyes; and after the ordinary interval she followed him into the inner room to take his order.

His order was evidently a usual one. 'I want, please,' he said with precision, 'one halfpenny bun and a small cup of black coffee.' An instant before the girl could turn away he added, 'Also, I want you to marry me.'

The young lady of the shop stiffened suddenly, and said: 'Those are jokes I don't allow.'

The red-haired young man lifted grey eyes of an unexpected gravity.

'Really and truly,' he said, 'it's as serious – as serious as the halfpenny bun. It is expensive, like the bun; one pays for it. It is indigestible, like the bun. It hurts.'

The dark young lady had never taken her dark eyes off him, but seemed to be studying him with almost tragic exactitude. At the end of her scrutiny she had something like the shadow of a smile, and she sat down in a chair.

'Don't you think,' observed Angus, absently, 'that it's rather cruel to eat these halfpenny buns? They might grow up into penny buns. I shall give up these brutal sports when we are married.'

The dark young lady rose from her chair and walked to the window, evidently in a state of strong but not unsympathetic cogitation. When at last she swung round again with an air of resolution, she was bewildered to observe that the young man was carefully laying out on the table various objects from the shop-window. They included a pyramid of highly coloured sweets, several plates of sandwiches, and the two decanters containing that mysterious port and sherry which are peculiar to pastry-cooks. In the middle of this neat arrangement he had carefully let down the enormous load of white sugared cake which had been the huge ornament of the window.

'What on earth are you doing?' she asked.

'Duty, my dear Laura,' he began.

'Oh, for the Lord's sake, stop a minute,' she cried, 'and don't talk to me in that way. I mean what is all that?'

'A ceremonial meal, Miss Hope.'

'And what is *that*?' she asked impatiently, pointing to the mountain of sugar.

'The wedding-cake, Mrs. Angus,' he said.

The girl marched to that article, removed it with some clatter, and put it back in the shop-window; she then returned, and, putting her elegant elbows on the table, regarded the young man not unfavourably, but with considerable exasperation.

'You don't give me any time to think,' she said.

'I'm not such a fool,' he answered; 'that's my Christian humility.'

She was still looking at him; but she had grown considerably graver behind the smile.

'Mr. Angus,' she said steadily, 'before there is a minute more of this nonsense I must tell you something about myself as shortly as I can.'

'Delighted,' replied Angus gravely. 'You might tell me something about myself, too, while you are about it.'

'Oh, do hold your tongue and listen,' she said. 'It's nothing that I'm ashamed of, and it isn't even anything that I'm specially sorry about. But what would you say if there were something that is no business of mine and yet is my nightmare?'

'In that case,' said the man seriously, 'I should suggest that you bring back the cake.'

'Well, you must listen to the story first,' said Laura, persistently. 'To begin with, I must tell you that my father owned the inn called the "Red Fish" at Ludbury, and I used to serve people in the bar.'

'I have often wondered,' he said, 'why there was a kind of a Christian air about this one confectioner's shop.'

'Ludbury is a sleepy, grassy little hole in the Eastern Counties, and the only kind of people who ever came to the "Red Fish" were occasional commercial travellers, and for the rest, the most awful people you can see, only you've never seen them. I mean little, loungy men, who had just enough to live on, and had nothing to do but lean about in bar-rooms and bet on horses, in bad clothes that were just too good for them. Even these wretched young rotters were not very common at our house; but there were two of them that were a lot too common – common in every sort of way. They both lived on money of their own, and were wearisomely idle and over-dressed. But yet I was a bit sorry for them, because I half believe they slunk into our little empty bar because each of them had a slight deformity; the sort of thing that some yokels laugh at. It wasn't exactly a deformity either; it was more an oddity. One of them was a surprisingly small man, something like a dwarf, or at least like a jockey. He was not at all jockeyish to look at, though, he had a round black head and a well-trimmed black beard, bright eyes like a bird's; he jingled money in his pockets; he jangled a great gold watch chain; and he never turned up except dressed just too much like a gentleman to be one. He was no fool, though, though a futile idler; he was curiously clever at all kinds of things that couldn't be the slightest use; a sort of impromptu conjuring; making fifteen matches set fire to each other like a regular firework; or cutting a banana or some such thing into a dancing doll. His name was Isidore Smythe; and I can see him still, with his little dark face, just coming up to the counter, making a jumping kangaroo out of five cigars.

'The other fellow was more silent and more ordinary; but somehow he alarmed me much more than poor little Smythe. He was very tall and slight, and light-haired; his nose had a high bridge, and he might almost have been handsome in a spectral sort of way; but he had one of the most appalling squints I have ever seen or heard of. When he looked straight at you, you didn't know where you were yourself, let alone what he was looking at. I fancy this sort of disfigurement embittered the poor chap a little; for while Smythe was ready to show off his monkey tricks anywhere, James Welkin (that was the squinting man's name) never did anything except soak in our bar parlour, and go for great walks by himself in the flat, grey country all round. All the same, I think Smythe, too, was a little sensitive about being so small, though he carried it off more smartly. And so it was that I was really puzzled, as well as startled, and very sorry, when they both offered to marry me in the same week.

'Well, I did what I've since thought was perhaps a silly thing. But, after all, these freaks were my friends in a way; and I had a horror of their thinking I refused them for the real reason, which was that they were so impossibly ugly. So I made up some gas of another sort, about never meaning to marry anyone who hadn't carved his way in the world. I said it was a point of principle with me not to live on money that was just inherited like theirs. Two days after I had talked in this well-meaning sort of way, the whole trouble began. The first thing I heard was that both of them had gone off to seek their fortunes, as if they were in some silly fairy tale.

'Well, I've never seen either of them from that day to this. But I've had two letters from the little man called Smythe, and really they were rather exciting.'

'Ever heard of the other man?' asked Angus.

'No, he never wrote,' said the girl, after an instant's hesitation. 'Smythe's first letter was simply to say that he had started out walking with Welkin to London; but Welkin was such a good walker that the little man dropped out of it, and took a rest by the roadside. He happened to be picked up by some travelling show, and, partly because he was nearly a dwarf, and partly because he was really a clever little wretch, he got on quite well in the show business, and was soon sent up to the Aquarium, to do some tricks that I forgot. That was his first letter. His second was much more of a startler, and I only got it last week.'

The man called Angus emptied his coffee-cup and regarded her with mild and patient eyes. Her own mouth took a slight twist of laughter as she resumed: 'I suppose you've seen on the hoardings all about this "Smythe's Silent Service"? Or you must be the only person that hasn't. Oh, I don't know much about it, it's some clockwork invention for doing all the housework by machinery. You know the sort of thing: "Press a button – A Butler who Never Drinks." "Turn a handle – Ten Housemaids who Never Flirt." You must have seen the advertisements. Well, whatever these machines are, they are making pots of money; and they are making it all for that little imp whom I knew down in Ludbury. I can't help feeling pleased the poor little chap has fallen on his feet; but the plain fact is, I'm in terror of his turning up any minute and telling me he's carved his way in the world – as he certainly has.'

'And the other man?' repeated Angus with a sort of obstinate quietude.

Laura Hope got to her feet suddenly. 'My friend,' she said: 'I think you are a witch. Yes, you are quite right. I have not seen a line of the other man's writing; and I have no more notion than the dead of what or where he is. But it is of him that I am frightened. It is he who is all about my path. It is he who has half driven me mad. Indeed, I think he has driven me mad; for I have felt him where he could not have been, and I have heard his voice when he could not have spoken.'

'Well, my dear,' said the young man, cheerfully, 'if he were Satan himself, he is done for now you have told somebody. One goes mad all alone, old girl. But when was it you fancied you felt and heard our squinting friend?'

'I heard James Welkin laugh as plainly as I hear you speak,' said the girl, steadily. 'There was nobody there, for I stood just outside the shop at the corner, and could see down both streets at once. I had forgotten how he laughed, though his laugh was as odd as his squint. I had not thought of him for nearly a year. But it's a solemn truth that a few seconds later the first letter came from his rival.'

'Did you ever make the spectre speak or squeak, or anything?' asked Angus, with some interest.

Laura suddenly shuddered, and then said with an unshaken voice: 'Yes. Just when I had finished reading the second letter from Isidore Smythe announcing his success, just then, I heard Welkin say: "He shan't have you, though." It was quite plain, as if he were in the room. It is awful; I think I must be mad.'

'If you really were mad,' said the young man, 'you would think you must be sane. But certainly there seems to me to be something a little rum about this unseen gentleman. Two heads are better than one – I spare you allusions to any other organs – and really, if you would allow me, as a sturdy, practical man, to bring back the wedding-cake out of the window — '

Even as he spoke, there was a sort of steely shriek in the street outside, and a small motor, driven at devilish speed, shot up to the door of the shop and stuck there. In the same flash of time a small man in a shiny top hat stood stamping in the outer room.

Angus, who had hitherto maintained hilarious ease from motives of mental hygiene, revealed the strain of his soul by striding abruptly out of the inner room and confronting the newcomer. A glance at him was quite sufficient to confirm the savage guesswork of a man in love. This very dapper but dwarfish figure, with the spike of black beard carried insolently forward, the clever unrestful eyes, the neat but very nervous fingers, could be none other than the man just described to him: Isidore Smythe, who made dolls out of banana skins and matchboxes: Isidore Smythe, who made millions out of undrinking butlers and unflirting housemaids of metal. For a moment the two men, instinctively understanding each other's air of possession, looked at each other with that curious cold generosity which is the soul of rivalry.

Mr. Smythe, however, made no allusion to the ultimate ground of their antagonism, but said simply and explosively: 'Has Miss Hope seen that thing on the window?'

'On the window?' repeated the staring Angus.

'There's no time to explain other things,' said the small millionaire shortly. 'There's some tomfoolery going on here that has to be investigated.'

He pointed his polished walking-stick at the window, recently depleted by the bridal preparations of Mr. Angus; and that gentleman was astonished to see along the front of the glass a long strip of paper pasted, which had certainly not been on the window when he had looked through it some time before. Following the energetic Smythe outside into the street, he found that some yard and a half of stamp paper had been carefully gummed along the glass outside, and on this was written in straggly characters: 'If you marry Smythe, he will die.'

'Laura,' said Angus, putting his big red head into the shop, 'you're not mad.'

'It's the writing of that fellow Welkin,' said Smythe gruffly. 'I haven't seen him for years, but he's always bothering me. Five times in the last fortnight he's had threatening letters left at my flat, and I can't even find out who leaves them, let alone if it is Welkin himself. The porter of the flats swears that no suspicious characters have been seen, and here he has pasted up a sort of dado on a public shop window, while the people in the shop — '

'Quite so,' said Angus modestly, 'while the people in the shop were having tea. Well, sir, I can assure you I appreciate your common sense in dealing so directly with the matter. We can talk about other things afterwards. The fellow cannot be very far off yet, for I swear there was no paper there when I went last to the window, ten or fifteen minutes ago. On the other hand, he's too far off to be chased, as we don't even know the direction. If you'll take my advice, Mr. Smythe, you'll put this at once in the hands of some energetic inquiry man, private rather than public. I know an extremely clever fellow, who has set up in business five minutes from here in your car. His name's Flambeau, and though his youth was a bit stormy, he's a strictly honest man now, and his brains are worth money. He lives in Lucknow Mansions, Hampstead.'

'That is odd,' said the little man, arching his black eyebrows. 'I live myself in Himalaya Mansions round the corner. Perhaps you might care to come with me; I can go to my rooms and sort out these queer Welkin documents, while you run round and get your friend the detective.'

'You are very good,' said Angus politely. 'Well, the sooner we act the better.'

Both men, with a queer kind of impromptu fairness, took the same sort of formal farewell of the lady, and both jumped into the brisk little car. As Smythe took the wheel and they turned the great corner of the street, Angus was amused to see a gigantesque poster of 'Smythe's Silent Service,' with a picture of a huge headless iron doll, carrying a saucepan with the legend, 'A Cook Who is Never Cross.'

'I use them in my own flat,' said the little black-bearded man, laughing, 'partly for advertisement, and partly for real convenience. Honestly, and all above board, those big clockwork dolls of mine do bring you coals or claret or a time-table quicker than any live servants I've ever known, if you know which knob to press. But I'll never deny, between ourselves, that such servants have their disadvantages, too.'

'Indeed?' said Angus; 'is there something they can't do?'

'Yes,' replied Smythe coolly; 'they can't tell me who left those threatening letters at my flat.'

The man's motor was small and swift like himself; in fact, like his domestic service, it was of his own invention. If he was an advertising quack, he was one who believed in his own wares. The sense of something tiny and flying was accentuated as they swept up long white curves of road in the dead but open daylight of evening. Soon the white curves came sharper and dizzier; they were upon ascending spirals, as they say in the modern religions. For, indeed, they were cresting a corner of London which is almost as precipitous as Edinburgh, if not quite so picturesque. Terrace rose above terrace, and the special tower of flats they sought, rose above them all to almost Egyptian height, gilt by the level sunset. The change, as they turned the corner and entered the crescent known as Himalaya Mansions, was as abrupt as the opening of a window; for they found that pile of flats sitting above London as above a green sea of slate. Opposite to the mansions, on the other side of the gravel crescent, was a bushy enclosure more like a steep hedge or dyke than a garden, and some way below that ran a strip of artificial water, a sort of canal, like the moat of that embowered fortress. As the car swept round the crescent it passed, at one corner, the stray stall of a man selling chestnuts; and right away at the other end of the curve, Angus could see a dim blue policeman walking slowly. These were the only human shapes in that high suburban solitude; but he had an irrational sense that they expressed the speechless poetry of London. He felt as if they were figures in a story.

The little car shot up to the right house like a bullet, and shot out its owner like a bomb shell. He was immediately inquiring of a tall commissionaire in shining braid, and a short porter in shirt sleeves, whether anybody or anything had been seeking his apartments. He was assured that nobody and nothing had passed these officials since his last inquiries; whereupon he and the slightly bewildered Angus were shot up in the lift like a rocket, till they reached the top floor.

'Just come in for a minute,' said the breathless Smythe. 'I want to show you those Welkin letters. Then you might run round the corner and fetch your friend.' He pressed a button concealed in the wall, and the door opened of itself.

It opened on a long, commodious ante-room, of which the only arresting features, ordinarily speaking, were the rows of tall half-human mechanical figures that stood up on both sides like tailors' dummies. Like tailors' dummies they were headless; and like tailors' dummies they had a handsome unnecessary humpiness in the shoulders, and a pigeon-breasted protuberance of chest; but barring this, they were not much more like a human figure than any automatic machine at a station that is about the human height. They had two great hooks like arms, for carrying trays; and they were painted pea-green, or vermilion, or black for convenience of distinction; in every other way they were only automatic machines and nobody would have looked twice at them. On this occasion, at least, nobody did. For between the two rows of these domestic dummies lay something more interesting than most of the mechanics of the world. It was a white, tattered scrap of paper scrawled with red ink; and the agile inventor had snatched it up almost as soon as the door flew open. He handed it to Angus without a word. The red ink on it actually was not dry, and the message ran: 'If you have been to see her today, I shall kill you.'

There was a short silence, and then Isidore Smythe said quietly: 'Would you like a little whisky? I rather feel as if I should.'

'Thank you; I should like a little Flambeau,' said Angus, gloomily. 'This business seems to me to be getting rather grave. I'm going round at once to fetch him.'

'Right you are,' said the other, with admirable cheerfulness. 'Bring him round here as quick as you can.'

But as Angus closed the front door behind him he saw Smythe push back a button, and one of the clockwork images glided from its place and slid along a groove in the floor carrying a tray with syphon and decanter. There did seem something a trifle weird about leaving the little man alone among those dead servants, who were coming to life as the door closed.

Six steps down from Smythe's landing the man in shirt sleeves was doing something with a pail. Angus stopped to extract a promise, fortified with a prospective bribe, that he would remain in that place until the return with the detective, and would keep count of any kind of stranger coming up those stairs. Dashing down to the front hall he then laid similar charges of vigilance on the commissionaire at the front door, from whom he learned the simplifying circumstance that there was no back door. Not content with this, he captured the floating policeman and induced him to stand opposite the entrance and watch it; and finally paused an instant for a pennyworth of chestnuts, and an inquiry as to the probable length of the merchant's stay in the neighbourhood.

The chestnut seller, turning up the collar of his coat, told him he should probably be moving shortly, as he thought it was going to snow. Indeed, the evening was growing grey and bitter, but Angus, with all his eloquence, proceeded to nail the chestnut man to his post.

'Keep yourself warm on your own chestnuts,' he said earnestly. 'Eat up your whole stock; I'll make it worth your while. I'll give you a sovereign if you'll wait here till I come back, and then tell me whether any man, woman, or child has gone into that house where the commissionaire is standing.'

He then walked away smartly, with a last look at the besieged tower.

'I've made a ring round that room, anyhow,' he said. 'They can't all four of them be Mr. Welkin's accomplices.'

Lucknow Mansions were, so to speak, on a lower platform of that hill of houses, of which Himalaya Mansions might be called the peak. Mr. Flambeau's semi-official flat was on the ground floor, and presented in every way a marked contrast to the American machinery and cold hotel-like luxury of the flat of the Silent Service. Flambeau, who was a friend of Angus, received him in a rococo artistic den behind his office, of which the ornaments were sabres, harquebuses, Eastern curiosities, flasks of Italian wine, savage cooking-pots, a plumy Persian cat, and a small dusty-looking Roman Catholic priest, who looked particularly out of place.

'This is my friend, Father Brown,' said Flambeau. 'I've often wanted you to meet him. Splendid weather, this; a little cold for Southerners like me.'

'Yes, I think it will keep clear,' said Angus, sitting down on a violet-striped Eastern ottoman.

'No,' said the priest quietly; 'it has begun to snow.'

And indeed, as he spoke, the first few flakes, foreseen by the man of chestnuts, began to drift across the darkening window-pane.

'Well,' said Angus heavily. 'I'm afraid I've come on business, and rather jumpy business at that. The fact is, Flambeau, within a stone's throw of your house is a fellow who badly wants your help; he's perpetually being haunted and threatened by an invisible enemy – a scoundrel whom nobody has even seen.' As Angus proceeded to tell the whole tale of Smythe and Welkin beginning with Laura's story, and going on with his own, the supernatural laugh at the corner of two empty streets, the strange distinct words spoken in an empty room, Flambeau grew more and more vividly concerned, and the little priest seemed to be left out of it, like a piece of furniture. When it came to the scribbled stamp-paper pasted on the window, Flambeau rose, seeming to fill the room with his huge shoulders.

'If you don't mind,' he said, 'I think you had better tell me the rest on the nearest road to this man's house. It strikes me, somehow, that there is no time to be lost.'

'Delighted,' said Angus, rising also, 'though he's safe enough for the present, for I've set four men to watch the only hole to his burrow.'

They turned out into the street, the small priest trundling after them with the docility of a small dog. He merely said, in a cheerful way, like one making conversation: 'How quick the snow gets thick on the ground.'

As they threaded the steep side streets already powdered with silver, Angus finished his story; and by the time they reached the crescent with the towering flats, he had leisure to turn his attention to the four sentinels. The chestnut seller, both before and after receiving a sovereign, swore stubbornly that he had watched the door and seen no visitor enter. The policeman was even more emphatic. He said he had had experience of crooks of all kinds, in top hats and in rags; he wasn't so green as to expect suspicious characters to look suspicious; he looked out for anybody, and, so help him, there had been nobody. And when all three men gathered round the gilded commissionaire, who still stood smiling astride of the porch, the verdict was more final still.

'I've got a right to ask any man, duke or dustman, what he wants in these flats,' said the genial and gold-laced giant, 'and I'll swear there's been nobody to ask since this gentleman went away.'

The unimportant Father Brown, who stood back, looking modestly at the pavement, here ventured to say meekly: 'Has nobody been up and down stairs, then, since the snow began to fall? It began while we were all round at Flambeau's.'

'Nobody's been in here, sir, you can take it from me,' said the official, with beaming authority.

'Then I wonder what that is?' said the priest, and stared at the ground blankly like a fish.

The others all looked down also; and Flambeau used a fierce exclamation and a French gesture. For it was unquestionably true that down the middle of the entrance guarded by the man in gold lace, actually between the arrogant, stretched legs of that colossus, ran a stringy pattern of grey footprints stamped upon the white snow.

'God!' cried Angus involuntarily; 'the Invisible Man!'

Without another word he turned and dashed up the stairs, with Flambeau following; but Father Brown still stood looking about him in the snow-clad street as if he had lost interest in his query.

Flambeau was plainly in a mood to break down the door with his big shoulder; but the Scotsman, with more reason, if less intuition, fumbled about on the frame of the door till he found the invisible button; and the door swung slowly open.

It showed substantially the same serried interior; the hall had grown darker, though it was still struck here and there with the last crimson shafts of sunset, and one or two of the headless machines had been moved from their places for this or that purpose, and stood here and there about the twilit place. The green and red of their coats were all darkened in the dusk, and their likeness to human shapes slightly increased by their very shapelessness. But in the middle of them all, exactly where the paper with the red ink had lain, there lay something that looked very like red ink spilled out of its bottle. But it was not red ink.

With a French combination of reason and violence Flambeau simply said 'Murder!' and, plunging into the flat, had explored every corner and cupboard of it in five minutes. But if he expected to find a corpse he found none. Isidore Smythe simply was not in the place, either dead or alive. After the most tearing search the two men met each other in the outer hall with streaming faces and staring eyes. 'My friend,' said Flambeau, talking French in his excitement, 'not only is your murderer invisible, but he makes invisible also the murdered man.'

Angus looked round at the dim room full of dummies, and in some Celtic corner of his Scotch soul a shudder started. One of the life-size dolls stood immediately overshadowing the blood stain, summoned, perhaps, by the slain man an instant before he fell. One of the high-shouldered hooks that served the thing for arms, was a little lifted and Angus had suddenly the horrid fancy that poor Smythe's own iron child had struck him down. Matter had rebelled, and these machines had killed their master. But even so, what had they done with him?

'Eaten him?' said the nightmare at his ear; and he sickened for an instant at the idea of rent, human remains absorbed and crushed into all that acephalous clockwork.

He recovered his mental health by an emphatic effort, and said to Flambeau: 'Well, there it is. The poor fellow has evaporated like a cloud and left a red streak on the floor. The tale does not belong to this world.'

'There is only one thing to be done,' said Flambeau, 'whether it belongs to this world or the other, I must go down and talk to my friend.'

They descended, passing the man with the pail, who again asseverated that he had let no intruder pass, down to the commissionaire and the hovering chestnut man, who rightly reasserted their own watchfulness. But when Angus looked round for his fourth confirmation he could not see it, and called out with some nervousness: 'Where is the policeman?'

'I beg your pardon,' said Father Brown; 'that is my fault. I just sent him down the road to investigate something – that I just thought worth investigating.'

'Well, we want him back pretty soon,' said Angus abruptly, 'for the wretched man upstairs has not only been murdered, but wiped out.'

'How?' asked the priest.

'Father,' said Flambeau, after a pause, 'upon my soul I believe it is more in your department than mine. No friend or foe has entered the house, but Smythe is gone, as if stolen by the fairies. If that is not supernatural, I — '

As he spoke they were all checked by an unusual sight; the big blue policeman came round the corner of the crescent running. He came straight up to Brown.

'You're right, sir,' he panted, 'they've just found poor Mr. Smythe's body in the canal down below.'

Angus put his hand wildly to his head. 'Did he run down and drown himself?' he asked.

'He never came down, I'll swear,' said the constable, 'and he wasn't drowned either, for he died of a great stab over the heart.'

'And yet you saw no one enter?' said Flambeau in a grave voice.

'Let us walk down the road a little,' said the priest.

As they reached the other end of the crescent he observed abruptly: 'Stupid of me! I forgot to ask the policeman something. I wonder if they found a light brown sack.'

'Why a light brown sack?' asked Angus, astonished.

'Because if it was any other coloured sack, the case must begin over again,' said Father Brown; 'but if it was a light brown sack, why, the case is finished.'

'I am pleased to hear it,' said Angus with hearty irony. 'It hasn't begun, so far as I am concerned.'

'You must tell us all about it,' said Flambeau, with a strange heavy simplicity, like a child.

Unconsciously they were walking with quickening steps down the long sweep of road on the other side of the high crescent, Father Brown leading briskly, though in silence. At last he said with an almost touching vagueness: 'Well, I'm afraid you'll think it so prosy. We always begin at the abstract end of things, and you can't begin this story anywhere else.

'Have you ever noticed this – that people never answer what you say? They answer what you mean – or what they think you mean. Suppose one lady says to another in a country house, "Is anybody staying with you?" the lady doesn't answer "Yes; the butler, the three footmen, the parlour-maid, and so on," though the parlour-maid may be in the room, or the butler behind her chair. She says: "There is *nobody* staying with us," meaning nobody of the sort you mean. But suppose a doctor inquiring into an epidemic asks, "Who is staying in the house?" then the lady will remember the butler, the parlour-maid, and the rest. All language is used like that; you never get a question answered literally, even when you get it answered truly. When those four quite honest men said that no man had gone into the Mansions, they did not really mean that *no man* had gone into them. They meant no man whom they could suspect of being your man. A man did go into the house, and did come out of it, but they never noticed him.'

'An invisible man?' inquired Angus, raising his red eyebrows.

'A mentally invisible man,' said Father Brown.

A minute or two after he resumed in the same unassuming voice, like a man thinking his way. 'Of course, you can't think of such a

man, until you do think of him. That's where his cleverness comes
in. But I came to think of him through two or three little things
in the tale Mr. Angus told us. First, there was the fact that this
Welkin went for long walks. And then there was the vast lot of
stamp-paper on the window. And then, most of all, there were
the two things the young lady said – things that couldn't be true.
Don't get annoyed,' he added hastily, noting a sudden movement
of the Scotsman's head; 'she thought they were true all right, but
they couldn't be true. A person *can't* be quite alone in a street a
second before she receives a letter. She can't be quite alone in a
street when she starts reading a letter just received. There must
be somebody pretty near her; he must be mentally invisible.'

'Why must there be somebody near her?' asked Angus.

'Because,' said Father Brown: 'barring carrier-pigeons, somebody must have brought her the letter.'

'Do you really mean to say,' asked Flambeau, with energy, 'that
Welkin carried his rival's letters to his lady?'

'Yes,' said the priest. 'Welkin carried his rival's letters to his
lady. You see, he had to.'

'Oh, I can't stand much more of this,' exploded Flambeau. 'Who
is this fellow? What does he look like? What is the usual get-up of
a mentally invisible man?'

'He is dressed rather handsomely in red, blue and gold,' replied
the priest promptly with decision, 'and in this striking, and even
showy costume he entered Himalaya Mansions under eight human
eyes; he killed Smythe in cold blood, and came down into the street
again carrying the dead body in his arms — '

'Reverend sir,' cried Angus, standing still, 'are you raving mad,
or am I?'

'You are not mad,' said Brown, 'only a little unobservant. You
have not noticed such a man as this, for example.'

He took three quick strides forward, and put his hand on the
shoulder of an ordinary passing postman who had bustled by them
unnoticed under the shade of the trees.

'Nobody ever notices postmen, somehow,' he said thoughtfully;
'yet they have passions like other men, and even carry large bags
where a small corpse can be stowed quite easily.'

The postman, instead of turning naturally, had ducked and

tumbled against the garden fence. He was a lean fair-bearded man of very ordinary appearance, but as he turned an alarmed face over his shoulder, all three men were fixed with an almost fiendish squint.

Flambeau went back to his sabres, purple rugs and Persian cat, having many things to attend to. John Turnbull Angus went back to the lady at the shop, with whom that imprudent young man contrives to be extremely comfortable. But Father Brown walked those snow-covered hills under the stars for many hours with a murderer, and what they said to each other will never be known.

AUTOBIOGRAPHY

THE STYLE is the man; and there is plenty of truth in the opinion that Chesterton reveals as much about himself in the biographies of Dickens and Browning as he does in his *Autobiography*. Dates, facts, actions are less important than eras, feelings and thoughts. He shows himself through a telescope rather than a microscope. For facts we must go to Maisie Ward or another biographer, but for a sense of the man as a whole and what formed his mind and tastes, the *Autobiography* is invaluable and, even though it was the last work he completed, makes an excellent introduction to the rest of Chesterton's writings.

Many autobiographies are content to be chronicles; not Chesterton's. He comments and reappraises all the time from the standpoint of a man at the end of his life. He gives meaning to episodes he recounts by putting them in the context of his whole knowledge. He explains, confesses, wonders, sighs with regret, chuckles and shakes his head. The result is not the usual self-justifying document concerned to 'put the record straight' but the portrait of an ordinary fallible man who can delight in the very lack of straightness that the record reveals.

There are portraits of his friends, musings upon war, sociology, history and politics; there are questions, anecdotes, arguments and asides. Chesterton is never the hero, just a man among many others caught in a tangled web of astonishing beauty and astonishing silliness which refuses to yield up the clue to its untangling. The emotion that one identifies most strongly in the *Autobiography* is gratitude; gratitude for a family, a home, a country and a life spent in discovery, discourse and delight.

The *Autobiography* is full of good things but Chesterton is perhaps at his best when describing childhood. Not only is he good – and unsentimental – about childhood in general, he is revealing about the springs of his own imagination and his understanding of what is real, true and important. Here, then, is Chapter II of Chesterton's *Autobiography*: 'The Man with the Golden Key'.

The Man with the Golden Key

The very first thing I can ever remember seeing with my own eyes was a young man walking across a bridge. He had a curly moustache and an attitude of confidence verging on swagger. He carried in his hand a disproportionately large key of a shining yellow metal and wore a large golden or gilded crown. The bridge he was crossing sprang on the one side from the edge of a highly perilous mountain chasm, the peaks of the range rising fantastically in the distance; and at the other end it joined the upper part of the tower of an almost excessively castellated castle. In the castle tower there was one window, out of which a young lady was looking. I cannot remember in the least what she looked like; but I will do battle with anyone who denies her superlative good looks.

To those who may object that such a scene is rare in the home life of house-agents living immediately to the north of Kensington High Street, in the later seventies of the last century, I shall be compelled to admit, not that the scene was unreal, but that I saw it through a window more wonderful than the window in the tower; through the proscenium of a toy theatre constructed by my father; and that (if I am really to be pestered about such irrelevant details) the young man in the crown was about six inches high and proved on investigation to be made of cardboard. But it is strictly true to say that I saw him before I can remember seeing anybody else; and that, so far as my memory is concerned, this was the sight on which my eyes first opened in this world. And the scene has to me a sort of aboriginal authenticity impossible to describe; something at the back of all my thoughts; like the very back-scene of the theatre of things. I have no shadow of recollection of what the young man was doing on the bridge, or of what he proposed to do with the key; though a later and wearier knowledge of literature and legend hints to me that he was not improbably going to release the lady from captivity. It is a not unamusing detail of psychology that, though I can remember no other characters in the story, I do remember noting that the crowned gentleman had a moustache and no beard, with a vague inference that there was another crowned gentleman who had a beard as well. We may safely guess, I imagine, that the bearded one was by way of being a wicked king; and we should not need much more converging evidence to convict him of having locked up the lady in the tower. All the rest is gone; scenes, subject, story, characters; but that one scene glows in my memory like a glimpse of some incredible paradise; and, for all I know, I shall still remember it when all other memory is gone out of my mind.

Apart from the fact of it being my first memory, I have several reasons for putting it first. I am no psychologist, thank God; but if psychologists are still saying what ordinary sane people have always said: that early impressions count considerably in life, I recognize a sort of symbol of all that I happen to like in imagery and ideas. All my life I have loved edges; and the boundary-line that brings one thing sharply against another. All my life I have loved frames and limits; and I will maintain that the largest wilderness looks larger seen through a window. To the grief of all grave dramatic critics, I will still assert that the perfect drama must strive to rise to the higher ecstasy of the peep-show. I have also a pretty taste in abysses and bottomless chasms and everything else that emphasizes a fine shade of distinction between one thing and another; and the warm affection I have always felt for bridges is connected with the fact that the dark and dizzy arch accentuates the chasm even more than the chasm itself. I can no longer behold the beauty of the princess; but I can see it in the bridge that the prince crossed to reach her. And I believe that in feeling these things from the first, I was feeling the fragmentary suggestions of a philosophy I have since found to be the truth. For it is upon that point of truth that there might perhaps be a quarrel between the more material psychologists and myself. If any man tells me that I only take pleasure in the mysteries of the window and the bridge because I saw these models of them when I was a baby, I shall take the liberty of telling him that he has not thought the thing out. To begin with, I must have seen thousands of other things before as well as after; and there must have been an element of selection and some reason for selection. And, what is still more obvious, to date the occasion does not even begin to deal with the fact. If some laborious reader of little books on child-psychology cries out to me in glee and cunning: 'You only like romantic things like toy theatres because your father showed you a toy theatre in your childhood,' I shall reply with gentle and Christian patience: 'Yes, fool, yes. Undoubtedly your explanation is, in that sense, the true one. But what you are saying, in your witty way, is simply that I associate these things with happiness because I was so happy. It does not even begin to consider the question of why I was so happy. Why should looking through a square hole, at yellow pasteboard, lift anybody into the seventh heaven of happiness at any time of life? Why should it specially do so at that time of life? That is the psychological fact that you have to explain; and I have never seen any sort of rational explanation.'

I apologize for this parenthesis; and for mentioning child psychology or anything else that can bring a blush to the cheek. But it happens to be a point on which I think some of our psycho-analysts display rather unblushing cheek. I do not wish my remarks confused with the horrible and degrading heresy that our minds are merely manufactured by accidental conditions, and therefore have no ultimate relation to truth at all. With all possible apologies to the freethinkers, I still propose to hold myself free to think. And anybody who will think for two minutes will see that this thought is the end of all thinking. It is useless to argue at all, if all our conclusions are warped by our conditions. Nobody can correct anybody's bias, if all mind is all bias.

The interlude is now over, thank you; and I will proceed to the more practical relations between my memory and my story. And it will first be necessary to say something about memory itself; and the reliability of such stories. I have begun with this fragment of a fairy play in a toy theatre, because it also sums up most clearly the strongest influences upon my childhood. I have said that the toy theatre was made by my father; and anybody who has ever tried to make such a theatre or mount such a play, will know that this alone stands for a remarkable round of crafts and accomplishments. It involves being in much more than the common sense the stage carpenter, being the architect and the builder and the draughtsman and the landscape-painter and the story-teller all in one. And, looking back on my life, and the relatively unreal and indirect art that I have attempted to practise, I feel that I have really lived a much narrower life than my father's.

His mere name, of course, is enough to recall wider memories. One of my first memories is playing in the garden under the care of a girl with ropes of golden hair; to whom my mother afterwards called out from the house: 'You are an angel'; which I was disposed to accept without metaphor. She is now living in Vancouver as Mrs. Kidd; and she and her sister had more to do with enlivening my early years than most. Since then, I have met what used to be called the wits of the age; but I have never known wittier conversation. Among my first memories also are those seascapes that were blue flashes to boys of my generation: North Berwick with the cone of green hill that seemed like the hill absolute; and a French seaside associated with little girls, the daughters of my father's old friend Mawer Cowtan, whom I shall not forget. But indeed I had a whole background of cousins: Tom Gilbert (my godfather, who gave me his last and my first name) had a large family of daughters, and my uncle Sidney a large family of sons; and they all still move in my memory almost like a male and female chorus in a great Greek play. The eldest of the boys, the one whom I once knew best, was killed with my brother in the Great War; but many of the others, I am glad to say, are still friends as well as relations. All these are memorable memories; but they do not resolve that first individual speculation about memory itself. The girl with the yellow hair is an early memory, in the sense in which some of the others have inevitably become later memories, at once expanded and effaced.

Really, the things we remember are the things we forget. I mean that when a memory comes back sharply and suddenly, piercing the protection of oblivion, it appears for an instant exactly as it really was. If we think of it often, while its essentials doubtless remain true, it becomes more and more our own memory of the thing rather than the thing remembered. I had a little sister who died when I was a child. I have little to go on; for she was the only subject about which my father did not talk. It was the one dreadful sorrow of his abnormally happy and even merry existence; and it is strange to think that I never spoke to him about it to the day of his death. I do not remember her dying; but I remember her falling off a rocking-horse. I know, from experience of bereavements only a little later, that children feel with exactitude, without a word of explanation, the emotional tone or tint of a house of mourning. But in this case, the greater catastrophe must somehow have become confused and identified with the smaller one. I always felt it as a tragic memory, as if she had been thrown by a real horse and killed. Something must have painted and repainted the picture in my mind; until I suddenly became conscious about the age of eighteen that it had become the picture of Amy Robsart lying at the foot of the stairs, flung down by Varney and another villain. This is the real difficulty about remembering anything; that we have remembered too much – for we have remembered too often.

I will take another example of this psychological trick, though it involves the anticipation of much later events in my life. One of these glimpses of my own prehistoric history is a memory of a long upper room filled with light (the light that never was on sea or land) and of somebody carving or painting with white paint the deal head of a hobby-horse; the head almost archaic in its simplification. Ever since that day my depths have been stirred by even a wooden post painted white; and more so by any white horse in the street; and it was like meeting a friend in a fairy tale to find myself under the sign of the White Horse at Ipswich on the first day of my honeymoon. But for that very reason, this image has remained and memory has constantly returned to it; and I have even done my best to deface and spoil the purity of the White Horse by writing an interminable ballad about it. A man does not generally manage to forget his wedding-day; especially such a highly comic wedding-day as mine. For the family remembers against me a number of now familiar legends, about the missing of trains, the losing of luggage, and other things counted yet more eccentric. It is alleged against me, and with perfect truth, that I stopped on the way to drink a glass of milk in one shop and to buy a revolver with cartridges in another. Some have seen these as singular wedding-presents for a bridegroom to give to himself; and if the bride had known less of him, I suppose she might have fancied that he was a suicide or a murderer or, worst of all, a teetotaller. They seemed to me the most natural things in the world. I did not buy the pistol to murder myself or my wife; I never was really modern. I bought it because it was the great adventure of my youth, with a general notion of protecting her from the pirates doubtless infesting the Norfolk Broads, to which we were bound; where, after all, there are still a suspiciously large number of families with Danish names. I shall not be annoyed if it is called childish; but obviously it was rather a reminiscence of boyhood, and not of childhood. But the ritual consumption of the glass of milk really was a reminiscence of childhood. I stopped at that particular dairy because I had always drunk a glass of milk there when walking with my mother in my infancy. And it seemed to me a fitting ceremonial to unite the two great relations of a man's life. Outside the shop there was the figure of a White Cow as a sort of pendant to the figure of the White Horse; the one standing at the beginning of my new journey and the other at the end. But the point is here that the very fact of these allegories having been acted over again, at the stage of marriage and maturity, does in a sense transform them, and does in some sense veil even while it invokes the original visions of the child. The sign of the White Horse has been repainted, and only in that sense painted out. I do not so much remember it as remember remembering it. But if I really want to be realistic about those remote days, I must scratch around till I find something not too much blunted to scratch me: something sufficiently forgotten to be remembered. I make the experiment at this moment as I write. Searching for those lost surroundings, I recall for the first time, at this moment, that there was another shop, next to the milk-shop, which had some mysterious charm for my childhood; and then I recall that it was an oil and colour shop, and they sold gold paint smeared inside shells; and there was a sort of pale pointed chalks I have been less familiar with of late. I do not think here of the strong colours of the common paint-box, like crimson-lake and prussian-blue, much as I exulted and still exult in them. For another boy called Robert Louis Stevenson has messed about with my colours upon that sort of palette; and I have grown up to enjoy them in print as well as in paint. But when I remember that these forgotten crayons contained a stick of 'light-red', seemingly a more commonplace colour, the point of that dull red pencil pricks me as if it could draw red blood.

From this general memory about memory I draw a certain inference. What was wonderful about childhood is that anything in it was a wonder. It was not merely a world full of miracles; it was a miraculous world. What gives me this shock is almost anything I really recall; not the things I should think most worth recalling. This is where it differs from the other great thrill of the past, all that is connected with first love and the romantic passion; for that, though equally poignant, comes always to a point; and is narrow like a rapier piercing the heart, whereas the other was more like a hundred windows opened on all sides of the head.

I have made here a sort of psychological experiment in memory. I have tried to think of the things I forget adjoining the things I remember; and in the childish case, though they are without form, I am sure they are of the same tint. I have long remembered the milk-shop; I have only just remembered the oil-shop; I have no notion at all about the next shop to the oil-shop. I am sure it was a shop shining with the same lost light of morning; because it was in the same street under the same sky. I have no notion on what street the row of windows in the long uplifted room looked out, when the white horse head was carved. But I feel in a flash that it was a happy street; or, if we must be pedantic, a street in which I should have been happy. Now it is not like that with even the happiest hours of the later things called love-affairs. I have already mentioned how my honeymoon began before the White Cow of my childhood; but of course I had in my time been myself a calf, not to say a moon-calf, in the sort of calf-love that dances in the moonshine long before the honeymoon. Those day-dreams also are wrecks of something divine; but they have the colour of sunset rather than the broad daylight. I have walked across wide fields at evening and seen, as a mere distant dot in a row of houses, one particular window and just distinguishable head; and been uplifted as with roaring trumpets as if by the salute of Beatrice. But it did not, and does not, make me think the other windows and houses were all almost equally interesting; and that is just what the glimpse of the babies' wonderland does. We have read countless pages about love brightening the sun and making the flowers more flamboyant; and it is true in a sense; but not in the sense I mean. It changes the world; but the baby lived in a changeless world; or rather the man feels that it is he who has changed. He has changed long before he comes near to the great and glorious trouble of the love of woman; and that has in it something new and concentrated and crucial; crucial in the true sense of being as near as Cana to Calvary. In the later case, what is loved becomes *instantly* what may be lost.

My point here is that we can test the childish mood by thinking, not only of what was there, but of what must have been there. I think of the backs of houses of which I saw only the fronts; the streets that stretched away behind the streets I knew; the things that remained round the corner; and they still give me a thrill. One of the sports of the imagination, a game I have played all my life, was to take a certain book with pictures of old Dutch houses, and think not of what was in the pictures, but of all that was out of the pictures, the unknown corners and side-streets of the same quaint town. The book was one my father had written and illustrated himself, merely for home consumption. It was typical of him that, in the Pugin period he had worked at Gothic illumination; but when he tried again, it was in another style of the dark Dutch Renaissance, the grotesque scroll-work that suggests wood-carving more than stone-cutting. He was the sort of man who likes to try everything once. This was the only book he ever wrote; and he never bothered to publish it.

My father might have reminded people of Mr. Pickwick, except that he was always bearded and never bald; he wore spectacles and had all the Pickwickian evenness of temper and pleasure in the humours of travel. He was rather quiet than otherwise, but his quietude covered a great fertility of notions; and he certainly liked taking a rise out of people. I remember, to give one example of a hundred such inventions, how he gravely instructed some grave ladies in the names of flowers; dwelling especially on the rustic names given in certain localities. 'The country people call them Sailors' Pen-knives,' he would say in an off-hand manner, after affecting to provide them with the full scientific name, or, 'They call them Bakers' Bootlaces down in Lincolnshire, I believe'; and it is a fine example of human simplicity to note how far he found he could safely go in such instructive discourse. They followed him without revulsion when he said lightly: 'Merely a sprig of wild bigamy.' It was only when he added that there was a local variety known as Bishop's Bigamy, that the full depravity of his character began to dawn on their minds. It was possibly this aspect of his unavailing amiability that is responsible for an entry I find in an ancient minute-book, of mock trials conducted by himself and his brothers; that Edward Chesterton was tried for the crime of

Aggravation. But the same sort of invention created for children the permanent anticipation of what is profoundly called a Surprise. And it is this side of the business that is relevant here.

His versatility both as an experimentalist and a handy man, in all such matters, was amazing. His den or study was piled high with the stratified layers of about ten or twelve creative amusements; water-colour painting and modelling and photography and stained glass and fretwork and magic lanterns and medieval illumination. I have inherited, or I hope imitated, his habit of drawing; but in every other way I am emphatically an unhandy man. There had been some talk of his studying art professionally in his youth; but the family business was obviously safer; and his life followed the lines of a certain contented and ungrasping prudence, which was extraordinarily typical of him and all his blood and generation. He never dreamed of turning any of these plastic talents to any mercenary account, or of using them for anything but his own private pleasure and ours. To us he appeared to be indeed the Man with the Golden Key, a magician opening the gates of goblin castles or the sepulchres of dead heroes; and there was no incongruity in calling his lantern a magic-lantern. But all this time he was known to the world, and even the next-door neighbours, as a very reliable and capable though rather unambitious business man. It was a very good first lesson in what is also the last lesson of life; that in everything that matters, the inside is much larger than the outside. On the whole I am glad that he was never an artist. It might have stood in his way in becoming an amateur. It might have spoilt his career; his private career. He could never have made a vulgar success of all the thousand things he did so successfully.

If I made a generalization about the Chestertons, my paternal kinsfolk (which may be dangerous, for there are a lot of them still alive), I should say that they were and are extraordinarily English. They have a perceptible and prevailing colour of good nature, of good sense not untinged with dreaminess, and a certain tranquil loyalty in their personal relations which was very notable even in one, like my brother Cecil, who in his public relations was supremely pugnacious and provocative. I think this sort of sleepy sanity rather an English thing; and in comparison it may not be entirely fanciful to suppose there was something French, after all, in the make-up of my mother's family; for, allowing for the usual admixture, they ran smaller in stature, often darker in colouring, tough, extraordinarily tenacious, prejudiced in a humorous fashion and full of the fighting spirit. But whatever we may guess in such matters (and nobody has yet done anything but guess about heredity), it was for another purpose that I mentioned the savour of something racial about such a stock. English in so many things, the Chestertons were supremely English in their natural turn for hobbies. It is an element in this sort of old English business man which divides him most sharply from the American business man; and to some extent from the new English business man, who is copying the American. When the American begins to suggest that, 'salesmanship can be an art,' he means that an artist ought to put all his art into his salesmanship. The old-fashioned Englishman, like my father, sold houses for his living, but filled his own house with his life.

A hobby is not a holiday. It is not *merely* a momentary relaxation necessary to the renewal of work; and in this respect it must be sharply distinguished from much that is called sport. A good game is a good thing, but it is not the same thing as a hobby; and many go golfing or shooting grouse because this is a concentrated form of recreation; just as what our contemporaries find in whisky is a concentrated form of what our fathers found diffused in beer. If half a day is to take a man out of himself, or make a new man of him, it is better done by some sharp competitive excitement like sport. But a hobby is not half a day, but half a lifetime. It would be truer to accuse the hobbyist of living a double life. And hobbies, especially such hobbies as the toy theatre, have a character that runs parallel to practical professional effort, and is not merely a reaction from it. It is not merely taking exercise; it is doing work. It is not merely exercising the body instead of the mind, an excellent, but now largely a recognized thing. It is exercising the rest of the mind; now an almost neglected thing. When Browning, that typical Victorian, says that he likes to know a butcher paints and a baker writes poetry, he would not be satisfied with the statement that a butcher plays tennis or a baker golf. And my father and uncles, also typical Victorians of the sort that followed Browning, were all marked in varying degrees by this taste for having their own tastes. One of them gave all his spare time to gardening and has somewhere in the horticultural records a chrysanthemum named after him, dating from the first days when chrysanthemums came to us from the islands of the Rising Sun. Another travelled in an ordinary commercial fashion, but made a most amazing collection of cranks and quacks, fitted to fill a far better memoir than this, whom he had met in his wanderings, and with whom he had argued and sympathized and quoted Browning and George Macdonald, and done I fancy not a little good, for he was himself a most interesting man; above all, interesting because he was interested. But in my own household, as I have said, it was not a question of one hobby, but a hundred hobbies, piled on top of each other; and it is a personal accident, or perhaps a personal taste, that the one which has clung to my memory through life is the hobby of the toy theatre. In any case, watching such work has made one great difference to my life and views to this day.

I cannot do much, by the standard of my nursery days. But I have learned to love seeing things done; not the handle that ultimately causes them to be done, but the hand that does them. If my father had been some common millionaire owning a thousand mills that made cotton, or a million machines that made cocoa, how much smaller he would have seemed. And this experience has made me profoundly sceptical of all the modern talk about the necessary dullness of domesticity; and the degrading drudgery that only has to make puddings and pies. Only to make things! There is no greater thing to be said of God Himself than that He makes things. The manufacturer cannot even manufacture things; he can only pay to have them manufactured. And (in the same way) I am now incurably afflicted with a faint smile, when I hear a crowd of frivolous people, who could not make anything to save their lives, talking about the inevitable narrowness and stuffiness of the Victorian home. We managed to make a good many things in our Victorian home which people now buy at insane prices from Art and Craft Shops; the sort of shops that have quite as much craft as art. All the things that happened in the house, or were in any sense done on the premises, linger in my imagination like a legend; and as much as any, those connected with the kitchen or the pantry. Toffee still tastes nicer to me than the most expensive chocolates which Quaker millionaires sell by the million; and mostly because we made toffee for ourselves.

No. 999 in the vast library-catalogue of the books I have never written (all of them so much more brilliant and convincing than the books that I have written) is the story of a successful city man who seemed to have a dark secret in his life; and who was eventually discovered by the detectives still playing with dolls or tin soldiers or some undignified antic of infancy. I may say with all modesty that I am that man, in everything except his solidity of repute and his successful commercial career. It was perhaps even more true, in that sense, of my father before me; but I for one have never left off playing, and I wish there were more time to play. I wish we did not have to fritter away on frivolous things, like lectures and literature, the time we might have given to serious, solid and constructive work like cutting out cardboard figures and pasting coloured tinsel upon them. When I say this, I come to the third reason for taking the toy theatre as a text; and it is one about which there will be much misunderstanding, because of the repetitions and the stale sentiment that have somehow come to cling to it. It is one of those things that are always misunderstood, because they have been too often explained.

I am inclined to contradict much of the modern Cult of the Child at Play. Through various influences of a recent and rather romantic culture, the Child has become rather the Spoilt Child. The true beauty has been spoilt by the rather unscrupulous emotion of mature persons, who have themselves lost much of their sense of reality. The worst heresy of this school is that a child is concerned only with make-believe. For this is interpreted in the sense, at once sentimental and sceptical, that there is not much difference between make-belief and belief. But the real child does not confuse fact and fiction. He simply likes fiction. He acts it, because he cannot as yet write it or even read it; but he never allows his moral sanity to be clouded by it. To him no two things could possibly be more totally contrary than playing at robbers and stealing sweets. No possible amount of playing at robbers would ever bring him an inch nearer to thinking it is really right to rob. I saw the distinction perfectly clearly when I was a child; I wish I saw it half as clearly now. I played at being a robber for hours together at the end of the garden; but it never had anything to do with the temptation I had to sneak a new paint-box out of my father's room. I was not *being* anything false; I was simply writing before I could write. Fortunately, perhaps, for the condition of the back-garden, I early transferred my dreams to some rude resemblance to writing; chiefly in the form of drawing straggling and sprawling maps of fabulous countries, inhabited by men of incredible shapes and colours and bearing still more incredible names. But though I might fill the world with dragons, I never had the slightest real doubt that heroes ought to fight with dragons.

I must stop to challenge many child-lovers for cruelty to children. It is quite false to say that the child dislikes a fable that has a moral. Very often he likes the moral more than the fable. Adults are reading their own more weary mockery into a mind still vigorous enough to be entirely serious. Adults liked the comic Sandford and Merton. Children liked the real Sandford and Merton. At least I know I liked it very much, and felt the heartiest faith in the Honest Farmer and the Noble Negro. I venture to dwell on the point if only in parenthesis: for on this also there is a current misunderstanding. Indeed there is what may be called a current cant; and none the less so because it is a cant against cant. It is now so common as to be conventional to express impatience with priggish and moralizing stories for children; stories of the old-fashioned sort that concern things like the sinfulness of theft; and as I am recalling an old-fashioned atmosphere, I cannot refrain from testifying on the psychology of the business.

Now I must heartily confess that I often adored priggish and moralizing stories. I do not suppose I should gain a subtle literary pleasure from them now; but that is not the point in question. The men who denounce such moralizings are men; they are not children. But I believe multitudes would admit their early affection for the moral tale, if they still had the moral courage. And the reason is perfectly simple. Adults have reacted against such morality, because they know that it often stands for immorality. They know that such platitudes have been used by hypocrites and pharisees, by cunning or perversion. But the child knows nothing about cunning or perversion. He sees nothing but the moral ideals themselves, and he simply sees that they are true. Because they are.

There is another blunder made by the modern cynic about the moralizing story-teller. The former always imagines that there is an element of corruption, in his own cynical manner, about the idea of reward, about the position of the child who can say, as in Stevenson's verses: 'Every day when I've been good, I get an orange after food.' To the man made ignorant by experience this always appears as a vulgar *bribe* to the child. The modern philosopher knows that it would require a very large bribe indeed to induce *him* to be good. It therefore seems to the modern philosopher what it would seem to the modern politician to say: 'I will give you fifty thousand pounds when you have, on some one definite and demonstrated occasion, kept your word.' The solid price seems something quite distinct from the rare and reluctant labour. But it does not seem like that to the child. It would not seem like that to the child, if the Fairy Queen said to the Prince: 'You will receive the golden apple from the magic tree when you have fought the dragon.' For the child is not a Manichee. He does not think that good things are in their nature separate from being good. In other words, he does not, like the reluctant realist, regard goodness as a bad thing. To him the goodness and the gift and the golden apple, that is called an orange, are all parts of one substantial paradise and naturally go together. In other words, he regards himself as normally on amiable terms with the natural authorities; not normally as quarrelling or bargaining with them. He has the ordinary selfish obstacles and misunderstandings; but he does not, in his heart, regard it as odd that his parents should be good to him, to the extent of an orange, or that he should be good to them, to the extent of some elementary experiments in good behaviour. He has no sense of being corrupted. It is only we, who have eaten the forbidden apple (or orange) who think of pleasure as a bribe.

My main purpose here, however, is to say this. To me my whole childhood has a certain quality, which may be indescribable but is not in the least vague. It is rather more definite than the difference between pitch dark and daylight, or between having a toothache and not having a toothache. For the sequel of the story, it is necessary to attempt this first and hardest chapter of the story: and I must try to state somehow what I mean by saying that my own childhood was of quite a different kind, or quality, from the rest of my very undeservedly pleasant and cheerful existence.

Of this positive quality, the most general attribute was clearness. Here it is that I differ, for instance, from Stevenson, whom I so warmly admire; and who speaks of the child as moving with his head in a cloud. He talks of the child as normally in a dazed day-dream, in which he cannot distinguish fancy from fact. Now children and adults are both fanciful at times; but that is not what, in my mind and memory, distinguishes adults from children. Mine is a memory of a sort of white light on everything, cutting things out very clearly, and rather emphasizing their solidity. The point is that the white light had a sort of wonder in it, as if the world were as new as myself; but not that the world was anything but a real world. I am much more disposed *now* to fancy that an apple-tree in the moonlight is some sort of ghost or grey nymph; or to see the furniture fantastically changing and crawling at twilight, as in some story of Poe or Hawthorne. But when I was a child I had a sort of confident astonishment in contemplating the apple-tree as an apple-tree. I was quite sure of it, and also sure of the surprise of it; as sure, to quote the perfect popular proverb, as sure as God made little apples. The apples might be little as I was: but they were solid and so was I. There was something of an eternal morning about the mood; and I liked to see a fire lit more than to imagine faces in the firelight. Brother Fire, whom St. Francis loved, did seem more like a brother than those dream-faces which come to men who have known other emotions than brotherhood. I do not know whether I ever, as the phrase goes, cried for the moon; but I am sure that I should have expected it to be solid like some colossal snowball; and should always have had more appetite for moons than for mere moonshine. Only figures of speech can faintly express the fact; but it was a fact and not a figure of speech. What I said first about the toy theatre may be urged in contradiction, and as an example of delight in a mere illusion.

In that case, what I said first about the toy theatre will be entirely misunderstood. In fact, there was in that business nothing of illusion or of disillusion. If this were a ruthless realistic modern story, I should of course give a most heartrending account of how my spirit was broken with disappointment, on discovering that the prince was only a painted figure. But this is not a ruthless realistic modern story. On the contrary, it is a true story. And the truth is that I do not remember that I was in any way deceived or in any way undeceived. The whole point is that I did like the toy theatre even when I knew it was a toy theatre. I did like the cardboard figures, even when I found they were of cardboard. The white light of wonder that shone on the whole business was not any sort of trick; indeed the things that now shine most in my memory were many of them mere technical accessories; such as the parallel sticks of white wood that held the scenery in place; a white wood that is still strangely mixed in my imaginative instincts with all the holy trade of the Carpenter. It was the same with any number of other games or pretences in which I took delight; as in the puppet-show of Punch and Judy. I not only knew that the figures were made of wood, but I wanted them to be made of wood. I could not imagine such a resounding thwack being given except by a wooden stick on a wooden head. But I took the sort of pleasure that a primitive man might have taken in a primitive craft, in seeing that they were carved and painted into a startling and grimacing caricature of humanity. I was pleased that the piece of wood was a face; but I was also pleased that the face was a piece of wood. That did not mean that the drama of wood, like the other drama of cardboard, did not reveal to me real ideas and imaginations, and give me glorious glimpses into the possibilities of existence. Of course, the child did not analyze himself then; and the man cannot analyze him now. But I am certain he was not merely tricked or trapped. He enjoyed the suggestive function of art exactly as an art critic enjoys it; only he enjoyed it a jolly sight more. For the same reason I do not think that I myself was ever very much worried about Santa Claus, or that alleged whisper of the little boy that Father Christmas 'is only your father'. Perhaps the word 'only' would strike all children as the *mot juste*.

My fixed idolatry of Punch and Judy illustrated the same fact and the same fallacy. I was not only grateful for the fun, but I came to feel grateful for the very fittings and apparatus of the fun; the four-cornered tower of canvas with the one square window at the top, and everything down to the minimum of conventional and obviously painted scenery. Yet these were the very things I ought to have torn and rent in rage, as the trappings of imposture, if I had really regarded the explanation as spoiling the experience. I was pleased, and not displeased, when I discovered that the magic figures could be moved by three human fingers. And I was right; for those three human fingers are more magical than any magic fingers; the three fingers which hold the pen and the sword and the bow of the violin; the very three fingers that the priest lifts in benediction as the emblem of the Blessed Trinity. There was no conflict between the two magics in my mind.

I will here sum up in four statements, which will look very like puzzles upon this page. I can assure the reader that they have a relevance to the ultimate upshot of this book. Having littered the world with millions of essays for a living, I am doubtless prone to let this story stray into a sort of essay; but I repeat that it is not an essay but a story. So much so, that I am here employing a sort of device from a detective story. In the first few pages of a police novel, there are often three or four hints rather to rouse curiosity than allay it; so that the curate's start of recognition, the cockatoo's scream in the night, the burnt blotting-paper or the hasty avoidance of the subject of onions, is exhibited in the beginning though not explained until the end. So it is with the dull and difficult interlude of this chapter; a mere introspection about infancy which is not introspective. The patient reader may yet discover that these dark hints have something to do with the ensuing mystery of my misguided existence, and even with the crime that comes before the end. Anyhow, I will set them down here, without discussion of anything which they foreshadow.

First; my life unfolded itself in the epoch of evolution, which really only means unfolding. But many of the evolutionists of that epoch really seemed to mean by evolution the unfolding of what is not there. I have since, in a special sense, come to believe in development; which means the unfolding of what is there. Now it may seem both a daring and a doubtful boast, if I claim that in my childhood I was all there. At least, many of those who knew me best were quite doubtful about it. But I mean that the distinctions I make here were all there; I was not conscious of them but I contained them. In short, they existed in infancy in the condition called implicit; though they certainly did not then express themselves in what is commonly called implicit obedience.

Second; I knew, for instance, that pretending is not deceiving. I could not have defined the distinction if it had been questioned; but that was because it had never occurred to me that it could be questioned. It was merely because a child understands the nature of art, long before he understands the nature of argument. Now it is still not uncommon to say that images are idols and that idols are dolls. I am content to say here that even dolls are not idols, but in the true sense images. The very word images means things necessary to imagination. But not things contrary to reason; no, not even in a child. For imagination is almost the opposite of illusion.

Third; I have noted that I enjoyed Punch and Judy as a drama and not a dream; and indeed the whole extraordinary state of mind I strive to recapture was really the very reverse of a dream. It was rather as if I was more wideawake then than I am now, and moving in broader daylight, which was to our broad daylight what daylight is to dusk. Only, of course, to those seeing the last gleam of it through the dusk, the light looks more uncanny than any darkness. Anyhow, it looks quite different; of that I am absolutely and solidly certain; though in such a subjective matter of sensation there can be no demonstration. What was the real meaning of that difference? I have some sort of a notion now; but I will not mention it at this stage of the story.

Fourth: it will be quite natural, it will also be quite wrong, to infer from all this that I passed a quite exceptionally comfortable childhood in complete contentment; or else that my memory is merely a sundial that has only marked the sunny hours. But that is not in the least what I mean; that is quite a different question. I was often unhappy in childhood like other children; but happiness and unhappiness seemed of a different texture or held on a different tenure. I was very often naughty in childhood like other children; and I never doubted for a moment the moral of all the moral tales; that, as a general principle, people ought to be unhappy when they have been naughty. That is, I held the whole idea of repentance and absolution implicit but not unfolded in my mind. To add to all this, I was by no means unacquainted with pain, which is a pretty unanswerable thing; I had a fair amount of toothache and especially earache; and few can bemuse themselves into regarding earache as a form of epicurean hedonism. But here again there is a difference. For some unaccountable reason, and in some indescribable way, the pain did not leave on my memory the sort of stain of the intolerable or mysterious that it leaves on the mature mind. To all these four facts I can testify; exactly as if they were facts like my loving a toy gun or climbing a tree. Their meaning, in the murder or other mystery, will appear later.

For I fear I have prolonged preposterously this note on the nursery; as if I had been an unconscionable time, not dying but being born, or at least being brought up. Well, I believe in prolonging childhood; and I am not sorry that I was a backward child. But I can only say that this nursery note is necessary if all the rest is to be anything but nonsense; and not even nursery nonsense. In the chapters that follow, I shall pass to what are called real happenings, though they are far less real. Without giving myself any airs of the adventurer or the globetrotter, I may say I have seen something of the world; I have travelled in interesting places and talked to interesting men; I have been in political quarrels often turning into faction fights; I have talked to statesmen in the hour of the destiny of States; I have met most of the great poets and prose writers of my time; I have travelled in the track of some of the whirlwinds and earthquakes in the ends of the earth; I have lived in houses burned down in the tragic wars of Ireland; I have walked through the ruins of Polish palaces left behind by the Red Armies; I have heard talk of the secret signals of the Ku Klux Klan upon the borders of Texas; I have seen the fanatical Arabs come up from the desert to attack the Jews in Jerusalem. There are many journalists who have seen more of such things than I; but I have been a journalist and I have seen such things; there will be no difficulty in filling other chapters with such things; but they will be unmeaning, if nobody understands that they still mean less to me than Punch and Judy on Campden Hill.

In a word; I have never lost the sense that this was my real life; the real beginning of what should have been a more real life; a lost experience in the land of the living. It seems to me that when I came out of the house and stood on that hill of houses, where the roads sank steeply towards Holland Park, and terraces of new red houses could look out across a vast hollow and see far away the sparkle of the Crystal Palace (and seeing it was a juvenile sport in those parts), I was subconsciously certain then, as I am consciously certain now, that there was the white and solid road and the worthy beginning of the life of man; and that it is man who afterwards darkens it with dreams or goes astray from it in self-deception. It is only the grown man who lives a life of make-believe and pretending; and it is he who has his head in a cloud.

At this time, of course, I did not even know that this morning light could be lost; still less about any controversies as to whether it could be recovered. So far the disputes of that period passed over my head like storms high up in air; and as I did not foresee the problem I naturally did not foresee any of my searches for a solution. I simply looked at the procession in the street as I looked at the processions in the toy theatre; and now and then I happened to see curious things, twopence coloured rather than a penny plain, which were worthy of the wildest pageants of the toy theatre. I remember once walking with my father along Kensington High Street, and seeing a crowd of people gathered by a rather dark and narrow entry on the southern side of that thoroughfare. I had seen crowds before; and was quite prepared for their shouting or shoving. But I was not prepared for what happened next. In a flash a sort of ripple ran along the line and all these eccentrics went down on their knees on the public pavement. I had never seen people play any such antics except in church; and I stopped and stared. Then I realized that a sort of little dark cab or carriage had drawn up opposite the entry; and out of it came a ghost clad in flames. Nothing in the shilling paintbox had ever spread such a conflagration of scarlet, such lakes of lake; or seemed so splendidly likely to incarnadine the multitudinous sea. He came on with all his glowing draperies like a great crimson cloud of sunset, lifting long frail fingers over the crowd in blessing. And then I looked at his face and was startled with a contrast; for his face was dead pale like ivory and very wrinkled and old, fitted together out of naked nerve and bone and sinew; with hollow eyes in shadow; but not ugly; having in every line the ruin of great beauty. The face was so extraordinary that for a moment I even forgot such perfectly scrumptious scarlet clothes.

We passed on; and then my father said, 'Do you know who that was? That was Cardinal Manning.'

Then one of his artistic hobbies returned to his abstracted and humorous mind; and he said:

'He'd have made his fortune as a model.'

THE POEMS

IN HIS NOVEL *Manalive*, Chesterton has his hero, Innocent Smith, utter these ringing words:

> I don't deny that there should be priests to remind men that they will one day die, I only say that at certain strange epochs it is necessary to have another kind of priests, called poets, actually to remind men that they are not dead yet.

Now it is unfair to ascribe to an author the sentiments which he puts into the mouth of one of his characters; but perhaps it is less unfair to Chesterton than it might be to some. Indeed, a study of Chesterton's whole output would reveal that Smith's opinion is actually very close to that of Chesterton. But if that was what he thought poetry was meant to do, it cannot be said that he was himself an entirely successful poet. Chesterton's verse can be enjoyed and defended on all sorts of grounds, but not for revealing life in all its richness and variety. His poems are never less than good because he was too fond of language and too much of a craftsman to produce slapdash work or to be satisfied with anything less than absolute precision in the matter of rhyme and metre. A Chesterton poem will always convince; it may enlighten or surprise, but it will not yield up new insights on reading after reading; it will not become part of our vision of the world, nor will it stand comparison with the true poets who were his contemporaries: Housman, for instance, Hardy, Yeats, Frost, Monro, Edward Thomas, T. S. Eliot.

Anyone who considers such a comparison as unfair has already, tacitly, put Chesterton out of the front rank of poets. The interesting question is why, given that he saw the poet as a kind of priest with all the resonances and depths which that image implies, he could not perform that priestly task. It was to do with the way he perceived the world.

A poem may be almost anything: a love lyric, a meditation, a vignette, a story, an argument, a satire, a shout, a squib, a description, a puzzle, an atmosphere, a conversation, a sigh; the list could be extended almost to infinity. For Chesterton it was nearly always an argument. Even when it is not quite an argument, rhetoric will always win out over understatement or powerful imagery. In an era when rhetoric has been all but forgotten and images are everything, Chesterton's rhetoric is a welcome antidote to loose thinking or a kind of hit-and-miss pointillism of words. But still it will not do: rhetoric alone does not make poetry. He treats his subjects rather as Father Brown complains men and women are treated by scientists 'in a dry impartial light'. We feel that everything is 'out there' to be used rather than inside to be struggled with and experienced. It is too often a defiant logic, intensely seen but not intensely felt. There are exceptions, of course, and perhaps his best poetry is his religious poetry where such a method seems to be more at home; a continuation of the metaphysical line which stretches back to Donne, Cowley and Crashaw. I choose those names carefully, for only very occasionally does Chesterton attain the warmth and directness of Herbert or Vaughan.

But if all this militated against Chesterton's writing great poetry, it was precisely what made him a writer of light verse par excellence. All these faults are immediately translated into virtues. What was 'mere' technique, logic-chopping, playfulness, objectivity and waspish wit becomes a prerequisite. Here he is in another great line which includes Lear, Butler, Carroll, Hood and W. S. Gilbert; even, perhaps, Pope.

That something seems to have supplanted poetry in his mind and his ambitions is clear from the fact that his first two volumes were of poetry, and a writer usually starts as he means to carry on. But polemic, journalism and the cut and thrust of debate, once discovered, took hold of his imagination and, if it never quenched his poetry, it certainly got in the way. Chesterton himself seems to be admitting something of the sort when he writes:

The poet writing his name upon a score of little pages in the silence of his study, may or may not have an intellectual right to despise the journalist; but I greatly doubt whether he would not morally be the better if he saw the great lights burning on through darkness into dawn, and heard the roar of the printing wheels weaving the destinies of another day. Here at least is a school of labour and of some rough humility, the largest work ever published anonymously since the great Christian Cathedrals.

That is more than a mere comparison of the poet and the journalist. 'A score of little pages' is the nearest thing Chesterton gets to a sneer. The poet is not writing verses, he is writing 'his name', and the implication is one of egotism and unreality, especially when compared with the labour and 'rough humility' of the journalist.

It may be that it was not just temperament which prevented Chesterton from writing poetry as opposed to verse. It may be that he was just too contented and genial a man, and too secure in his own beliefs, to plumb the depths of experience and even anguish that produce great poetry.

But even when he is denying himself the power of lived experience explored in a vital and unique diction, Chesterton is never less than interesting. Occasionally, as in 'The Donkey' which has rightly found its way into scores of anthologies, he hits on something that perfectly fits his mode of thought and of expression, with marvellous results.

His best serious poem is undoubtedly the epic-length 'The Ballad of the White Horse' which, unfortunately, is far too long to reproduce here and does not lend itself to being quoted piecemeal. It is a genuine ballad on the life of King Alfred and, as Maisie Ward points out, it celebrates the three great loves of Chesterton's life: his country, his wife and his faith.[18] During the First World War it was more often read than Shakespeare if we believe the stories; and it was so well-known that, during the Second World War, two stanzas from it formed virtually the whole of the first leader in *The Times*:

I tell you naught for your comfort,
Yea, naught for your desire,
Save that the sky grows darker yet
And the sea rises higher.

Night shall be thrice night over you,
And heaven an iron cope.
Do you have joy without a cause,
Yea, faith without a hope?

Months later, in more optimistic circumstances, *The Times* was able to revisit the poem and quote another passage:

'The high tide!' King Alfred cried.
'The high tide and the turn!'

It is hardly known today, which is a pity because Chesterton's reputation as a serious poet must rest on this poem much more than on his short pieces.

His light verse is what we remember today: drinking songs, ballads, satires and nonsense. W. H. Auden could not point to one of Chesterton's comic verses that was not a triumphant success. If this seems to be going too far, we may let Chesterton take himself down a peg or two:

I know they are better than many books that are published, but Heaven knows that is not saying much. In support of some of my work I would fight to the last. But with regard to this occasional verse I feel a humbug. To publish a book of my nonsense verses seems to me exactly like summoning the whole of the people of Kensington to see me smoke cigarettes.

What comes naturally is easy to despise. We do not have to believe him even if we believe he means it.

The Rolling English Road

Before the Roman came to Rye or out to Severn
  strode,
The rolling English drunkard made the rolling
  English road.
A reeling road, a rolling road, that rambles round
  the shire,
And after him the parson ran, the sexton and the
  squire;
A merry road, a mazy road, and such as we did
  tread
The night we went to Birmingham by way of
  Beachy Head.

I knew no harm of Bonaparte and plenty of the
  Squire,
And for to fight the Frenchman I did not much
  desire;
But I did bash their baggonets because they came
  arrayed
To straighten out the crooked road an English
  drunkard made,
Where you and I went down the lane with ale-mugs
  in our hands,
The night we went to Glastonbury by way of
  Goodwin Sands.

His sins they were forgiven him; or why do flowers
  run
Behind him; and the hedges all strengthening in
  the sun?
The wild thing went from left to right and knew
  not which was which,
But the wild rose was above him when they found
  him in the ditch.
God pardon us, nor harden us; we did not see so
  clear

The night we went to Bannockburn by way of
  Brighton Pier.

My friends, we will not go again or ape an ancient
  rage,
Or stretch the folly of our youth to be the shame
  of age,
But walk with clearer eyes and ears this path that
  wandereth,
And see undrugged in evening light the decent inn
  of death;
For there is good news yet to hear and fine things
  to be seen,
Before we go to Paradise by way of Kensal Green.

Commercial Candour

*(On the Outside of a Sensational Novel is
Printed the Statement: 'The Back of the
Cover will Tell you the Plot')*

Our fathers to creed and tradition were tied,
They opened a book to see what was inside,
And of various methods they deemed not the worst
Was to find the first chapter and look at it first.
And so from the first to the second they passed,
Till in servile routine they arrived at the last.
But a literate age, unbenighted by creed,
Can find on two boards all it wishes to read;
For the front of the cover shows somebody shot
And the back of the cover will tell you the plot.

Between, that the book may be handily padded,
Some pages of mere printed matter are added,
Expanding the theme, which in case of great need
The curious reader might very well read

With the zest that is lent to a game worth the
   winning,
By knowing the end when you start the beginning;
While our barbarous sires, who would read every
   word
With a morbid desire to find out what occurred
Went drearily drudging through Dickens and Scott.
But the back of the cover will tell you the plot.

The wild village folk in earth's earliest prime
Could often sit still for an hour at a time
And hear a blind beggar, nor did the tale pall
Because Hector must fight before Hector could fall:
Nor was Scheherazade required, at the worst,
To tell her tales backwards and finish them first;
And the minstrels who sang about battle and
   banners
Found the rude camp-fire crowd had some notion
   of manners.
Till Forster (who pelted the people like crooks,
The Irish with buckshot, the English with books),
Established the great educational scheme
Of compulsory schooling, that glorious theme.
Some learnt how to read, and the others forgot,
And the back of the cover will tell you the plot.

O Genius of Business! O marvellous brain,
Come in place of the priests and the warriors to
   reign!
O Will to Get On that makes everything go —
O Hustle! O Pep! O Publicity! O!
Shall I spend three-and-sixpence to purchase the
   book,
Which we all can pick up on the bookstall and
   look?
Well, it may appear strange, but I think I shall not,
For the back of the cover will tell you the plot.

Gloria in Profundis

There has fallen on earth for a token
A god too great for the sky.
He has burst out of all things and broken
The bounds of eternity:
Into time and the terminal land
He has strayed like a thief or a lover,
For the wine of the world brims over,
Its splendour is spilt on the sand.

Who is proud when the heavens are humble,
Who mounts if the mountains fall,
If the fixed stars topple and tumble
And a deluge of love drowns all —
Who rears up his head for a crown,
Who holds up his will for a warrant,
Who strives with the starry torrent,
When all that is good goes down?

For in dread of such falling and failing
The fallen angels fell
Inverted in insolence, scaling
The hanging mountain of hell:
But unmeasured of plummet and rod
Too deep for their sight to scan,
Outrushing the fall of man
Is the height of the fall of God.

Glory to God in the Lowest
The spout of the stars in spate —
Where the thunderbolt thinks to be slowest
And the lightning fears to be late:
As men dive for a sunken gem
Pursuing, we hunt and hound it,
The fallen star that has found it
In the cavern of Bethlehem.

The World State

Oh, how I love Humanity,
　　With love so pure and pringlish,
And how I hate the horrid French,
　　Who never will be English!

The International Idea,
　　The largest and the clearest,
Is welding all the nations now,
　　Except the one that's nearest.

This compromise has long been known,
　　This scheme of partial pardons,
In ethical societies
　　And small suburban gardens —

The villas and the chapels where
　　I learned with little labour
The way to love my fellow-man
　　And hate my next-door neighbour.

A Ballad of Abbreviations

The American's a hustler, for he says so,
　　And surely the American must know.
He will prove to you with figures why it pays so
　　Beginning with his boyhood long ago.
When the slow-maturing anecdote is ripest,
　　He'll dictate it like a Board of Trade Report,
And because he has no time to call a typist,
　　He calls her a Stenographer for short.

He is never known to loiter or malinger,
　　He rushes, for he knows he has 'a date';
He is always on the spot and full of ginger,

Which is why he is invariably late.
When he guesses that it's getting even later,
   His vocabulary's vehement and swift,
And he yells for what he calls the Elevator,
   A slang abbreviation for a lift.

Then nothing can be nattier or nicer
   For those who like a light and rapid style
Than to trifle with a work of Mr. Dreiser
   As it comes along in waggons by the mile.
He has taught us what a swift selective art meant
   By description of his dinners and all that,
And his dwelling, which he says is an Apartment,
   Because he cannot stop to say a flat.

We may whisper of his wild precipitation,
   That its speed is rather longer than a span,
But there really is a definite occasion
   When he does not use the longest word he can.
When he substitutes, I freely make admission,
   One shorter and much easier to spell;
If you ask him what he thinks of Prohibition,
   He may tell you quite succinctly it is Hell.

The Secret People

Smile at us, pay us, pass us; but do not quite forget;
For we are the people of England, that never have
   spoken yet.
There is many a fat farmer that drinks less cheerfully,
There is many a free French peasant who is richer
   and sadder than we.
There are no folk in the whole world so helpless or
   so wise.
There is hunger in our bellies, there is laughter in
   our eyes;

You laugh at us and love us, both mugs and eyes
are wet:
Only you do not know us. For we have not spoken
yet.

The fine French kings came over in a flutter of flags
and dames.
We liked their smiles and battles, but we never could
say their names.
The blood ran red to Bosworth and the high French
lords went down;
There was naught but a naked people under a naked
crown.
And the eyes of the King's Servants turned terribly
every way,
And the gold of the King's Servants rose higher
every day.
They burnt the homes of the shaven men, that had
been quaint and kind,
Till there was no bed in a monk's house, nor food
that man could find.
The inns of God where no man paid, that were the
wall of the weak,
The King's Servants ate them all. And still we did
not speak.

And the face of the King's Servants grew greater
than the King:
He tricked them, and they trapped him, and stood
round him in a ring.
The new grave lords closed round him, that had
eaten the abbey's fruits,
And the men of the new religion, with their bibles
in their boots,
We saw their shoulders moving, to menace or
discuss,
And some were pure and some were vile; but none
took heed of us.

We saw the King as they killed him, and his face
   was proud and pale;
And a few men talked of freedom, while England
   talked of ale.

A war that we understood not came over the world
   and woke
Americans, Frenchmen, Irish; but we knew not the
   things they spoke.

They talked about rights and nature and peace and
   the people's reign:
And the squires, our masters, bade us fight; and
   scorned us never again.
Weak if we be for ever, could none condemn us then;
Men called us serfs and drudges; men knew that
   we were men.
In foam and flame at Trafalgar, on Albuera plains,
We did and died like lions, to keep ourselves in
   chains
We lay in living ruins; firing and fearing not
The strange fierce face of the Frenchmen who knew
   for what they fought,
And the man who seemed to be more than man we
   strained against and broke;
And we broke our own rights with him. And still
   we never spoke.

Our patch of glory ended; we never heard guns
   again.
But the squire seemed struck in the saddle; he was
   foolish, as if in pain.
He leaned on a staggering lawyer, he clutched a
   cringing Jew,
He was stricken; it may be, after all, he was stricken
   at Waterloo.
Or perhaps the shades of the shaven men, whose
   spoil is in his house,

Come back in shining shapes at last to spoil his last
   carouse:
We only know the last sad squires ride slowly
   towards the sea,
And a new people takes the land: and still it is
   not we.

They have given us into the hand of new unhappy
   lords,
Lords without anger and honour, who dare not carry
   their swords.
They fight by shuffling papers; they have bright
   dead alien eyes;
They look at our labour and laughter as a tired man
   looks at flies.
And the load of their loveless pity is worse than the
   ancient wrongs,
Their doors are shut in the evening; and they know
   no songs.

We hear men speaking for us of new laws strong
   and sweet,
Yet is there no man speaketh as we speak in the
   street.
It may be we shall rise the last as Frenchmen rose
   the first,
Our wrath come after Russia's wrath and our wrath
   be the worst.
It may be we are meant to mark with our riot and
   our rest
God's scorn for all men governing. It may be beer
   is best.
But we are the people of England; and we have
   not spoken yet.
Smile at us, pay us, pass us. But do not quite
   forget.

Elegy in a Country Churchyard

The men that worked for England
They have their graves at home:
And bees and birds of England
About the cross can roam.

But they that fought for England,
Following a falling star,
Alas, alas for England
They have their graves afar.

And they that rule in England,
In stately conclave met,
Alas, alas for England
They have no graves as yet.

The Sword of Surprise

Sunder me from my bones, O sword of God,
Till they stand stark and strange as do the trees;
That I whose heart goes up with the soaring woods
May marvel as much at these.

Sunder me from my blood that in the dark
I hear that red ancestral river run,
Like branching buried floods that find the sea
But never see the sun.

Give me miraculous eyes to see my eyes,
Those rolling mirrors made alive in me,
Terrible crystal more incredible
Than all the things they see.

Sunder from me my soul, that I may see
The sins like streaming wounds, the life's brave beat:
Till I shall save myself, as I would save
A stranger in the street.

The Donkey

When fishes flew and forests walked
    And figs grew upon thorn,
Some moment when the moon was blood
    Then surely I was born.

With monstrous head and sickening cry
    And ears like errant wings,
The devil's walking parody
    On all four-footed things.

The tattered outlaw of the earth,
    Of ancient crooked will;
Starve, scourge, deride me: I am dumb,
    I keep my secret still.

Fools! For I also had my hour;
    One far fierce hour and sweet:
There was a shout about my ears,
    And palms before my feet.

Wine and Water

Old Noah he had an ostrich farm and fowls on
    the largest scale,
He ate his egg with a ladle in an egg-cup big as
    a pail,
And the soup he took was Elephant Soup and the
    fish he took was Whale,
But they all were small to the cellar he took when
    he set out to sail,
And Noah he often said to his wife when he sat
    down to dine,
'I don't care where the water goes if it doesn't get
    into the wine.'

The cataract of the cliff of heaven fell blinding off
  the brink
As if it would wash the stars away as suds go down
  a sink,
The seven heavens came roaring down for the throats
  of hell to drink,
And Noah he cocked his eye and said, 'It looks
  like rain, I think,
The water has drowned the Matterhorn as deep as
  a Mendip mine,
But I don't care where the water goes if it doesn't
  get into the wine.'

But Noah he sinned, and we have sinned; on tipsy
  feet we trod,
Till a great big black teetotaller was sent to us for
  a rod,
And you can't get wine at a P.S.A., or chapel, or
  Eisteddfod,
For the Curse of Water has come again because of
  the wrath of God,
And water is on the Bishop's board and the Higher
  Thinker's shrine,
But I don't care where the water goes if it doesn't
  get into the wine.

The Shakespeare Memorial

Lord Lilac thought it rather rotten
That Shakespeare should be quite forgotten,
And therefore got on a Committee
With several chaps out of the City,
And Shorter and Sir Herbert Tree,
Lord Rothschild and Lord Rosebery,
And F.C.G. and Comyns Carr,
Two dukes and a dramatic star,

Also a clergyman now dead;
And while the vain world careless sped
Unheeding the heroic name —
The souls most fed with Shakespeare's flame
Still sat unconquered in a ring,
Remembering him like anything.

Lord Lilac did not long remain,
Lord Lilac did not come again.
He softly lit a cigarette
And sought some other social set
Where, in some other knots or rings,
People were doing cultured things,
– Miss Zwilt's Humane Vivarium
– The little men that paint on gum
– The exquisite Gorilla Girl. . . .
He sometimes, in this giddy whirl
(Not being really bad at heart),
Remembered Shakespeare with a start —
But not with that grand constancy
Of Clement Shorter, Herbert Tree,
Lord Rosebery and Comyns Carr
And all the other names there are;
Who stuck like limpets to the spot,
Lest they forgot, lest they forgot.

Lord Lilac was of slighter stuff;
Lord Lilac had had quite enough.

Antichrist, or the Reunion
of Christendom: An Ode

*'A Bill which has shocked the conscience of
every Christian community in Europe.' – Mr.
F. E. Smith, on the Welsh Disestablishment Bill.*

Are they clinging to their crosses,
                          F. E. Smith,
Where the Breton boat-fleet tosses,
                          Are they, Smith?
Do they, fasting, trembling, bleeding,
    Wait the news from this our city?
Groaning 'That's the Second Reading!'
    Hissing 'There is still Committee!'
If the voice of Cecil falters,
    If McKenna's point has pith,
Do they tremble for their altars?
                          Do they, Smith?

Russian peasants round their pope
                          Huddled, Smith,
Hear about it all, I hope,
                          Don't they, Smith?
In the mountain hamlets clothing
    Peaks beyond Caucasian pales,
Where Establishment means nothing
    And they never heard of Wales,
Do they read it all in Hansard
    With a crib to read it with —
'Welsh Tithes: Dr. Clifford Answered.'
                          Really, Smith?

In the lands where Christians were,
                          F. E. Smith,
In the little lands laid bare,
                          Smith, O Smith!

Where the Turkish bands are busy,
  And the Tory name is blessed
Since they hailed the Cross of Dizzy
  On the banners from the West!
Men don't think it half so hard if
  Islam burns their kin and kith,
Since a curate lives in Cardiff
               Saved by Smith.

It would greatly, I must own,
            Soothe me, Smith!
If you left this theme alone,
            Holy Smith!
For your legal cause or civil
  You fight well and get your fee;
For your God or dream or devil
  You will answer, not to me.
Talk about the pews and steeples
  And the cash that goes therewith!
But the souls of Christian peoples . . .
            Chuck it, Smith!

Joseph

If the stars fell; night's nameless dreams
  Of bliss and blasphemy came true,
If skies were green and snow were gold,
  And you loved me as I love you;

O long light hands and curled brown hair,
  And eyes where sits a naked soul;
Dare I even then draw near and burn
  My fingers in the aureole?

Yes, in the one wise foolish hour
  God gives this strange strength to a man.

He can demand, though not deserve,
  Where ask he cannot, seize he can.

But once the blood's wild wedding o'er,
  Were not dread his, half dark desire,
To see the Christ-child in the cot,
  The Virgin Mary by the fire?

The Wise Men

The house from which the heavens are fed,
  The old strange house that is our own,
Where tricks of words are never said,
And Mercy is as plain as bread,
  And Honour is as hard as stone.

Go humbly, humble are the skies,
  And low and large and fierce the Star;
So very near the Manger lies
  That we may travel far.

Hark! Laughter like a lion wakes
  To roar to the resounding plain,
And the whole heaven shouts and shakes,
  For God Himself is born again,
And we are little children walking
  Through the snow and rain.

Step softly, under snow or rain,
  To find the place where men can pray;
The way is all so very plain
  That we may lose the way.

Oh, we have learnt to peer and pore
  On tortured puzzles from our youth,
We know all labyrinthine lore,

We are the three wise men of yore,
    And we know all things but the truth.

We have gone round and round the hill
    And lost the wood among the trees,
And learnt long names for every ill,
And served the mad gods, naming still
    The furies the Eumenides.

The gods of violence took the veil
    Of vision and philosophy,
The Serpent that brought all men bale,
He bites his own accursed tail,
    And calls himself Eternity.

Go humbly . . . it has hailed and snowed . . .
    With voices low and lanterns lit;
So very simple is the road,
    That we may stray from it.

The world grows terrible and white,
    And blinding white the breaking day;
We walk bewildered in the light,
For something is too large for sight,
    And something much too plain to say.

The Child that was ere worlds begun
    (. . . We need but walk a little way,
We need but see a latch undone . . .)
The Child that played with moon and sun
    Is playing with a little hay.

A Curse in Free Verse

(This is the only rhyme admitted: otherwise the enchanting lyric is all that the most fastidious fashionable taste could require):

I CURSE PARADOX —
I curse the contradictory inconsistencies of the Modern Mind:
I curse and curse and curse . . .

Those who dogmatise about the folly of dogma:
Those who moralise about the non-existence of morals:
Those who say people are too stupid to educate their children
But not too stupid to educate each other's:
Those who say we can be certain of nothing.
Because we are so certain of all the exploded evolutionary
    hypotheses
That show we can be certain of nothing . . .
But what are all these inconsistencies —
Compared with the conduct of Those Who
Deliberately Call Their House Christmas Cottage,
And then go away from it at Christmas?

I hate those who wage and win twenty unjust wars
And then say 'The World now requires Peace',
Who then make a League for Peace and use it to make
    another War:
I hate those who intemperately denounce Beer and call it
    Temperance;
Those who deny what science says about Cancer
And what Christianity says about Calvary
And Call the Contradiction Christian Science.
I hate those who want to Rise out of Barbarism
By running about naked and grubbing up roots and herbs;
But what are all these aversions . . . ?
Compared with the blighting blistering horror and hatred
With which I regard
THOSE WHO CALL THEIR HOUSE CHRISTMAS
COTTAGE AND THEN GO AWAY FROM IT AT
CHRISTMAS?

        (The Poet is removed, cursing . . .)

THE ESSAYS

CHESTERTON, whatever else one might say of him, was a man who knew his own mind. He was never afraid to express his own personal convictions; never one to pass up a chance to show how the world, seen in a proper perspective, reinforced the deepest-held beliefs of Chesterton. Such a method is often dismissed as mere axe-grinding, but that is an odd criticism of a man who has set himself up as an axe-grinder. If we despise Chesterton for using the journalistic essay to make a point or to illustrate his philosophy, then we must also agree to condemn farmers for their agriculture, composers for their tiresome habit of continually writing music, and holly trees for their signal failure to produce musk roses or medlars. Besides, the twist at the end (in 'The Twelve Men' for example) is not so much a tagged-on moral as a clinching of the whole argument. It is as if an extra light has suddenly been switched on, not as if all the existing lights had suddenly been re-focused. What Chesterton was doing as a journalist was engaging in a direct democratic appeal to his readers about subjects, topical or general, which were disputed or disputable. He can address subjects such as censorship, national pride, justice, history, literature or progress; but he is just as revealing about these huge matters of morality, balance and truth when he is dealing with seemingly fanciful subjects such as walking in the rain, lying in bed or eating cheese. Such essays are further illustrations of what he pointed to in his poem 'The Wise Men':

> The way is all so very plain
> That we may lose the way.

He shows, over and over again, that a person is all of a piece: that unspoken attitudes are often uninspected attitudes which can soak into and spoil other parts of our intellect and emotion and behaviour. We have to be aware. We may believe ourselves to be walking down a chosen road; but are we sure that it is not merely an habitually attractive rut?

Perhaps if there is one single thing that, above all else, we should thank Chesterton for, it is this awareness. He is awake and he is alive and, even if we decide to disagree with him, he can be relied on to rouse us from our torpor, to make us confront his huge claims, to make us partake of his own vitality.

In *The Screwtape Letters* C. S. Lewis describes exactly the dangers that Chesterton was aware of and fighting against. Screwtape writes to his subordinate, Wormwood:

> The use of Fashions in thought is to distract the attention of men from their real dangers. We direct the fashionable outcry of each generation against those vices of which it is least in danger and fix its approval on the virtue nearest to that vice which we are trying to make endemic. The game is to have them all running about with fire extinguishers whenever there is a flood, and all crowding to that side of the boat which is already nearly gunwhale under. Thus we make it fashionable to expose the dangers of enthusiasm at the very moment when they are all really becoming worldly and lukewarm; a century later, when we are really making them all Byronic and drunk with emotion, the fashionable outcry is directed against the dangers of the mere 'understanding'. Cruel ages are put on their guard against Sentimentality, feckless and idle ones against Respectability, lecherous ones against Puritanism; and whenever all men are really hastening to be slaves or tyrants we make Liberalism the prime bogey.[19]

It is often said of great thinkers that they are against the tide of current thought; it might be truer to say that they are against the tide of thoughtlessness.

The delight of these essays and the quality of the writing will not need pointing out to anyone who reads them. What may need reinforcement is the importance that Chesterton attached to them. He was, on the whole, dismissive of all his books that were written as such. Of his novels he said 'I have spoilt a number of jolly good ideas in my time' and, asked by a friend of E. C. Bentley to inscribe his name in *Orthodoxy*, he wrote on the title-page 'Bosh. By G. K. Chesterton'. He even referred to his finest poem as 'an interminable ballad'. But, even after he had established himself firmly enough to be able to write poetry, criticism, critical works or apologetics for the rest of his life, he chose to continue as a journalist: to face a weekly deadline for at least one and often several more essays or editorials or broadcasts. Either his love or his duty or both led him to the onerous life of the journalist. It may have been because he wanted constant challenge and stimulus; it may have been because he felt that journalism afforded him the widest and most varied readership. It was certainly not the desire for an easy life.

The essays, almost by definition, represent Chesterton at his most typical. He wrote more of them than anything else and the short time allowed for their composition is a guarantee that we shall meet the true, instinctive Chesterton and not a carefully assembled persona. They are also a guarantee of the integrity of the longer works. The wide-ranging intellect that can pick out a metaphor from Renaissance painting here, an image from archaeology there, from poetry, history, mythology or political philosophy is not one which is bound to reference books or a painstaking dredging through card-indexes – it is the real thing: it is a well-stocked mind and a creative mind that bubbles over, that makes everything its own and arranges it into a pattern. We find that mind in the essays as clearly as we do in *The Everlasting Man* or *Autobiography*.

The principal feeling that comes across in the essays is one of performance. Chesterton is onstage, giving a display. Linguistic vitality is added to an urgent enthusiasm, a marvellous humour and an unexpected idea – or at least, to an idea that becomes gradually more and more unexpected as the essay proceeds. The overall effect is like watching a conjurer, a comedian and a virtuoso musician; and it is irresistible. Even when it is over the reader is left with at least one kernel of thought, if not three or four, which can provide a source of meditation for many an hour. He points to the tip of an iceberg and leaves us to don the diving suits. He is an animator and entertainer and an irritant. Some of his casual asides are so perceptive that they could be turned into whole theses. Here is one about George Eliot:

> Her air is bright and intellectually even exciting; but it is like the air of a cloudless day on the parade of Brighton. She sees people clearly, but not through an atmosphere. And she can conjure up storms in the conscious, but not in the subconscious mind.

Before the essays are read perhaps a final word needs to be said about the very word 'journalist'. It is a job that has taken the place of 'engine driver' in the minds of aspirant youth, if we are to believe the sociologists. But, while more people want to be journalists than anything else, the word has, in some quarters, become synonymous with hasty, ungrammatical, inaccurate writing that panders to the lowest tastes and desires. It is tempting to deduce, therefore, that the education system is actually doing a fine job in fitting people for the career of their choice. There has always been a divide between literature and journalism but some have made it out to be greater than it is. Obviously there is an uncrossable gulf between, say, a John Donne poem and a football world cup report in the *Sun*. There is a divide between *Anna Karenina* and the most considered article in a quality newspaper. But between the two there is a great deal of space to occupy and it is, in some ways, a matter of taste whether one considers Defoe, Cobbett, Johnson, Lamb, Carlyle, Wells, Orwell and Connolly – to name but eight out of scores – as journalists or literary writers. They could be either or both; and today the distinction is even more blurred. If Chesterton wished to be known as a journalist then we should not argue; but maybe we should revise our opinions on what journalism is capable of and what we should feel entitled to expect from it.

From Some Policemen and a Moral

The other day I was nearly arrested by two excited policemen in a wood in Yorkshire. I was on a holiday, and was engaged in that rich and intricate mass of pleasures, duties, and discoveries which for the keeping off of the profane we disguise by the exoteric name of Nothing. At the moment in question I was throwing a big Swedish knife at a tree, practising (alas, without success) that useful trick of knife-throwing by which men murder each other in Stevenson's romances.

Suddenly the forest was full of two policemen; there was something about their appearance in and relation to the greenwood that reminded me, I know not how, of some happy Elizabethan comedy. They asked what the knife was, who I was, why I was throwing it, what my address was, trade, religion, opinions on the Japanese war, name of favourite cat, and so on. They also said I was damaging the tree; which was, I am sorry to say, not true, because I could not hit it. The peculiar philosophical importance, however, of the incident was this. After some half-hour's animated conversation, the exhibition of an envelope, an unfinished poem, which was read with great care, and, I trust, with some profit, and one or two other subtle detective strokes, the elder of the two knights became convinced that I really was what I professed to be, that I was a journalist, that I was on the *Daily News* (this was the real stroke; they were shaken with a terror common to all tyrants), that I lived in a particular place as stated, and that I was stopping with particular people in Yorkshire, who happened to be wealthy and well-known in the neighbourhood.

In fact the leading constable became so genial and complimentary at last that he ended up by representing himself as a reader of my work. And when that was said, everything was settled. They acquitted me and let me pass.

'But,' I said, 'what of this mangled tree? It was to the rescue of that Dryad, tethered to the earth, that you rushed like knight-errants. You, the higher humanitarians, are not deceived by the seeming stillness of the green things, a stillness like the stillness of the cataract, a headlong and crashing silence. You know that a tree is but a creature tied to the ground by one leg. You will not let assassins with their Swedish daggers shed the green blood of such a being. But if so, why am I not in custody; where are my gyves? Produce, from some portion of your persons, my mouldy straw and my grated window. The facts of which I have just convinced you, that my name is Chesterton, that I am a journalist, that I am living with the well-known and philanthropic Mr Blank of Ilkley, cannot have anything to do with the question of whether I have been guilty of cruelty to vegetables. The tree is none the less damaged, even though it may reflect with a dark pride that it was wounded by a gentleman connected with the Liberal press. Wounds in the bark do not more rapidly close up because they are inflicted by people who are stopping with Mr Blank of Ilkley. That tree, the ruin of its former self, the wreck of what was once a giant of the forest, now splintered and laid low by the brute superiority of a Swedish knife, that tragedy, constable, cannot be wiped out even by stopping for several months more with some wealthy person. It is incredible that you have no legal claim to arrest even the most august and fashionable persons on this charge. For if so, why did you interfere with me at all?'

I made the later and larger part of this speech to the silent wood, for the two policemen had vanished almost as quickly as they came. It is very possible, of course, that they were fairies. In that case the somewhat illogical character of their view of crime, law, and personal responsibility would find a bright and elfish explanation; perhaps if I had lingered in the glade till moonrise I might have seen rings of tiny policemen dancing on the sward; or running about with glow-worm belts, arresting grasshoppers for damaging blades of grass. But taking the bolder hypothesis, that they really were policemen, I find myself in a certain difficulty. I was certainly accused of something which was either an offence or was not. I was let off because I proved I was a guest at a big house. The inference seems painfully clear; either it is not a proof of infamy to throw a knife about in a lonely wood, or else it is a proof of innocence to know a rich man. Suppose a very poor person, poorer even than a journalist, a navvy or unskilled labourer, tramping in search of work, often changing his lodgings, often, perhaps, failing in his rent. Suppose he had read Stevenson's novels. Suppose he had been intoxicated with the green gaiety of the ancient wood. Suppose he had thrown knives at trees and could give no description of a dwelling-place except that he had been fired out of the last. As I walked home through a cloudy and purple twilight I wondered how he would have got on.

The Slavery of Free Verse

The truth most needed today is that the end is never the right end. The beginning is the right end at which to begin. The modern man has to read everything backwards; as when he reads journalism first and history afterwards – if at all. He is like a blind man exploring an elephant, and condemned to begin at the very tip of its tail. But he is still more unlucky; for when he has a first principle, it is generally the very last principle that he ought to have. He starts, as it were, with one infallible dogma about the elephant; that its tail is its trunk. He works the wrong way round on principle; and tries to fit all the practical facts to his principle. Because the elephant has no eyes in its tail-end, he calls it a blind elephant; and expatiates on its ignorance, superstition and need of compulsory education. Because it has no tusks at its tail-end, he says that tusks are a fantastic flourish attributed to a fabulous creature, an ivory chimera that must have come through the ivory gate. Because it does not as a rule pick up things with its tail, he dismisses the magical story that it can pick up things with its trunk. He probably says it is plainly a piece of anthropomorphism to suppose that an elephant can pack its trunk. The result is that he becomes as pallid and worried as a pessimist; the world to him is not only an elephant, but a white elephant. He does not know what to do with it, and cannot be persuaded of the perfectly simple explanation; which is that he has not made the smallest real attempt to make head or tail of the animal. He will not begin at the right end; because he happens to have come first on the wrong end.

But in nothing do I feel this modern trick, of trusting to a fag-end rather than a first principle, more than in the modern treatment of poetry. With this or that particular metrical form, or unmetrical form, or unmetrical formlessness, I might be content or not, as it achieved some particular effect or not. But the whole general tendency, regarded as an emancipation, seems to me more or less of an enslavement. It seems founded on one subconscious idea; that talk is freer than verse; and that verse, therefore, should claim the freedom of talk. But talk, especially in our time, is not free at all. It is tripped up by trivialities, tamed by conventions, loaded with dead words, thwarted by a thousand meaningless things. It does not liberate the soul so much, when a man can say, 'You always look so nice', as when he can say, 'But your eternal summer shall not fade.' The first is an awkward and constrained sentence ending with the weakest word ever used, or rather misused, by man. The second is like the gesture of a giant or the sweeping flight of an archangel; it has the very rush of liberty. I do not despise the man who says the first, because he *means* the second; and what he means is more important than what he says. I have always done my best to emphasize the inner dignity of these daily things, in spite of their dull externals; but I do not think it an improvement that the inner spirit itself should grow more external and more dull. It is thought right to discourage numbers of prosaic people trying to be poetical; but I think it much more of a bore to watch numbers of poetical people trying to be prosaic. In short, it is another case of tail-foremost philosophy; instead of watering the laurel hedge of the cockney villa, we bribe the cockney to brick in the plant of Apollo.

I have always had the fancy that if a man were really free, he would talk in rhythm and even in rhyme. His most hurried postcard would be a sonnet; and his most hasty wires like harp-strings. He would breathe a song into the telephone; a song which would be a lyric or an epic, according to the time involved in awaiting the call; or in his inevitable altercation with the telephone girl, the duel would be also a duet. He would express his preference among the dishes at dinner in short impromptu poems, combining the more mystical gratitude of grace with a certain epigrammatic terseness, more convenient for domestic good feeling. If Mr. Yeats can say, in exquisite verse, the exact number of bean rows he would like on his plantation, why not the number of beans he would like on his plate? If he can issue a rhymed request to procure the honey-bee, why not to pass the honey? Misunderstandings might arise at first with the richer and more fantastic poets; and Francis Thompson might have asked several times for 'the gold skins of undelirious wine' before anybody understood that he wanted the grapes. Nevertheless, I will maintain that his magnificent phrase would be a far more real expression of God's most glorious gift of the vine, than if he had simply said in a peremptory manner 'grapes'; especially if the culture of compulsory education had carefully taught him to pronounce it as if it were 'gripes'. And if a man could ask for a potato in the form of a poem, the poem would not be merely a more romantic but a much more realistic rendering of a potato. For a potato is a poem; it is even an ascending scale of poems; beginning at the root, in subterranean grotesques in the Gothic manner, with humps like the deformities of a goblin and eyes like a beast of Revelation, and rising up through the green shades of the earth to a crown that has the shape of stars and the hue of heaven.

But the truth behind all this is that expressed in that very ancient mystical notion, the music of the spheres. It is the idea that, at the back of everything, existence begins with a harmony and not a chaos; and, therefore, when we really spread our wings and find a wider freedom, we find it in something more continuous and recurrent, and not in something more fragmentary and crude. Freedom is fullness, especially fullness of life; and a full vessel is more rounded and complete than an empty one, and not less so. To vary Browning's phrase, we find in prose the broken arcs, in poetry the perfect round. Prose is not the freedom of poetry; rather prose is the fragments of poetry. Prose, at least in the prosaic sense, is poetry interrupted, held up and cut off from its course; the chariot of Phoebus stopped by a block in the Strand. But when it begins to move again at all, I think we shall find certain old-fashioned things move with it, such as repetition and even measure, rhythm and even rhyme. We shall discover with horror that the wheels of the chariot go round and round; and even that the horses of the chariot have the usual number of feet.

Anyhow, the right way to encourage the cortège is not to put the cart before the horse. It is not to make poetry more poetical by ignoring what distinguishes it from prose. There may be many new ways of making the chariot move again; but I confess that most of the modern theorists seem to me to be lecturing on a new theory of its mechanics, while it is standing still. If a wizard before my very eyes works a miracle with a rope, a boy and a mango plant, I am only theoretically interested in the question of a sceptic, who asks why it should not be done with a garden hose, a maiden aunt and a monkey-tree. Why not, indeed, if he can do it? If a saint performs a miracle tomorrow, by turning a stone into a fish, I shall be the less concerned at being asked in the abstract, why a man should not also turn a camp-stool into a cockatoo; but let him do it, and not merely explain how it can be done. It is certain that words such as 'birds' and 'sweet', which are as plain as 'fish' or 'stone', can be combined in such a miracle as 'Bare ruined quires where late the sweet birds sang'. So far as I can follow my own feelings, the metre and fall of the feet, even the rhyme and place in the sonnet, have a great deal to do with producing such an effect. I do not say there is no other way of producing such an effect. I only ask, not without longing, where else in this wide and weary time is it produced? I know I cannot produce it; and I do not in fact feel it when I hear *vers libres*. I know not where is that Promethean heat; and, even to express my ignorance, I am glad to find better words than my own.

The Glory of Grey

I suppose, that, taking this summer as a whole, people will not call it an appropriate time for praising the English climate. But for my part I will praise the English climate till I die – even if I die of the English climate. There is no weather so good as English weather. Nay, in a real sense there is no weather at all anywhere but in England. In France you have much sun and some rain; in Italy you have hot winds and cold winds; in Scotland and Ireland you have rain, either thick or thin; in America you have hells of heat and cold, and in the Tropics you have sunstrokes varied by thunderbolts. But all these you have on a broad and brutal scale, and you settle down into contentment or despair. Only in our own romantic country do you have the strictly romantic thing called Weather; beautiful and changing as a woman. The great English landscape painters (neglected now like everything that is English) have this salient distinction: that the Weather is not the atmosphere of their pictures; it is the subject of their pictures. They paint portraits of the Weather. The Weather sat to Constable. The Weather posed for Turner; and a deuce of a pose it was. This cannot truly be said of the greatest of their continental models or rivals. Poussin and Claude painted objects, ancient cities or perfect Arcadian shepherds through a clear medium of the climate. But in the English painters Weather is the hero; with Turner an Adelphi hero, taunting, flashing and fighting, melodramatic but really magnificent. The English climate, a tall and terrible protagonist, robed in rain and thunder and snow and sunlight, fills the whole canvas and the whole foreground. I admit the superiority of many other French things besides French art. But I will not yield an inch on the superiority of English weather and weather-painting. Why, the French have not even got a word for Weather; and you must ask for the weather in French as if you were asking for the time in English.

Then, again, variety of climate should always go with stability of abode. The weather in the desert is monotonous; and as a natural consequence the Arabs wander about, hoping it may be different somewhere. But an Englishman's house is not only his castle; it is his fairy castle. Clouds and colours of every varied dawn and eve are perpetually touching and turning it from clay to gold, or from gold to ivory. There is a line of woodland beyond a corner of my garden which is literally different on every one of the three hundred and sixty-five days. Sometimes it seems as near as a hedge, and sometimes as far as a faint and fiery evening cloud. The same principle (by the way) applies to the difficult problem of wives. Variability is one of the virtues of a woman. It avoids the crude requirement of polygamy. So long as you have one good wife you are sure to have a spiritual harem.

Now, among the heresies that are spoken in this matter is the habit of calling a grey day a 'colourless' day. Grey is a colour, and can be a very powerful and pleasing colour. There is also an insulting style of speech about 'one grey day just like another'. You might as well talk about one green tree just like another. A grey clouded sky is indeed a canopy between us and the sun; so is a green tree, if it comes to that. But the grey umbrellas differ as much as the green in their style and shape, in their tint and tilt. One day may be grey like steel, and another grey like dove's plumage. One may seem grey like the smoke of substantial kitchens. No things could seem further apart than the doubt of grey and the decision of scarlet. Yet grey and red can mingle, as they do in the morning clouds: and also in a sort of warm smoky stone of which they build the little towns in the west country. In those towns even the houses that are wholly grey have a glow in them as if their secret firesides were such furnaces of hospitality as faintly to transfuse the walls like walls of cloud. And wandering in those westland parts I did once really find a sign-post pointing up a steep crooked path to a town that was called Clouds. I did not climb up to it; I feared that either the town would not be good enough for the name, or I should not be good enough for the town. Anyhow, the little hamlets of the warm grey stone have a geniality which is not achieved by all the artistic scarlet of the suburbs; as if it were better to warm one's hands at the ashes of Glastonbury than at the painted flames of Croydon.

Again, the enemies of grey (those astute, daring and evil-minded men) are fond of bringing forward the argument that colours suffer in grey weather, and that strong sunlight is necessary to all the hues of heaven and earth. Here again there are two words to be said; and it is essential to distinguish. It is true that sun is needed to burnish and bring into bloom the tertiary and dubious colours: the colour of peat, pea-soup, Impressionist sketches, brown velvet coats, olives, grey and blue slates, the complexions of vegetarians, the tinge of volcanic rock, chocolate, cocoa, mud, soot, slime, old boots; the delicate shades of these do need the sunlight to bring out the faint beauty that often clings to them. But if you have a healthy negro taste in colour, if you choke your garden with poppies and geraniums, if you paint your house sky-blue and scarlet, if you wear, let us say, a golden top-hat and a crimson frock-coat, you will not only be visible on the greyest day, but you will notice that your costume and environment produce a certain singular effect. You will find, I mean, that rich colours actually look more luminous on a grey day, because they are seen against a sombre background and seem to be burning with a lustre of their own. Against a dark sky all flowers look like fireworks. There is something strange about them, at once vivid and secret, like flowers traced in fire in the phantasmal garden of a witch. A bright blue sky is necessarily the high light of the picture; and its brightness kills all the bright blue flowers. But on a grey day the larkspur looks like fallen heaven; the red daisies are really the red lost eyes of day; and the sunflower is the vice-regent of the sun.

Lastly, there is this value about the colour that men call colourless; that it suggests in some way the mixed and troubled average of existence, especially in its quality of strife and expectation and promise. Grey is a colour that always seems on the eve of changing to some other colour; of brightening into blue or blanching into white or bursting into green and gold. So we may be perpetually reminded of the indefinite hope that is in doubt itself; and when there is grey weather in our hills or grey hairs in our heads, perhaps they may still remind us of the morning.

The Appetite of Earth

I was walking the other day in a kitchen garden, which I find has somehow got attached to my premises, and I was wondering why I liked it. After a prolonged spiritual self-analysis I came to the conclusion that I like a kitchen garden because it contains things to eat. I do not mean that a kitchen garden is ugly; a kitchen garden is often very beautiful. The mixture of green and purple on some monstrous cabbage is much subtler and grander than the mere freakish and theatrical splashing of yellow and violet on a pansy. Few of the flowers merely meant for ornament are so ethereal as a potato. A kitchen garden is as beautiful as an orchard; but why is it that the word 'orchard' sounds as beautiful as the word 'flower-garden', and yet also sounds more satisfactory? I suggest again my extraordinarily dark and delicate discovery: that it contains things to eat.

The cabbage is a solid; it can be approached from all sides at once; it can be realized by all senses at once. Compared with that the sunflower, which can only be seen, is a mere pattern, a thing painted on a flat wall. Now, it is this sense of the solidity of things that can only be uttered by the metaphor of eating. To express the cubic content of a turnip, you must be all round it at once. The only way to get all round a turnip at once is to eat the turnip. I think any poetic mind that has loved solidity, the thickness of trees, the squareness of stones, the firmness of clay, must have sometimes wished that they were things to eat. If only brown peat tasted as good as it looks; if only white fir-wood were digestible! We talk rightly of giving stones for bread: but there are in the Geological Museum certain rich crimson marbles, certain split stones of blue and green, that make me wish my teeth were stronger.

Somebody staring into the sky with the same ethereal appetite declared that the moon was made of green cheese. I never could conscientiously accept the full doctrine. I am Modernist in this matter. That the moon is made of cheese I have believed from childhood; and in the course of every month a giant (of my acquaintance) bites a big round piece out of it. This seems to me a doctrine that is above reason, but not contrary to it. But that the cheese is green seems to be in some degree actually contradicted by the senses and the reason; first because if the moon were made of green cheese it would be inhabited; and second because if it were made of green cheese it would be green. A blue moon is said to be an unusual sight; but I cannot think that a green one is much more common. In fact, I think I have seen the moon looking like every other sort of cheese except a green cheese. I have seen it look exactly like a cream cheese: a circle of warm white upon a warm faint violet sky above a cornfield in Kent. I have seen it look very like a Dutch cheese, rising a dull red copper disk amid masts and dark waters at Honfleur. I have seen it look like an ordinary sensible Chedder [sic] cheese in an ordinary sensible Prussian blue sky; and I have once seen it so naked and ruinous-looking, so strangely lit up, that it looked like a Gruyère cheese, that awful volcanic cheese that has horrible holes in it, as if it had come in boiling unnatural milk from mysterious and unearthly cattle. But I have never yet seen the lunar cheese green; and I incline to the opinion that the moon is not old enough. The moon, like everything else, will ripen by the end of the world; and in the last days we shall see it taking on those volcanic sunset colours, and leaping with that enormous and fantastic life.

But this is a parenthesis; and one perhaps slightly lacking in prosaic actuality. Whatever may be the value of the above speculations, the phrase about the moon and green cheese remains a good example of this imagery of eating and drinking on a large scale. The same huge fancy is in the phrase 'if all the trees were bread and cheese', which I have cited elsewhere in this connection; and in that noble nightmare of a Scandinavian legend, in which Thor drinks the deep sea near dry out of a horn. In an essay like the present (first intended as a paper to be read before the Royal Society) one cannot be too exact; and I will concede that my theory of the gradual virescence of our satellite is to be regarded rather as an alternative theory than as a law finally demonstrated and universally accepted by the scientific world. It is a hypothesis that holds the field, as the scientists say of a theory when there is no evidence for it so far.

But the reader need be under no apprehension that I have suddenly gone mad, and shall start biting large pieces out of the trunks of trees; or seriously altering (by large semi-circular mouthfuls) the exquisite outline of the mountains. This feeling for expressing a fresh solidity by the image of eating is really a very old one. So far from being a paradox of perversity, it is one of the oldest commonplaces of religion. If anyone wandering about wants to have a good trick or test for separating the wrong idealism from the right, I will give him one on the spot. It is a mark of false religion that it is always trying to express concrete facts as abstract; it calls sex affinity; it calls wine alcohol; it calls brute starvation the economic problem. The test of true religion is that its energy drives exactly the other way; it is always trying to make men feel truths as facts; always trying to make abstract things as plain and solid as concrete things; always trying to make men, not merely admit the truth, but see, smell, handle, hear, and devour the truth. All great spiritual scriptures are full of the invitation not to test, but to taste, not to examine, but to eat. Their phrases are full of living water and heavenly bread, mysterious manna and dreadful wine. Worldliness, and the polite society of the world, has despised this instinct of eating; but religion has never despised it. When we look at a firm, fat, white cliff of chalk at Dover, I do not suggest that we should desire to eat it; that would be highly abnormal. But I really mean that we should think it good to eat; good for someone else to eat. For, indeed, someone else is eating it; the grass that grows upon its top is devouring it silently, but, doubtless, with an uproarious appetite.

On Mr. Thomas Gray

A newspaper appeared with the news, which it seemed to regard as exciting and even alarming news, that Gray did not write the 'Elegy in a Country Churchyard' in the churchyard of Stoke Poges, but in some other country churchyard of the same sort in the same country. What effect the news will have on the particular type of American tourist who has chipped pieces off trees and tombstones, when he finds that the chips come from the wrong trees, or the wrong tombstones, I do not feel impelled to inquire. Nor, indeed, do I know whether the new theory is proved or not. Nor do I care whether the new theory is proved or not. What is most certainly proved, if it needed any proving, is the complete lack of imagination, in many journalists and archaeologists, about how any poet writes any poem.

In such a controversy it is implied, generally on both sides, that what happens is something like this. The poet comes and sits on a tombstone, or wherever he was supposed to sit, in the one and only churchyard of Stoke Poges, or whatever place be the rival of Stoke Poges. He hears the Curfew; and there is a dreadful doubt and dispute about whether anybody sitting among the tombs of Stoke Poges can hear the Curfew, which does really ring from Windsor, though I imagine it sounds pretty much like any other bell at evening. Then the poet produces a portable pen and ink. preferably a large quill and a scroll (the poet in question lived before the time of fountain-pens), and writes down the first line: 'The curfew tolls the knell of parting day.' Then he looks round to make quite sure that there are some lowing herds winding over that particular lea, that the ploughman is present and doing his duty in plodding homeward his weary way, and that all the other fittings are in the offing. Later, he will have to insist peremptorily on an ivy-mantled tower being in the immediate neighbourhood, inhabited by an (if possible) moping owl. It will not be the only owl involved in the business. If there are not all these correct conditions provided on the spot, he will not be able to write the Elegy. If, on the other hand, they are all there and everything has been properly provided, he will then write the whole of the Elegy, steadily, right through, and not roll up his scroll or rise from his tombstone until he has left the unfortunate young man in the poem finally safe in the bosom of his Father and his God. Then he will go home to tea; and I should imagine he would need it, after so prolonged and sustained a literary effort achieved in such damp and clammy conditions. That, with very little exaggeration, is what is really suggested by those who talk about Gray writing the poem in this place or that place, and under this or that condition of local colour.

Now, I should have thought that anybody would know that poetry is not written like that. But perhaps, in this case, even a bad poet is better than a good critic. Anybody who has ever written any verse, good, bad, or indifferent, will know that calculations of this sort are calculations about the incalculable. Gray might have written the poem, or any part of the poem, in any place on the map; he might have visited the New Stoke Poges or the Old Stoke Poges, or quite probably both, or possibly neither. But, if I may be allowed to pick out one thread of speculation from a thousand threads of possibility, I would suggest that the 'Elegy in a Country Churchyard', even if it did refer to one particular churchyard, is very likely to have been begun, continued, and ended rather like this:

Mr. Thomas Gray was sitting one evening in a coffee-house; let us hope a coffee-house that did not confine itself to coffee. Something or other, a fiddle or a few glasses of wine, or a good dinner, had thrown him into a mood of musing, of pleasant musing, though touched with a manly and generous melancholy. His thoughts turned round and round, as they do at such times, the tantalizing old riddle of what we really feel about life and death; about the toy God gave us which is beautiful and brittle, yet certainly not trivial. He said to himself: 'After all, who doesn't really feel that it really matters, with all its botherations? . . . A queer business . . . pleasing . . . anxious . . .' Then something stirred quicker within him, and he said to himself, in warm poetic emotion —

> For who tytumpty tumpty tumpty tum,
> This pleasing anxious being e'er resign'd.

Then his impulse gathered speed and power; and he struck the table and said the next line straight off —

> Left the warm precincts of the cheerful day.

He said that line several times. He liked it very much. Then it was almost a matter of form, certainly a matter of facility, to put the tail on the verse —

> Nor cast one longing, ling'ring look behind.

Then he got up and put on his hat. He left the warm precincts of the cheerful coffee-house, and went home and forgot all about it.

Some time afterwards, perhaps quite a long time afterwards, he was walking in the countryside at dusk. It is quite possible that he was walking in Stoke Poges, or through Stoke Poges, or through any number of other places in the neighbourhood. Perhaps he did hear the Curfew, or what he thought was the Curfew, or what he pretended was the Curfew. He made up another verse or two about the twilight landscape, full of the same spirit of stoical thankfulness and genial resignation. Then he noticed, with great joy, that they would work into the same metre as the lines he had made up in the coffee-house. They were very much in the same mood. But he did not write many of the verses in the churchyard. Possibly he did not write any of the verses in the churchyard. It is more likely that the third act has for its scene Mr. Gray's private study, lined with classics in old leather bindings, and adorned with the celebrated cat and the bowl of goldfish. There he jotted down disjointed verses, and began to put them together; until it looked as if they might some day make a poem. But, subject to any information that may

exist on the subject, it would not in the ordinary way surprise me
to learn that it was a devil of a long time before they did make
a poem. It is most likely, in the abstract, that he got sick of it
half-way through, and chucked it away, and found it again years
afterwards. It is extremely likely that there was another very long
interval, when he was just finishing it, but could not finish finishing
it. Many a man writing such a poem has held it up for a year for
want of one verse. Nor would the newspaper assist him, in such a
difficulty, by pointing out that there was another churchyard much
more suitable than that of Stoke Poges.

Now, it is possible – nay, it is probable – that there is not one
word of truth in this particular description of the proceedings of
Mr. Gray. I have not read any of the literary and biographical
records of Mr. Gray, at least for a long time; and there are plenty
of records to read. It is quite likely that there are details of his
daily life that destroy altogether the details I have here suggested.
It is even possible that, by some amazing eccentricity, he did
write the whole thing in a churchyard; or, by some unscrupulous
exaggeration, pretended that he had done so. But my story is a
great deal nearer to the normal story of the production of a poem
than any story that supposes particular places and conditions to be
necessary to the poem. Even if Gray did write with all the stage
properties stuck up around him, the lowing cow, the plodding
ploughman, the moping owl, they were not the materials of the
poem; and he would probably have written pretty much the same
sort of poem without them. All this business of clues and tests is not
criticism. It is a very good thing that people are applying literature
to detective stories and detectives. But it is not a good thing to
apply detectives to literature. Gray's unmistakable footmark or
favourite tobacco-ash may be found in Stoke Poges or anywhere
else. But it is not in those ashes that there lived his wonted fires.

The real relation of Gray's great poem to the present stage of
our history will probably not be understood until a later stage. Yet
the poem is a monument, a trophy, and, at the same time, a beacon
or signal, standing up as solid and significant as the monument
stands up in the Stoke Poges fields. Many poems have been written
since, and grown more fashionable, if not more famous, which
have not the particular meaning for the modern world stored up

in this very storied urn. For Gray wrote at the very beginning of a certain literary epoch of which we, perhaps, stand at the very end. He represented that softening of the Classic which slowly turned it into the Romantic. We represent that ultimate hardening of the Romantic which has turned it into the Realistic. Both changes have, of course, been criticized in their time by the more conservative critics. Dr. Johnson said, probably with a partly humorous impatience, that Gray had only proved that he 'could be dull in a new way'. And most of us will agree that the modern realistic writers, who have in their turn replaced the romantic writers, have indubitably discovered a marvellous and amazing number of new ways of being dull.

But the change, as it hung uncompleted in Gray, strangely resembled the twilight changes of that landscape which the poem describes. Indeed, the whole episode has a curious, almost uncanny, harmony that even includes coincidence. Concerned as he was with a fine shade of twilight, it is even odd that his name was Gray. The whole legend is like that of something colourless and classical fading into mere shadow. For something was, indeed, fading before the eyes of Thomas Gray, the poet, and it was something that he did not wish to see fade. It may be noted that the first impression, especially in the first verses, is one of things moving away from the poet and leaving him alone. We see only the back of the ploughman, so to speak, as he plods away into the darkness; the herds of cattle have the perspective of vanishing things; for a whole world was indeed passing out of the sight and reach of that learned and sensitive and secluded gentleman, who represented the culture of eighteenth-century England, and could only watch a twilight transformation which he could not understand. For when the ploughman comes back out of that twilight, he will come back different. He will be either a scientific works-manager or an entirely new kind of agrarian citizen, great as in the first days of Rome; a free peasant or a servant of alien machinery; but never the same again.

I am not very fond of committees and societies of specialists or amateurs who sit upon this or that sort of problem; but in the particular problem of the preservation of the rural and cultural traditions of our own countryside, I cannot see at the moment that any other machinery is possible. And it seems to me that the Penn-Gray Society is a good example of a machine suited to its work and doing work that is wanted. The trouble is that the typical cultured Englishman, like Gray or the traditional admirer of Gray, was generally a certain kind of gentleman, of the sort that had some kind of country seat. Since then, to continue the figure, the gentleman with the country seat has rather fallen between two stools. He is no longer so rich and powerful as a landlord. He generally has not become so rich and powerful as a local politician. There were any number of men, of course, who appreciated the country without owning a country seat. But if they were not the sort of men to own a country seat, still less were they the sort of men to stand for a county council. And, as the old organization of England went, the organization that has been gradually dying since the days of Gray, men of this artistic sort were mostly attached in some more or less indirect way to the gentry. That is the point; that, for good or ill, it was the system peculiar to a gentry. It was never, for instance, the system peculiar to a peasantry. When there is anything like a peasantry, even as there is in Scotland, it was possible to produce a peasant poet like Burns. And the memory of a peasant like Burns would be preserved by other peasants, even if there were nobody else to preserve it. But nobody could expect the agricultural labourers to preserve the memory of a scholar like Gray. It is amusing to remember that Burns put a verse from the Elegy as a motto to his own homely and pungent picture of peasant life; as some thought, consciously stressing the contrast between his own realism and the scholar's classicism:

> Let not Ambition mock their useful toil,
> Their homely joys, and destiny obscure;
> Nor Grandeur hear, with a disdainful smile,
> The short and simple annals of the poor.

Indeed, I rather fancy that, in citing those rather patronizing lines, it was the poor poet who had the disdainful smile.

But we must take the rough with the smooth in that noble aristocratic story that has made South England like a garden among the nations. And with it weakened the only organization for protecting the art and antiquities of rural life. Gray could not be a popular poet like Burns; at least, not in that sort of rural life. Perhaps there is a hint of it in his own phrase; that the Village Milton would have remained mute and inglorious. Perhaps he deliberately did not finish the tale of the Village Hampden, who was possibly a poacher but could not possibly be a peasant. Anyhow, the old organization of culture has weakened; and the new organization of local politics is not an organization of culture. There can be a culture of peasants, but not a culture of petty politicians. In this dilemma there is nothing to be done except to work through groups of sympathetic individuals, students or artists or lovers of landscape, who take the trouble to support each other in defending the tradition of the national history and poetry. Otherwise the whole country will be swept bare for the sort of motorist to whom every object is an obstacle to rushing from nowhere to nowhere. Roads will not be roads, for there will be no places for them to go to; there will be only those ominously called arterial, and resembling, indeed, those open and spouting arteries that are an inevitable sign of death. I should say the ultimate moral is that we ought to have made up our minds between real aristocracy and real democracy, and should have either preserved a gentry or created a peasantry. But the immediate moral is that we must preserve what we can of all that reminds us that rural life was a civilization and not a savagery, and especially support such groups as the society here in question, which is defending the great tradition of Gray.

On Lying in Bed

Lying in bed would be an altogether perfect and supreme experience if only one had a coloured pencil long enough to draw on the ceiling. This, however, is not generally a part of the domestic apparatus on the premises. I think myself that the thing might be managed with several pails of Aspinall and a broom. Only if one worked in a really sweeping and masterly way, and laid on the colour in great washes, it might drip down again on one's face in floods of rich and mingled colour like some strange fairy rain; and that would have its disadvantages. I am afraid it would be necessary to stick to black and white in this form of artistic composition. To that purpose, indeed, the white ceiling would be of the greatest possible use; in fact, it is the only use I think of a white ceiling being put to.

But for the beautiful experiment of lying in bed I might never have discovered it. For years I have been looking for some blank spaces in a modern house to draw on. Paper is much too small for any really allegorical design; as Cyrano de Bergerac says, 'Il me faut des géants.' But when I tried to find these fine clear spaces in the modern rooms such as we all live in I was continually disappointed. I found an endless pattern and complication of small objects hung like a curtain of fine links between me and my desire. I examined the walls; I found them to my surprise to be already covered with wallpaper, and I found the wallpaper to be already covered with very uninteresting images, all bearing a ridiculous resemblance to each other. I could not understand why one arbitrary symbol (a symbol apparently entirely devoid of any religious or philosophical significance) should thus be sprinkled all over my nice walls like a sort of smallpox. The Bible must be referring to wallpapers, I think, when it says, 'Use not vain repetitions, as the Gentiles do.' I found the Turkey carpet a mass of unmeaning colours, rather like the Turkish Empire, or like the sweetmeat called Turkish Delight. I do not exactly know what Turkish Delight really is; but I suppose it is Macedonian Massacres. Everywhere that I went forlornly, with my pencil or my paint brush, I found that others had unaccountably been before me, spoiling the walls, the curtains, and the furniture with their childish and barbaric designs.

Nowhere did I find a really clear space for sketching until this occasion when I prolonged beyond the proper limit the process of lying on my back in bed. Then the light of that white heaven broke upon my vision, that breadth of mere white which is indeed almost the definition of Paradise, since it means purity and also means freedom. But alas! like all heavens, now that it is seen it is found to be unattainable; it looks more austere and more distant than the blue sky outside the window. For my proposal to paint on it with the bristly end of a broom has been discouraged – never mind by whom; by a person debarred from all political rights – and even my minor proposal to put the other end of the broom into the kitchen fire and turn it into charcoal has not been conceded. Yet I am certain that it was from persons in my position that all the original inspiration came for covering the ceilings of palaces and cathedrals with a riot of fallen angels or victorious gods. I am sure that it was only because Michael Angelo was engaged in the ancient and honourable occupation of lying in bed that he ever realized how the roof of the Sistine Chapel might be made into an awful imitation of a divine drama that could only be acted in the heavens.

The tone now commonly taken towards the practice of lying in bed is hypocritical and unhealthy. Of all the marks of modernity that seem to mean a kind of decadence, there is none more menacing and dangerous than the exaltation of very small and secondary matters of conduct at the expense of very great and primary ones, at the expense of eternal ties and tragic human morality. If there is one thing worse than the modern weakening of major morals it is the modern strengthening of minor morals. Thus it is considered more withering to accuse a man of bad taste than of bad ethics. Cleanliness is not next to godliness nowadays, for cleanliness is made an essential and godliness is regarded as an offence. A playwright can attack the institution of marriage so long as he does not misrepresent the manners of society, and I have met Ibsenite pessimists who thought it wrong to take beer but right to take prussic acid. Especially this is so in matters of hygiene; notably such matters as lying in bed. Instead of being regarded, as it ought to be, as a matter of personal convenience and adjustment, it has come to be regarded by many as if it were a part of essential morals to get up early in the morning. It is upon the whole part of practical wisdom; but there is nothing good about it or bad about its opposite.

Misers get up early in the morning; and burglars, I am informed, get up the night before. It is the great peril of our society that all its mechanism may grow more fixed while its spirit grows more fickle. A man's minor actions and arrangements ought to be free, flexible, creative; the things that should be unchangeable are his principles, his ideals. But with us the reverse is true; our views change constantly; but our lunch does not change. Now, I should like men to have strong and rooted conceptions, but as for their lunch, let them have it sometimes in the garden, sometimes in bed, sometimes on the roof, sometimes in the top of a tree. Let them argue from the same first principles, but let them do it in a bed, or a boat, or a balloon. This alarming growth of good habits really means a too great emphasis on those virtues which mere custom can ensure, it means too little emphasis on those virtues which custom can never quite ensure, sudden and splendid virtues of inspired pity or of inspired candour. If ever that abrupt appeal is made to us we may fail. A man can get used to getting up at five o'clock in the morning. A man cannot very well get used to being burnt for his opinions; the first experiment is commonly fatal. Let us pay a little more attention to these possibilities of the heroic and the unexpected. I dare say that when I get out of this bed I shall do some deed of an almost terrible virtue.

For those who study the great art of lying in bed there is one emphatic caution to be added. Even for those who can do their work in bed (like journalists), still more for those whose work cannot be done in bed (as, for example, the professional harpooners of whales), it is obvious that the indulgence must be very occasional. But that is not the caution I mean. The caution is this: if you do lie in bed, be sure you do it without any reason or justification at all. I do not speak, of course, of the seriously sick. But if a healthy man lies in bed, let him do it without a rag of excuse; then he will get up a healthy man. If he does it for some secondary hygienic reason, if he has some scientific explanation, he may get up a hypochondriac.

The Fear of the Film

Long lists are being given of particular cases in which children have suffered in spirits or health from alleged horrors of the cinema. One child is said to have had a fit after seeing a film; another to have been sleepless with some fixed idea taken from a film; another to have killed his father with a carving knife through having seen a knife used in a film. This may possibly have occurred; though if it did, anybody of common sense would prefer to have details about that particular child rather than about that particular picture. But what is supposed to be the practical moral of it, in any case? Is it that the young should never see a story with a knife in it? Are they to be brought up in complete ignorance of 'The Merchant of Venice' because Shylock flourishes a knife for a highly disagreeable purpose? Are they never to hear of Macbeth, lest it should slowly dawn upon their trembling intelligence that it is a dagger that they see before them? It would be more practical to propose that a child should never see a real carving-knife, and still more practical that he should never see a real father. All that may come; the era of preventive and prophetic science has only begun. We must not be impatient. But when we come to the cases of morbid panic after some particular exhibition, there is yet more reason to clear the mind of cant. It is perfectly true that a child will have the horrors after seeing some particular detail. It is quite equally true that nobody can possibly predict what that detail will be. It certainly need not be anything so obvious as a murder or even a knife. I should have thought anybody who knew anything about children, or for that matter anybody who had been a child, would know that these nightmares are quite incalculable. The hint of horror may come by any chance in any connection. If the cinema exhibited nothing but views of country vicarages or vegetarian restaurants, the ugly fancy is as likely to be stimulated by these things as by anything else. It is like seeing a face in the carpet; it makes no difference that it is the carpet at the vicarage.

I will give two examples from my own most personal circle; I could give hundreds from hearsay. I know a child who screamed steadily for hours if he had been taken past the Albert Memorial. This was not a precocious precision or excellence in his taste in architecture. Nor was it a premature protest against all that gimcrack German culture which nearly entangled us in the downfall of the barbaric tyranny. It was the fear of something which he himself described with lurid simplicity as The Cow with the India-rubber Tongue. It sounds rather a good title for a creepy short story. At the base of the Albert Memorial (I may explain for those who have never enjoyed that monument) are four groups of statuary representing Europe, Asia, Africa, and America. America especially is very overwhelming; borne onward on a snorting bison who plunges forward in a fury of western progress, and is surrounded with Red Indians, Mexicans, and all sorts of pioneers, O pioneers, armed to the teeth. The child passed this transatlantic tornado with complete coolness and indifference. Europe however is seated on a bull so mild as to look like a cow; the tip of its tongue is showing and happened to be discoloured by weather; suggesting, I suppose, a living thing coming out of the dead marble. Now nobody could possibly foretell that a weather-stain would occur in that particular place, and fill that particular child with that particular fancy. Nobody is likely to propose meeting it by forbidding graven images, like the Moslems and the Jews. Nobody has said (as yet) that it is bad morals to make a picture of a cow. Nobody has even pleaded that it is bad manners for a cow to put its tongue out. These things are utterly beyond calculation; they are also beyond counting, for they occur all over the place, not only to morbid children but to any children. I knew this particular child very well, being a rather older child myself at the time. He certainly was not congenitally timid or feeble-minded; for he risked going to prison to expose the Marconi Scandal and died fighting in the Great War.

Here is another example out of scores. A little girl, now a very normal and cheerful young lady, had an insomnia of insane terror entirely arising from the lyric of 'Little Bo-Peep'. After an inquisition like that of the confessor or the psycho-analyst, it was found that the word 'bleating' had some obscure connection in her mind with the word 'bleeding'. There was thus perhaps an added horror in the phrase 'heard'; in hearing rather than seeing the flowing of blood. Nobody could possibly provide against that sort of mistake. Nobody could prevent the little girl from hearing about sheep, any more than the little boy from hearing about cows. We might abolish all nursery rhymes; and as they are happy and popular and used with universal success, it is very likely that we shall. But the whole point of the mistake about that phrase is that it might have been a mistake about any phrase. We cannot foresee all the fancies that might arise, not only out of what we say, but of what we do not say. We cannot avoid promising a child a caramel lest he should think we say cannibal, or conceal the very word 'hill' lest it should sound like 'hell'.

All the catalogues and calculations offered us by the party of caution in this controversy are therefore quite worthless. It is perfectly true that examples can be given of a child being frightened of this, that or the other. But we can never be certain of his being frightened of the same thing twice. It is not on the negative side, by making lists of vetoes, that the danger can be avoided; it can never indeed be entirely avoided. We can only fortify the child on the positive side by giving him health and humour and a trust in God; not omitting (what will much mystify the moderns) an intelligent appreciation of the idea of authority, which is only the other side of confidence, and which alone can suddenly and summarily cast out such devils. But we may be sure that most modern people will not look at it in this way. They will think it more scientific to attempt to calculate the incalculable. So soon as they have realized that it is not so simple as it looks, they will try to map it out, however complicated it may be. When they discover that the terrible detail need not be a knife, but might just as well be a fork, they will only say there is a fork complex as well as a knife complex. And that increasing complexity of complexes is the net in which liberty will be taken.

Instead of seeing in the odd cases of the cow's tongue or the bleating sheep the peril of their past generalizations, they will see them only as starting points for new generalizations. They will get yet another theory out of it. And they will begin acting on the theory long before they have done thinking about it. They will start out with some new and crude conception that sculpture has made children scream or that nursery rhymes have made children sleepless; and the thing will be a clause in a programme of reform before it has begun to be a con-clusion in a serious story of psychology. That is the practical problem about modern liberty which the critics will not see; of which eugenics is one example and all this amateur child-psychology is another. So long as an old morality was in black and white like a chess-board, even a man who wanted more of it made white was certain that no more of it would be made black. Now he is never certain what vices may not be released, but neither is he certain what virtues may be forbidden. Even if he did not think it wrong to run away with a married woman, he knew that his neighbours only thought it wrong because the woman was married. They did not think it wrong to run away with a red-haired woman, or a left-handed woman, or a woman subject to headaches. But when we let loose a thousand eugenical speculations, all adopted before they are verified and acted on even before they are adopted, he is just as likely as not to find himself separated from the woman for those or any other reasons. Similarly there was something to be said for restrictions, even rather puritanical and provincial restrictions, upon what children should read or see, so long as they fenced in certain fixed departments like sex or sensational tortures. But when we begin to speculate on whether other sensations may not stimulate as dangerously as sex, those other sensations may be as closely controlled as sex. When, let us say, we hear that the eye and brain are weakened by the rapid turning of wheels as well as by the most revolting torturing of men, we have come into a world in which cartwheels and steam-engines may become as obscene as racks and thumbscrews. In short, so long as we *combine* ceaseless and often reckless scientific speculation with rapid and often random social reform, the result must inevitably be not anarchy but ever-increasing tyranny. There must be a ceaseless and almost mechanical multiplication of things forbidden. The resolution to cure all the ills that flesh is heir to, combined with the guess-work about all possible ills that flesh and nerve and brain-cell may be heir to – these two things conducted simultaneously must inevitably spread a sort of panic of prohibition. Scientific imagination and social reform between them will quite logically and almost legitimately have made us slaves. This seems to me a very clear, a very fair and a very simple point of public criticism; and I am much mystified about why so many publicists cannot even see what it is, but take refuge in charges of anarchism, which firstly are not true, and secondly have nothing to do with it.

On Abolishing Sunday

The report that the Bolshevist Government had abolished Sunday might be read in several ways. Some of the Bolshevists were of the race which might be expected to substitute Saturday. Others have a marked intellectual affinity to the great religion which, oddly enough, selects Friday. The Moslem day of rest is Friday; and when I was in Jerusalem, very quaint results sometimes followed from the three religious festivals coming on the three successive days. It was complained that the Jews took an unfair advantage of the fact that their Sabbath ceases at sunset; but, anyhow, it was highly significant of a universal human need that the three great cosmopolitan communions, which all disagreed about the choice of a sacred day, all agreed in having one. They had fought and persecuted and oppressed and exploited each other in all sorts of ways. But they all had the profound human instinct of a Truce of God, in which men should, if possible, leave off fighting, and even (if the thought be conceivable) leave off exploiting.

If the Bolshevists have really declared war on the intrinsic idea of a common Day of Rest, it is not perhaps the first point in which they have proved themselves much stupider than Jews, Turks, infidels and heretics. We all tend to talk naturally about antiquated pedantry. But the most pedantic sort of pedant is he who is too limited to be antiquated. He is cut off from antiquity and therefore from humanity; he will learn nothing from things, but only from theories; and, in the very act of claiming to teach by experiment, refuses to learn by experience. There could hardly be a stronger example of this sort of deaf and dull impatience than a merely destructive attitude towards Sabbaths and special days. The fact that men have always felt them necessary only makes this sort of prig more certain that they are unnecessary. Their universality, even in variety, ought to warn him that he is dealing with something deep and delicate – something at once subtle and stubborn. I do not say that he is bound to consider them right; but he is bound to consider them. And he never does consider them, because he finds it the line of least resistance to condemn them. It is almost enough for him that mankind has always desired something; he will instantly set to work to deliver mankind from anything that it has always desired. Sooner or later, we shall doubtless see a movement for freeing men from the old and barbarous custom of eating food. We have already, for that matter, seen something like a movement for delivering them from the fantastic habit of drinking drinks. We shall have revolutionists denouncing the degrading necessity of going to bed at night. After all, the prostrate posture might be considered servile or touched with the superstitions of the suppliant. The true active, alert, and self-respecting citizen may reasonably be expected to stand upright for twenty-four hours on end. The progressive philosopher may be required to walk in his sleep, and even to talk in his sleep; and, considering what he says and where he walks to, it seems likely enough. Anyhow, the same sort of dehumanized philosophy which destroys the recurrence of one day in seven may well disregard the recurrence of six hours in twenty-four. We may see a vast intellectual revolt against the Slavery of Sleep. I can vividly imagine the pamphlets and the posters; the elaborate statistics showing that, if people never stopped working, they would produce more than they do at present; the lucid diagrams setting forth the loss to labour by the fact that few men are actually at work in their factories while they are asleep in their beds. These scientific demonstrations are always so close and cogent. I can almost see the rows of figures showing successively in the case of coal, cotton, butter, boot-laces, pork and pig-iron, that in every single example more work would be done if everybody could only go on working. It is true that this sort of argument is generally of most ultimate use to Capitalism. But so is Bolshevism.

But these true friends of Capitalism, who still call themselves Communists, do not, of course, mean that nobody should have any leisure, any more than that nobody should have any sleep. The Communists would say that there should be shifts of labour, and frequent recurrences of leisure; but so would the Capitalists. They would say that the labour should be organized for all, and the leisure given in turn to each individual; but so would the Capitalists. There is really not much difference in the general plan of the factory system presided over by the collectivism of Moscow and the individualism of Detroit. It is only fair to say that Mr. Ford has forgotten what anybody ever meant by Individualism, quite as completely as the Bolshevist leaders have forgotten what they themselves originally meant by Bolshevism. The holiday is given to the individual, but there is nothing individual about it. It is given by an impersonal power by a mechanical rotation, over which the individual himself has no power. It is not given to him on his birthday, or the day of his patron saint, or even on the day that he would personally prefer; God forbid! – or, rather (as the Bolshevists would say), Godlessness forbid.

But, even apart from the failure of the solitary holiday to be a personal holiday, there is a deeper objection to the disappearance of a social holiday. It lies deep in the mysteries of human nature, the one thing which the pedantic revolutionist is always too impatient to understand. He will study mathematics in a week and metaphysics in a fortnight; and as for economics, he has picked up the whole truth about them by looking at a little pamphlet in the lunch-hour. But he will not study Man; he dodges that science by simply dismissing all the elements he cannot understand as superstitions. Now one thing that is essential to man is rhythm; and not merely a rhythm in his own life, but to some extent in the living world around him. I will even remark, chiefly for the pleasure of annoying the scientific sociologist, that the most profound and practical truth of the matter is found in the statement that God made the world in six days and rested on the seventh day. In other words, there is a rhythm at the back of things, and in the beginning and nature of the universe; and there must be something of the same kind in the social and secular manifestations of the world. Men are not happy if things always *look* the same; it is recognized in practice in the common medical case for what is called a 'change'. The mere fact that a man has not got to do any work himself on Tuesday is a very small part of the general sense of release or refreshment that exists in an institution like Sunday. I once ventured to use the expression (though I put it into the mouth of a bull-terrier), 'the smell of Sunday morning'. And I am prepared to say that there is such a thing, though my own sense of smell is very deficient compared with a bull-terrier's. There is something in the very light and air of a world in which most people are not working, or not working as much or in the same way as usual, which satisfies the subconscious craving for crisis and fulfilment. If men have nothing but an endless series of days which look alike, it would matter little whether they were days of leisure or labour. They would not give that particular sense of something achieved, or, at least, of something measured; of the image of God resting on the seventh day. It is a psychological fact that such monotony would take on a character as of mathematical insanity. It would be like the endless corridors of a nightmare. Men have always known this by instinct, Pagans as well as Christians. And when all humanity has agreed on the necessity for something, we may be perfectly certain that some sort of humanitarian will want to destroy it.

The Romantic in the Rain

The middle classes of modern England are quite fanatically fond of washing; and are often enthusiastic for teetotalism. I cannot therefore comprehend why it is that they exhibit a mysterious dislike of rain. Rain, that inspiring and delightful thing, surely combines the qualities of these two ideals with quite a curious perfection. Our philanthropists are eager to establish public baths everywhere. Rain surely is a public bath; it might almost be called mixed bathing. The appearance of persons coming fresh from this great natural lustration is not perhaps polished or dignified; but for the matter of that, few people are dignified when coming out of a bath. But the scheme of rain in itself is one of an enormous purification. It realizes the dream of some insane hygienist: it scrubs the sky. Its giant brooms and mops seem to reach the starry rafters and starless corners of the cosmos; it is a cosmic spring-cleaning.

If the Englishman is really fond of cold baths, he ought not to grumble at the English climate for being a cold bath. In these days we are constantly told that we should leave our little special possessions and join in the enjoyment of common social institutions and a common social machinery. I offer the rain as a thoroughly Socialistic institution. It disregards that degraded delicacy which has hitherto led each gentleman to take his shower-bath in private.

It is a better shower-bath, because it is public and communal; and, best of all, because somebody else pulls the string.

As for the fascination of rain for the water drinker, it is a fact the neglect of which I simply cannot comprehend. The enthusiastic water drinker must regard a rainstorm as a sort of universal banquet and debauch of his own favourite beverage. Think of the imaginative intoxication of the wine drinker if the crimson clouds sent down claret or the golden clouds hock. Paint upon primitive darkness some such scenes of apocalypse, towering and gorgeous skyscapes in which champagne falls like fire from heaven or the dark skies grow purple and tawny with the terrible colours of port. All this must the wild abstainer feel, as he rolls in the long soaking grass, kicks his ecstatic heels to heaven, and listens to the roaring rain. It is he, the water drinker, who ought to be the true bacchanal of the forests; for all the forests are drinking water. Moreover, the forests are apparently enjoying it: the trees rave and reel to and fro like drunken giants; they clash boughs as revellers clash cups; they roar undying thirst and howl the health of the world.

All around me as I write is a noise of Nature drinking: and Nature makes a noise when she is drinking, being by no means refined. If I count it Christian mercy to give a cup of cold water to a sufferer, shall I complain of these multitudinous cups of cold water handed round to all living things; a cup of water for every shrub; a cup of water for every weed? I would be ashamed to grumble at it. As Sir Philip Sidney said, their need is greater than mine – especially for water.

There is a wild garment that still carries nobly the name of a wild Highland clan: a clan come from those hills where rain is not so much an incident as an atmosphere. Surely every man of imagination must feel a tempestuous flame of Celtic romance spring up within him whenever he puts on a mackintosh. I could never reconcile myself to carrying an umbrella; it is a pompous Eastern business, carried over the heads of despots in the dry, hot lands. Shut up, an umbrella is an unmanageable walking-stick; open, it is an inadequate tent. For my part, I have no taste for pretending to be a walking pavilion; I think nothing of my hat, and precious little of my head. If I am to be protected against wet, it must be by some closer and more careless protection, something that I can forget altogether. It might be a Highland plaid. It might be that yet more Highland thing, a mackintosh.

And there is really something in the mackintosh of the military qualities of the Highlander. The proper cheap mackintosh has a blue and white sheen as of steel or iron; it gleams like armour. I like to think of it as the uniform of that ancient clan in some of its old and misty raids. I like to think of all the Mackintoshes, in their mackintoshes, descending on some doomed Lowland village, their wet waterproofs flashing in the sun or moon. For indeed this is one of the real beauties of rainy weather, that while the amount of original and direct light is commonly lessened, the number of things that reflect light is unquestionably increased. There is less sunshine, but there are more shiny things, such beautifully shiny things as pools and puddles and mackintoshes. It is like moving in a world of mirrors.

And indeed this is the last and not the least gracious of the casual works of magic wrought by rain: that while it decreases light, yet it doubles it. If it dims the sky, it brightens the earth. It gives the roads (to the sympathetic eye) something of the beauty of Venice. Shallow lakes of water reiterate every detail of earth and sky; we dwell in a double universe. Sometimes walking upon bare and lustrous pavements, wet under numerous lamps, a man seems a black blot on all that golden looking-glass and could fancy he was flying in a yellow sky. But wherever trees and towns hang head downwards in a pigmy puddle, the sense of Celestial topsy-turvydom is the same. This bright, wet, dazzling confusion of shape and shadow, of reality and reflection, will appeal strongly to anyone with the transcendental instinct about this dreamy and dual life of ours. It will always give a man the strange sense of looking down at the skies.

The Romance of Rhyme

The poet in the comic opera, it will be remembered (I hope), claimed for his aesthetic authority that 'Hey diddle diddle will rank as an idyll, if I pronounce it chaste'. In face of a satire which still survives the fashion it satirized, it may require some moral courage seriously to pronounce it chaste, or to suggest that the nursery rhyme in question has really some of the qualities of an idyll. Of its chastity, in the vulgar sense, there need be little dispute, despite the scandal of the elopement of the dish with the spoon, which would seem as free from grossness as the loves of the triangles. And though the incident of the cow may have something of the moonstruck ecstasy of Endymion, that also has a silvery coldness about it worthy of the wilder aspects of Diana. The truth more seriously tenable is that this nursery rhyme is a complete and compact model of the nursery short story. The cow jumping over the moon fulfils to perfection the two essentials of such a story for children. It makes an effect that is fantastic out of objects that are familiar; and it makes a picture that is at once incredible and unmistakable. But it is yet more tenable, and here more to the point, that this nursery rhyme is emphatically a rhyme. Both the lilt and the jingle are just right for their purpose, and are worth whole libraries of elaborate literary verse for children. And the best proof of its vitality is that the satirist himself has unconsciously echoed the jingle even in making the joke. The metre of that nineteenth-century satire is the metre of the nursery rhyme. 'Hey diddle diddle, the cat and the fiddle' and 'Hey diddle diddle will rank as an idyll' are obviously both dancing to the same ancient tune; and that by no means the tune the old cow died of, but the more exhilarating air to which she jumped over the moon.

The whole history of the thing called rhyme can be found between those two things: the simple pleasure of rhyming 'diddle' to 'fiddle', and the more sophisticated pleasure of rhyming 'diddle' to 'idyll'. Now the fatal mistake about poetry, and more than half of the fatal mistake about humanity, consists in forgetting that we should have the first kind of pleasure as well as the second. It might be said that we should have the first pleasure as the basis of the second; or yet more truly, the first pleasure inside the second. The fatal metaphor of progress, which means leaving things behind us, has utterly obscured the real idea of growth, which means leaving things inside us. The heart of the tree remains the same, however many rings are added to it; and a man cannot leave his heart behind by running hard with his legs. In the core of all culture are the things that may be said, in every sense, to be learned by heart. In the innermost part of all poetry is the nursery rhyme, the nonsense that is too happy even to care about being nonsensical. It may lead on to the more elaborate nonsense of the Gilbertian line, or even the far less poetic nonsense of some of the Browningesque rhymes. But the true enjoyment of poetry is always in having the simple pleasure as well as the subtle pleasure. Indeed it is on this primary point that so many of our artistic and other reforms seem to go wrong. What is the matter with the modern world is that it is trying to get simplicity in everything except the soul. Where the soul really has simplicity it can be grateful for anything – even complexity. Many peasants have to be vegetarians, and their ordinary life is really a simple life. But the peasants do not despise a good dinner when they can get it; they wolf it down with enthusiasm, because they have not only the simple life but the simple spirit. And it is so with the modern modes of art which revert, very rightly, to what is 'primitive'. But their moral mistake is that they try to combine the ruggedness that should belong to simplicity with a superciliousness that should only belong to satiety. The last Futurist draughtsmanship, for instance, evidently has the aim of drawing a tree as it might be drawn by a child of ten. I think the new artists would admit it; nor do I merely sneer at it. I am willing to admit, especially for the sake of argument, that there is a truth of philosophy and psychology in this attempt to attain the clarity even through the crudity of childhood. In this sense I can see what a man is driving at when he draws a tree merely as a stick with smaller sticks standing out of it. He may be trying to trace, in black and white or grey, a primeval and almost pre-natal illumination; that it is very remarkable that a stick should exist, and still more remarkable that a stick should stick up or stick out. He may be similarly enchanted with his own stick of charcoal or grey chalk; he may be enraptured, as a child is, with the mere fact that it makes a mark on the paper – a highly poetic fact in itself. But the child does not despise the real tree for being different from his drawing of the tree. He does not despise Uncle Humphrey because that talented amateur can really draw a tree. He does not think less of the real sticks because they are live sticks, and can grow and branch and curve in a way uncommon in walking-sticks. Because he has a single eye he can enjoy a double pleasure. This distinction, which seems strangely neglected, may be traced again in the drama and most other domains of art. Reformers insist that the audiences of simpler ages were content with bare boards or rudimentary scenery if they could hear Sophocles or Shakespeare talking a language of the gods. They were very properly contented with plain boards. But they were not discontented with pageants. The people who appreciated Antony's oration as such would have appreciated Aladdin's palace as such. They did not think gilding and spangles substitutes for poetry and philosophy, because they are not. But they did think gilding and spangles great and admirable gifts of God, because they are.

But the application of this distinction here is to the case of rhyme in poetry. And the application of it is that we should never be ashamed of enjoying a thing as a rhyme as well as enjoying it as a poem. And I think the modern poets who try to escape from the rhyming pleasure, in pursuit of a freer poetical pleasure, are making the same fundamentally fallacious attempt to combine simplicity with superiority. Such a poet is like a child who could take no pleasure in a tree because it looked like a tree, or a playgoer who could take no pleasure in the Forest of Arden because it looked like a forest. It is not impossible to find a sort of prig who professes that he could listen to literature in any scenery, but strongly objects to good scenery. And in poetical criticism and creation there has also appeared the prig who insists that any new poem must avoid the sort of melody that makes the beauty of any old song. Poets must put away childish things, including the child's pleasure in the mere sing-song of irrational rhyme. It may be hinted that when poets put away childish things they will put away poetry. But it may be well to say a word in further justification of rhyme as well as poetry, in the child as well as the poet. Now, the neglect of this nursery instinct would be a blunder, even if it were merely an animal instinct or an automatic instinct. If a rhyme were to a man merely what a bark is to a dog, or a crow to a cock, it would be clear that such natural things cannot be merely neglected. It is clear that a canine epic, about Argus instead of Ulysses, would have a beat ultimately consisting of barks. It is clear that a long poem like *Chantecler*, written by a real cock, would be to the tune of Cock-a-doodle-doo. But in truth the nursery rhyme has a nobler origin; if it be ancestral it is not animal; its principle is a primary one, not only in the body but in the soul.

Milton prefaced *Paradise Lost* with a ponderous condemnation of rhyme. And perhaps the finest and even the most familiar line in the whole of *Paradise Lost* is really a glorification of rhyme. 'Seasons return, but not to me return,' is not only an echo that has all the ring of a rhyme in its form, but it happens to contain nearly all the philosophy of rhyme in its spirit. The wonderful word 'return' has, not only in its sound but in its sense, a hint of the whole secret of song. It is not merely that its very form is a fine example of a certain quality in English, somewhat similar to that which Mrs. Meynell admirably analyzed in the case of words like 'unforgiven'. It is that it describes poetry itself, not only in a mechanical but a moral sense. Song is not only a recurrence, it is a return. It does not merely, like the child in the nursery, take pleasure in seeing the wheels go round. It also wishes to go back as well as round; to go back to the nursery where such pleasures are found. Or to vary the metaphor slightly, it does not merely rejoice in the rotation of a wheel on the road, as if it were a fixed wheel in the air. It is not only the wheel but the waggon that is returning. That labouring caravan is always travelling towards some camping-ground that it has lost and cannot find again. No lover of poetry needs to be told that all poems are full of that noise of returning wheels; and none more than the poems of Milton himself. The whole truth is obvious, not merely in the poem, but even in the two words of the title. All poems might be bound in one book under the title of *Paradise Lost*. And the only object of writing *Paradise Lost* is to turn it, if only by a magic and momentary illusion, into *Paradise Regained*.

It is in this deeper significance of return that we must seek for the peculiar power in the recurrence we call rhyme. It would be easy enough to reply to Milton's strictures on rhyme in the spirit of a sensible if superficial liberality by saying that it takes all sorts to make a world, and especially the world of the poets. It is evident enough that Milton might have been right to dispense with rhyme without being right to despise it. It is obvious that the peculiar dignity of his religious epic would have been weakened if it had been a rhymed epic, beginning:

> Of man's first disobedience and the fruit
> Of that forbidden tree whose mortal root.

But it is equally obvious that Milton himself would not have tripped on the light fantastic toe with quite so much charm and cheerfulness in the lines:

> But come thou Goddess fair and free
> In heaven yclept Euphrosyne

if the goddess had been yclept something else, as, for the sake of argument, Syrinx. Milton in his more reasonable moods would have allowed rhyme in theory a place in all poetry, as he allowed it in practice in his own poetry. But he would certainly have said at this time, and possibly at all times, that he allowed it an inferior place, or at least a secondary place. But is its place secondary; and is it in any sense inferior?

The romance of rhyme does not consist merely in the pleasure of a jingle, though this is a pleasure of which no man should be ashamed. Certainly most men take pleasure in it, whether or not they are ashamed of it. We see it in the older fashion of prolonging the chorus of a song with syllables like 'rumty tumty' or 'tooral looral'. We see it in the similar but later fashion of discussing whether a truth is objective or subjective, or whether a reform is constructive or destructive, or whether an argument is deductive or inductive: all bearing witness to a very natural love for those nursery rhyme recurrences which make a sort of song without words, or at least without any kind of intellectual significance. But something much deeper is involved in the love of rhyme as distinct from other poetic forms, something which is perhaps too deep and subtle to be described. The nearest approximation to the truth I can think of is something like this: that while all forms of genuine verse recur, there is in rhyme a sense of return to exactly the same place. All modes of song go forward and backward like the tides of a sea; but in the great sea of Homeric or Virgilian hexameters, the sea that carried the labouring ships of Ulysses and Aeneas, the thunder of the breakers is rhythmic, but the margin of the foam is necessarily irregular and vague. In rhyme there is rather a sense of water poured safely into one familiar well, or (to use a nobler metaphor) of ale poured safely into one familiar flagon. The armies of Homer and Virgil advance and retreat over a vast country, and suggest vast and very profound sentiments about it, about whether it is their own country or only a strange country. But when the old nameless ballad boldly rhymes 'the bonny ivy tree' to 'my ain countree' the vision at once dwindles and sharpens to a very vivid image of a single soldier passing under the ivy that darkens his own door. Rhythm deals with similarity, but rhyme with identity. Now in the one word identity are involved perhaps the deepest and certainly the dearest human things. He who is homesick does not desire houses or even homes. He who is lovesick does not want to see all the women with whom he might have fallen in love. Only he who is sea-sick, perhaps, may be said to have a cosmopolitan craving for all lands or any kind of land. And this is probably why sea-sickness, like cosmopolitanism, has never yet been a high inspiration to song. Songs, especially the most poignant of them, generally refer to some absolute, to some positive place or person for whom no similarity is a substitute. In such a case all approximation is merely asymptotic. The prodigal returns to his father's house and not the house next door, unless he is still an imperfectly sober prodigal; the lover desires his lady and not her twin sister, except in old complications of romance; and even the spiritualist is generally looking for a ghost and not merely for ghosts. I think the intolerable torture of spiritualism must be a doubt about identity. Anyhow, it will generally be found that where this call for the identical has been uttered most ringingly and unmistakably in literature, it has been uttered in rhyme. Another purpose for which this pointed and definite form is very much fitted is the expression of dogma, as distinct from doubt or even opinion. This is why, with all allowance for a decline in the most classical effects of the classical tongue, the rhymed Latin of the medieval hymns does express what it had to express in a very poignant poetical manner, as compared with the reverent agnosticism so nobly uttered in the rolling unrhymed metres of the ancients. For even if we regard the matter of the medieval verses as a dream, it was at least a vivid dream, a dream full of faces, a dream of love and of lost things. And something of the same spirit runs in a vaguer way through proverbs and phrases that are not exactly religious, but rather in a rude sense philosophical, but which all move with the burden of returning; things to be felt only in familiar fragments . . . *on revient toujours* . . . it's the old story – it's love that makes the world go round; and all roads lead to Rome: we might almost say that all roads lead to Rhyme.

Milton's revolt against rhyme must be read in the light of history. Milton is the Renascence [*sic*] frozen into a Puritan form: the beginning of a period which was in a sense classic, but was in a still more definite sense aristocratic. There the Classicist was the artistic aristocrat because the Calvinist was the spiritual aristocrat. The seventeenth century was intensely individualistic; it had both in the noble and the ignoble sense a respect for persons. It had no respect whatever for popular traditions; and it was in the midst of its purely logical and legal excitement that most of the popular traditions died. The Parliament appeared and the people disappeared. The arts were put under patrons, where they had once been under patron saints. The schools and colleges at once strengthened and narrowed the New Learning, making it something rather peculiar to one country and one class. A few men talked a great deal of good Latin, where all men had once talked a little bad Latin. But they talked even the good Latin so that no Latinist in the world could understand them. They confined all study of the classics to that of the most classical period, and grossly exaggerated the barbarity and barrenness of patristic Greek or medieval Latin. It is as if a man said that because the English translation of the Bible is perhaps the best English in the world, therefore Addison and Pater and Newman are not worth reading. We can imagine what men in such a mood would have said of the rude rhymed hexameters of the monks; and it is not unnatural that they should have felt a reaction against rhyme itself. For the history of rhyme is the history of something else, very vast and sometimes invisible, certainly somewhat indefinable, against which they were in aristocratic rebellion.

That thing is difficult to define in impartial modern terms. It might well be called Romance, and that even in a more technical sense, since it corresponds to the rise of the Romance languages as distinct from the Roman language. It might more truly be called Religion, for historically it was the gradual re-emergence of Europe through the Dark Ages, because it still had one religion, though no longer one rule. It was, in short, the creation of Christendom. It may be called Legend, for it is true that the most overpowering presence in it is that of omnipresent and powerful popular legend; so that things that may never have happened, or, as some say, could never have happened, are nevertheless rooted in our racial memory like things that have happened to ourselves. The whole Arthurian Cycle, for instance, seems something more real than reality. If the faces in that darkness of the Dark Ages, Lancelot and Arthur and Merlin and Mordred, are indeed faces in a dream, they are like faces in a real dream: a dream in a bed and not a dream in a book. Subconsciously at least, I should be much less surprised if Arthur were to come again than I should be if the Superman were to come at all. Again, the thing might be called Gossip: a noble name, having in it the name of God and one of the most generous and genial of the relations of men. For I suppose there has seldom been a time when such a mass of culture and good traditions of craft and song have been handed down orally, by one universal buzz of conversation, through centuries of ignorance down to centuries of greater knowledge. Education must have been an eternal *viva voce* examination; but the men passed their examination. At least they went out in such rude sense masters of art as to create the Song of Roland and the round Roman arches that carry the weight of so many Gothic towers. Finally, of course, it can be called ignorance, barbarism, black superstition, a reaction towards obscurantism and old night; and such a view is eminently complete and satisfactory, only that it leaves behind it a sort of weak wonder as to why the very youngest poets do still go on writing poems about the sword of Arthur and the horn of Roland.

All this was but the beginning of a process which has two great points of interest. The first is the way in which the medieval movement did rebuild the old Roman civilization; the other was the way in which it did not. A strange interest attaches to the things which had never existed in the pagan culture and did appear in the Christian culture. I think it is true of most of them that they had a quality that can very approximately be described as popular, or perhaps as vulgar, as indeed we still talk of the languages which at that time liberated themselves from Latin as the vulgar tongues. And to many Classicists these things would appear to be vulgar in a more vulgar sense. They were vulgar in the sense of being vivid almost to excess, of making a very direct and unsophisticated appeal to the emotions. The first law of heraldry was to wear the heart upon the sleeve. Such medievalism was the reverse of mere mysticism, in the sense of mere mystery; it might more truly be described as sensationalism. One of these things, for instance, was a hot and even an impatient love of colour. It learned to paint before it could draw, and could afford the twopence coloured long before it could manage the penny plain. It culminated at last, of course, in the energy and gaiety of the Gothic; but even the richness of Gothic rested on a certain psychological simplicity. We can contrast it with the classic by noting its popular passion for telling a story in stone. We may admit that a Doric portico is a poem, but no one would describe it as an anecdote. The time was to come when much of the imagery of the cathedrals was to be lost; but it would have mattered the less that it was defaced by its enemies if it had not been already neglected by its friends. It would have mattered less if the whole tide of taste among the rich had not turned against the old popular masterpieces. The Puritans defaced them, but the Cavaliers did not truly defend them. The Cavaliers also were aristocrats of the new classical culture, and used the word Gothic in the sense of barbaric. For the benefit of the Teutonists we may note in parenthesis that, if this phrase meant that Gothic was despised, it also meant that Goths were despised. But when the Cavaliers came back, after the Puritan interregnum, they restored not in the style of Pugin but in the style of Wren. The very thing we call the Restoration, which was the restoration of King Charles, was also the restoration of St. Paul's. And it was a very modern restoration.

So far we might say that simple people do not like simple things. This is certainly true if we compare the classic with these highly-coloured things of medievalism, or all the vivid visions which first began to glow in the night of the Dark Ages. Now, one of these things was the romantic expedient called rhyme. And even in this, if we compare the two, we shall see something of the same paradox by which the simple like complexities and the complex like simplicities. The ignorant liked rich carvings and melodious and often ingenious rhymes. The learned liked bare walls and blank verse. But in the case of rhyme it is peculiarly difficult to define the double and yet very definite truth. It is difficult to define the sense in which rhyme is artifical and the sense in which it is simple. In truth it is simple because it is artificial. It is an artifice of the kind enjoyed by children and other poetic people; it is a toy. As a technical accomplishment it stands at the same distance from the popular experience as the old popular sports. Like swimming, like dancing, like drawing the bow, anybody can do it, but nobody can do it without taking the trouble to do it; and only a few can do it very well. In a hundred ways it was akin to that simple and even humble energy that made all the lost glory of the guilds. Thus their rhyme was useful as well as ornamental. It was not merely a melody but also a mnemonic; just as their towers were not merely trophies but beacons and belfries. In another aspect rhyme is akin to rhetoric, but of a very positive and emphatic sort; the coincidence of sound giving the effect of saying, 'It is certainly so.' Shakespeare realized this when he rounded off a fierce or romantic scene with a rhymed couplet. I know that some critics do not like this, but I think there is a moment when a drama ought to become a melodrama. Then there is a much older effect of rhyme that can only be called mystical, which may seem the very opposite of the utilitarian, and almost equally remote from the rhetorical. Yet it shares with the former the tough texture of something not easily forgotten, and with the latter the touch of authority which is the aim of all oratory. The thing I mean may be found in the fact that so many of the old proverbial prophecies, from Merlin to Mother Shipton, were handed down in rhyme. It can be found in the very name of Thomas the Rhymer.

But the simplest way of putting this popular quality is in a single word: it is a song. Rhyme corresponds to a melody so simple that it goes straight like an arrow to the heart. It corresponds to a chorus so familiar and obvious that all men can join in it. I am not disturbed by the suggestion that such an arrow of song, when it hits the heart, may entirely miss the head. I am not concerned to deny that the chorus may sometimes be a drunken chorus, in which men have lost their heads to find their tongues. I am not defending but defining; I am trying to find words for a large but elusive distinction between certain things that are certainly poetry and certain other things which are also song. Of course it is only an accident that Horace opens his greatest series of odes by saying that he detests the profane populace and wishes to drive them from his temple of poetry. But it is the sort of accident that is almost an allegory. There is even a sense in which it has a practical side. When all is said, *could* a whole crowd of men sing the 'Descende Coelo', that noble ode, as a crowd can certainly sing the 'Dies Irae', or for that matter 'Down among the Dead Men'? Did Horace himself sing the Horatian odes in the sense in which Shakespeare could sing, or could hardly help singing, the Shakespearean songs? I do not know, having no kind of scholarship on these points. But I do not feel that it could have been at all the same thing; and my only purpose is to attempt a rude description of that thing. Rhyme is consonant to the particular kind of song that can be a popular song, whether pathetic or passionate or comic; and Milton is entitled to his true distinction; nobody is likely to sing *Paradise Lost* as if it were a song of that kind. I have tried to suggest my sympathy with rhyme, in terms true enough to be accepted by the other side as expressing their antipathy for it. I have admitted that rhyme is a toy and even a trick, of the sort that delights children. I have admitted that every rhyme is a nursery rhyme. What I will never admit is that anyone who is too big for the nursery is big enough for the Kingdom of God, though the God were only Apollo.

A good critic should be like God in the great saying of a Scottish mystic. George Macdonald said that God was easy to please and hard to satisfy. That paradox is the poise of all good artistic appreciation. Without the first part of the paradox appreciation perishes, because it loses the power to appreciate. Good criticism, I repeat, combines the subtle pleasure in a thing being done well with the simple pleasure in it being done at all. It combines the pleasure of the scientific engineer in seeing how the wheels work together to a logical end with the pleasure of the baby in seeing the wheels go round. It combines the pleasure of the artistic draughtsman in the fact that his lines of charcoal, light and apparently loose, fall exactly right and in a perfect relation with the pleasure of the child in the fact that the charcoal makes marks of any kind on the paper. And in the same fashion it combines the critic's pleasure in a poem with the child's pleasure in a rhyme. The historical point about this kind of poetry, the rhymed romantic kind, is that it rose out of the Dark Ages with the whole of this huge popular power behind it, the human love of a song, a riddle, a proverb, a pun or a nursery rhyme; the sing-song of innumerable children's games, the chorus of a thousand camp-fires and a thousand taverns. When poetry loses its link with all these people who are easily pleased it loses all its power of giving pleasure. When a poet looks down on a rhyme it is, I will not say as if he looked down on a daisy (which might seem possible to the more literal-minded), but rather as if he looked down on a lark because he had been up in a balloon. It is cutting away the very roots of poetry; it is revolting against nature because it is natural, against sunshine because it is bright, or mountains because they are high, or moonrise because it is mysterious. The freezing process began after the Reformation with a fastidious search for finer yet freer forms; today it has ended in formlessness.

But the joke of it is that even when it is formless it is still fastidious. The new anarchic artists are not ready to accept everything. They are not ready to accept anything except anarchy. Unless it observes the very latest conventions of unconventionality, they would rule out anything classic as coldly as any classic ever ruled out anything romantic. But the classic was a form; and there was even a time when it was a new form. The men who invented Sapphics did invent a new metre; the introduction of Elizabethan blank verse was a real revolution in literary form. But *vers libre*, or nine-tenths of it, is not a new metre any more than sleeping in a ditch is a new school of architecture. It is no more a revolution in literary form than eating meat raw is an innovation in cookery. It is not even original, because it is not creative; the artist does not invent anything, but only abolishes something. But the only point about it, that is to my present purpose, is expressed in the word 'pride'. It is not merely proud in the sense of being exultant, but proud in the sense of being disdainful. Such outlaws are more exclusive than aristocrats; and their anarchical arrogance goes far beyond the pride of Milton and the aristocrats of the New Learning. And this final refinement has completed the work which the saner aristocrats began, the work now most evident in the world: the separation of art from the people. I need not insist on the sensational and self-evident character of that separation. I need not recommend the modern poet to attempt to sing his *vers libres* in a public house. I need not even urge the young Imagist to read out a number of his disconnected Images to a public meeting. The thing is not only admitted but admired. The old artist remained proud in spite of his unpopularity; the new artist is proud because of his unpopularity; perhaps it is his chief ground for pride.

Dwelling as I do in the Dark Ages, or at latest among the medieval fairy tales, I am yet moved to remember something I once read in a modern fairy tale. As it happens, I have already used the name of George Macdonald; and in the best of his books there is a description of how a young miner in the mountains could always drive away the subterranean goblins if he could remember and repeat any kind of rhyme. The impromptu rhymes were often doggerel, as was the dog-Latin of many monkish hexameters or the burden of many rude Border ballads. But I have a notion that they drove away the devils, blue devils of pessimism and black devils of pride. Anyhow Madame Montessori, who has apparently been deploring the educational effects of fairy tales, would probably see in me a pitiable example of such early perversion, for that image which was one of my first impressions seems likely enough to be one of my last; and when the noise of many new and original musical instruments, with strange shapes and still stranger noises, has passed away like a procession, I shall hear in the succeeding silence only a rustle and scramble among the rocks and a boy singing on the mountain.

On the Comic Spirit

Not so long ago the author of what was counted the wittiest of recent comedies produced another comedy, which was received

with booing; and even, among those who would hardly descend
to booing, received with boredom. As I have never seen either
the play called a success or the play called a failure, I am naturally
not going to pronounce on the merits of the playwright. But
the contrast suggests certain considerations about the position
of modern comedy which may do something to solve the riddle.
Everybody agrees that the comedies in question are what is called
'modern'; which seems to mean that they are comedies about
cocktails and artificial complexions and people who walk about
in a languid manner, when they are supposed to be taking part in
a wild dance of liberty and the joy of life. In the recent case some
apparently felt that the appearance of a film hero in blue pyjamas
was a little absurd. To some of us, I grieve to say, the appearance
of a film hero is always absurd, even when the film has wholly
discoloured his sleeping-suit. But even to these too sensitive souls
the hero is only felt to be absurd because he is supposed to be
heroic. And that involves a truth which may have something to
do with the reaction against this comedy. It might be stated by
saying that, where there is flippancy, there cannot be irony.

It is obvious on the surface that all fun depends on some sort of
solemnity. The Bishop of Rumti-foo is a funny figure because the
Bishop of Rome is a serious figure. A horrible thought crosses my
mind, at this moment, that perhaps there are some in the new world
who know nothing of the Bishop of Rumti-foo and his missionary
efforts; who may even look him up in a clerical directory or consult
the atlas for the discovery of his diocese. I do not know how many
people now read the *Bab Ballads*; but those who do will find many
inventions much more amusing than any of the cocktail comedies.
To those who have ever known the work, it may possibly recall the
particular figure, if I say that the Bishop of Rumti-foo had another
link of association with the Bishop of Rome. His name was Peter.
He preached to the cannibals of Rumti-foo and persuaded them to
wear clothes; generally to wear his own cast clothes; so that each of
those wild barbarians presented the appearance of an imperfectly
or hastily attired Anglican bishop. But his most famous exploit was
learning to dance; not at all in a languid modern manner, but in a
wild and fantastic manner, to amuse the islanders of Rumti-foo.
And this alone will serve to illustrate the contrast needed for

comedy. It seemed very funny in the *Bab Ballads* that a bishop should fling himself about into wild attitudes like an acrobat; or indeed that a bishop should dance at all. But I imagine that there were high priests of old hieratic cults who really did dance at high solemnities, as David danced before the Ark. Those people did not think there was anything funny about a high priest dancing; because a high priest was simply a man who danced. And just as there is no fun in it when everything is serious, so there is no fun in it when everything is funny. A man who thinks the high priests of Rome and Rumti-foo equally absurd and antiquated, will not see any difference between them and the wild priest of the primitive cult; or between the dancing dervish and the dancing David. Some regard ecclesiastical emblems, last lumber of an abandoned barbarism, as things to be dismissed as grotesque and meaningless. And they would see very little difference between the insignia of the Bishop of Rumti-foo and the fetishes or totems of the tribe of savages among whom that excellent missionary discharged his mission. Suppose that we have really agreed to class clericalism with cannibalism. It will then be no longer possible to make fun of a bishop by imagining him clad (or unclad) like a cannibal. It will be impossible to make any more comic contrast than we should feel between the ways of the Sandwich Islanders and those of the Solomon Islanders. There will be no more comedy in the confusion than there would be in the confusion between one set of savages who baked their missionaries and another set of savages who boiled them. Where both are equally grotesque objects, there is no effect of the grotesque. There must be something serious that is respected, even in order that it may be satirized. There may be something amusing in a bishop's gaiters; but only because they are a bishop's. Take somebody who has never heard of a bishop and show him over a huge emporium which sells nothing but gaiters, and it is doubtful whether even the ten-thousandth gaiter which he takes up to gaze at will of itself move him to peals of mirth. Modern comedy seems to be collecting gaiters and to have somehow mislaid the bishop and consequently missed the joke.

Now, when we talk of the artificial and superficial character of the old comedies, we do not mean exactly the same thing. The comedies of Congreve or Sheridan did not, for the moment, take the world seriously. But they did not describe a world in which nobody took anything seriously. The respectable things were there, if only to be treated with disrespect. Moreover, the respectable things were respected things. There were a hundred indications that the things being mocked were things that were generally and normally revered. A dialogue of Congreve may be flippant, in the sense that he keeps entirely on the surface. But he does not imply that there is no solid ground under the surface. The old comedy is like a scene of people dancing a minuet on a very polished floor; but it is a polished oak floor. The new comedy is like a scene of people dancing the Charleston on a sheet of ice – of very thin ice. Both floors are very smooth; both floors are very slippery; on both floors undignified accidents occur from time to time. But we know that the Congreve character will not sink through the floor; that the earth will not open and swallow him; that he will not fall with a crash into the wine-cellar and destroy dozens of fine old port. In the other case we feel that the whole thing may dissolve; and there is nothing under that hard and glittering ice except water; sometimes, I fear, rather dirty water. But, anyhow, the old scoffer was dancing on something solid, even if he was dancing on his mother's grave. And the quaint old custom of paying some respect to graves, and even to mothers, was necessary to the grotesque effect even of that dance of death. But the comedy of ice melts very easily into mere colourless water; and the mockers of everything are really mockers of nothing. Unstable as water, they shall not excel.

For in a world where everything is ridiculous, nothing can be ridiculed. You cannot unmask a mask; when it is admittedly as hollow as a mask. You cannot turn a thing upside down, if there is no theory about when it is right way up. If life is really so formless that you cannot make head or tail of it, you cannot pull its tail; and you certainly cannot make it stand on its head. Now there is a certain degree of frivolity that becomes formlessness. If the comic writer has not, at the back of his mind, either his own theory of life which he thinks right, or somebody else's theory of life which he thinks wrong, or at least some negative notion that somebody is wrong in thinking it wrong, he has really nothing to write about. He attempts to produce a sort of comedy in which everybody is indifferent to everything and to everybody else; but you cannot create excitement by the collision of several different boredoms. Boredom is dangerously infectious; and has a way of spreading across the footlights. The reason is that there is not in the frivolity any touch of the serious, and therefore none of the satiric. The satirist is no longer set down to make fun of a bishop; he is set down all alone in the cold world to make fun of a gaiter. The old aesthetes used to explain that Art is unmoral, rather than immoral. It would be rather truer to say that Art can be immoral, but cannot be unmoral. Unmoral comedy is rapidly ceasing to be comic.

The Twelve Men

The other day, while I was meditating on morality and Mr. H. Pitt, I was, so to speak, snatched up and put into a jury box to try people. The snatching took some weeks, but to me it seemed something sudden and arbitrary. I was put into this box because I lived in Battersea, and my name began with a C. Looking round me, I saw that there were also summoned and in attendance in the court whole crowds and processions of men, all of whom lived in Battersea, and all of whose names began with a C.

It seems that they always summon jurymen in this sweeping alphabetical way. At one official blow, so to speak, Battersea is denuded of all its C's, and left to get on as best it can with the rest of the alphabet. A Cumberpatch is missing from one street – a Chizzolpop from another – three Chucksterfields from Chucksterfield House; the children are crying out for an absent Cadgerboy; the woman at the street corner is weeping for her Coffintop, and will not be comforted. We settle down with a rollicking ease into our seats (for we are a bold, devil-may-care race, the C's of Battersea), and an oath is administered to us in a totally inaudible manner by an individual resembling an Army surgeon in his second childhood. We understand, however, that we are to well and truly try the case between our sovereign lord the King and the prisoner at the bar, neither of whom has put in an appearance as yet.

Just when I was wondering whether the King and the prisoner

were, perhaps, coming to an amicable understanding in some adjoining public house, the prisoner's head appears above the barrier of the dock; he is accused of stealing bicycles, and he is the living image of a great friend of mine. We go into the matter of the stealing of the bicycles. We do well and truly try the case between the King and the prisoner in the affair of the bicycles. And we come to the conclusion, after a brief but reasonable discussion, that the King is not in any way implicated. Then we pass on to a woman who neglected her children, and who looks as if somebody or something had neglected her. And I am one of those who fancy that something had.

All the time that the eye took in these light appearances and the brain passed these light criticisms, there was in the heart a barbaric pity and fear which men have never been able to utter from the beginning, but which is the power behind half the poems of the world. The mood cannot even inadequately be suggested, except faintly by this statement that tragedy is the highest expression of the infinite value of human life. Never had I stood so close to pain; and never so far away from pessimism. Ordinarily, I should not have spoken of these dark emotions at all, for speech about them is too difficult; but I mention them now for a specific and particular reason to the statement of which I will proceed at once. I speak of these feelings because out of the furnace of them there came a curious realization of a political or social truth. I saw with a queer and indescribable kind of clearness what a jury really is, and why we must never let it go.

The trend of our epoch up to this time has been consistently towards specialism and professionalism. We tend to have trained soldiers because they fight better, trained singers because they sing better, trained dancers because they dance better, specially instructed laughers because they laugh better, and so on and so on. The principle has been applied to law and politics by innumerable modern writers. Many Fabians have insisted that a greater part of our political work should be performed by experts. Many legalists have declared that the untrained jury should be altogether supplanted by the trained judge.

Now, if this world of ours were really what is called reasonable, I do not know that there would be any fault to find with this. But the true result of all experience and the true foundation of all religion is this. That the four or five things that it is most practically essential that a man should know, are all of them what people call paradoxes. That is to say, that though we all find them in life to be mere plain truths, yet we cannot easily state them in words without being guilty of seeming verbal contradictions. One of them, for instance, is the unimpeachable platitude that the man who finds most pleasure for himself is often the man who least hunts for it. Another is the paradox of courage; the fact that the way to avoid death is not to have too much aversion to it. Whoever is careless enough of his bones to climb some hopeless cliff above the tide may save his bones by that carelessness. Whoever will lose his life, the same shall save it; an entirely practical and prosaic statement.

Now, one of these four or five paradoxes which should be taught to every infant prattling at his mother's knee is the following: that the more a man looks at a thing, the less he can see it, and the more a man learns a thing the less he knows it. The Fabian argument of the expert, that the man who is trained should be the man who is trusted, would be absolutely unanswerable if it were really true that a man who studied a thing and practised it every day went on seeing more and more of its significance. But he does not. He goes on seeing less and less of its significance. In the same way, alas! we all go on every day, unless we are continually goading ourselves into gratitude and humility, seeing less and less of the significance of the sky or the stones.

Now, it is a terrible business to mark a man out for the vengeance of men. But it is a thing to which a man can grow accustomed, as he can to other terrible things; he can even grow accustomed to the sun. And the horrible thing about all legal officials, even the best, about all judges, magistrates, barristers, detectives, and policemen, is not that they are wicked (some of them are good), not that they are stupid (several of them are quite intelligent), it is simply that they have got used to it.

Strictly they do not see the prisoner in the dock; all they see is the usual man in the usual place. They do not see the awful court of judgment; they only see their own workshop. Therefore, the instinct of Christian civilization has most wisely declared that into their judgments there shall upon every occasion be infused fresh blood and fresh thoughts from the streets. Men shall come in who can see the court and the crowd, and coarse faces of the policemen and the professional criminals, the wasted faces of the wastrels, the unreal faces of the gesticulating counsel, and see it all as one sees a new picture or a play hitherto unvisited.

Our civilization has decided, and very justly decided, that determining the guilt or innocence of men is a thing too important to be trusted to trained men. It wishes for light upon that awful matter, it asks men who know no more law than I know, but who can feel the things that I felt in the jury box. When it wants a library catalogued, or the solar system discovered, or any trifle of that kind, it uses up its specialists. But when it wishes anything done which is really serious, it collects twelve of the ordinary men standing round. The same thing was done, if I remember right, by the Founder of Christianity.

The Pseudo-Scientific Books

There is a certain kind of modern book which must, if possible, be destroyed. It ought to be blown to pieces with the dynamite of some great satirist like Swift or Dickens. As it is, it must be patiently hacked into pieces even by some plodding person like myself. I will do it, as George Washington said, with my little hatchet; though it might take a long time to do it properly. The kind of book I mean is the pseudo-scientific book. And by this I do not mean that the man who writes it is a conscious quack or that he knows nothing; I mean that he proves nothing; he simply gives you all his cocksure, and yet shaky, modern opinions and calls it science. Books are coming out with so-called scientific conclusions – books in which there is actually no scientific argument at all. They simply affirm all the notions that happen to be fashionable in loose 'intellectual' clubs, and call them the conclusions of research. But I am no more awed by the flying fashions among prigs than I am by the flying fashions among snobs. Snobs say they have the right kind of hat; prigs say they have the right kind of head. But in both cases I should like some evidence beyond their own habit of staring at themselves in the glass. Suppose I were to write about the current fashions in dress something like this: 'Our ignorant and superstitious ancestors had straight hat-brims; but the advance of reason and equality has taught us to have curly hat-brims; in early times shirt-fronts are triangular, but science has shown that they ought to be round; barbaric peoples had loose trousers, but enlightened and humane peoples have tight trousers', and so on, and so on. You would naturally rebel at this simple style of argument. You would say 'But, hang it all, give us some facts. Prove that the new fashions are more enlightened. Prove that men think better in the new hats. Prove that men run faster in the new trousers.'

I have just read a book which has been widely recommended, which is introduced to the public by Dr. Saleeby, and which is, I understand, written by a Swiss scientist of great distinction. It is called *Sexual Ethics*, by Professor Forel. I began to read the book, therefore, with respect. I finished reading it with stupefaction. The Swiss Professor is obviously an honest man, though too Puritanical to my taste, and I am told that he does really know an enormous lot about insects. But as for the conception of proving a case, as for any notion that a 'new' opinion needs proof, and that it is not enough, when you knock down great institutions, to say that you don't like them – it is clear that no such conceptions have ever crossed his mind. Science says that man has no conscience. Science says that man and woman must have the same political powers. Science says that sterile unions are morally free and without rule. Science says that it is wrong to drink fermented liquor. And all this with a splendid indifference to the two facts – first, that 'Science' does not say these things at all, for numbers of great scientists say exactly the opposite; and second, that if Science did say these things, a person reading a book of rationalistic ethics might be permitted to ask why. Professor Forel may have mountains of evidence which he has no space to exhibit. We will give him the benefit of that doubt, and pass on to points where any thinking man is capable of judging him.

Where this sort of scientific writer is seen in all his glory is in his first abstract arguments about the nature of morality. He is immense; he is at once simple and monstrous, like a whale. He always has one dim principle or prejudice: to prove that there is

nothing separate or sacred about the moral sense. Professor Forel
holds this prejudice with all possible decorum and propriety. He
always trots out three arguments to prove it; like three old
broken-kneed elephants. Professor Forel duly trots them out.
They are supposed to show that there is no such thing positively
existing as the conscience; and they might just as easily be used
to show that there are no such things as wings or whiskers, or toes
or teeth, or boots or books, or Swiss Professors.

The first argument is that man has no conscience because some
men are quite mad, and therefore not particularly conscientious.
The second argument is that man has no conscience because some
men are more conscientious than others. And the third is that man
has no conscience because conscientious men in different countries
and quite different circumstances often do very different things.
Professor Forel applies these arguments eloquently to the question
of human consciences; and I really cannot see why I should not
apply them to the question of human noses. Man has no nose
because now and then a man has no nose – I believe that Sir
William Davenant, the poet, had none. Man has no nose because
some noses are longer than others or can smell better than others.
Man has no nose because not only are noses of different shapes, but
(oh, piercing sword of scepticism!) some men use their noses and
find the smell of incense nice, while some use their noses and find
it nasty. Science therefore declares that man is normally noseless;
and will take this for granted for the next four or five hundred
pages, and will treat all the alleged noses of history as the quaint
legends of a credulous age.

I do not mention these views because they are original, but
exactly because they are not. They are only dangerous in Professor
Forel's book because they can be found in a thousand books of
our epoch. This writer solemnly asserts that Kant's idea of an
ultimate conscience is a fable because Mohammedans think it
wrong to drink wine, while English officers think it right. Really
he might just as well say that the instinct of self-preservation is
a fable because some people avoid brandy in order to live long,
and some people drink brandy in order to save their lives. Does
Professor Forel believe that Kant, or anybody else, thought that
our consciences gave us direct commands about the details of diet

or social etiquette? Did Kant maintain that, when we had reached a certain stage of dinner, a supernatural voice whispered in our ear 'Asparagus'; or that the marriage between almonds and raisins was a marriage that was made in heaven? Surely it is plain enough that all these social duties are deduced from primary moral duties – and may be deduced wrong. Conscience does not suggest 'asparagus', but it does suggest amiability, and it is thought by some to be an amiable act to accept asparagus when it is offered to you. Conscience does not respect fish and sherry; but it does respect any innocent ritual that will make men feel alike. Conscience does not tell you not to drink your hock after your port. But it does tell you not to commit suicide; and your mere naturalistic reason tells you that the first act may easily approximate to the second.

Christians encourage wine as something which will benefit men. Teetotallers discourage wine as something that will destroy men. Their conscientious conclusions are different, but their consciences are just the same. Teetotallers say that wine is bad because they think it moral to say what they think. Christians will not say that wine is bad because they think it immoral to say what they don't think. And a triangle is a three-sided figure. And a dog is a four-legged animal. And Queen Anne is dead. We have, indeed, come back to alphabetical truths. But Professor Forel has not yet even come to them. He goes on laboriously repeating that there cannot be a fixed moral sense, because some people drink wine and some people don't. I cannot imagine how it was that he forgot to mention that France and England cannot have the same moral sense, because Frenchmen drive cabs on the right side of the road and Englishmen on the left.

On Experience

It will be remarked that Experience which was once claimed by the aged is now claimed exclusively by the young. There used to be a system of morals and metaphysics that was specially known as the Experience Philosophy, but those who advanced it were grim rationalists and utilitarians who were already old in years, or more commonly old before their time. We all now know that Experience now stands rather for the philosophy of those who claim to be young long after their time. But they preach something that may in a sense be called an Experience Philosophy; though some of the experiences seem to me the reverse of philosophical. So far as I can make it out, it consists of two dogmas: first, that there is no such thing as right or wrong; and secondly, that they themselves have a right to experience. How they manage to have any rights if there is no such thing as right, I do not know; nor do they. But perhaps the philosophy was best summed up in a phrase I saw recently in a very interesting and important American magazine; quoted from one of the more wild and fanciful of the American critics. I have not the text before me, but the substance of the remark was this. The critic demanded indignantly to know how many ordinary American novelists had any Experiences outside those of earning their bread, pottering about in a farm or a farm house, helping to mind the baby, etc. The question struck me as striking at the very root of all the rot and corruption and imbecility of the times.

On the face of it, of course, the whole question is rather a joke; only that these gay pleasure-seekers and revellers in the joy of life have seldom been known to see a joke. We might politely inquire exactly how much Experience is needed to equip a novelist to write novels. How many marks does he get for being vamped or for being intoxicated; and which are the particular discreditable acts by which he can get credits? How many liaisons give him this singular rank as a literary liaison officer; and how many double lives does it take to constitute Life? Is it only after a fourth divorce that he may write his first novel? For my part, I do not see why the same principle should not be applied to all the other Ten Commandments as well as to that particular Commandment. It should surely be obvious that if love affairs are necessary to the writing of this particular sort of love story, then it follows that a life of crime is necessary to the writing of any kind of crime story. I have myself made arrangements (on paper) for no less than fifty-two murders in my time; they took the form of short stories; and I shall expose myself to the withering contempt of the young sages of Experience when I confess that I am not really a murderer, and have never yet committed an actual murder. And what about all the other forms of criminal Experience? Must a writer be a forger; and manufacture other men's names, before he is allowed to make his own? Must there be a journalistic apprenticeship in picking pockets as well as in picking brains; and have we to look to the establishment of an Academy of Anarchy, with the power of conferring degrees? Novelists might proudly print after their names the letters indicating the degrees they had taken; such as F.Y.B., meaning 'Five Years for Burglary', or T.N.H., for 'Twice Nearly Hanged'. Altogether, it may be said that writers do not rob, but it may be fortunate that robbers do not write; it is possible that the wild and wicked criminal might after all make almost as dull a novelist as the novelist.

It would also be easy enough to attack the fallacy upon the facts. Everybody who has any real experience knows that good writing should not necessarily come from people with many experiences. Some of the art which is closest to life has been produced under marked limitations of living. Its prestige has generally lasted longer than the splash made by sensational social figures. Jane Austen has already survived Georges Sand. Even the most modern critic, if he is really a critic, will admit that Jane Austen is really realistic in a sense in which Georges Sand is only romantic. She was indeed a flaming, fashionable figure created entirely by the Romantic Movement; but Jane Austen did not belong to any movement; she does not move; but she stays. And though I do not agree with the too common depreciation of Byron, it is true that all his somewhat excessive Experience, in the new or juvenile sense, has not prevented people feeling him to be the very reverse of realistic; and in some ways strangely unreal.

But there is, of course, a much deeper objection to the whole of this new sort of Experience Philosophy; which is quite sufficiently exposed in the very examples I quoted from the magazine. There are certainly all sorts of experiences; some great and some small. But the small ones are those which the critic imagines to be great; and the great ones are those that he contemptuously dismisses as small. There are no more universal affairs than those which he imagines to be little and local. There are no events more tremendous than those which he regards as trivial. There are no experiences more exciting than those which he dully imagines to be dull. To take his own example, a literary man who cannot see that a baby is marvellous could not see that anything was marvellous. He has certainly no earthly logical reason for regarding a movie vamp as marvellous. The movie vamp is only what happens to the baby when it goes wrong; but, from a really imaginative and intellectual standpoint, there is nothing marvellous about either of them except what is already marvellous in the mere existence of the baby. But this sort of moralist or immoralist has a queer, half-baked prejudice; to the effect that there is no good in anything until it has gone bad. It is supposed to be a part of Experience for the woman to be a vamp; but not for the woman to be a mother. Although it stares us all in the face, as a stark fact of common sense; that child-bearing really is an experience, and a highly realistic experience; while the other sort of experiment may not really be an experience at all. It may be in the exact sense mere play acting; and, as the game is now played, the main preoccupation is to prevent its ending with an addition to the cast of characters. Whatever happens, it must not be the means of bringing on the scene a new, breathing, thinking, conscious creature like a baby. That would not be life.

Now, if there is one thing of which I have been certain since my boyhood, and grow more certain as I advance in age, it is that nothing is poetical if plain daylight is not poetical; and no monster should amaze us if the normal man does not amaze. All this talk of waiting for experiences in order to write, is simply a confession of incapacity to experience anything. It is a confession of never having felt the big facts; in such experiences as babyhood and the baby. A paralytic of this deaf and dumb description imagines he can be healed in strange waters or after strange wanderings; and announces himself ready to drink poisons that they may stimulate him like drugs. But it is futile for him to suppose that this sort of quackery will teach him how to be a writer; for he has been from the first admittedly blind to everything that is worth writing about. He will find nothing in the wilderness but the broken shards or ruins of what should have been sacred in his own home; and if he can really make nothing of the second he will certainly make nothing of the first. The whole theory rests on a ridiculous confusion, by which it is supposed that certain primary principles or relations will become interesting when they are damaged, but are bound to be depressing when they are intact.

None of those who are perpetually suggesting this view ever state it thus plainly; for they are incapable of making plain statements, just as they are incapable of feeling plain things. But the point they have to prove, if they really want their Experience Philosophy accepted by those who do not care for catch words, is that the high perils, pleasures, and creative joys of life do not occur on the high road of life; but only in certain crooked and rambling by-paths made entirely by people who have lost their way. As yet they have not even begun to prove it; and in any case, and in every sense, it could be disproved by a baby.

The Book of Job

The Book of Job is among the other Old Testament Books both a philosophical riddle and a historical riddle. It is the philosophical riddle that concerns us in such an introduction as this; so we may dismiss first the few words of general explanation or warning which should be said about the historical aspect. Controversy has long raged about which parts of this epic belong to its original scheme and which are interpolations of considerably later date. The doctors disagree, as it is the business of doctors to do; but upon the whole, trend of investigation has always been in the direction of maintaining that the parts interpolated, if any, were the prose prologue and epilogue and possibly the speech of the young man who comes in with an apology at the end. I do not profess to be competent to decide such questions. But whatever decision the reader may come to concerning them, there is a general truth to be remembered in this connection. When you deal with any ancient artistic creation do not suppose that it is anything against it that it grew gradually. The Book of Job may have grown gradually just as Westminster Abbey grew gradually. But the people who made the old folk poetry, like the people who made Westminster Abbey, did not attach that importance to the actual date and the actual author, that importance which is entirely the creation of the almost insane individualism of modern times. We may put aside the case of Job, as one complicated with religious difficulties, and take any other, say the case of the *Iliad*. Many people have maintained the characteristic formula of modern scepticism, that Homer was not written by Homer, but by another person of the same name. Just in the same way many have maintained that Moses was not Moses but another person called Moses. But the thing really to be remembered in the matter of the *Iliad* is that if other people did interpolate the passages, the thing did not create the same sense of shock as would be created by such proceedings in these individualistic times. The creation of the tribal epic was to some extent regarded as a tribal work, like the building of the tribal temple. Believe then, if you will, that the prologue of Job and the epilogue and the speech of Elihu are things inserted after the original work was composed. But do not suppose that such insertions have that obvious and spurious character which would belong to any insertions in a modern individualistic book. Do not regard the insertions as you would regard a chapter in George Meredith which you afterwards found had not been written by George Meredith, or half a scene in Ibsen which you found had been cunningly sneaked in by Mr. William Archer. Remember that this old world which made these old poems like the *Iliad* and Job, always kept the tradition of what it was making. A man could almost leave a poem to his son to be finished as he would have finished it, just as a man could leave a field to his son, to be reaped as he would have reaped it. What is called Homeric unity may be a fact or not. The *Iliad* may have been written by one man. It may have been written by a hundred men. But let us remember that there was more unity in those times in a hundred men than there is unity now in one man. Then a city was like one man. Now one man is like a city in civil war.

Without going, therefore, into questions of unity as understood by the scholars, we may say of the scholarly riddle that the book has unity in the sense that all great traditional creations have unity; in the sense that Canterbury Cathedral has unity. And the same is broadly true of what I have called the philosophical riddle. There is a real sense in which the Book of Job stands apart from most of the books included in the canon of the Old Testament. But here again those are wrong who insist on the entire absence of unity. Those are wrong who maintain that the Old Testament is a mere loose library; that it has no consistency or aim. Whether the result was achieved by some supernal spiritual truth, or by a steady national tradition, or merely by an ingenious selection in after times, the books of the Old Testament have a quite perceptible unity. To attempt to understand the Old Testament without realizing this main idea is as absurd as it would be to study one of Shakespeare's plays without realizing that the author of them had any philosophical object at all. It is as if a man were to read the history of Hamlet, Prince of Denmark, thinking all the time that he was reading what really purported to be the history of an old Danish pirate prince. Such a reader would not realize at all that Hamlet's procrastination was on the part of the poet intentional. He would merely say, 'How long Shakespeare's hero does take to kill his enemy.' So speak the Bible smashers, who are unfortunately always at bottom Bible worshippers. They do not understand the special tone and intention of the Old Testament; they do not understand its main idea, which is the idea of all men being merely the instruments of a higher power.

Those, for instance, who complain of the atrocities and treacheries of the judges and prophets of Israel have really got a notion in their head that has nothing to do with the subject. They are too Christian. They are reading back into the pre-Christian scriptures a purely Christian idea – the idea of saints, the idea that the chief instruments of God are very particularly good men. This is a deeper, a more daring, and a more interesting idea than the old Jewish one. It is the idea that innocence has about it something terrible which in the long run makes and re-makes empires and the world. But the Old Testament idea was much more what may be called the common-sense idea, that strength is strength, that cunning is cunning, that worldly success is worldly success, and that Jehovah uses these things for His own ultimate purpose, just as He uses natural forces or physical elements. He uses the strength of a hero as He uses that of a Mammoth – without any particular respect for the Mammoth. I cannot comprehend how it is that so many simple-minded sceptics have read such stories as the fraud of Jacob and supposed that the man who wrote it (whoever he was) did not know that Jacob was a sneak just as well as we do. The primeval human sense of honour does not change so much as that. But these simple-minded sceptics are, like the majority of modern sceptics, Christians. They fancy that the patriarchs must be meant for patterns; they fancy that Jacob was being set up as some kind of saint; and in that case I do not wonder that they are a little startled. That is not the atmosphere of the Old Testament at all. The heroes of the Old Testament are not the sons of God, but the slaves of God, gigantic and terrible slaves, like the genii, who were the slaves of Aladdin.

The central idea of the great part of the Old Testament may be called the idea of the loneliness of God. God is not only the chief character of the Old Testament; God is properly the only character in the Old Testament. Compared with His clearness of purpose all the other wills are heavy and automatic, like those of animals; compared with His actuality all the sons of flesh are shadows. Again and again the note is struck, 'With whom hath he taken counsel?' 'I have trodden the wine press alone, and of the peoples there was no man with me.' All the patriarchs and prophets are merely His tools or weapons; for the Lord is a man of war. He uses Joshua like an axe or Moses like a measuring-rod. For Him Samson is only a sword and Isaiah a trumpet. The saints of Christianity are supposed to be like God, to be, as it were, little statuettes of Him. The Old Testament hero is no more supposed to be of the same nature as God than a saw or a hammer is supposed to be of the same shape as the carpenter. This is the main key and characteristic of the Hebrew scriptures as a whole. There are, indeed, in those scriptures innumerable instances of the sort of rugged humour, keen emotion, and powerful individuality which is never wanting in great primitive prose and poetry. Nevertheless the main characteristic remains; the sense not merely that God is stronger than man, not merely that God is more secret than man, but that He means more, that He knows better what He is doing, that compared with Him we have something of the vagueness, the unreason, and the vagrancy of the beasts that perish. 'It is He that sitteth above the earth, and the inhabitants thereof are as grasshoppers.' We might almost put it thus. The book is so intent upon asserting the personality of God that it almost asserts the impersonality of man. Unless this gigantic cosmic brain has conceived a thing, that thing is insecure and void; man has not enough tenacity to ensure its continuance. 'Except the Lord build the house their labour is but lost that build it. Except the Lord keep the city the watchman watcheth but in vain.'

Everywhere else, then, the Old Testament positively rejoices in the obliteration of man in comparison with the divine purpose. The Book of Job stands definitely alone because the Book of Job definitely asks, 'But what is the purpose of God?' Is it worth the sacrifice even of our miserable humanity? Of course it is easy enough to wipe out our own paltry wills for the sake of a will that is grander and kinder. Let God use His tools; let God break His tools. But what is He doing and what are they being broken for? It is because of this question that we have to attack as a philosophical riddle the riddle of the Book of Job.

The present importance of the Book of Job cannot be expressed adequately even by saying that it is the most interesting of ancient books. We may almost say of the Book of Job that it is the most interesting of modern books. In truth, of course, neither of the two phrases covers the matter, because fundamental human religion and fundamental human irreligion are both at once old and new; philosophy is either eternal or it is not philosophy. The modern habit of saying, 'This is my opinion, but I may be wrong', is entirely irrational. If I say that it may be wrong I say that it is not my opinion. The modern habit of saying, 'Every man has a different philosophy; this is my philosophy and it suits me': the habit of saying this is mere weakmindedness. A cosmic philosophy is not constructed to fit a man; a cosmic philosophy is constructed to fit a cosmos. A man can no more possess a private religion than he can possess a private sun and moon.

The first of the intellectual beauties of the Book of Job is that it is all concerned with this desire to know the actuality; the desire to know what is, and not merely what seems. If moderns were writing the book we should probably find that Job and his Comforters got on quite well together by the simple operation of referring their differences to what is called the temperament, saying that the comforters were by nature 'optimists' and Job by nature a 'pessimist'. And they would be quite comfortable, as people can often be, for some time at least, by agreeing to say what is obviously untrue. For if the word 'pessimist' means anything at all, then emphatically Job is not a pessimist. His case alone is sufficient to refute the modern absurdity of referring everything to physical temperament. Job does not in any sense look at life in a gloomy way. If wishing to be happy and being quite ready to be happy constitute an optimist, Job is an optimist; he is an outraged and insulted optimist. He wishes the universe to justify itself, not because he wishes it to be caught out, but because he really wishes it to be justified. He demands an explanation from God, but he does not do it at all in the spirit in which Hampden might demand an explanation from Charles I. He does it in the spirit in which a wife might demand an explanation from her husband whom she really respected. He remonstrates with his Maker because he is proud of his Maker. He even speaks of the Almighty as his enemy, but he never doubts, at the back of his mind, that his enemy has some kind of a case which he does not understand. In a fine and famous blasphemy he says, 'Oh, that mine adversary had written a book!' It never really occurs to him that it could possibly be a bad book. He is anxious to be convinced, that is, he thinks that God could convince him. In short, we may say again that if the word optimist means anything (which I doubt) Job is an optimist. He shakes the pillars of the world and strikes insanely at the heavens; he lashes the stars, but it is not to silence them; it is to make them speak.

In the same way we may speak of the official optimists, the Comforters of Job. Again, if the word pessimist means anything (which I doubt) the comforters of Job may be called pessimists rather than optimists. All that they really believe is not that God is good but that God is so strong that it is much more judicious to call Him good. It would be the exaggeration of censure to call them evolutionists; but they have something of the vital error of the evolutionary optimist. They will keep on saying that everything in the universe fits into everything else: as if there were anything comforting about a number of nasty things all fitting into each other. We shall see later how God in the great climax of the poem turns this particular argument upside down.

When, at the end of the poem, God enters (somewhat abruptly), is struck the sudden and splendid note which makes the thing as great as it is. All the human beings through the story, and Job especially, have been asking questions of God. A more trivial poet would have made God enter in some sense or other in order to answer the questions. By a touch truly to be called inspired, when God enters, it is to ask a number more questions on His own account. In this drama of scepticism God Himself takes up the role of sceptic. He does what all the great voices defending religion have always done. He does, for instance, what Socrates did. He turns rationalism against itself. He seems to say that if it comes to asking questions, He can ask some questions which will fling down and flatten out all conceivable human questioners. The poet by an exquisite intuition has made God ironically accept a kind of controversial equality with His accusers. He is willing to regard it as if it were a fair intellectual duel: 'Gird up now thy loins like a man; for I will demand of thee, and answer thou me.' The everlasting adopts an enormous and sardonic humility. He is quite willing to be prosecuted. He only asks for the right which every prosecuted person possesses; He asks to be allowed to cross-examine the witness for the prosecution. And He carries yet further the correctness of the legal parallel. For the first question, essentially speaking, which He asks of Job is the question that any criminal accused by Job would be most entitled to ask. He asks Job who he is. And Job, being a man of candid intellect, takes a little time to consider, and comes to the conclusion that he does not know.

This is the first great fact to notice about the speech of God, which is the culmination of the inquiry. It represents all human sceptics routed by a higher scepticism. It is this method, used sometimes by supreme and sometimes by mediocre minds, that has ever since been the logical weapon of the true mystic. Socrates, as I have said, used it when he showed that if you only allowed him enough sophistry he could destroy all the sophists. Jesus Christ used it when He reminded the Sadducees, who could not imagine the nature of marriage in heaven, that if it came to that they had not really imagined the nature of marriage at all. In the break up of Christian theology in the eighteenth century, Butler used it, when he pointed out that rationalistic arguments could be used as much against vague religion as against doctrinal religion, as much against rationalist ethics as against Christian ethics. It is the root and reason of the fact that men who have religious faith have also philosophic doubt, like Cardinal Newman, Mr. Balfour, or Mr. Mallock. These are the small streams of the delta; the Book of Job is the first great cataract that creates the river. In dealing with the arrogant asserter of doubt, it is not the right method to tell him to stop doubting. It is rather the right method to tell him to go on doubting, to doubt a little more, to doubt every day newer and wilder things in the universe, until at last, by some strange enlightenment, he may begin to doubt himself.

This, I say, is the first fact touching the speech; the fine inspiration by which God comes in at the end, not to answer riddles, but to propound them. The other great fact which, taken together with this one, makes the whole work religious instead of merely philosophical, is that other great surprise which makes Job suddenly satisfied with the mere presentation of something impenetrable. Verbally speaking the enigmas of Jehovah seem darker and more desolate than the enigmas of Job; yet Job was comfortless before the speech of Jehovah and is comforted after it. He has been told nothing, but he feels the terrible and tingling atmosphere of something which is too good to be told. The refusal of God to explain His design is itself a burning hint of His design. The riddles of God are more satisfying than the solutions of man.

Thirdly, of course, it is one of the splendid strokes that God rebukes alike the man who accused, and the men who defended Him; that He knocks down pessimists and optimists with the same hammer.

And it is in connection with the mechanical and supercilious comforters of Job that there occurs the still deeper and finer inversion of which I have spoken. The mechanical optimist endeavours to justify the universe avowedly upon the ground that it is a rational and consecutive pattern. He points out that the fine thing about the world is that it can all be explained. That is one point, if I may put it so, on which God, in return, is explicit to the point of violence. God says, in effect, that if there is one fine thing about the world, as far as men are concerned, it is that it cannot be explained. He insists on the inexplicableness of everything: 'Hath the rain a father? . . . Out of whose womb came the ice?' He goes farther, and insists on the positive and palpable unreason of things: 'Hast thou sent the rain upon the desert where no man is, and upon the wilderness wherein there is no man?' God will make man see things, if it is only against the black background of nonentity. God will make Job see a startling universe if He can only do it by making Job see an idiotic universe. To startle man God becomes for an instant a blasphemer; one might almost say that God becomes for an instant an atheist. He unrolls before Job a long panorama of created things, the horse, the eagle, the raven, the wild ass, the peacock, the ostrich, the crocodile. He so describes each of them that it sounds like a monster walking in the sun. The whole is a sort of psalm or rhapsody of the sense of wonder. The maker of all things is astonished at the things He has Himself made.

This we may call the third point. Job puts forward a note of interrogation; God answers with a note of exclamation. Instead of proving to Job that it is an explicable world, He insists that it is a much stranger world than Job ever thought it was. Lastly, the poet has achieved in this speech, with that unconscious artistic accuracy found in so many of the simpler epics, another and much more delicate thing. Without once relaxing the rigid impenetrability of Jehovah in His deliberate declaration, he has contrived to let fall here and there in the metaphors, in the parenthetical imagery, sudden and splendid suggestions that the secret of God is a bright and not a sad one – semi-accidental suggestions, like light seen for an instant through the cracks of a closed door. It would be difficult to praise too highly, in a purely poetical sense, the instinctive exactitude and ease with which these more optimistic insinuations are let fall in other connections, as if the Almighty Himself were scarcely aware that He was letting them out. For instance, there is that famous passage where Jehovah with devastating sarcasm asks Job where he was when the foundations of the world were laid, and then (as if merely fixing a date) mentions the time when the sons of God shouted for joy. One cannot help feeling, even upon this meagre information, that they must have had something to shout about. Or again, when God is speaking of snow and hail in the mere catalogue of the physical cosmos, He speaks of them as a treasury that He has laid up against the day of battle – a hint of some huge Armageddon in which evil shall be at last overthrown.

Nothing could be better, artistically speaking, than this optimism breaking through agnosticism like fiery gold round the edges of a black cloud. Those who look superficially at the barbaric origin of the epic may think it fanciful to read so much artistic significance into its casual similes or accidental phrases. But no one who is well acquainted with great examples of semi-barbaric poetry, as in the Song of Roland or the old ballads, will fall into this mistake. No one who knows what primitive poetry is, can fail to realize that while its conscious form is simple some of its finer effects are subtle. The *Iliad* contrives to express the idea that Hector and Sarpedon have a certain tone or tint of sad and chivalrous resignation, not bitter enough to be called pessimism and not jovial enough to be called optimism; Homer could never have said this in elaborate words. But somehow he contrives to say it in simple words. The Song of Roland contrives to express the idea that Christianity imposes upon its heroes a paradox: a paradox of great humility in the matter of their sins combined with great ferocity in the matter of their ideas. Of course the Song of Roland could not say this; but it conveys this. In the same way the Book of Job must be credited with many subtle effects which were in the author's soul without being, perhaps, in the author's mind. And of these by far the most important remains even yet to be stated. I do not know, and I doubt whether even scholars know, if the Book of Job had a great effect or had any effect upon the after development of Jewish thought. But if it did have any effect it may have saved them from an enormous collapse and decay. Here in this book the question is really asked whether God invariably punishes vice with terrestrial punishment and rewards virtue with terrestrial prosperity. If the Jews had answered that question wrong they might have lost all their influence in human history. They might have sunk even down to the level of modern well-educated society. For when once people have begun to believe that prosperity is the reward of virtue their next calamity is obvious. If prosperity is regarded as the reward of virtue it will be regarded as the symptom of virtue. Men will leave off the heavy task of making good men successful. They will adopt the easier task of making our successful men good. This, which has happened throughout modern commerce and journalism, is the ultimate Nemesis of the wicked optimism of the comforters of Job. If the Jews could be saved from it, the Book of Job saved them. The Book of Job is chiefly remarkable, as I have insisted throughout, for the fact that it does not end in a way that is conventionally satisfactory. Job is not told that his misfortunes were due to his sins or a part of any plan for his improvement. But in the prologue we see Job tormented not because he was the worst of men, but because he was the best. It is the lesson of the whole work that man is most comforted by paradoxes; and it is by all human testimony the most reassuring. I need not suggest what a high and strange history awaited this paradox of the best man in the worst fortune. I need not say that in the freest and most philosophical sense there is one Old Testament figure who is truly a type; or say what is pre-figured in the wounds of Job.

THE FICTION

THE NOVELIST is, above all, a man or woman without a point of view; someone who is content to explore an idea or a situation without hankering after right answers, without manipulating the characters into mere mouthpieces, without making the reader feel that everything is being subtly, or not so subtly, directed and twisted in order to fulfil a preconceived pattern. Chesterton's habit of mind made it virtually impossible for him to work in this way. When one of your tasks is always to have an answer to whatever questions the universe may ask, it is difficult to allow your creations to doubt, to undergo the random and meaningless, even to suffer. Novels raise questions, novels are untidy; they suggest and they explore. But Chesterton answered questions, he tidied life up; he taught and he proved. Perhaps that is the fate of a man who is uniquely adjusted and contented.

Chesterton could recognize greatness in others, and where it lay. Dickens springs immediately to mind; and it is no coincidence perhaps that the two poets he singled out for special study, Chaucer and Browning, are as near to novelists in their methods as any poet is likely to get. But, even though he knew why Dickens was great, he could not attain that greatness himself. He could not create a real, living, breathing character. For a man so concerned with the soul it is perhaps surprising that he consistently failed to convince us that his characters had souls in any but the most abstract sense. Metaphysics are there in his fiction, abundantly there, but as a scaffolding, a kind of exoskeleton. The inner life is missing: everything happens outside. We are told, but we are not shown. Chesterton's fiction will never move us to tears any more than the capture of a king moves us in a game of chess. In a sense he seems so busy establishing that we have one foot in eternity that he does not bother to place the other foot firmly enough in this world. He may be telling us the truth, but it is not a felt truth. This is all the more surprising in that Chesterton was certainly capable of feeling and exploring his feelings as he demonstrates in his essays.

Where he excels is in the sort of writing that depends on the clever, surprising or implacably logical outworking of a single idea, however bizarre, which is why the short story, and particularly the detective story, was the form which suited him best. The novels never really became anything more than extended short stories, episodic and lacking in that vital ingredient – true character.

Even Father Brown is not a true character in novelistic terms. He is a fascinating and successful creation, rather like Sherlock Holmes. But, like Holmes, he is a given quantity; he will not change or mature, or reveal hidden depths. Read the stories in any order and you will find no development, no deepening, no danger that he will ever act out of character. He may seem to, but that will be a device or a paradox which, once we have understood it, will serve to show that he was acting in character all along had we only the wit or the foresight to have seen it.

This is not to say that the novels of Chesterton cannot be read with great pleasure. We do not always want *Tess of the D'Urbervilles* or *Madame Bovary*. Even if he is never a great novelist he is never a bad writer. Those who enjoy the rest of Chesterton's writing will find as much wit, perceptiveness and sheer gusto in the fiction as they will anywhere else.

Probably the best is *The Man Who Was Thursday* which starts with the advantage of a superb title, even if acquaintance has dulled it a little. Writing about *A Midsummer Night's Dream* Chesterton says:

> Here is the pursuit of the man we cannot catch, the flight from the man we cannot see; here is the perpetual returning to the same place, here is the crazy alteration in the very objects of our desire, the substitution of one face for another face, the putting of the wrong souls in the wrong bodies, the fantastic disloyalties of the night.

All of which is a very good introduction to the atmosphere of Chesterton's own nightmare, *The Man Who Was Thursday*. It has, at once, the inconsequence of a dream, and the compulsion of a dream; a chase, a tangle, a bewilderment. It has been admired by writers as different as Tolkien, T. S. Eliot and Jose Luis Borges. It is tempting to analyze the book and untangle some of its undoubted mysteries, but there is a special Hell reserved for those who give away the plot of a book when their job is merely to excite the taste for reading it, and Chesterton knew it (see *Commercial Candour* on page 103). But perhaps it is not giving too much away to quote Chesterton's own clues to the book. This is from an article printed in *The Illustrated London News* on the day before he died. He begins by bemoaning the fact that so many critics give themselves problems by failing to read the title or the title-page of the books they are reviewing and miss the point of the story. He continues:

It is odd that one example occurred in my own case . . . in a book called *The Man Who Was Thursday*. It was a very melodramatic sort of moonshine, but it had a kind of notion in it; and the point is that it described, first a band of the last champions of order fighting against what appeared to be a world of anarchy, and then the discovery that the mysterious master both of the anarchy and the order was the same sort of elemental elf who had appeared to be rather too like a pantomime ogre. This line of logic, or lunacy, led many to infer that this equivocal being was meant for a serious description of the Deity; and my work even enjoyed a temporary respect among those who like the Deity to be so described. But this error was entirely due to the fact that they had read the book but had not read the title-page. In my case, it is true, it was a question of a subtitle rather than a title. The book was called *The Man Who Was Thursday*: *A Nightmare*. It was not intended to describe the real world as it was, or as I thought it was, even when my thoughts were considerably less settled than they are now. It was intended to describe the world of wild doubt and despair which the pessimists were generally describing at that date; with just a gleam of hope in some double meaning of the doubt, which even the pessimists felt in some fitful fashion.

It is certainly the most vivid and memorable of all Chesterton's

THE FICTION 195

novels. There is more mystery and more ambiguity here than in any other of his works. The lack of characterization and the episodic nature of his plotting are here not flaws so much as advantages. A chase is, by its very nature, a sequence of episodes; thus, Chesterton's weakness is turned to strength.

Since Chesterton is a farceur and fabulist, his stories really become comprehensible only when they are over, which means that any extract is going to be incomprehensible or teasing or both. The first three chapters of *The Man Who Was Thursday* will certainly tease and, it is to be hoped, will lead the reader to finding the book and finishing it. It gets stranger and even more intriguing. Though Chesterton's novels may not have been pivotal at the time they were written one must point to this particular book as a precursor of Stephen Fry's similarly puzzling and nightmarish *The Liar*.

Occasionally Chesterton was too paradoxical for his own good. A series of short stories called *Tales of the Longbow* are little more than extended and rather groanworthy puns. These stories illustrate how even the most metaphorical of English idioms may be literally enacted. Thus, a very straight-laced gentleman in a very conservative community begins to wear a cabbage on his head that he might finally fulfil in action the expression 'I'll eat my hat'. The stories are never less than crafty and composed, but after the first couple the joke begins to pall. *The Club of Queer Trades* is much more successful. Again it is a series of bizarre short stories, but they are much more witty and puzzling than the *Tales of the Longbow*. Their surreal quality can only be fully appreciated as incident piles on incident. As a taster, here is Chesterton's delineation of the Club's policy:

The nature of this society, such as we afterwards discovered it to be, is soon and simply told. It is an eccentric and Bohemian Club, of which the absolute condition of membership lies in this, that the candidate must have invented the method by which he earns his living. It must be an entirely new trade. The exact definition of this requirement is given in the two principal rules. First, it must not be a mere application or variation of an existing trade. Thus, for instance, the Club would not admit an insurance agent simply because instead of insuring men's furniture against being burnt in a fire, he insured, let us say, their trousers against being torn by a mad dog. The principle (as Sir Bradcock Burnaby-Bradcock, in the extraordinarily eloquent and soaring speech to the club on the occasion of the question being raised in the Stormby Smith affair, said wittily and keenly) is the same. Secondly, the trade must be a genuine commercial source of income, the support of its inventor. Thus the club would not receive a man simply because he chose to pass his days collecting broken sardine tins, unless he could drive a roaring trade in them. Professor Chick made that quite clear. And when one remembers what Professor Chick's own new trade was, one doesn't know whether to laugh or cry.

A similar framework is used for a book which few have noticed and fewer have praised; a book whose very title is a paradox, *Four Faultless Felons*. There are four stories, one for each felon and, without forgoing the wit, the intrigue and the satire, Chesterton seems to have found here a new vein of seriousness. There is a touching quality about each of the stories however outrageous its premise. The characters are not quasi-allegorical figures as they are in *The Ball and the Cross* or cardboard cut-outs as in *The Flying Inn*. They are perhaps the nearest Chesterton comes to painting truly human and moving characters even though they are lightly sketched. Each story is about eighty pages long and divided into chapters. It may be that to have allowed himself a slower pace and a little more room forced him into creating a story that mattered to his characters and therefore has more resonance, more than a simple geometrical truth, for his readers. It was the last of his novels to be published in his lifetime.

The Man Who Was Thursday:
A Nightmare

I
The Two Poets of Saffron Park

The suburb of Saffron Park lay on the sunset side of London, as red and ragged as a cloud of sunset. It was built of a bright brick throughout; its skyline was fantastic, and even its ground plan was wild. It had been the outburst of a speculative builder, faintly tinged with art, who called its architecture sometimes Elizabethan and sometimes Queen Anne, apparently under the impression that the two sovereigns were identical. It was described with some justice as an artistic colony, though it never in any definable way produced any art. But although its pretensions to be an intellectual centre were a little vague, its pretensions to be a pleasant place were quite indisputable. The stranger who looked for the first time at the quaint red houses could only think how very oddly shaped the people must be who could fit in to them. Nor when he met the people was he disappointed in this respect. The place was not only pleasant, but perfect, if once he could regard it not as a deception but rather as a dream. Even if the people were not 'artists', the whole was nevertheless artistic. That young man with the long, auburn hair and the impudent face – that young man was not really a poet; but surely he was a poem. That old gentleman with the wild, white beard and the wild, white hat – that venerable humbug was not really a philosopher; but at least he was the cause of philosophy in others. That scientific gentleman with the bald, egg-like head and the bare, bird-like neck had no real right to the airs of science that he assumed. He had not discovered anything new in biology; but what biological creature could he have discovered more singular than himself? Thus, and thus only, the whole place had properly to be regarded; it had to be considered not so much as a workshop for artists, but as a frail but finished work of art. A man who stepped into its social atmosphere felt as if he had stepped into a written comedy.

More especially this attractive unreality fell upon it about nightfall, when the extravagant roofs were dark against the afterglow and the whole insane village seemed as separate as a drifting cloud. This again was more strongly true of the many nights of local festivity, when the little gardens were often illuminated, and the big Chinese lanterns glowed in the dwarfish trees like some fierce and monstrous fruit. And this was strongest of all on one particular evening, still vaguely remembered in the locality, of which the auburn-haired poet was the hero. It was not by any means the only evening of which he was the hero. On many nights those passing by his little back garden might hear his high, didactic voice laying down the law to men and particularly to women. The attitude of women in such cases was indeed one of the paradoxes of the place. Most of the women were of the kind vaguely called emancipated, and professed some protest against male supremacy. Yet these new women would always pay to a man the extravagant compliment which no ordinary woman ever pays to him, that of listening while he is talking. And Mr. Lucian Gregory, the red-haired poet, was really (in some sense) a man worth listening to, even if one only laughed at the end of it. He put the old cant of the lawlessness of art and the art of lawlessness with a certain impudent freshness which gave at least a momentary pleasure. He was helped in some degree by the arresting oddity of his appearance, which he worked, as the phrase goes, for all it was worth. His dark red hair parted in the middle was literally like a woman's, and curved into the slow curls of a virgin in a pre-Raphaelite picture. From within this almost saintly oval, however, his face projected suddenly broad and brutal, the chin carried forward with a look of cockney contempt. This combination at once tickled and terrified the nerves of a neurotic population. He seemed like a walking blasphemy, a blend of the angel and the ape.

This particular evening, if it is remembered for nothing else, will be remembered in that place for its strange sunset. It looked like the end of the world. All the heaven seemed covered with a quite vivid and palpable plumage; you could only say that the sky was full of feathers, and of feathers that almost brushed the face.

Across the great part of the dome they were grey, with the strangest tints of violet and mauve and an unnatural pink or pale green; but towards the west the whole grew past description, transparent and passionate, and the last red-hot plumes of it covered up the sun like something too good to be seen. The whole was so close about the earth, as to express nothing but a violent secrecy. The very empyrean seemed to be a secret. It expressed that splendid smallness which is the soul of local patriotism. The very sky seemed small.

I say that there are some inhabitants who may remember the evening if only by that oppressive sky. There are others who may remember it because it marked the first appearance in the place of the second poet of Saffron Park. For a long time the red-haired revolutionary had reigned without a rival; it was upon the night of the sunset that his solitude suddenly ended. The new poet, who introduced himself by the name of Gabriel Syme, was a very mild-looking mortal, with a fair, pointed beard and faint, yellow hair. But an impression grew that he was less meek than he looked. He signalized his entrance by differing with the established poet, Gregory, upon the whole nature of poetry. He said that he (Syme) was a poet of law, a poet of order; nay, he said he was a poet of respectability. So all the Saffron Parkers looked at him as if he had that moment fallen out of that impossible sky.

In fact, Mr. Lucian Gregory, the anarchic poet, connected the two events.

'It may well be,' he said, in his sudden lyrical manner, 'it may well be on such a night of clouds and cruel colours that there is brought forth upon the earth such a portent as a respectable poet. You say you are a poet of law; I say you are a contradiction in terms. I only wonder there were not comets and earthquakes on the night you appeared in this garden.'

The man with the meek blue eyes and the pale, pointed beard endured these thunders with a certain submissive solemnity. The third party of the group, Gregory's sister Rosamond, who had her brother's braids of red hair, but a kindlier face underneath them, laughed with such mixture of admiration and disapproval as she gave commonly to the family oracle.

Gregory resumed in high oratorical good humour.

'An artist is identical with an anarchist,' he cried. 'You might transpose the words anywhere. An anarchist is an artist. The man who throws a bomb is an artist, because he prefers a great moment to everything. He sees how much more valuable is one burst of blazing light, one peal of perfect thunder, than the mere common bodies of a few shapeless policemen. An artist disregards all governments, abolishes all conventions. The poet delights in disorder only. If it were not so, the most poetical thing in the world would be the Underground Railway.'

'So it is,' said Mr Syme.

'Nonsense!' said Gregory, who was very rational when anyone else attempted paradox. 'Why do all the clerks and navvies in the railway trains look so sad and tired, so very sad and tired? I will tell you. It is because they know that the train is going right. It is because they know that whatever place they have taken a ticket for that place they will reach. It is because after they have passed Sloane Square they know that the next station must be Victoria, and nothing but Victoria. Oh, their wild rapture! oh, their eyes like stars and their souls again in Eden, if the next station were unaccountably Baker Street!'

'It is you who are unpoetical,' replied the poet Syme. 'If what you say of clerks is true, they can only be as prosaic as your poetry. The rare, strange thing is to hit the mark; the gross, obvious thing is to miss it. We feel it is epical when man with one wild arrow strikes a distant bird. Is it not also epical when man with one wild engine strikes a distant station? Chaos is dull; because in chaos the train might indeed go anywhere, to Baker Street or to Bagdad. But man is a magician, and his whole magic is in this, that he does say Victoria, and lo! it is Victoria. No, take your books of mere poetry and prose; let me read a time table, with tears of pride. Take your Byron, who commemorates the defeats of man; give me Bradshaw, who commemorates his victories. Give me Bradshaw, I say!'

'Must you go?' inquired Gregory sarcastically.

'I tell you,' went on Syme with passion, 'that every time a train comes in I feel that it has broken past batteries of besiegers, and that man has won a battle against chaos. You say contemptuously that when one has left Sloane Square one must come to Victoria. I say that one might do a thousand things instead, and that whenever

I really come there I have the sense of hair-breadth escape. And when I hear the guard shout out the word "Victoria", it is not an unmeaning word. It is to me the cry of a herald announcing conquest. It is to me indeed "Victoria", it is the victory of Adam.'

Gregory wagged his heavy, red head with a slow and sad smile.

'And even then,' he said, 'we poets always ask the question, "And what is Victoria now that you have got there?" You think Victoria is like the New Jerusalem. We know that the New Jerusalem will only be like Victoria. Yes, the poet will be discontented even in the streets of heaven. The poet is always in revolt.'

'There again,' said Syme irritably, 'what is there poetical about being in revolt? You might as well say that it is poetical to be sea-sick. Being sick is a revolt. Both being sick and being rebellious may be the wholesome thing on certain desperate occasions; but I'm hanged if I can see why they are poetical. Revolt in the abstract is – revolting. It's mere vomiting.'

The girl winced for a flash at the unpleasant word, but Syme was too hot to heed her.

'It is things going right,' he cried, 'that is poetical! Our digestions, for instance, going sacredly and silently right, that is the foundation of all poetry. Yes, the most poetical thing, more poetical than the flowers, more poetical than the stars – the most poetical thing in the world is not being sick.'

'Really,' said Gregory superciliously, 'the examples you choose— '

'I beg your pardon,' said Syme grimly, 'I forgot we had abolished all conventions.'

For the first time a red patch appeared on Gregory's forehead.

'You don't expect me,' he said, 'to revolutionize society on this lawn?'

Syme looked straight into his eyes and smiled sweetly.

'No, I don't,' he said; 'but I suppose that if you were serious about your anarchism, that is exactly what you would do.'

Gregory's big bull's eyes blinked suddenly like those of an angry lion, and one could almost fancy that his red mane rose.

'Don't you think, then,' he said in a dangerous voice, 'that I am serious about my anarchism?'

'I beg your pardon?' said Syme.

'Am I not serious about my anarchism?' cried Gregory, with knotted fists.

'My dear fellow!' said Syme, and strolled away.

With surprise, but with a curious pleasure, he found Rosamond Gregory still in his company.

'Mr Syme,' she said, 'do the people who talk like you and my brother often mean what they say? Do you mean what you say now?'

Syme smiled.

'Do you?' he asked.

'What do you mean?' asked the girl, with grave eyes.

'My dear Miss Gregory,' said Syme gently, 'there are many kinds of sincerity and insincerity. When you say "Thank you" for the salt, do you mean what you say? No. When you say "The world is round", do you mean what you say? No. It is true, but you don't mean it. Now, sometimes a man like your brother really finds a thing he does mean. It may be only a half-truth, quarter-truth, tenth-truth; but then he says more than he means – from sheer force of meaning it.'

She was looking at him from under level brows; her face was grave and open, and there had fallen upon it the shadow of that unreasoning responsibility which is at the bottom of the most frivolous woman, the maternal watch which is as old as the world.

'Is he really an anarchist, then?' she asked.

'Only in that sense I speak of,' replied Syme; 'or if you prefer it, in that nonsense.'

She drew her broad brows together and said abruptly —

'He wouldn't really use – bombs or that sort of thing?'

Syme broke into a great laugh, that seemed too large for his slight and somewhat dandified figure.

'Good Lord, no!' he said, 'that has to be done anonymously.'

And at that the corners of her own mouth broke into a smile, and she thought with a simultaneous pleasure of Gregory's absurdity and of his safety.

Syme strolled with her to a seat in the corner of the garden, and continued to pour out his opinions. For he was a sincere man, and in spite of his superficial airs and graces, at root a humble one. And it is always the humble man who talks too much; the proud man watches himself too closely. He defended respectability with violence and exaggeration. He grew passionate in his praise of tidiness and propriety. All the time there was a smell of lilac all round him. Once he heard very faintly in some distant street a barrel-organ begin to play, and it seemed to him that his heroic words were moving to a tiny tune from under or beyond the world.

He stared and talked at the girl's red hair and amused face for what seemed to be a few minutes; and then, feeling that the groups in such a place should mix, rose to his feet. To his astonishment, he discovered the whole garden empty. Everyone had gone long ago, and he went himself with a rather hurried apology. He left with a sense of champagne in his head, which he could not afterwards explain. In the wild events which were to follow this girl had no part at all; he never saw her again until all his tale was over. And yet, in some indescribable way, she kept recurring like a motive in music through all his mad adventures afterwards, and the glory of her strange hair ran like a red thread through those dark and ill-drawn tapestries of the night. For what followed was so improbable, that it might well have been a dream.

When Syme went out into the starlit street, he found it for the moment empty. Then he realized (in some odd way) that the silence was rather a living silence than a dead one. Directly outside the door stood a street lamp, whose gleam gilded the leaves of the tree that bent out over the fence behind him. About a foot from the lamp-post stood a figure almost as rigid and motionless as the lamp-post itself. The tall hat and long frock-coat were black; the face, in an abrupt shadow, was almost as dark. Only a fringe of fiery hair against the light, and also something aggressive in the attitude, proclaimed that it was the poet Gregory. He had something of the look of a masked bravo waiting sword in hand for his foe.

He made a sort of doubtful salute, which Syme somewhat more formally returned.

'I was waiting for you,' said Gregory. 'Might I have a moment's conversation?'

'Certainly. About what?' asked Syme in a sort of weak wonder.

Gregory struck out with his stick at the lamp-post, and then at the tree.

'About *this* and *this*,' he cried; 'about order and anarchy. There is your precious order, that lean, iron lamp, ugly and barren; and there is anarchy, rich, living, reproducing itself – there is anarchy, splendid in green and gold.'

'All the same,' replied Syme patiently, 'just at present you only see the tree by the light of the lamp. I wonder when you would ever see the lamp by the light of the tree.' Then after a pause he said, 'But may I ask if you have been standing out here in the dark only to resume our little argument?'

'No,' cried out Gregory, in a voice that rang down the street, 'I did not stand here to resume our argument, but to end it for ever.'

The silence fell again, and Syme, though he understood nothing, listened instinctively for something serious. Gregory began in a smooth voice and with a rather bewildering smile.

'Mr Syme,' he said, 'this evening you succeeded in doing something rather remarkable. You did something to me that no man born of woman has ever succeeded in doing before.'

'Indeed!'

'Now I remember,' resumed Gregory reflectively, 'one other person succeeded in doing it. The captain of a penny steamer (if I remember correctly) at Southend. You have irritated me.'

'I am very sorry,' replied Syme with gravity.

'I am afraid my fury and your insult are too shocking to be wiped out even with an apology,' said Gregory very calmly. 'No duel could wipe it out. If I struck you dead I could not wipe it out. There is only one way by which that insult can be erased, and that way I choose. I am going, at the possible sacrifice of my life and honour, to *prove* to you that you were wrong in what you said.'

'In what I said?'

'You said I was not serious about being an anarchist.'

'There are degrees of seriousness,' replied Syme. 'I have never doubted that you were perfectly sincere in this sense, that you thought what you said well worth saying, that you thought a paradox might wake men up to a neglected truth.'

Gregory stared at him steadily and painfully.

'And in no other sense,' he asked, 'you think me serious? You think me a *flâneur* who lets fall occasional truths. You do not think that in a deeper, a more deadly sense, I am serious.'

Syme struck his stick violently on the stones of the road.

'Serious!' he cried. 'Good Lord! is this street serious? Are these damned Chinese lanterns serious? Is the whole caboodle serious? One comes here and talks a pack of bosh, and perhaps some sense as well, but I should think very little of a man who didn't keep something in the background of his life that was more serious than all this talking – something more serious, whether it was religion or only drink.'

'Very well,' said Gregory, his face darkening, 'you shall see something more serious than either drink or religion.'

Syme stood waiting with his usual air of mildness until Gregory again opened his lips.

'You spoke just now of having a religion. Is it really true that you have one?'

'Oh,' said Syme with a beaming smile, 'we are all Catholics now.'

'Then may I ask you to swear by whatever gods or saints your religion involves that you will *not* reveal what I am now going to tell you to any son of Adam, and especially not to the police? Will you swear that! If you will take upon yourself this awful abnegation, if you will consent to burden your soul with a vow that you should never make and a knowledge you should never dream about, I will promise you in return — '

'You will promise me in return?' inquired Syme, as the other paused.

'I will promise you a very entertaining evening.' Syme suddenly took off his hat.

'Your offer,' he said, 'is far too idiotic to be declined. You say that a poet is always an anarchist. I disagree; but I hope at least that he is always a sportsman. Permit me, here and now, to swear as a Christian, and promise as a good comrade and a fellow-artist, that I will not report anything of this, whatever it is, to the police. And now, in the name of Colney Hatch, what is it?'

'I think,' said Gregory, with placid irrelevancy, 'that we will call a cab.'

He gave two long whistles, and a hansom came rattling down the road. The two got into it in silence. Gregory gave through the trap the address of an obscure public-house on the Chiswick bank of the river. The cab whisked itself away again, and in it these two fantastics quitted their fantastic town.

II
The Secret of Gabriel Syme

The cab pulled up before a particularly dreary and greasy beershop, into which Gregory rapidly conducted his companion. They seated themselves in a close and dim sort of bar-parlour, at a stained wooden table with one wooden leg. The room was so small and dark, that very little could be seen of the attendant who was summoned, beyond a vague and dark impression of something bulky and bearded.

'Will you take a little supper?' asked Gregory politely. 'The *pâté de foie gras* is not good here, but I can recommend the game.'

Syme received the remark with stolidity, imagining it to be a joke. Accepting the vein of humour, he said, with a well-bred indifference —

'Oh, bring me some lobster mayonnaise.'

To his indescribable astonishment, the man only said 'Certainly, sir!' and went away apparently to get it.

'What will you drink?' resumed Gregory, with the same careless yet apologetic air. 'I shall only have a *crème de menthe* myself; I have dined. But the champagne can really be trusted. Do let me start you with a half-bottle of Pommery at least?'

'Thank you!' said the motionless Syme. 'You are very good.'

His further attempts at conversation, somewhat disorganized in themselves, were cut short finally as by a thunderbolt by the actual appearance of the lobster. Syme tasted it, and found it particularly good. Then he suddenly began to eat with great rapidity and appetite.

'Excuse me if I enjoy myself rather obviously!' he said to Gregory, smiling. 'I don't often have the luck to have a dream like this. It is new to me for a nightmare to lead to a lobster. It is commonly the other way.'

'You are not asleep, I assure you,' said Gregory. 'You are, on the contrary, close to the most actual and rousing moment of your existence. Ah, here comes your champagne! I admit that there may be a slight disproportion, let us say, between the inner arrangements of this excellent hotel and its simple and unpretentious exterior. But that is all our modesty. We are the most modest men that ever lived on earth.'

'And who are *we*?' asked Syme, emptying his champagne glass.

'It is quite simple,' replied Gregory. '*We* are the serious anarchists, in whom you do not believe.'

'Oh!' said Syme shortly. 'You do yourselves well in drinks.'

'Yes, we are serious about everything,' answered Gregory.

Then after a pause he added —

'If in a few moments this table begins to turn round a little, don't put it down to your inroads into the champagne. I don't wish you to do yourself an injustice.'

'Well, if I am not drunk, I am mad,' replied Syme with perfect calm; 'but I trust I can behave like a gentleman in either condition. May I smoke?'

'Certainly!' said Gregory, producing a cigar-case. 'Try one of mine.'

Syme took the cigar, clipped the end off with a cigar-cutter out of his waistcoat pocket, put it in his mouth, lit it slowly, and let out a long cloud of smoke. It is not a little to his credit that he performed these rites with so much composure, for almost before he had begun them the table at which he sat had begun to revolve, first slowly, and then rapidly, as if at an insane séance.

'You must not mind it,' said Gregory; 'it's a kind of screw.'

'Quite so,' said Syme placidly, 'a kind of screw. How simple that is!'

The next moment the smoke of his cigar, which had been wavering across the room in snaky twists, went straight up as if from a factory chimney, and the two, with their chairs and table, shot down through the floor as if the earth had swallowed them. They went rattling down a kind of roaring chimney as rapidly as a lift cut loose, and they came with an abrupt bump to the bottom.

But when Gregory threw open a pair of doors and let in a red subterranean light, Syme was still smoking, with one leg thrown over the other, and had not turned a yellow hair.

Gregory led him down a low, vaulted passage, at the end of which was the red light. It was an enormous crimson lantern, nearly as big as a fireplace, fixed over a small but heavy iron door. In the door there was a sort of hatchway or grating, and on this Gregory struck five times. A heavy voice with a foreign accent asked him who he was. To this he gave the more or less unexpected reply, 'Mr. Joseph Chamberlain.' The heavy hinges began to move; it was obviously some kind of password.

Inside the doorway the passage gleamed as if it were lined with a network of steel. On a second glance, Syme saw that the glittering pattern was really made up of ranks and ranks of rifles and revolvers, closely packed or interlocked.

'I must ask you to forgive me all these formalities,' said Gregory; 'we have to be very strict here.'

'Oh, don't apologize,' said Syme. 'I know your passion for law and order', and he stepped into the passage lined with the steel weapons. With his long, fair hair and rather foppish frock-coat, he looked a singularly frail and fanciful figure as he walked down that shining avenue of death.

They passed through several such passages, and came out at last into queer steel chamber with curved walls, almost spherical in shape, but presenting, with its tiers of benches, something of the appearance of a scientific lecture-theatre. There were no rifles or pistols in this apartment, but round the walls of it were hung more dubious and dreadful shapes, things that looked like the bulbs of iron plants, or the eggs of iron birds. They were bombs, and the very room itself seemed like the inside of a bomb. Syme knocked his cigar ash off against the wall, and went in.

'And now, my dear Mr Syme,' said Gregory, throwing himself in an expansive manner on the bench under the largest bomb, 'now we are quite cosy, so let us talk properly. Now no human words can give you any notion of why I brought you here. It was one of those quite arbitrary emotions, like jumping off a cliff or falling in love. Suffice it to say that you were an inexpressibly irritating fellow, and, to do you justice, you are still. I would break twenty oaths of secrecy for the pleasure of taking you down a peg. That way you have of lighting a cigar would make a priest break the seal of confession. Well, you said that you were quite certain I was not a serious anarchist. Does this place strike you as being serious?'

'It does seem to have a moral under all its gaiety,' assented Syme; 'but may I ask you two questions? You need not fear to give me information, because, as you remember, you very wisely extorted from me a promise not to tell the police, a promise I shall certainly keep. So it is in mere curiosity that I make my queries. First of all, what is it really all about? What is it you object to? You want to abolish Government?'

'To abolish God!' said Gregory, opening the eyes of a fanatic. 'We do not only want to upset a few despotisms and police regulations; that sort of anarchism does exist, but it is a mere branch of the Nonconformists. We dig deeper and we blow you higher. We wish to deny all those arbitrary distinctions of vice and virtue, honour and treachery, upon which mere rebels base themselves. The silly sentimentalists of the French Revolution talked of the Rights of Man! We hate Rights as we hate Wrongs. We have abolished Right and Wrong.'

'And Right and Left,' said Syme with a simple eagerness, 'I hope you will abolish them too. They are much more troublesome to me.'

'You spoke of a second question,' snapped Gregory.

'With pleasure,' resumed Syme. 'In all your present acts and surroundings there is a scientific attempt at secrecy. I have an aunt who lived over a shop, but this is the first time I have found people living from preference under a public house. You have a heavy iron door. You cannot pass it without submitting to the humiliation of calling yourself Mr. Chamberlain. You surround yourself with steel instruments which make the place, if I may say so, more impressive than homelike. May I ask why, after taking all this trouble to barricade yourselves in the bowels of the earth, you then parade your whole secret by talking about anarchism to every silly woman in Saffron Park?'

Gregory smiled.

'The answer is simple,' he said. 'I told you I was a serious anarchist, and you did not believe me. Nor do *they* believe

me. Unless I took them into this infernal room they would not
believe me.'

Syme smoked thoughtfully, and looked at him with interest.
Gregory went on.

'The history of the thing might amuse you,' he said. 'When first
I became one of the New Anarchists I tried all kinds of respectable
disguises. I dressed up as a bishop. I read up all about bishops in
our anarchist pamphlets, in *Superstition the Vampire* and *Priests of
Prey*. I certainly understood from them that bishops are strange
and terrible old men keeping a cruel secret from mankind. I was
misinformed. When on my first appearing in episcopal gaiters in
a drawing-room I cried out in a voice of thunder, 'Down! down!
presumptuous human reason!' they found out in some way that I
was not a bishop at all. I was nabbed at once. Then I made up
as a millionaire; but I defended Capital with so much intelligence
that a fool could see that I was quite poor. Then I tried being
a major. Now I am a humanitarian myself, but I have, I hope,
enough intellectual breadth to understand the position of those
who, like Nietzsche, admire violence – the proud, mad war of
Nature and all that, you know. I threw myself into the major.
I drew my sword and waved it constantly. I called out 'Blood!'
abstractedly, like a man calling for wine. I often said, 'Let the weak
perish; it is the Law.' Well, well, it seems majors don't do this. I
was nabbed again. At last I went in despair to the President of the
Central Anarchist Council, who is the greatest man in Europe.'

'What is his name?' asked Syme.

'You would not know it,' answered Gregory. 'That is his
greatness. Cæsar and Napoleon put all their genius into being
heard of, and they *were* heard of. He puts all his genius into
not being heard of, and he is not heard of. But you cannot be
for five minutes in the room with him without feeling that Cæsar
and Napoleon would have been children in his hands.'

He was silent and even pale for a moment, and then resumed —

'But whenever he gives advice it is always something as startling
as an epigram, and yet as practical as the Bank of England. I said
to him, "What disguise will hide me from the world? What can I
find more respectable than bishops and majors?" He looked at me
with his large but indecipherable face. "You want a safe disguise,

do you? You want a dress which will guarantee you harmless; a dress in which no one would ever look for a bomb?" I nodded. He suddenly lifted his lion's voice. "Why, then, dress up as an *anarchist*, you fool!" he roared so that the room shook. "Nobody will ever expect you to do anything dangerous then." And he turned his broad back on me without another word. I took his advice, and have never regretted it. I preached blood and murder to those women day and night, and – by God! – they would let me wheel their perambulators.'

Syme sat watching him with some respect in his large, blue eyes.

'You took me in,' he said. 'It is really a smart dodge.'

Then after a pause he added —

'What do you call this tremendous President of yours?'

'We generally call him Sunday,' replied Gregory with simplicity. 'You see, there are seven members of the Central Anarchist Council, and they are named after days of the week. He is called Sunday, by some of his admirers Bloody Sunday. It is curious you should mention the matter because the very night you have dropped in (if I may so express it) is the night on which our London branch, which assembles in this room, has to elect its own deputy to fill a vacancy in the Council. The gentleman who has for some time past played, with propriety and general applause, the difficult part of Thursday, has died quite suddenly. Consequently, we have called a meeting this very evening to elect a successor.'

He got to his feet and strolled across the room with a sort of smiling embarrassment.

'I feel somehow as if you were my mother, Syme,' he continued casually. 'I feel that I can confide anything to you, as you have promised to tell nobody. In fact, I will confide to you something that I would not say in so many words to the anarchists who will be coming to the room in about ten minutes. We shall, of course, go through a form of election; but I don't mind telling you that it is practically certain what the result will be.' He looked down for a moment modestly. 'It is almost a settled thing that I am to be Thursday.'

'My dear fellow,' said Syme heartily, 'I congratulate you. A great career!'

Gregory smiled in deprecation, and walked across the room, talking rapidly.

'As a matter of fact, everything is ready for me on this table,' he said, 'and the ceremony will probably be the shortest possible.'

Syme also strolled across to the table, and found lying across it a walking-stick, which turned out on examination to be a sword-stick, a large Colt's revolver, a sandwich case, and a formidable flask of brandy. Over the chair, beside the table, was thrown a heavy-looking cape or cloak.

'I have only to get the form of election finished,' continued Gregory with animation, 'then I snatch up this cloak and stick, stuff these other things into my pocket, step out of a door in this cavern, which opens on the river, where there is a steam-tug already waiting for me, and then – then – oh, the wild joy of being Thursday!' And he clasped his hands.

Syme, who had sat down once more with his usual insolent languor, got to his feet with an unusual air of hesitation.

'Why is it,' he asked vaguely, 'that I think you are quite a decent fellow? Why do I positively like you, Gregory?' He paused a moment, and then added with a sort of fresh curiosity, 'Is it because you are such an ass?'

There was a thoughtful silence again, and then he cried out —

'Well, damn it all! this is the funniest situation I have ever been in in my life, and I am going to act accordingly. Gregory, I gave you a promise before I came into this place. That promise I would keep under red-hot pincers. Would you give me, for my own safety, a little promise of the same kind?'

'A promise?' asked Gregory, wondering.

'Yes,' said Syme very seriously, 'a promise. I swore before God that I would not tell your secret to the police. Will you swear by Humanity, or whatever beastly thing you believe in, that you will not tell my secret to the anarchists?'

'Your secret?' asked the staring Gregory. 'Have you got a secret?'

'Yes,' said Syme, 'I have a secret.' Then after a pause, 'Will you swear?'

Gregory glared at him gravely for a few moments, and then said abruptly —

'You must have bewitched me, but I feel a furious curiosity about you. Yes, I will swear not to tell the anarchists anything you tell me. But look sharp, for they will be here in a couple of minutes.'

Syme rose slowly to his feet and thrust his long, white hands into his long, grey trousers' pockets. Almost as he did so there came five knocks on the outer grating, proclaiming the arrival of the first of the conspirators.

'Well,' said Syme slowly, 'I don't know how to tell you the truth more shortly than by saying that your expedient of dressing up as an aimless poet is not confined to you or your President. We have known the dodge for some time at Scotland Yard.'

Gregory tried to spring up straight, but he swayed thrice.

'What do you say?' he asked in an inhuman voice.

'Yes,' said Syme simply, 'I am a police detective. But I think I hear your friends coming.'

From the doorway there came a murmur of 'Mr Joseph Chamberlain.' It was repeated twice and thrice and then thirty times, and the crowd of Joseph Chamberlains (a solemn thought) could be heard trampling down the corridor.

III
The Man Who Was Thursday

Before one of the fresh faces could appear at the doorway, Gregory's stunned surprise had fallen from him. He was beside the table with a bound, and a noise in his throat like a wild beast. He caught up the Colt's revolver and took aim at Syme. Syme did not flinch, but he put up a pale and polite hand.

'Don't be such a silly man,' he said, with the effeminate dignity of a curate. 'Don't you see it's not necessary? Don't you see that we're both in the same boat? Yes, and jolly sea-sick.'

Gregory could not speak, but he could not fire either, and he looked his question.

'Don't you see we've checkmated each other?' cried Syme. 'I can't tell the police you are an anarchist. You can't tell the anarchists I'm a policeman. I can only watch you, knowing what you are; you can only watch me, knowing what I am. In short, it's a lonely, intellectual duel, my head against yours. I'm a policeman deprived of the help of the police. You, my poor fellow, are an anarchist deprived of the help of that law and organization which is so essential to anarchy. The one solitary difference is in your favour. You are not surrounded by inquisitive policemen; I am surrounded by inquisitive anarchists. I cannot betray you, but I might betray myself. Come, come! wait and see me betray myself. I shall do it so nicely.'

Gregory put the pistol slowly down, still staring at Syme as if he were a sea-monster.

'I don't believe in immortality,' he said at last, 'but if, after all this, you were to break your word, God would make a hell only for you, to howl in for ever.'

'I shall not break my word,' said Syme sternly, 'nor will you break yours. Here are your friends.'

The mass of the anarchists entered the room heavily, with a slouching and somewhat weary gait; but one little man, with a black beard and glasses – a man somewhat of the type of Mr. Tim Healy – detached himself, and bustled forward with some papers in his hand.

'Comrade Gregory,' he said, 'I suppose this man is a delegate?'

Gregory, taken by surprise, looked down and muttered the name of Syme; but Syme replied almost pertly —

'I am glad to see that your gate is well enough guarded to make it hard for anyone to be here who was not a delegate.'

The brow of the little man with the black beard was, however, still contracted with something like suspicion.

'What branch do you represent?' he asked sharply.

'I should hardly call it a branch,' said Syme, laughing; 'I should call it at the very least a root.'

'What do you mean?'

'The fact is,' said Syme serenely, 'the truth is I am a Sabbatarian. I have been specially sent here to see that you show a due observance of Sunday.'

The little man dropped one of his papers, and a flicker of fear went over all the faces of the group. Evidently the awful President, whose name was Sunday, did sometimes send down such irregular ambassadors to such branch meetings.

'Well, comrade,' said the man with the papers after a pause, 'I suppose we'd better give you a seat in the meeting?'

'If you ask my advice as a friend,' said Syme with severe benevolence, 'I think you'd better.'

When Gregory heard the dangerous dialogue end, with a sudden safety for his rival, he rose abruptly and paced the floor in painful thought. He was, indeed, in an agony of diplomacy. It was clear that Syme's inspired impudence was likely to bring him out of all merely accidental dilemmas. Little was to be hoped from them. He could not himself betray Syme, partly from honour, but partly also because, if he betrayed him and for some reason failed to destroy him, the Syme who escaped would be a Syme freed from all obligation of secrecy, a Syme who would simply walk to the nearest police station. After all, it was only one night's discussion, and only one detective who would know of it. He would let out as little as possible of their plans that night, and then let Syme go, and chance it.

He strode across to the group of anarchists, which was already distributing itself along the benches.

'I think it is time we began,' he said; 'the steam-tug is waiting on the river already. I move that Comrade Buttons takes the chair.'

This being approved by a show of hands, the little man with the papers slipped into the presidential seat.

'Comrades,' he began, as sharp as a pistol-shot, 'our meeting tonight is important, though it need not be long. This branch has always had the honour of electing Thursdays for the Central European Council. We have elected many and splendid Thursdays. We all lament the sad decease of the heroic worker who occupied the post until last week. As you know, his services to the cause were considerable. He organized the great dynamite coup of Brighton which, under happier circumstances, ought to have killed everybody on the pier. As you also know, his death was as self-denying as his life, for he died through his faith in a hygienic mixture of chalk and water as a substitute for milk, which beverage he regarded as barbaric, and as involving cruelty to the cow. Cruelty, or anything approaching to cruelty, revolted him always. But it is not to acclaim his virtues that we are met, but for a harder task. It is difficult properly to praise his qualities, but it is more difficult to replace them. Upon you, comrades, it devolves this evening to choose out of the company present the man who shall be Thursday. If any comrade suggests a name I will put it to the vote. If no comrade suggests a name, I can only tell myself that that dear dynamiter, who is gone from us, has carried into the unknowable abysses the last secret of his virtue and his innocence.'

There was a stir of almost inaudible applause, such as is sometimes heard in church. Then a large old man, with a long and venerable white beard, perhaps the only real working-man present, rose lumberingly and said —

'I move that Comrade Gregory be elected Thursday,' and sat lumberingly down again. 'Does anyone second?' asked the chairman.

A little man with a velvet coat and pointed beard seconded.

'Before I put the matter to the vote,' said the chairman, 'I will call on Comrade Gregory to make a statement.'

Gregory rose amid a great rumble of applause. His face was deadly pale, so that by contrast his queer red hair looked almost scarlet. But he was smiling and altogether at ease. He had made up his mind, and he saw his best policy quite plain in front of him like a white road. His best chance was to make a softened and ambiguous speech, such as would leave on the detective's mind the impression that the anarchist brotherhood was a very mild affair after all. He believed in his own literary power, his capacity for suggesting fine shades and picking perfect words. He thought that with care he could succeed, in spite of all the people around him, in conveying an impression of the institution, subtly and delicately false. Syme had once thought that anarchists, under all their bravado, were only playing the fool. Could he not now, in the hour of peril, make Syme think so again?

'Comrades,' began Gregory, in a low but penetrating voice, 'it is not necessary for me to tell you what is my policy, for it is your policy also. Our belief has been slandered, it has been disfigured, it has been utterly confused and concealed, but it has never been altered. Those who talk about anarchism and its dangers go everywhere and anywhere to get their information, except to us, except to the fountain head. They learn about anarchists from sixpenny novels; they learn about anarchists from tradesmen's newspapers; they learn about anarchists from *Ally Sloper's Half-Holiday* and the *Sporting Times*. They never learn about anarchists from anarchists. We have no chance of denying the mountainous slanders which are heaped upon our heads from one end of Europe to another. The man who has always heard that we are walking plagues has never heard our reply. I know that he will not hear it tonight, though my passion were to rend the roof. For it is deep, deep under the earth that the persecuted are permitted to assemble, as the Christians assembled in the Catacombs. But if, by some incredible accident, there were here tonight a man who all his life had thus immensely misunderstood us, I would put this question to him: "When those Christians met in those Catacombs, what sort of moral reputation had they in the streets above? What tales were told of their atrocities by one educated Roman to another? Suppose" (I would say to him), "suppose that we are only repeating that still mysterious paradox of history. Suppose we seem as shocking as the Christians because we are really as harmless as the Christians. Suppose we seem as mad as the Christians because we are really as meek.'"

The applause that had greeted the opening sentences had been gradually growing fainter, and at the last word it stopped suddenly. In the abrupt silence, the man with the velvet jacket said, in a high, squeaky voice —

'I'm not meek!'

'Comrade Witherspoon tells us,' resumed Gregory, 'that he is not meek. Ah, how little he knows himself! His words are, indeed, extravagant; his appearance is ferocious, and even (to an ordinary taste) unattractive. But only the eye of a friendship as deep and delicate as mine can perceive the deep foundation of solid meekness which lies at the base of him, too deep even for himself to see. I repeat, we are the true early Christians, only that we come too late. We are simple, as they were simple – look at Comrade Witherspoon. We are modest, as they were modest – look at me. We are merciful — '

'No, no!' called out Mr Witherspoon with the velvet jacket.

'I say we are merciful,' repeated Gregory furiously, 'as the early Christians were merciful. Yet this did not prevent their being accused of eating human flesh. We do not eat human flesh — '

'Shame!' cried Witherspoon. 'Why not?'

'Comrade Witherspoon,' said Gregory, with a feverish gaiety, 'is anxious to know why nobody eats him (laughter). In our society, at any rate, which loves him sincerely, which is founded upon love — '

'No, no!' said Witherspoon, 'down with love.'

'Which is founded upon love,' repeated Gregory, grinding his teeth, 'there will be no difficulty about the aims which we shall pursue as a body, or which I should pursue were I chosen as the representative of that body. Superbly careless of the slanders that represent us as assassins and enemies of human society, we shall pursue with moral courage and quiet intellectual pressure, the permanent ideals of brotherhood and simplicity.'

Gregory resumed his seat and passed his hand across his forehead. The silence was sudden and awkward, but the chairman rose like an automaton, and said in a colourless voice —

'Does anyone oppose the election of Comrade Gregory?'

The assembly seemed vague and sub-consciously disappointed, and Comrade Witherspoon moved restlessly on his seat and muttered in his thick beard. By the sheer rush of routine, however, the motion would have been put and carried. But as the chairman was opening his mouth to put it, Syme sprang to his feet and said in a small and quiet voice —

'Yes, Mr Chairman, I oppose.'

The most effective fact in oratory is an unexpected change in the voice. Mr Gabriel Syme evidently understood oratory. Having said these first formal words in a moderated tone and with a brief simplicity, he made his next word ring and volley in the vault as if one of the guns had gone off.

'Comrades!' he cried, in a voice that made every man jump out of his boots, 'have we come here for this? Do we live underground like rats in order to listen to talk like this? This is talk we might listen to while eating buns at a Sunday School treat. Do we line these walls with weapons and bar that door with death lest anyone should come and hear Comrade Gregory saying to us, "Be good, and you will be happy," "Honesty is the best policy," and "Virtue is its own reward"? There was not a word in Comrade Gregory's address to which a curate could not have listened with pleasure (hear, hear). But I am not a curate (loud cheers), and I did not listen to it with pleasure (renewed cheers). The man who is fitted to make a good curate is not fitted to make a resolute, forcible, and efficient Thursday (hear, hear).

'Comrade Gregory has told us, in only too apologetic a tone, that we are not the enemies of society. But I say that we are the enemies of society, and so much the worse for society. We are the enemies of society, for society is the enemy of humanity, its oldest and its most pitiless enemy (hear, hear). Comrade Gregory has told us (apologetically again) that we are not murderers. There I agree. We are not murderers, we are executioners (cheers).'

Ever since Syme had risen Gregory had sat staring at him, his face idiotic with astonishment. Now in the pause his lips of clay parted, and he said, with an automatic and lifeless distinctness —

'You damnable hypocrite!'

Syme looked straight into those frightful eyes with his own pale blue ones, and said with dignity —

'Comrade Gregory accuses me of hypocrisy. He knows as well as I do that I am keeping all my engagements and doing nothing but my duty. I do not mince words. I do not pretend to. I say that Comrade Gregory is unfit to be Thursday for all his amiable qualities. He is unfit to be Thursday because of his amiable qualities. We do not want the Supreme Council of Anarchy infected with a maudlin mercy (hear, hear). This is no time for ceremonial politeness, neither is it a time for ceremonial modesty. I set myself against Comrade Gregory as I would set myself against all the Governments of Europe, because the anarchist who has given himself to anarchy has forgotten modesty as much as he has forgotten pride (cheers). I am not a man at all. I am a cause (renewed cheers). I set myself against Comrade Gregory as impersonally and as calmly as I should choose one pistol rather than another out of that rack upon the wall; and I say that rather than have Gregory and his milk-and-water methods on the Supreme Council, I would offer myself for election — '

His sentence was drowned in a deafening cataract of applause.

The faces, that had grown fiercer and fiercer with approval as his tirade grew more and more uncompromising, were now distorted with grins of anticipation or cloven with delighted cries. At the moment when he announced himself as ready to stand for the post of Thursday, a roar of excitement and assent broke forth, and became uncontrollable, and at the same moment Gregory sprang to his feet, with foam upon his mouth, and shouted against the shouting.

'Stop, you blasted madmen!' he cried, at the top of a voice that tore his throat. 'Stop, you — '

But louder than Gregory's shouting and louder than the roar of the room came the voice of Syme, still speaking in a peal of pitiless thunder —

'I do not go to the Council to rebut that slander that calls us murderers; I go to earn it (loud and prolonged cheering). To the priest who says these men are the enemies of religion, to the judge who says these men are the enemies of law, to the fat parliamentarian who says these men are the enemies of order and public decency, to all these I will reply, "You are false kings, but you are true prophets. I am come to destroy you, and to fulfil your prophecies."'

The heavy clamour gradually died away, but before it had ceased Witherspoon had jumped to his feet, his hair and beard all on end, and had said —

'I move, as an amendment, that Comrade Syme be appointed to the post.'

'Stop all this, I tell you!' cried Gregory, with frantic face and hands. 'Stop it, it is all — '

The voice of the chairman clove his speech with a cold accent.

'Does anyone second this amendment?' he said.

A tall, tired man, with melancholy eyes and an American chin beard, was observed on the back bench to be slowly rising to his feet. Gregory had been screaming for some time past; now there was a change in his accent, more shocking than any scream.

'I end all this!' he said, in a voice as heavy as stone. 'This man cannot be elected. He is a — '

'Yes,' said Syme, quite motionless, 'what is he?'

Gregory's mouth worked twice without sound; then slowly the blood began to crawl back into his dead face.

'He is a man quite inexperienced in our work,' he said, and sat down abruptly.

Before he had done so, the long, lean man with the American beard was again upon his feet, and was repeating in a high American monotone —

'I beg to second the election of Comrade Syme.'

'The amendment will, as usual, be put first,' said Mr Buttons, the chairman, with mechanical rapidity.

'The question is that Comrade Syme — '

Gregory had again sprung to his feet, panting and passionate.

'Comrades,' he cried out, 'I am not a madman.'

'Oh, oh!' said Mr Witherspoon.

'I am not a madman,' reiterated Gregory, with a frightful sincerity which for a moment staggered the room, 'but I give you a counsel which you can call mad if you like. No, I will not call it a counsel, for I can give you no reason for it. I will call it a command. Call it a mad command, but act upon it. Strike, but hear me! Kill me but obey me! Do not elect this man.'

Truth is so terrible, even in fetters, that for a moment Syme's slender and insane victory swayed like a reed. But you could not have guessed it from Syme's bleak blue eyes. He merely began —

'Comrade Gregory commands — '

Then the spell was snapped, and one anarchist called out to Gregory —

'Who are you? You are not Sunday'; and another anarchist added in a heavier voice, 'And you are not Thursday.'

'Comrades,' cried Gregory, in a voice like that of a martyr who in an ecstasy of pain has passed beyond pain, 'it is nothing to me whether you detest me as a tyrant or detest me as a slave. If you will not take my command, accept my degradation. I kneel to you. I throw myself at your feet. I implore you. Do not elect this man.'

'Comrade Gregory,' said the chairman after a painful pause, 'this is really not quite dignified.'

For the first time in the proceedings there was for a few seconds a real silence. Then Gregory fell back in his seat, a pale wreck of a man, and the chairman repeated, like a piece of clock-work suddenly started again —

'The question is that Comrade Syme be elected to the post of Thursday on the General Council.'

The roar rose like the sea, the hands rose like a forest, and three minutes afterwards Mr. Gabriel Syme, of the Secret Police Service, was elected to the post of Thursday on the General Council of the Anarchists of Europe.

Everyone in the room seemed to feel the tug waiting on the river, the sword-stick and the revolver, waiting on the table. The instant the election was ended and irrevocable, and Syme had received the paper proving his election, they all sprang to their feet, and the fiery groups moved and mixed in the room. Syme found himself, somehow or other, face to face with Gregory, who still regarded him with a stare of stunned hatred. They were silent for many minutes.

'You are a devil!' said Gregory at last.

'And you are a gentleman,' said Syme with gravity.

'It was you that entrapped me,' began Gregory, shaking from head to foot, 'entrapped me into — '

'Talk sense,' said Syme shortly. 'Into what sort of devils' parliament have you entrapped me, if it comes to that? You made me swear before I made you. Perhaps we are both doing what we think right. But what we think right is so damned different that there can be nothing between us in the way of concession. There is nothing possible between us but honour and death,' and he pulled the great cloak about his shoulders and picked up the flask from the table.

'The boat is quite ready,' said Mr Buttons, bustling up. 'Be good enough to step this way.'

With a gesture that revealed the shopwalker, he led Syme down a short, iron-bound passage, the still agonized Gregory following feverishly at their heels. At the end of the passage was a door, which Buttons opened sharply, showing a sudden blue and silver picture of the moonlit river, that looked like a scene in a theatre. Close to the opening lay a dark, dwarfish steamlaunch, like a baby dragon with one red eye.

Almost in the act of stepping on board, Gabriel Syme turned to the gaping Gregory.

'You have kept your word,' he said gently, with his face in shadow. 'You are a man of honour, and I thank you. You have kept it even down to a small particular. There was one special thing you promised me at the beginning of the affair, and which you have certainly given me by the end of it.'

'What do you mean?' cried the chaotic Gregory. 'What did I promise you?'

'A very entertaining evening,' said Syme, and he made a military salute with the sword-stick as the steamboat slid away.

The Moderate Murderer

Chapter I
The Man with the Green Umbrella

The new Governor was Lord Tallboys, commonly called Top-hat Tallboys, because of his attachment to that uncanny erection, which he continued to carry balanced on his head as calmly among the palm-trees of Egypt as among the lamp-posts of Westminster. Certainly he carried it calmly enough in lands where few crowns were safe from toppling. The district he had come out to govern may here be described, with diplomatic vagueness, as a strip on the edge of Egypt and called for our convenience Polybia. It is an old story now; but one which many people had reason to remember for many years; and at the time it was an imperial event. One Governor was killed, another Governor was nearly killed; but in this story we are concerned only with one catastrophe; and that was rather a personal and even private catastrophe.

Top-hat Tallboys was a bachelor and yet he brought a family with him. He had a nephew and two nieces of whom one, as it happened, had married the Deputy Governor of Polybia, the man who had been called to rule during the interregnum after the murder of the previous ruler. The other niece was unmarried; her name was Barbara Traill; and she may well be the first figure to cross the stage of this story.

For indeed she was rather a solitary and striking figure, raven dark and rich in colouring with a very beautiful but rather sullen profile, as she crossed the sandy spaces and came under the cover of one long low wall which alone threw a strip of shadow from the sun, which was sloping towards the desert horizon. The wall itself was a quaint example of the patchwork character of that borderland of East and West. It was actually a line of little villas, built for clerks and small officials, and thrown out as by a speculative builder whose speculations spread to the ends of the earth. It was a strip of Streatham amid the ruins of Heliopolis. Such oddities are not unknown, when the oldest countries are turned into the newest colonies. But in this case the young woman, who was not without imagination, was conscious of a quite fantastic contrast.

Each of these dolls' houses had its toy shrubs and plants and its narrow oblong of back garden running down to the common and continuous garden wall; and it was just outside this wall that there ran the rough path, fringed with a few hoary and wrinkled olives. Outside the fringe there faded away into infinity the monstrous solitude of sand. Only there could still be detected on that last line of distance a faint triangular shape; a sort of mathematical symbol whose unnatural simplicity has moved all poets and pilgrims for five thousand years. Anyone seeing it really for the first time, as the girl did, can hardly avoid uttering a cry: 'The Pyramids!'

Almost as she said it a voice said in her ear, not loud but with alarming clearness and very exact articulation: 'The foundations were traced in blood and in blood shall they be traced anew. These things are written for our instruction.'

It has been said that Barbara Traill was not without imagination; it would be truer to say that she had rather too much. But she was quite certain she had not imagined the voice; though she certainly could not imagine where it came from. She appeared to be absolutely alone on the little path which ran along the wall and led to the gardens round the Governorate. Then she remembered the wall itself, and looking sharply over her shoulder, she fancied she saw for one moment a head peering out of the shadow of a sycamore, which was the only tree of any size for some distance; since she had left the last of the low sprawling olives two hundred yards behind. Whatever it was, it had instantly vanished; and somehow she suddenly felt frightened; more frightened at its disappearance than its appearance. She began to hurry along the path to her uncle's residence at a pace that was a little like a run. It was probably through this sudden acceleration of movement that she seemed to become aware, rather abruptly, that a man was marching steadily in front of her along the same track towards the gates of the Governorate.

He was a very large man; and seemed to take up the whole of the narrow path. She had something of the sensation, with which she was already slightly acquainted, of walking behind a camel through the narrow and crooked cracks of the Eastern town. But this man planted his feet as firmly as an elephant; he walked, one might say, even with a certain pomp, as if he were in a procession.

He wore a long frock-coat and his head was surmounted by a tower of scarlet, a very tall red fez, rather taller than the top-hat of Lord Tallboys. The combination of the red Eastern cap and the black Western clothes is common enough among the *Effendi* class in those countries. But somehow it seemed novel and incongruous in this case, for the man was very fair and had a big blonde beard blown about in the breeze. He might have been a model for the idiots who talk of the Nordic type of European; but somehow he did not look like an Englishman. He carried hooked on one finger a rather grotesque green umbrella or parasol, which he twirled idly like a trinket. As he was walking slower and slower and Barbara was walking fast and wanted to walk faster, she could hardly repress an exclamation of impatience and something like a request for room to pass. The large man with the beard immediately faced round and stared at her; then he lifted a monocle and fixed it in his eye and instantly smiled his apologies. She realized that he must be short-sighted and that she had been a mere blur to him a moment before; but there was something else in the change of his face and manner, something that she had seen before, but to which she could not put a name.

He explained, with the most formal courtesy, that he was going to leave a note for an official at the Governorate; and there was really no reason for her to refuse him credence or conversation. They walked a little way together, talking of things in general; and she had not exchanged more than a few sentences before she realized that she was talking to a remarkable man.

We hear much in these days about the dangers of innocence; much that is false and a little that is true. But the argument is almost exclusively applied to sexual innocence. There is a great deal that ought to be said about the dangers of political innocence. That most necessary and most noble virtue of patriotism is very often brought to despair and destruction, quite needlessly and prematurely, by the folly of educating the comfortable classes in a false optimism about the record and security of the Empire. Young people like Barbara Traill have often never heard a word about the other side of the story, as it would be told by Irishmen or Indians or even French Canadians; and it is the fault of their parents and their papers if they often pass abruptly from a stupid Britishism to an equally stupid Bolshevism. The hour of Barbara Traill was come; though she probably did not know it.

'If England keeps her promises,' said the man with the beard, frowning, 'there is still a chance that things may be quiet.'

And Barbara had answered, like a schoolboy:

'England always keeps her promises.'

'The Waba have not noticed it,' he answered with an air of triumph.

The omniscient are often ignorant. They are often especially ignorant of ignorance. The stranger imagined that he was uttering a very crushing repartee; as perhaps he was, to anybody who knew what he meant. But Barbara had never heard of the Waba. The newspapers had seen to that.

'The British Government,' he was saying, 'definitely pledged itself two years ago to a complete scheme of local autonomy. If it is a complete scheme, all will be well. If Lord Tallboys has come out here with an incomplete scheme, a compromise, it will be very far from well. I shall be very sorry for everybody, but especially for my English friends.'

She answered with a young and innocent sneer, 'Oh yes – I suppose you are a great friend of the English.'

'Yes,' he replied calmly. 'A friend: but a candid friend.'

'Oh, I know all about that sort,' she said with hot sincerity. 'I know what they mean by a candid friend. I've always found it meant a nasty, sneering, sneaking, treacherous friend.'

He seemed stung for an instant and answered, 'Your politicians have no need to learn treachery from the Egyptians.' Then he added abruptly: 'Do you know on Lord Jaffray's raid they shot a child? Do you know anything at all? Do you even know how England tacked on Egypt to her Empire?'

'England has a glorious Empire,' said the patriot stoutly.

'England had a glorious Empire,' he said. 'So had Egypt.'

They had come, somewhat symbolically, to the end of their common path and she turned away indignantly to the gate that led into the private gardens of the Governor. As she did so he lifted his green umbrella and pointed with a momentary gesture at the dark line of the desert and the distant Pyramid. The afternoon had already reddened into evening, and the sunset lay in long bands of burning crimson across the purple desolation of that dry inland sea.

'A glorious Empire,' he said. 'An Empire on which the sun never sets. Look . . . the sun is setting in blood.'

She went through the iron gate like the wind and let it clang behind her. As she went up the avenue towards the inner gardens, she lost a little of her impatient movement and began to trail along in the rather moody manner which was more normal to her. The colours and shadows of that quieter scene seemed to close about her; this place was for the present her nearest approach to home; and at the end of the long perspective of gaily coloured garden walks, she could see her sister Olive picking flowers.

The sight soothed her; but she was a little puzzled about why she should need any soothing. She had a deeply disquieting sense of having touched something alien and terrible, something fierce and utterly foreign, as if she had stroked some strange wild beast of the desert. But the gardens about her and the house beyond had already taken on a tone or tint indescribably English, in spite of the recent settlement and the African sky. And Olive was so obviously choosing flowers to put into English vases or to decorate English dinner-tables, with decanters and salted almonds.

But as she drew nearer to that distant figure, it grew more puzzling. The blossoms grasped in her sister's hand looked like mere ragged and random handfuls, torn away as a man lying on the turf would idly tear out grass, when he is abstracted or angry. A few loose stalks lay littered on the path; it seemed as if the heads had been merely broken off as if by a child. Barbara did not know why she took in all these details with a slow and dazed eye, before she looked at the central figure they surrounded. Then Olive looked up and her face was ghastly. It might have been the face of Medea in the garden, gathering the poisonous flowers.

Chapter II
The Boy Who Made a Scene

Barbara Traill was a girl with a good deal of the boy about her. This is very commonly said about modern heroines. None the less, the present heroine would be a very disappointing modern heroine. For, unfortunately, the novelists who call their heroines boyish obviously know nothing whatever about boys. The girl they depict, whether we happen to regard her as a bright young thing or a brazen little idiot, is at any rate in every respect the complete contrary of a boy. She is sublimely candid; she is lightly shallow; she is uniformly cheerful; she is entirely unembarrassed; she is everything that a boy is not. But Barbara really was rather like a boy. That is, she was rather shy, obscurely imaginative, capable of intellectual friendships and at the same time of emotional brooding over them; capable of being morbid and by no means incapable of being secretive. She had that sense of misfit which embarrasses so many boys; the sense of the soul being too big to be seen or confessed, and the tendency to cover the undeveloped emotions with a convention. One effect of it was that she was of the sort troubled by Doubt. It might have been religious doubt; at the moment it was a sort of patriotic doubt; though she would have furiously denied that there was any doubt about the matter. She had been upset by her glimpse of the alleged grievances of Egypt or the alleged crimes of England; and the face of the stranger, the white face with the golden beard and the glaring monocle, had come to stand for the tempter or the spirit that denies. But the face of her sister suddenly banished all such merely political problems. It brought her back with a shock to much more private problems; indeed to much more secret problems; for she had never admitted them to anyone but herself.

The Traills had a tragedy; or rather, perhaps, something that Barbara's brooding spirit had come to regard as the dawn of a tragedy. Her younger brother was still a boy; it might more truly be said that he was still a child. His mind had never come to a normal maturity; and though opinions differed about the nature of the deficiency, she was prone in her black moods to take the darkest view and let it darken the whole house of Tallboys. Thus it happened that she said quickly, at the sight of her sister's strange expression:

'Is anything wrong about Tom?'

Olive started slightly, and then said, rather crossly than otherwise: 'No, not particularly . . . Uncle has put him with a tutor here, and they say he's getting on better . . . Why do you ask? There's nothing special the matter with him.'

'Then I suppose,' said Barbara, 'that there is something special the matter with you.'

'Well,' answered the other, 'isn't there something the matter with all of us?'

With that she turned abruptly and went back towards the house, dropping the flowers she had been making a pretence of gathering; and her sister followed, still deeply disturbed in mind.

As they came near the portico and veranda, she heard the high voice of her uncle Tallboys, who was leaning back in a garden chair and talking to Olive's husband, the Deputy Governor. Tallboys was a lean figure with a large nose and ears standing out from his stalk of a head; like many men of that type he had a prominent Adam's apple and talked in a full-throated gobbling fashion. But what he said was worth listening to; though he had a trick of balancing one clause against another, with alternate gestures of his large loose hands, which some found a trifle irritating. He was also annoyingly deaf. The Deputy Governor, Sir Harry Smythe, was an amusing contrast; a square man with a rather congested face, the colour high under the eyes, which were very light and clear, and two parallel black bars of brow and moustache; which gave him rather a look of Kitchener, until he stood up and looked stunted by the comparison. It also gave him a rather misleading look of bad temper; for he was an affectionate husband and a good-humoured comrade, if a rather stubborn party man. For the rest the conversation was enough to show that he had a military point of view, which is sufficiently common and even commonplace.

'In short,' the Governor was saying, 'I believe the Government scheme is admirably adapted to meet a somewhat difficult situation. Extremists of both types will object to it; but extremists object to everything.'

'Quite so,' answered the other; 'the question isn't so much whether they object as whether they can make themselves objectionable.'

Barbara, with her new and nervous political interests, found herself interrupted in her attempt to listen to the political conversation by the unwelcome discovery that there were other people present. There was a very beautifully dressed young gentleman, with hair like black satin, who seemed to be the local secretary of the Governor; his name was Arthur Meade. There was an old man with a very obvious chestnut wig and a very unobvious, not to say inscrutable yellow face; who was an eminent financier known by the name of Morse. There were various ladies of the official circle who were duly scattered among these gentlemen. It seemed to be the tail end of a sort of afternoon tea; which made all the more odd and suspicious the strange behaviour of the only hostess, in straying to the other garden and tearing up the flowers. Barbara found herself set down beside a pleasant old clergyman with smooth silver hair, and an equally smooth silver voice, who talked to her about the Bible and the Pyramids. She found herself committed to the highly uncomfortable experience of pretending to conduct one conversation while trying to listen to another.

This was the more difficult because the Rev. Ernest Snow, the clergyman in question, had (for all his mildness) not a little gentle pertinacity. She received a confused impression that he held very strong views on the meaning of certain Prophecies in connection with the end of the world and especially with the destiny of the British Empire. He had that habit of suddenly asking questions which is so unkind to the inattentive listener. Thus, she would manage to hear a scrap of the talk between the two rulers of the province; the Governor would say, balancing his sentences with his swaying hands:

'There are two considerations and by this method we meet them both. On the one hand, it is impossible entirely to repudiate our pledge. On the other hand, it is absurd to suppose that the recent atrocious crime does not necessarily modify the nature of that pledge. We can still make sure that our proclamation is a proclamation of a reasonable liberty. We have therefore decided — '

And then, at that particular moment, the poor clergyman would pierce her consciousness with the pathetic question:

'Now how many cubits do you think that would be?'

A little while later she managed to hear Smythe, who talked much less than his companion, say curtly: 'For my part, I don't believe it makes much difference what proclamations you make.

There are rows here when we haven't got sufficient forces; and there are no rows when we have got sufficient forces. That's all.'

'And what is our position at present?' asked the Governor gravely.

'Our position is damned bad, if you ask me,' grumbled the other in a low voice. 'Nothing has been done to train the men; why, I found the rifle practice consisted of a sort of parlour game with a pea-shooter about twice a year. I've put up proper rifle butts beyond the olive walk there now; but there are other things. The munitions are not — '

'But in that case,' came the mild but penetrating voice of Mr. Snow, 'in that case what becomes of the Shunamites?'

Barbara had not the least idea what became of them; but in this case she felt she could treat it as a rhetorical question. She forced herself to listen a little more closely to the views of the venerable mystic; and she only heard one more fragment of the political conversation.

'Shall we really want all these military preparations?' asked Lord Tallboys rather anxiously. 'When do you think we shall want them?'

'I can tell you,' said Smythe with a certain grimness. 'We shall want them when you publish your proclamation of reasonable liberty.'

Lord Tallboys made an abrupt movement in the garden chair, like one breaking up a conference in some irritation; then he made a diversion by lifting a finger and signalling to his secretary Mr. Meade, who slid up to him and after a brief colloquy slid into the house. Released from the strain of State affairs, Barbara fell once more under the spell of the Church and the Prophetical Office. She still had only a confused idea of what the old clergyman was saying, but she began to feel a vague element of poetry in it. At least it was full of things that pleased her fancy like the dark drawings of Blake; prehistoric cities and blind and stony seers and kings who seemed clad in stone like their sepulchres the Pyramids. In a dim way she understood why all that stony and starry wilderness has been the playground of so many cranks. She softened a little towards the clerical crank and even accepted an invitation to his house on the day after the following, to see the documents and the definite proof about the Shunamites. But she was still very vague about what it was supposed to prove.

He thanked her and said gravely: 'If the prophecy is fulfilled now, there will be a grave calamity.'

'I suppose,' she said with a rather dreary flippancy, 'if the prophecy were not fulfilled, it would be an even greater calamity.'

Even as she spoke there was a stir behind some of the garden palms and the pale and slightly gaping face of her brother appeared above the palm-leaves. The next moment she saw just behind him the secretary and the tutor; it was evident that his uncle had sent for him. Tom Traill had the look of being too big for his clothes, which is not uncommon in the otherwise undeveloped; the gloomy good looks which he would otherwise have shared with his branch of the family were marred by his dark straight hair being brushed crooked and his habit of looking out of the corner of his eye at the corner of the carpet. His tutor was a big man of a dull and dusty exterior, apparently having the name of Hume. His broad shoulders were a little bowed like those of a drudge; though he was as yet hardly middle-aged. His plain and rugged face had a rather tired expression, as well it might. Teaching the defective is not always a hilarious parlour game.

Lord Tallboys had a brief and kindly conversation with the tutor. Lord Tallboys asked a few simple questions. Lord Tallboys gave a little lecture on education; still very kindly; but accompanied by the waving of the hands in rotation. On the one hand, the power to work was a necessity of life and could never be wholly evaded. On the other hand, without a reasonable proportion of pleasure and repose even work would suffer. On the one hand . . . it was at this point that the Prophecy was apparently fulfilled and a highly regrettable Calamity occurred at the Governor's tea-party.

For the boy burst out abruptly into a sort of high gurgling crow and began to flap his hands about like the wings of a penguin; repeating over and over again, 'On the one hand. On the other hand. On the one hand. On the other hand. On the one hand. On the other hand . . . Golly!'

'Tom!' cried Olive on a sharp accent of agony and there was a ghastly silence over all the garden.

'Well,' said the tutor in a reasonable undertone, which was as clear as a bell in that stillness, 'you can't expect to have three hands, can you?'

'Three hands?' repeated the boy, and then after a long silence, 'Why, how could you?'

'One would have to be in the middle, like an elephant's trunk,' went on the tutor in the same colourless conversational tone. 'Wouldn't it be nice to have a long nose like an elephant so that you could turn it this way and that and pick up things on the breakfast table, and never let go of your knife and fork?'

'Oh, you're *mad*!' ejaculated Tom with a sort of explosion that had a queer touch of exultation.

'I'm not the only mad person in the world, old boy,' said Mr. Hume.

Barbara stood staring as she listened to this extraordinary conversation in that deadly silence and that highly unsuitable social setting. The most extraordinary thing about it was that the tutor said these crazy and incongruous things with an absolutely blank face.

'Didn't I ever tell you,' he said in the same heavy and indifferent voice, 'about the clever dentist who could pull out his own teeth with his own nose? I'll tell you tomorrow.'

He was still quite dull and serious; but he had done the trick. The boy was distracted from his dislike of his uncle by the absurd image, just as a child in a temper is distracted by a new toy. Tom was now only looking at the tutor and followed him everywhere with his eyes. Perhaps he was not the only member of his family who did so. For the tutor, Barbara thought, was certainly a very odd person.

There was no more political talk that day; but there was not a little political news on the next. On the following morning proclamations were posted everywhere announcing the just, reasonable and even generous compromise which His Majesty's Government was now offering as a fair and final settlement of the serious social problems of Polybia and Eastern Egypt. And on the following evening the news went through the town in one blast, like the wind of the desert, that Viscount Tallboys, Governor of Polybia, had been shot down by the last of the line of olives, at the corner of the wall.

Chapter III
The Man Who Could Not Hate

Immediately after leaving the little garden party, Tom and his tutor parted for the evening; for the former lived at the Governorate, while the latter had a sort of lodge or little bungalow higher up on the hill behind amid the taller trees. The tutor said in private what everybody had indignantly expected him to say in public; and remonstrated with the youth for his display of imitative drama.

'Well, I won't like him,' said Tom warningly, 'I'd like to kill him. His nose sticks out.'

'You can hardly expect it to stick in,' said Mr. Hume mildly. 'I wonder whether there's an old story about the man whose nose stuck in.'

'Is there?' demanded the other in the literal spirit of infancy.

'There may be tomorrow,' replied the tutor and began to climb the steep path to his abode.

It was a lodge built mostly of bamboo and light timber with a gallery running round outside, from which could be seen the whole district spread out like a map; the grey and green squares of the Governorate building and grounds; the path running straight under the low garden wall and parallel to the line of villas; the solitary sycamore breaking the line at one point and further along the closer rank of the olive trees, like a broken cloister, and then another gap and then the corner of the wall, beyond which spread brown slopes of desert, patched here and there with green, where the ground was being turfed as part of some new public works or the Deputy Governor's rapid reforms in military organization. The whole hung under him like a vast coloured cloud in the brief afterglow of the Eastern sunset; then it was rapidly rolled in the purple gloom in which the strong stars stood out over his head and seemed nearer than the things of earth.

He stood for some moments on the gallery looking down on the darkening landscape, his blunt features knotted in a frown of curious reflection. Then he went back into the room where he and his pupil had worked all day, or where he had worked to induce his pupil to consider the idea of working. It was a rather bare room and the few objects in it rather odd and varied. A few bookshelves showed very large and gaily coloured books containing the verses of Mr. Edward Lear and very small and shabby books containing the verses of the principal French and Latin poets. A rack of pipes, all hanging crooked, gave the inevitable touch of the bachelor; a fishing-rod and an old double-barrelled gun leaned dusty and disused in a corner; for it was long ago that this man, in other ways so remote from the sports of his countrymen, had indulged those two hobbies, chiefly because they were unsociable. But what was perhaps most curious of all, the desk and the floor were littered with geometrical diagrams treated in a manner unusual among geometers; for the figures were adorned with absurd faces or capering legs, such as a schoolboy adds to the squares and triangles on the blackboard. But the diagrams were drawn very precisely; as if the draughtsman had an exact eye and excelled in anything depending on that organ.

John Hume sat down at his desk and began to draw more diagrams. A little later he lit a pipe, and began to study those he had drawn; but he did not leave his desk or his preoccupations. So the hours went by amid an unfathomable stillness around that hillside hermitage; until the distant strains of a more or less lively band floated up from below, as a signal that a dance at the Governorate was already in progress. He knew there was a dance that night and took no notice of it; he was not sentimental, but some of the tunes stirred almost mechanical memories. The Tallboys family was a little old-fashioned, even for this rather earlier time. They were old-fashioned in not pretending to be any more democratic than they were. Their dependents were dependents, decently treated; they did not call themselves liberal because they dragged their sycophants into society. It had therefore never crossed the mind of the secretary or the tutor that the dance at the Governorate was any concern of theirs. They were also old-fashioned in the arrangements of the dance itself; and the date must also be allowed for. The new dances had only just begun to pierce; and nobody had dreamed of the wild and varied freedom of our new fashion, by which a person has to walk about all night with the same partner to the same tune. All this sense of distance, material and moral, in the old swaying waltzes moved through his subconsciousness and must be allowed for in estimating what he suddenly looked up and saw.

It seemed for one instant as if, in rising through the mist, the tune had taken outline and colour and burst into his room with the bodily presence of a song; for the blues and greens of her patterned dress were like notes of music and her amazing face came to him like a cry; a cry out of the old youth he had lost or never known. A princess flying out of fairyland would not have seemed more impossible than that girl from that ballroom, though he knew her well enough as the younger sister of his charge; and the ball was a few hundred yards away. Her face was like a pale face burning through a dream and itself as unconscious as a dreamer's; for Barbara Traill was curiously unconscious of that mask of beauty fixed on her brooding boyish soul. She had been counted less attractive than her sisters and her sulks had marked her almost as the ugly duckling. Nothing in the solid man before her told of the shock of realization in his mind. She did not even smile. It was also characteristic of her that she blurted out what she had to say at once, almost as crudely as her brother:

'I'm afraid Tom is very rude to you,' she said. 'I'm very sorry. How do you think he is getting on?'

'I think most people would say,' he said slowly at last, 'that I ought to apologize for his schooling more than you for his family. I'm sorry about his uncle; but it's always a choice of evils. Tallboys is a very distinguished man and can look after his own dignity, but I've got to look after my charge. And I know that is the right way with him. Don't you be worried about him. He's perfectly all right if you understand him; and it's only a matter of making up for lost time.'

She was listening, or not listening, with her characteristic frown of abstraction; she had taken the chair he offered her apparently without noticing it and was staring at the comical diagrams apparently without seeing them. Indeed, it might well have been supposed that she was not listening at all; for the next remark she made appeared to be about a totally different subject.

But she often had a habit of thus showing fragments of her mind; and there was more plan in the jig-saw puzzle than many people understood. Anyhow, she said suddenly, without lifting her eyes from the ludicrous drawing in front of her:

'I met a man going to the Governorate today. A big man with a long fair beard and a single eyeglass. Do you know who he is? He said all sorts of horrid things against England.'

Hume got to his feet with his hands in his pockets and the expression of one about to whistle. He stared at the girl and said softly:

'Hullo! Has he turned up again? I thought there was some trouble coming. Yes, I know him – they call him Dr. Gregory, but I believe he comes from Germany, though he often passes for English. He is a stormy petrel, anyhow; and wherever he goes there's a row. Some say we ought to have used him ourselves; I believe he once offered his talents to our Government. He's a very clever fellow and knows a frightful lot of the facts about these parts.'

'Do you mean,' she said sharply, 'that I'm to believe that man and all the things he said?'

'No,' said Hume. 'I shouldn't believe that man; not even if you believe all the things he said.'

'What do you mean?' she demanded.

'Frankly, I think he is a thoroughly bad egg,' said the tutor. 'He's got a pretty rotten reputation about women; I won't go into details, but he'd have gone to prison twice but for suborning perjury. I only say, whatever you may come to believe, don't believe in him.'

'He dared to say that our Government broke its word,' said Barbara indignantly.

John Hume was silent. Something in his silence affected her like a strain; and she said quite irrationally:

'Oh, for the Lord's sake say something! Do you know he dared to say that somebody on Lord Jaffray's expedition shot a child? I don't mind their saying England's cold and hard and all that; I suppose that's natural prejudice. But can't we stop these wild, wicked lies?'

'Well,' replied Hume rather wearily, 'nobody can say that Jaffray is cold and hard. The excuse for the whole thing was that he was blind drunk.'

'Then I am to take the word of that liar!' she said fiercely.

'He's a liar all right,' said the tutor gloomily. 'And it's a very dangerous condition of the press and the public, when only the liars tell the truth.'

Something of a massive gravity in his grim humour for the moment overpowered her breathless resentment; and she said in a quieter tone: 'Do you believe in this demand for self-government?'

'I'm not very good at believing,' he said. 'I find it very hard to believe that these people cannot live or breathe without votes, when they lived contentedly without them for fifty centuries when they had the whole country in their own hands. A Parliament may be a good thing; a top-hat may be a good thing; your uncle certainly thinks so. We may like or dislike our top-hats. But if a wild Turk tells me he has a natural born right to a top-hat, I can't help answering: "Then why the devil didn't you make one for yourself?"'

'You don't seem to care much for the Nationalists either,' she said.

'Their politicians are often frauds; but they're not alone in that. That's why I find myself forced into an intermediate position; a sort of benevolent neutrality. It simply seems to be a choice between a lot of blasted blackguards and a lot of damned drivelling, doddering idiots. You see I'm a Moderate.'

He laughed a little for the first time; and his plain face was suddenly altered for the better. She was moved to say in a more friendly tone:

'Well, we must prevent a real outbreak. You don't want all our people murdered.'

'Only a little murdered,' he said, still smiling. 'Yes, I think I should like some of them *rather* murdered. Not too much, of course; it's a question of a sense of proportion.'

'Now you're talking nonsense,' she said, 'and people in our position can't stand any nonsense. Harry says we may have to make an example.'

'I know,' he said. 'He made several examples when he was in

command here, before Lord Tallboys came out. It was vigorous – very vigorous. But I think I know what would be better than making an example.'

'And what is that?'

'Setting an example,' said Hume. 'What about our own politicians?'

She said suddenly: 'Well, why don't you do something yourself?'

There was a silence. Then he drew a deep breath. 'Ah, there you have me. I can't do anything myself. I am futile; naturally and inevitably futile. I suffer from a deadly weakness.'

She felt suddenly rather frightened; she had encountered his blank and empty eyes.

'I cannot hate,' he said. 'I cannot be angry.'

Something in his heavy voice seemed full of quality, like the fall of a slab of stone on a sarcophagus; she did not protest, and in her subconsciousness yawned a disappointment. She half realized the depth of her strange reliance and felt like one who had dug in the desert and found a very deep well; and found it dry.

When she went out on to the veranda the steep garden and plantation were grey in the moon; and a certain greyness spread over her own spirit; a mood of fatalism and of dull fear. For the first time she realized something of what strikes a Western eye in Eastern places as the unnaturalness of nature. The squat, limbless growth of the prickly pear was not like the green growths of home, springing on light stalks to lovely flowers like butterflies captured out of air. It was more like the dead blind bubbling of some green squalid slime: a world of plants that were as plain and flat as stones. She hated the hairy surface of some of the squat and swollen trees of that grotesque garden; the tufts here and there irritated her fancy as they might have tickled her face. She felt that even the big folded flowers, if they opened, would have a foul fragrance. She had a latent sense of the savour of faint horror, lying over all as lightly as the faint moonshine. Just as it had chilled her most deeply, she looked up and saw something that was neither plant nor tree, though it hung as still in the stillness; but it had the unique horror of a human face. It was a very white face, but bearded with gold like the Greek statues of gold and ivory; and at the temples were two golden curls, that might have been the horns of Pan.

For the moment that motionless head might indeed have been that of some terminal god of gardens. But the next moment it had found legs and came to life, springing out upon the pathway behind her. She had already gone some distance from the hut and was not far from the illuminated grounds of the Governorate, whence the music swelled louder as she went. Nevertheless, she swung round and faced the other way, looking desperately at the figure she recognized. He had abandoned his red fez and black frock-coat and was clad completely in white, like many tropical trippers; but it gave him in the moonlight something of the silver touch of a spectral harlequin. As he advanced he screwed the shining disk into his eye and it revealed in a flash the faint memory that had always escaped her. His face in repose was calm and classic and might have been the stone mask of Jove rather than Pan. But the monocle gathered up his features into a sneer and seemed to draw his eyes closer together; and she suddenly saw that he was no more a German than an Englishman. And though she had no anti-Semitic prejudice in particular, she felt somehow that in that scene there was something sinister in a fair Jew, as in a white negro.

'We meet under a yet more beautiful sky,' he said; she hardly heard what else he said. Broken phrases from what she had heard recently tumbled through her mind, mere words like 'reputation' and 'prison'; and she stepped back to increase the distance, but moving in the opposite direction from which she had come. Afterwards she hardly remembered what had happened; he had said other things; he had tried to stop her; and an instantaneous impression of crushing and startling strength, like a chimpanzee, surprised her into a cry. Then she stumbled and ran; but not in the direction of the house of her own people.

Mr. John Hume got out of his chair more quickly than was his wont and went to meet someone who stumbled up the stair without.

'My dear child,' he said, and put a hand on her shaking shoulder, giving and receiving a queer thrill like a dull electric shock. Then he went; moving quickly past her. He had seen something in the moonlight beyond and without descending the steps, sprang over the rail to the ground below, standing waist high in the wild and tangled vegetation. There was a screen of large leaves waving to and from between Barbara and the rapid drama that followed; but she saw, as in flashes of moonlight, the tutor dart across the path of the figure in white and heard the shock of blows and saw a kick like a catapult. There was a wheel of silver legs like the arms of the Isle of Man; and then out of the dense depth of the lower thicket a spout of curses in a tongue that was not English, nor wholly German, but which shrieked and chattered in all the Ghettoes of the world. But one strange thing remained even in her disordered memory; that when the figure in white had risen tottering and turned to plunge down the hill, the white face and the furious gesture of malediction were turned, not towards the assailant, but towards the house of the Governor.

The tutor was frowning ponderously as he came again up the veranda steps, as if over some of his geometrical problems. She asked him rather wildly what he had done and he answered in his heavy voice:

'I hope I half killed him. You know I am in favour of half measures.'

She laughed rather hysterically and cried: 'You said you could not be angry.'

Then they suddenly became very stiff and silent and it was with an almost fatuous formality that he escorted her down the slope to the very doors of the dancing-rooms. The sky behind the green pergolas of foliage was a vivid violet or some sort of blue that seemed warmer than any red; and the furry filaments of the great tree-trunks seemed like the quaint sea-beasts of childhood, which could be stroked and which unfolded their fingers. There was something upon them both beyond speech or even silence. He even went so far as to say it was a fine night.

'Yes,' she answered, 'it is a fine night'; and felt instantly as if she had betrayed some secret.

They went through the inner gardens to the gate of the vestibule, which was crowded with people in uniform and evening dress. They parted with the utmost formality; and that night neither of them slept.

Chapter IV
The Detective and the Parson

It was not until the following evening, as already noted, that the news came that the Governor had fallen by a shot from an unknown hand. And Barbara Traill received the news later than most of her friends; because she had departed rather abruptly that morning for a long ramble amid the ruins and plantations of palm, in the immediate neighbourhood. She took a sort of picnic basket with her, but light as was her visible luggage, it would be true to say that she went away to unpack upon a large scale. She went to unfold a sort of invisible *impedimenta* which had accumulated in her memories; especially her memories of the night before. This sort of impetuous solitude was characteristic of her; but it had an immediate effect which was rather fortunate in her case. For the first news was the worst; and when she returned the worst had been much modified. It was first reported that her uncle was dead; then that he was dying; finally that he had only been wounded and had every prospect of recovery. She walked with her empty basket straight into the hubbub of discussion about these things; and soon found that the police operations for the discovery and pursuit of the criminal were already far advanced. The inquiry was in the hands of a hard-headed, hatchet-faced officer named Hayter, the chief of the detective force; who was being actively seconded by young Meade, the secretary of the Governor. But she was rather more surprised to find her friend the tutor in the very centre of the group, being questioned about his own recent experiences.

The next moment she felt a strange sort of surge of subconscious annoyance, as she realized the subject-matter of the questions. The questioners were Meade and Hayter; but it was significant that they had just received the news that Sir Harry Smythe, with characteristic energy, had arrested Dr. Paulus Gregory, the dubious foreigner with the big beard. The tutor was being examined about his own last glimpse of that questionable public character; and Barbara felt a secret fury at finding the affair of the night before turned into a public problem of police. She felt as if she had come down in the morning to find the whole breakfast-table talking about some very intimate dream she had had in the middle of the night. For though she had carried that picture with her as she wandered among the tombs and the green thickets, she had felt it as something as much peculiar to herself as if she had had a vision in the wilderness. The bland, black-haired Mr. Meade was especially insinuating in his curiosity. She told herself, in a highly unreasonable fashion, that she had always hated Arthur Meade.

'I gather,' the secretary was saying, 'that you have excellent reasons of your own for regarding this man as a dangerous character.'

'I regard him as a rotter and I always did,' replied Hume in a rather sulky and reluctant manner. 'I did have a bit of a kick up with him last night, but it didn't make any difference to my views, nor to his either, I should think.'

'It seems to me it might make a considerable difference,' persisted Meade. 'Isn't it true that he went away cursing not only you but especially the Governor? And he went away down the hill towards the place where the Governor was shot. It's true he wasn't shot till a good time after, and nobody seems to have seen his assailant; but he might have hung about in the woods and then crept out along the wall at dusk.'

'Having helped himself to a gun from the gun-tree that grows wild in these woods, I suppose,' said the tutor sardonically. 'I swear he had no gun or pistol on him when I threw him into the prickly pear.'

'You seem to be making the speech for the defence,' said the secretary with a faint sneer. 'But you yourself said he was a pretty doubtful character.'

'I don't think he is in the least a doubtful character,' replied the tutor in his stolid way. 'I haven't the least doubt about him myself. I think he is a loose, lying, vicious braggart and humbug; a selfish, sensual mountebank. So I'm pretty sure that he didn't shoot the Governor, whoever else did.'

Colonel Hayter cocked a shrewd eye at the speaker and spoke himself for the first time.

'Ah – and what do you mean by that exactly?'

'I mean what I say,' answered Hume. 'It's exactly because he's that sort of rascal that he didn't commit that sort of rascality. Agitators of his type never do things themselves; they incite other people; they hold meetings and send round the hat and then vanish, to do the same thing somewhere else. It's a jolly different sort of person that's left to take the risks of playing Brutus or Charlotte Corday. But I confess there are two other little bits of evidence, which I think clear the fellow completely.'

He put two fingers in his waistcoat pocket and slowly and thoughtfully drew out a round flat piece of glass with a broken string.

'I picked this up on the spot where we struggled,' he said. 'It's Gregory's eye-glass; and if you look through it you won't see anything, except the fact that a man who wanted a lens as strong as that could see next to nothing without it. He certainly couldn't see to shoot as far as the end of the wall from the sycamore, which is whereabouts they think the shot must have been fired from.'

'There may be something in that,' said Hayter, 'though the man might have had another glass, of course. You said you had a second reason for thinking him innocent.'

'The second reason,' said Hume, 'is that Sir Harry Smythe has just arrested him.'

'What on earth do you mean?' asked Meade sharply. 'Why, you brought us the message from Sir Harry yourself.'

'I'm afraid I brought it rather imperfectly,' said the other, in a dull voice. 'It's quite true Sir Harry has arrested the doctor, but he'd arrested him before he heard of the attempt on Lord Tallboys. He had just arrested him for holding a seditious meeting five miles away at Pentapolis, at which he made an eloquent speech, which must have reached its beautiful peroration about the time when Tallboys was being shot at, here at the corner of the road.'

'Good Lord!' cried Meade, staring, 'you seem to know a lot about this business.'

The rather sullen tutor lifted his head and looked straight at the secretary with a steady but rather baffling gaze.

'Perhaps I do know a little about it,' he said. 'Anyhow, I'm quite sure Gregory's got a good alibi.'

Barbara had listened to this curious conversation with a confused and rather painful attention; but as the case against Gregory seemed to be crumbling away, a new emotion of her own began to work its way to the surface. She began to realize that she had wanted Gregory to be made responsible, not out of any particular malice towards him, but because it would explain and dispose of the whole incident; and dismiss it from her mind along with another disturbing but hardly conscious thought. Now that the criminal had again become a nameless shadow, he began to haunt her mind with dreadful hints of identity and she had spasms of fear, in which that shadowy figure was suddenly fitted with a face.

As has been already noted, Barbara Traill was a little morbid about her brother and the tragedy of the Traills. She was an omnivorous reader; she had been the sort of schoolgirl who is always found in a corner with a book. And this means generally, under modern conditions, that she read everything she could not understand some time before she read anything that she could. Her mind was a hotch-potch of popular science about heredity and psycho-analysis; and the whole trend of her culture tended to make her pessimistic about everything. People in this mood never have any difficulty in finding reasons for their worst fears. And it was enough for her that, the very morning before her uncle was shot, he had been publicly insulted, and even crazily threatened, by her brother.

That sort of psychological poison works itself deeper and deeper into the brain. Barbara's broodings branched and thickened like a dark forest; and did not stop with the thought that a dull, undeveloped schoolboy was really a maniac and a murderer. The unnatural generalizations of the books she had read pushed her further and further. If her brother, why not her sister? If her sister, why not herself? Her memory exaggerated and distorted the distracted demeanour of her sister in the flower-garden, till she could almost fancy that Olive had torn up the flowers with her teeth. As is always the case in such unbalanced worry, all sorts of accidents took on a terrible significance. Her sister had said, 'Is there not something the matter with all of us?' What could that mean but such a family curse? Hume himself had said he was not the only mad person present. What else could that mean? Even Dr. Gregory had declared after talking to her, that her race was degenerate; did he mean that her family was degenerate? After all, he was a doctor, if he was a wicked one. Each of these hateful coincidences gave her a spiritual shock, so that she almost cried aloud when she thought of it. Meanwhile the rest of her mind went round and round in the iron circle of all such logic from hell. She told herself again and again that she was being morbid; and then told herself again and again that she was only morbid because she was mad. But she was not in the least mad; she was only young; and thousands of young people go through such a phase of nightmare; and nobody knows or helps.

But she was moved with a curious impulse in the search for help; and it was the same impulse that had driven her back across the moonlit glade to the wooden hut upon the hill. She was actually mounting that hill again, when she met John Hume coming down.

She poured out all her domestic terrors and suspicions in a flood, as she had poured out all her patriotic doubts and protests, with a confused confidence which rested on no defined reason or relation and yet was sure of itself.

'So there it is,' she said at the end of her impetuous monologue. 'I began by being quite sure that poor Tom had done it. But by this time I feel as if I might have done it myself.'

'Well, that's logical enough,' agreed Hume. 'It's about as sensible to say that you are guilty as that Tom is. And about as sensible to say the Archbishop of Canterbury is guilty as either of you.'

She attempted to explain her highly scientific guesses about heredity; and their effect was more marked. They succeeded at least in arousing this large and slow person to a sort of animation.

'Now the devil take all doctors and scientists,' he cried, 'or rather the devil take all novelists and newspaper men who talk about what even the doctors don't understand! People abuse the old nurses for frightening children with bogies which pretty soon became a joke. What about the new nurses who let children frighten themselves with all the black bogies they are supposed to take seriously? My dear girl, there is nothing the matter with your brother, any more than with you. He's only what they call a protected neurotic; which is their long-winded way of saying he has an extra skin that the Public School varnish won't stick on, but runs off like water off a duck's back. So much the better for him, as likely as not, in the long run. But even suppose he did remain a little more like a child than the rest of us. Is there anything particularly horrible about a child? Do you shudder when you think of your dog, merely because he's happy and fond of you and yet can't do the forty-eighth proposition of Euclid? Being a dog is not a disease. Being a child is not a disease. Even remaining a child is not a disease; don't you sometimes wish we could all remain children?'

She was of the sort that grapples with notions and suggestions one after another, as they come; and she stood silent; but her mind was busy like a mill. It was he who spoke again, and more lightly.

'It's like what we were saying about making examples. I think the world is much too solemn and severe about punishments; it would be far better if it were ruled like a nursery. People don't want penal servitude and execution and all the rest. What most people want is to have their ears boxed or be sent to bed. What fun it would be to take an unscrupulous millionaire and make him stand in the corner! Such an appropriate penalty.'

When she spoke again there was in her tones something of relief and a renewed curiosity.

'What do you do with Tom?' she asked, 'and what's the meaning of all those funny triangles?'

'I play the fool,' he replied gravely. 'What he wants is to have his attention aroused and fixed; and foolery always does that for children; very obvious foolery. Don't you know how they have always liked such images as the cow jumping over the moon? It's the educational effect of riddles. Well, I have to be the riddle. I have to keep him wondering what I mean or what I shall do next. It means being an ass; but it's the only way.'

'Yes,' she answered slowly, 'there's something awfully rousing about riddles . . . all sorts of riddles. Even that old parson with his riddles out of Revelations makes you feel he has something to live for . . . by the way, I believe we promised to go to tea there this afternoon; I've been in a state to forget everything.'

Even as she spoke she saw her sister Olive coming up the path attired in the unmistakable insignia of one paying calls, and accompanied by her sturdy husband, the Deputy-Governor, who did not often attend these social functions. They all went down the road together and Barbara was vaguely surprised to see ahead of them on the same road, not only the sleek and varnished figure of Mr. Meade the secreatary, but also the more angular outline of Colonel Hayter. The clergyman's invitation had evidently been a comprehensive one.

The Rev. Ernest Snow lived in a very modest manner in one of the little houses that had been erected in a row for the minor officials of the Governorate. It was at the back of this line of villas that the path ran along the garden wall and past the sycamore to the bunch of olives and finally to the corner where the Governor had fallen by the mysterious bullet. That path fringed the open desert and had all the character of a rude beaten path for the desert pilgrims. But walking on the other side, in front of the row of houses, a traveller might well have imagined himself in any London suburb, so regular were the ornamental railings and so identical the porticoes and the small front-garden plots. Nothing but a number distinguished the house of the clergyman; and the entrance to it was so prim and narrow that the group of guests from the Governorate had some difficulty in squeezing through it.

Mr. Snow bowed over Olive's hand with a ceremony that seemed to make his white hair a ghost of eighteenth-century powder, but also with something else that seemed at first a shade more difficult to define. It was something that went with the lowered voice and lifted hand of his profession at certain moments. His face was composed, but it would almost seem deliberately composed; and in spite of his grieved tone his eyes were very bright and steady. Barbara suddenly realized that he was conducting a funeral; and she was not far out.

'I need not tell you, Lady Smythe,' he said in the same soft accents, 'what sympathy we all feel in this terrible hour. If only from a public standpoint, the death of your distinguished uncle — '

Olive Smythe struck in with a rather wild stare.

'But my uncle isn't dead, Mr. Snow. I know they said so at first; but he only got a shot in his leg and he is trying to limp about already.'

A shock of transformation passed over the clergyman's face, too quick for most eyes to follow; it seemed to Barbara that his jaw dropped and when it readjusted itself, it was in a grin of utterly artificial congratulation.

'My dear lady,' he breathed, 'for this relief — '

He looked round a little vacantly at the furniture. Whether the Rev. Ernest Snow had remembered to prepare tea at tea-time, was not yet quite clear; but the preparations he had made seemed to be of a less assuaging sort. The little tables were loaded with large books, many of them lying open; and these were mostly traced with sprawling plans and designs, mostly architectural or generally archaeological, in some cases apparently astronomical or astrological, but giving as a whole a hazy impression of a magician's spells or a library of the black art.

'Apocalyptic studies,' he stammered, 'a hobby of mine. I believed that my calculations . . . These things are written for our instruction.'

And then Barbara felt a final stab of astonishment and alarm. For two facts became instantly and simultaneously vivid to her consciousness. The first was that the Rev. Ernest Snow had been reposing upon the fact of the Governor's death with something very like a solemn satisfaction, and had heard of his recovery with something quite other than relief. And the second was that he spoke with the same voice that had once uttered the same words, out of the shadow of the sycamore, that sounded in her ears like a wild cry for blood.

Chapter V
The Theory of Moderate Murder

Colonel Hayter, the Chief of the Police, was moving towards the inner rooms with a motion that was casual but not accidental. Barbara indeed had rather wondered why such an official had accompanied them on a purely social visit; and she now began to entertain dim and rather incredible possibilities. The clergyman had turned away to one of the bookstands and was turning over the leaves of a volume with feverish excitement; it seemed almost that he was muttering to himself. He was a little like a man looking up a quotation on which he has been challenged.

'I hear you have a very nice garden here, Mr. Snow,' said Hayter. 'I should rather like to look at your garden.'

Snow turned a startled face over his shoulder; he seemed at first unable to detach his mind from his preoccupation; then he said sharply but a little shakily, 'There's nothing to see in my garden; nothing at all. I was just wondering — '

'Do you mind if I have a squint at it?' asked Hayter indifferently; and shouldered his way to the back door. There was something resolute about his action that made the others trail vaguely after him, hardly knowing what they did. Hume, who was just behind the detective, said to him in an undertone:

'What do you expect to find growing in the old man's garden?'

Hayter looked over his shoulder with a grim geniality. 'Only a particular sort of tree you were talking of lately,' he said.

But when they went out into the neat and narrow strip of back garden, the only tree in sight was the sycamore spreading over the desert path; and Barbara remembered with another subconscious thrill that this was the spot from which, as the experts calculated, the bullet had been fired.

Hayter strode across the lawn and was seen stooping over something in the tangle of tropical plants under the wall. When he straightened himself again he was seen to be holding a long and heavy cylindrical object.

'Here is something fallen from the gun-tree you said grew in these parts,' he said grimly. 'Funny that the gun should be found in Mr. Snow's back garden, isn't it? Especially as it's a double-barrelled gun with one barrel discharged.'

Hume was staring at the big gun in the detective's hand; and for the first time his usually stolid face wore an expression of amazement and even consternation.

'Damn it all!' he said softly, 'I forgot about that. What a rotten fool I am!'

Few except Barbara even heard his strange whisper; and nobody could make any sense of it. Suddenly he swung round and addressed the whole company aloud, almost as if they were a public meeting.

'Look here,' he said, 'do you know what this means? This means that poor old Snow, who is probably still fussing over his hieroglyphics, is going to be charged with attempted murder.'

'It's a bit premature,' said Hayter, 'and some would say you were interfering in our job, Mr. Hume. But I owe you something for putting us right about the other fellow, when I admit we were wrong.'

'You were wrong about the other fellow and you are wrong about this fellow,' said Hume, frowning savagely. 'But I happened to be able to offer you evidence in the other case. What evidence can I give now?'

'Why should you have any evidence to give?' asked the other, very much puzzled.

'Well, I have,' said Hume, 'and I jolly well don't want to give it.' He was silent for a moment and then broke out in a sort of fury: 'Blast it all, can't you *see* how silly it is to drag in that silly old man? Don't you see he'd only fallen in love with his own prophecies of disaster, and was a bit put off when they didn't come true after all?'

'There are a good many more suspicious circumstances,' cut in Smythe curtly. 'There's the gun in the garden and the position of the sycamore.'

There was a long silence during which Hume stood with huge hunched shoulders frowning resentfully at his boots. Then he suddenly threw up his head and spoke with a sort of explosive lightness.

'Oh, well then, I must give my evidence,' he said, with a smile that was almost gay: 'I shot the Governor myself.'

There was a stillness as if the place had been full of statues; and for a few seconds nobody moved or spoke. Then Barbara heard her own voice in the silence, crying out:

'Oh, you didn't!'

A moment later the Chief of Police was speaking with a new and much more official voice:

'I should like to know whether you are joking,' he said, 'or whether you really mean to give yourself up for the attempted murder of Lord Tallboys.'

Hume held up one hand in an arresting gesture, almost like a public speaker. He was still smiling slightly, but his manner had grown more grave.

'Pardon me,' he said. 'Pardon me. Let us distinguish. The distinction is of great value to my self-esteem. I did not try to murder the Governor. I tried to shoot him in the leg and I did shoot him in the leg.'

'What is the sense of all this?' cried Smythe with impatience.

'I am sorry to appear punctilious,' said Hume calmly. 'Imputations on my morals I must bear, like other members of the criminal class. But imputations on my marksmanship I cannot tolerate; it is the only sport in which I excel.' He picked up the double-barrelled gun before they could stop him and went on rapidly: 'And may I draw attention to one technical point? This gun has two barrels and one is still undischarged. If any fool had shot Tallboys at that distance and not killed him, don't you think even a fool would have shot again, if that was what he wanted to do? Only, you see, it was not what I wanted to do.'

'You seem to fancy yourself a lot as a marksman,' said the Deputy-Governor rudely.

'Ah, you are sceptical,' replied the tutor in the same airy tone. 'Well, Sir Harry, you have yourself provided the apparatus of demonstration, and it will not take a moment. The targets which we owe to your patriotic efficiency are already set up, I think, on the slope just beyond the end of the wall.' Before anybody could move he had hopped up on to the low garden-wall, just under the shadow of the sycamore. From that perch he could see the long line of the butts stretching along the border of the desert.

'Suppose we say,' he said pleasantly, in the tone of a popular lecturer, 'that I put this bullet about an inch inside the white on the second target.'

The group awoke from its paralysis of surprise; Hayter ran forward and Smythe burst out with: 'Of all the damned tomfoolery — '

His sentence was drowned in the deafening explosion, and amid the echoes of it the tutor dropped serenely from the wall.

'If anybody cares to go and look,' he said, 'I think he will find the demonstration of my innocence – not indeed of shooting the

Governor, but of wanting to shoot him anywhere else but where I did shoot him.'

There was another silence; and then this comedy of unexpected happenings was crowned with another that was still more unexpected; coming from the one person whom everybody had naturally forgotten.

Tom's high crowing voice was suddenly heard above the crowd.

'Who's going to look?' he cried. 'Well, why don't you go and look?'

It was almost as if a tree in the garden had spoken. And indeed the excitement of events had worked upon that vegetating brain till it unfolded rapidly, as do some vegetables at the touch of chemistry. Nor was this all; for the next moment the vegetable had taken on a highly animal energy and hurled itself across the garden. They saw a whirl of lanky limbs against the sky as Tom Traill cleared the garden wall and went plunging away through the sand towards the targets.

'Is this place a lunatic asylum?' cried Sir Harry Smythe, his face still more congested with colour and a baleful light in his eyes, as if a big but buried temper was working its way to the surface.

'Come, Mr. Hume,' said Hayter in a cooler tone, 'everybody regards you as a very sensible man. Do you mean to tell me seriously that you put a bullet in the Governor's leg for no reason at all, not even murder.'

'I did it for an excellent reason,' answered the tutor, still beaming at him in a rather baffling manner. 'I did it because I am a sensible man. In fact, I am a Moderate Murderer.'

'And what the blazes may that be?'

'The philosophy of moderation in murder,' continued the tutor blandly, 'is one to which I have given some little attention. I was saying only the other day that what most people want is to be rather murdered; especially persons in responsible political situations. As it is, the punishments on both sides are far too severe. The merest touch or *soupçon* of murder is all that is required for purposes of reform. The little more and how much it is; the little less and the Governor of Polybia gets clean away, as Browning said.'

'Do you really ask me to believe,' snorted the Chief of Police, 'that you make a practice of potting every public man in the left leg?'

'No, no,' said Hume, with a sort of hasty solemnity. 'The treatment, I assure you, is marked with much more individual attention. Had it been the Chancellor of the Exchequer, I should perhaps have selected a portion of the left ear. In the case of the Prime Minister the tip of the nose would be indicated. But the point is the general principle that *something* should happen to these people, to arouse their dormant faculties by a little personal problem. Now if ever there was a man,' he went on with delicate emphasis, as if it were a scientific demonstration, 'if ever there was a man meant and marked out by nature to be rather murdered, it is Lord Tallboys. Other eminent men, very often, are just murdered; and everyone feels that the situation has been adequately met; that the incident is terminated. One just murders them and thinks no more about it. But Tallboys is a remarkable case; he is my employer and I know him pretty well. He is a good fellow, really. He is a gentleman, he is a patriot; what is more, he is really a liberal and reasonable man. But by being perpetually in office he has let that pompous manner get worse and worse, till it seems to grow on him, like his confounded top-hat. What is needed in such a case? A few days in bed, I decided. A few healthful weeks standing on one leg and meditating on that fine shade of distinction between oneself and God Almighty, which is so easily overlooked.'

'Don't listen to any more of this rubbish,' cried the Deputy-Governor. 'If he says he shot Tallboys, we've got to take him up for it, I suppose. He ought to know.'

'You've hit it at last, Sir Harry,' said Hume heartily, 'I'm arousing a lot of dormant intellects this afternoon.'

'We won't have any more of your joking,' cried Smythe with sudden fury; 'I'm arresting you for attempted murder.'

'I know,' answered the smiling tutor, 'that's the joke.'

At this moment there was another leap and scurry by the sycamore and the boy Tom hurled himself back into the garden, panting aloud:

'It's quite right. It's just where he said.'

For the rest of the interview, and until that strange group had broken up on the lawn, the boy continued to stare at Hume as only a boy can stare at somebody who has done something rather remarkable in a game. But as he and Barbara went back to the Governorate together, the latter indescribably dazed and bewildered, she found her companion curiously convinced of some view of his own, which he was hardly competent to describe. It was not exactly as if he disbelieved Hume or his story. It was rather as if he believed what Hume had not said, rather than what he had.

'It's a riddle,' repeated Tom with stubborn solemnity. 'He's awfully fond of riddles. He says silly things just to make you think. That's what we've got to do. He doesn't like you to give it up.'

'What we've got to do?' repeated Barbara.

'Think what it really means,' said Tom.

There was some truth perhaps in the suggestion that Mr. John Hume was fond of riddles; for he fired off one more of them at the Chief of Police, even as that official took him into custody.

'Well,' he said cheerfully, 'you can only half hang me because I'm only half a murderer. I suppose you have hanged people sometimes?'

'Occasionally, I'm sorry to say,' replied Colonel Hayter.

'Did you ever hang somebody to prevent him being hanged?' asked the tutor with interest.

Chapter VI
The Thing That Really Happened

It is not true that Lord Tallboys wore his top-hat in bed, during his brief indisposition. Nor is it true, as was more moderately alleged, that he sent for it as soon as he could stand upright and wore it as a finishing touch to a costume consisting of a green dressing-gown and red slippers. But it was quite true that he resumed his hat and his high official duties at the earliest possible opportunity; rather to the annoyance, it was said, of his subordinate the Deputy-Governor, who found himself for the second time checked in some of those vigorous military measures which are always more easily effected after the shock of a political outrage. In plain words, the Deputy-Governor was rather sulky.

He had relapsed into a red-faced and irritable silence; and when he broke it his friends rather wished he would relapse into it again. At the mention of the eccentric tutor, whom his department had taken into custody, he exploded with a special impatience and disgust. 'Oh, for God's sake don't tell me about that beastly madman and mountebank!' he cried, almost in the voice of one tortured and unable to tolerate a moment more of human folly. 'Why in the world we are cursed with such filthy fools . . . shooting him in the leg . . . moderate murderer . . . mouldy swine!'

'He's not a mouldy swine,' said Barbara Traill emphatically, as if it were an exact point of natural history. 'I don't believe a word of what you people are saying against him.'

'Do you believe what he is saying against himself?' asked her uncle, looking at her with screwed-up eyes and a quizzical expression. Tallboys was leaning on a crutch; in marked contrast to the sullenness of Sir Harry Smythe, he carried his disablement in a very plucky and pleasant fashion. The necessity of attending to the interrupted rhythm of his legs had apparently arrested the oratorical rotation of his hands. His family felt that they had never liked him so much before. It seemed almost as if there were some truth in the theory of the Moderate Murderer.

On the other hand, Sir Harry Smythe, usually so much more good-humoured with his family, seemed to be in an increasingly bad humour. The dark red of his complexion deepened, until by contrast there was something almost alarming about the light of his pale eyes.

'I tell you of all these measly, meddlesome blighters,' he began.

'And I tell you you know nothing about it,' retorted his sister-in-law. 'He isn't a bit like that; he — '

At this point, for some reason or other, it was Olive who intervened swiftly and quietly; she looked a little wan and worried.

'Don't let's talk about all that now,' she said hastily. 'Harry has got such a lot of things to do . . .'

'I know what I'm going to do,' said Barbara stubbornly. 'I'm going to ask Lord Tallboys, as Governor of this place, if he will let me visit Mr. Hume and see if *I* can find out what it means.'

She had become for some reason violently excited and her own voice sounded strangely in her ears. She had a dizzy impression of Harry Smythe's eyes standing out of his head in apoplectic anger and of Olive's face in the background growing more and more unnaturally pale and staring; and hovering over all, with something approaching to an elvish mockery, the benevolent amusement of her uncle. She felt as if he had let out too much, or that he had gained a new subtlety of perception.

Meanwhile John Hume was sitting in his place of detention, staring at a blank wall with an equally blank face. Accustomed as he was to solitude, he soon found something of a strain in two or three days and nights of the dehumanized solitude of imprisonment. Perhaps the fact most vivid to his immediate senses was being deprived of tobacco. But he had other and what some would call graver grounds of depression. He did not know what sort of sentence he would be likely to get for confessing to an attempt to wound the Governor. But he knew enough of political conditions and legal expedients to know that it would be easy to inflict heavy punishment immediately after the public scandal of the crime. He had lived in that outpost of civilization for the last ten years, till Tallboys had picked him up in Cairo; he remembered the violent reaction after the murder of the previous Governor, the way in which the Deputy-Governor had been able to turn himself into a despot and sweep the country with coercion acts and punitive expeditions, until his impulsive militarism had been a little moderated by the arrival of Tallboys with a compromise from the home Government. Tallboys was still alive and even, in a modified manner, kicking. But he was probably still under doctor's orders and could hardly be judge in his own cause; so that the autocratic Smythe would probably have another chance of riding the whirlwind and directing the storm. But the truth is that there was at the back of the prisoner's mind something that he feared much more than prison. The tiny point of panic, which had begun to worry and eat away even his rocky stolidity of mind and body, was the fear that his fantastic explanation had given his enemies another sort of opportunity. What he really feared was their saying he was mad and putting him under more humane and hygienic treatment.

And indeed, anyone watching his demeanour for the next hour

or so might be excused for entertaining doubts and fancies on the point. He was still staring before him in a rather strange fashion. But he was no longer staring as if he saw nothing; but rather as if he saw something. It seemed to himself that, like a hermit in his cell, he was seeing visions.

'Well, I suppose I am, after all,' he said aloud in a dead and distinct voice. 'Didn't St. Paul say something? . . . Wherefore, O King Agrippa, I was not disobedient to the heavenly vision . . . I have seen that heavenly one coming in at the door like that several times; and rather hoped it was real. But real people can't come through prison doors like that. . . . Once it came so that the room might have been full of trumpets and once with a cry like the wind and there was a fight and I found out that I could hate and that I could love. Two miracles on one night. Don't you think that must have been a dream – that is supposing you weren't a dream and could think anything? But I did rather hope you were real then.'

'Don't!' said Barbara Traill, 'I am real now.'

'Do you mean to tell me in cold blood that I am not mad,' asked Hume, still staring at her, 'and you are here?'

'You are the only sane person I ever knew,' she replied.

'Good Lord,' he said, 'then I've said a good deal just now that ought only to be said in lunatic asylums – or in heavenly visions.'

'You have said so much,' she said in a low voice, 'that I want you to say much more. I mean about the whole of this trouble. After what you have said . . . don't you think I might be allowed to know?'

He frowned at the table and then said rather more abruptly:

'The trouble was that I thought you were the last person who ought to know. You see, there is your family; and you might be brought into it, and one might have to hold one's tongue for the sake of someone you would care about.'

'Well,' she said steadily, 'I *have* been brought into it for the sake of someone I care about.'

She paused a moment and went on: 'The others never did anything for me. They would have let me go raving mad in a respectable flat, and so long as I was finished at a fashionable school, they wouldn't have cared if I'd finished myself with laudanum. I never really talked to anybody before. I don't want to talk to anybody else now.'

He sprang to his feet; something like an earthquake had shaken him at last out of his long petrified incredulity about happiness. He caught her by both hands and words came out of him he had never dreamed were within. And she, who was younger in years, only stared at him with a steady smile and starry eyes, as if she were older and wiser; and at the end only said:

'You will tell me now.'

'You must understand,' he said at last more soberly, 'that what I said was true. I was not making up fairy-tales to shield my long-lost brother from Australia, or any of that business in the novels. I really did put a bullet in your uncle, and I meant to put it there.'

'I know,' she said, 'but for all that I'm sure I don't know everything. I'm sure there is some extraordinary story behind all this.'

'No,' he answered. 'It isn't an extraordinary story; except an extraordinarily ordinary story.'

He paused a moment reflectively and then went on:

'It's really a particularly plain and simple story. I wonder it hasn't happened hundreds of times before. I wonder it hasn't been told in hundreds of stories before. It might so easily happen anywhere, given certain conditions.

'In this case you know some of the conditions. You know that sort of balcony that runs round my bungalow; and how one looks down from it and sees the whole landscape like a map. Well, I was looking down and saw all that flat plan of the place; the row of villas and the wall and path running behind it and the sycamore, and further on the olives and the end of the wall, and so out into the open slopes being laid out with turf and all the rest. But I saw what surprised me; that the rifle-range was already set up. It must have been a rush order; people must have worked all night. And even as I stared, I saw in the distance a dot that was a man standing by the nearest target, as if adding the last touches. Then he made a sort of signal to somebody away on the other side and moved very rapidly away from the place. Tiny as the figure looked, every gesture told me something; he was quite obviously clearing out just before the firing at the target was to begin. And almost at the same moment

I saw something else. Well, I saw one thing, anyhow. I saw why Lady Smythe is worried, and wandered distracted in the garden.'

Barbara stared; but he went on: 'Travelling along the path from the Governorate and towards the sycamore was a familiar shape. It just showed above the long garden wall in sharp outline like a shape in a shadow pantomime. It was the top-hat of Lord Tallboys. Then I remembered that he always went for a constitutional along this path and out on to the slopes beyond; and I felt an overwhelming suspicion that he did not know that the space beyond was already a firing-ground. You know he is very deaf; and I sometimes doubt whether he hears all the things officially told to him; sometimes I fear they are told so that he cannot hear. Anyhow, he had every appearance of marching straight across as usual; and there came over me in a cataract a solid, an overwhelming and a most shocking certainty.

'I will not say much about that now. I will say as little as I can for the rest of my life. But there were things I knew and you probably don't about the politics here and what had led up to that dreadful moment. Enough that I had good reason for my dread. Feeling vaguely that if things were interrupted there might be a fight, I snatched up my own gun and dashed down the slope towards the path, waving wildly and trying to hail or head him off. He didn't see me and couldn't hear me. I pounded along after him along the path, but he had too long a start. By the time I reached the sycamore, I knew I was too late. He was already half-way down the grove of olives and no mortal runner could reach him before he came to the corner.

'I felt a rage against the fool which a man looks against the background of fate. I saw his lean pompous figure with the absurd top-hat riding on top of it; and the large ears standing out from his head . . . the large, useless ears. There was something agonizingly grotesque about that unconscious back outlined against the plains of death. For I was certain that the moment he passed the corner that field would be swept by the fire, which would cut across at right angles to his progress. I could think of only one thing to do and I did it. Hayter thought I was mad when I asked him if he had ever hanged a man to prevent his being hanged. That is the sort of practical joke I played. I shot a man to prevent his being shot.

'I put a bullet in his calf and he dropped, about two yards from the corner. I waited a moment and saw that people were coming out of the last houses to pick him up. I did the only thing I really regret. I had a vague idea the house by the sycamore was empty, so I threw the gun over the wall into the garden, and nearly got that poor old ass of a parson into trouble. Then I went home and waited till they summoned me to give evidence about Gregory.'

He concluded with all his normal composure, but the girl was still staring at him with an abnormal attention and even alarm.

'But what was it all about,' she asked; 'who could have — ?'

'It was one of the best planned things I ever knew,' he said. 'I don't believe I could have proved anything. It would have looked just like an accident.'

'You mean,' she said, 'that it wouldn't have been.'

'As I said before, I don't want to say much about that now, but . . . Look here, you are the sort of person who likes to think about things. I'll just ask you to take two things and think about them; and then you can get used to the idea in your own way.

'The first thing is this. I am a Moderate, as I told you; I really am against all the Extremists. But when journalists and jolly fellows in clubs say that, they generally forget that there really are different sorts of Extremists. In practice they think only of revolutionary Extremists. Believe me, the reactionary Extremists are quite as likely to go to extremes. The history of faction fights will show acts of violence by Patricians as well as Plebeians, by Ghibellines as well as Guelphs, by Orangemen as well as Fenians, by Fascists as well as Bolshevists, by the Ku-Klux-Klan as well as the Black Hand. And when a politician comes from London with a compromise in his pocket – it is not only Nationalists who see their plans frustrated.

'The other point is more personal, especially to you. You once told me you feared for the family sanity, merely because you had bad dreams and brooded over things of your own imagination. Believe me, it's not the imaginative people who become insane. It's not they who are mad, even when they are morbid. They can always be woken up from bad dreams by broader prospects and brighter visions – because they are imaginative. The men who go mad are the unimaginative. The stubborn stoical men who have only room for one idea and take it literally. The sort of man who seems to be silent but stuffed to bursting, congested — '

'I know,' she said hastily; 'you needn't say it, because I believe I understand everything now. Let me tell you two things also; they are shorter; but they have to do with it. My uncle sent me here with an officer who has an order for your release . . . and the Deputy-Governor is going home . . . resignation on the grounds of ill-health.'

'Tallboys is no fool,' said John Hume, 'he has guessed.'

She laughed with a little air of embarrassment.

'I'm afraid he has guessed a good many things,' she said.

What the other things were is no necessary part of this story; but Hume proceeded to talk about them at considerable length during the rest of the interview; until the lady herself was moved to a somewhat belated protest. She said she did not believe that he could really be a Moderate after all.

ORTHODOXY *and* THE EVERLASTING MAN

FOR MOST PEOPLE, these two books represent the pinnacle of Chesterton's achievement as the sane, gentle explainer of Truth to the common man and woman. This may seem like arrogance but it is not: Chesterton genuinely believed himself to be the archetypal common man and would, no doubt, have been pleased with Ezra Pound's remark 'Chesterton *is* the mob'. *Orthodoxy* is confident but never stern; it affirms without condemning and, because it is a kind of spiritual autobiography rather than a moral treatise, it is never condescending. Chesterton is talking to himself as much as to any unknown reader.

Orthodoxy was written long before Chesterton became a Roman Catholic; it is not party propaganda. But so much has been spoken and written about the most important challenges and questions facing humanity, of which religion and, specifically Christianity, is not the least, that the truth can easily be obscured by all the verbosity it has inspired. Some of this, moreover, will undoubtedly have been uttered by the malevolent, the stupid, the ignorant or those who are simply misled. Chesterton wanted to get back to first principles and plain, simple words. As he explains himself:

> Long words go rattling by us like long railway trains. We know they are carrying thousands who are too tired or too indolent to walk and think for themselves. It is a good exercise to try for once in a way to express any opinion one holds in words of one syllable. If you say 'The social utility of the indeterminate sentence is recognized by all criminologists as a part of our sociological evolution towards a more humane and scientific view of punishment,' you can go on talking like that for hours with hardly a movement of the grey matter

inside your skull. But if you begin 'I wish Jones to go to gaol and Brown to say when Jones shall come out,' you will discover, with a thrill of horror, that you are obliged to think. The long words are not the hard words, it is the short words that are hard.[20]

In 1905 Chesterton had published *Heretics*, a volume of essays that had originally appeared in the *Daily News* and exposed the contradictions and confusions in the philosophies of a number of eminent pontificators. A reply came from another journalist, G. S. Street, asking what was the 'orthodoxy' from which he judged these people. 'I will begin to worry about my philosophy,' said Mr. Street, 'when Mr. Chesterton has given us his.' In 1908 Chesterton published his reply in *Orthodoxy*. The title is dull, even when one understands its appropriateness; the book itself sparkles. He may have written as well elsewhere: he never wrote better.

In describing his method, Chesterton uses the image of a young man in a yacht who believes himself to have discovered a new land and finds that he has sailed round the world back to his starting point and discovered England. He raises his flag on a country that is already mapped and discovered. Thus, Chesterton says: 'I did try to found a heresy of my own; and when I had put the last touches to it, I discovered that it was orthodoxy.'

The core of *Orthodoxy* appears in an even earlier altercation that Chesterton enjoyed with the editor of the *Clarion*, Robert Blatchford. Blatchford was a rationalist who had published his philosophy in a volume entitled *God and My Neighbour*, and he then, rashly but bravely, offered the *Clarion* as an arena for debate on the issues he had raised. Chesterton responded, of course, and responded brilliantly. The following passage is particularly apposite to the arguments which he later developed in *Orthodoxy* but with different imagery.

When the secular thinker points out, dismissively, that both the Hebrew and the Christian religions began as local things, that their God was, essentially, a tribal god, Chesterton agrees:

This is an excellent example of one of the things that if I were conducting a detailed campaign I should use as an argument for the validity of Biblical experience. For if there really are some other and higher beings than ourselves, and if they, in some strange way, at some emotional crisis, really revealed themselves to rude poets or dreamers in very simple times, that these rude people should regard the revelation as local, and connect it with the particular hill or river where it happened, seems to me exactly what any reasonable human being would expect. It has a far more credible look than if they had talked cosmic philosophy from the beginning. If they had, I should have suspected 'priestcraft' and forgeries and third-century Gnosticism.

If there be such a thing as God, and He can speak to a child, and if God spoke to a child in the garden, the child would, of course, say that God lived in the garden. I should not think it any less likely to be true for that. If the child said: 'God is everywhere; an impalpable essence pervading and supporting all constituents of the Cosmos alike' – if, I say, the infant addressed me in the above terms, I should think he was much more likely to have been with the governess than with God.

So if Moses had said God was an Infinite Energy, I should be certain he had seen nothing extraordinary. As he said He was a Burning Bush, I think it very likely that he did see something extraordinary. For whatever be the Divine Secret, and whether or no it has (as all peoples have believed) sometimes broken bounds and surged into our world, at least it lies on the side furthest away from pedants and their definitions, and nearest to the silver souls of quiet people, to the beauty of bushes, and the love of one's native place.

Thus, then, in our last instance (out of hundreds that might be taken), we conclude in the same way. When the learned sceptic says: 'The visions of the Old Testament were local and rustic, and grotesque,' we shall answer: 'Of course. They were genuine.'

Thus, as I said at the beginning, I find myself, to start with, face to face with the difficulty that to mention the reasons that I have for believing in Christianity is, in many cases, simply to repeat those arguments which Mr. Blatchford, in some strange way, seems to regard as arguments against it. His book is really rich and powerful. He has undoubtedly set up these four great guns of which I have spoken. I have nothing to say against the size and ammunition of the guns. I only say that by some strange accident of arrangement he has set up those four pieces of artillery pointing at himself. If I were not so humane, I should say: 'Gentlemen of the Secularist Guard, fire first.'

A perfect example of what Chesterton meant when he said that he had learnt Christianity chiefly from its opponents.

The Everlasting Man, one of his longest books, falls into two distinct halves. The first half is a study of what kind of creature man is: not just an animal, different only in degree from all the other animals, but utterly different – and surprisingly different – in *kind*. The second half looks at the person of Jesus Christ and studies how He too is different from the rest of humanity again, crucially, not just in degree but in kind.

Just as the image of the yachtsman introduces Chesterton's thesis in *Orthodoxy*, the image of a boy leaving home and looking back to it captures the essence of his approach in *The Everlasting Man*. Both characters are, we are told, fugitives from stories once pondered but never written. Chesterton explains the significance of the image in the opening pages of his Introduction:

I conceived [the story] as a romance of those vast valleys with sloping sides, like those along which the ancient White Horses of Wessex are scrawled along the flanks of the hills. It concerned some boy whose farm or cottage stood on such a slope, and who went on his travels to find something, such as the effigy and grave of some giant; and when he was far enough from home he looked back and saw that his own farm and kitchen-garden, shining flat on the hill-side like the colours and quarterings of a shield, were but parts of some such gigantic figure, on which he had always lived, but which was too large and too close to be seen. That, I think, is a true picture of the progress of any real independent intelligence today; and that is the point of this book.

The point of this book, in other words, is that the next best thing to being really inside Christendom is to be really outside it.

By which Chesterton means from the point of view of being able to understand it. He was not talking about morality but clarity of vision. He makes this clear a page or two later:

Now the best relation to our spiritual home is to be near enough to love it. But the next best is to be far enough away not to hate it. It is the contention of these pages that while the best judge of Christianity is a Christian, the next best judge would be something more like a Confucian. The worst judge of all is the man now most ready with his judgments; the ill-educated Christian turning gradually into the ill-tempered agnostic, entangled in the end of a feud of which he never understood the beginning.

Clearly, we are very much back in the realms of *Orthodoxy*, especially in the seond half of the book. But we are encountering a slightly different Chesterton: more restrained, more expansive and less mercurial. *Andante* rather than *Allegro con Brio*. The books complement each other both in style and in content. Together they form a paradigm of Chesterton's characteristic strengths and graces as no other books can do.

Orthodoxy

Chapter IV
The Ethics of Elfland

When the business man rebukes the idealism of his office-boy, it is commonly in some such speech as this: 'Ah, yes, when one is young, one has these ideals in the abstract and these castles in the air; but in middle age they all break up like clouds, and one comes down to a belief in practical politics, to using the machinery one has and getting on with the world as it is.' Thus, at least, venerable and philanthropic old men now in their honoured graves used to talk to me when I was a boy. But since then I have grown up and have discovered that these philanthropic old men were telling lies. What has really happened is exactly the opposite of what they said would happen. They said that I should lose my ideals and begin to believe in the methods of practical politicians. Now, I have not lost my ideals in the least; my faith in fundamentals is exactly what it always was. What I have lost is my old childlike faith in practical politics. I am still as much concerned as ever about the Battle of Armageddon; but I am not so much concerned about the General Election. As a babe I leapt up on my mother's knee at the mere mention of it. No; the vision is always solid and reliable. The vision is always a fact. It is the reality that is often a fraud. As much as I ever did, more than I ever did, I believe in Liberalism. But there was a rosy time of innocence when I believed in Liberals.

I take this instance of one of the enduring faiths because, having now to trace the roots of my personal speculation, this may be counted, I think, as the only positive bias. I was brought up a Liberal, and have always believed in democracy, in the elementary liberal doctrine of a self-governing humanity. If any one finds the phrase vague or threadbare, I can only pause for a moment to explain that the principle of democracy, as I mean it, can be stated in two propositions. The first is this: that the things common to all men are more important than the things peculiar to any men. Ordinary things are more valuable than extraordinary things; nay, they are more extraordinary. Man is something more awful than men; something more strange. The sense of the miracle of humanity itself should be always more vivid to us than any marvels of power, intellect, art, or civilization. The mere man on two legs, as such, should be felt as something more heart-breaking than any music and more startling than any caricature. Death is more tragic even than death by starvation. Having a nose is more comic even than having a Norman nose.

This is the first principle of democracy: that the essential things in men are the things they hold in common, not the things they hold separately. And the second principle is merely this: that the political instinct or desire is one of these things which they hold in common. Falling in love is more poetical than dropping into poetry. The democratic contention is that government (helping to rule the tribe) is a thing like falling in love, and not a thing like dropping into poetry. It is not something analogous to playing the church organ, painting on vellum, discovering the North Pole (that insidious habit), looping the loop, being Astronomer Royal, and so on. For these things we do not wish a man to do at all unless he does them well. It is, on the contrary, a thing analogous to writing one's own love-letters or blowing one's own nose. These things we want a man to do for himself, even if he does them badly. I am not here arguing the truth of any of these conceptions; I know that some moderns are asking to have their wives chosen by scientists, and they may soon be asking, for all I know, to have their noses blown by nurses. I merely say that mankind does recognize these universal human functions, and that democracy classes government among them. In short, the democratic faith is this: that the most terribly important things must be left to ordinary men themselves – the mating of the sexes, the rearing of the young, the laws of the state. This is democracy; and in this I have always believed.

But there is one thing that I have never from my youth up been able to understand. I have never been able to understand where people got the idea that democracy was in some way opposed to tradition. It is obvious that tradition is only democracy extended through time. It is trusting to a consensus of common human voices rather than to some isolated or arbitrary record. The man who quotes some German historian against the tradition of the Catholic Church, for instance, is strictly appealing to aristocracy. He is appealing to the superiority of one expert against the awful authority of a mob. It is quite easy to see why a legend is treated, and ought to be treated, more respectfully than a book of history. The legend is generally made by the majority of people in the village, who are sane. The book is generally written by the one man in the village who is mad. Those who urge against tradition that men in the past were ignorant may go and urge it at the Carlton Club, along with the statement that voters in the slums are ignorant. It will not do for us. If we attach great importance to the opinion of ordinary men in great unanimity when we are dealing with daily matters, there is no reason why we should disregard it when we are dealing with history or fable. Tradition may be defined as an extension of the franchise. Tradition means giving votes to the most obscure of all classes, our ancestors. It is the democracy of the dead. Tradition refuses to submit to the small and arrogant oligarchy of those who merely happen to be walking about. All democrats object to men being disqualified by the accident of birth; tradition objects to their being disqualified by the accident of death. Democracy tells us not to neglect a good man's opinion, even if he is our groom; tradition asks us not to neglect a good man's opinion, even if he is our father. I, at any rate, cannot separate the two ideas of democracy and tradition; it seems evident to me that they are the same idea. We will have the dead at our councils. The ancient Greeks voted by stones; these shall vote by tombstones. It is all quite regular and official, for most tombstones, like most ballot papers, are marked with a cross.

I have first to say, therefore, that if I have had a bias, it was always a bias in favour of democracy, and therefore of tradition. Before we come to any theoretic or logical beginnings I am content to allow for that personal equation; I have always been more inclined to believe the ruck of hard-working people than to believe that special and troublesome literary class to which I belong. I prefer even the fancies and prejudices of the people who see life from the inside to the clearest demonstrations of the people who see life from the outside. I would always trust the old wives' fables against the old maids' facts. As long as wit is mother wit it can be as wild as it pleases.

Now, I have to put together a general position, and I pretend to no training in such things. I propose to do it, therefore, by writing down one after another the three or four fundamental ideas which I have found for myself, pretty much in the way that I found them. Then I shall roughly synthesize them, summing up my personal philosophy or natural religion; then I shall describe my startling discovery that the whole thing had been discovered before. It had been discovered by Christianity. But of these profound persuasions which I have to recount in order, the earliest was concerned with this element of popular tradition. And without the foregoing explanation touching tradition and democracy I could hardly make my mental experience clear. As it is, I do not know whether I can make it clear, but I now propose to try.

My first and last philosophy, that which I believe in with unbroken certainty, I learnt in the nursery. I generally learnt it from a nurse; that is, from the solemn and star-appointed priestess at once of democracy and tradition. The things I believed most then, the things I believe most now, are the things called fairy tales. They seem to me to be the entirely reasonable things. They are not fantasies: compared with them other things are fantastic. Compared with them religion and rationalism are both abnormal, though religion is abnormally right and rationalism abnormally wrong. Fairyland is nothing but the sunny country of common sense. It is not earth that judges heaven, but heaven that judges earth; so for me at least it was not earth that criticized elfland, but elfland that criticized the earth. I knew the magic beanstalk before I had tasted beans; I was sure of the Man in the Moon before I was certain of the moon. This was at one with all popular tradition. Modern minor poets are naturalists, and talk about the bush or the brook; but the singers of the old epics and fables were supernaturalists, and talked about the gods of brook and bush. That is what the moderns mean when they say that the ancients did not 'appreciate Nature', because they said that Nature was divine. Old nurses do not tell children about the grass, but about the fairies that dance on the grass; and the old Greeks could not see the trees for the dryads.

But I deal here with what ethic and philosophy come from being fed on fairy tales. If I were describing them in detail I could note many noble and healthy principles that arise from them. There is the chivalrous lesson of 'Jack the Giant Killer'; that giants should be killed because they are gigantic. It is a manly mutiny against pride as such. For the rebel is older than all the kingdoms, and the Jacobin has more tradition than the Jacobite. There is the lesson of 'Cinderella', which is the same as that of the Magnificat – *exaltavit humiles*. There is the great lesson of 'Beauty and the Beast'; that a thing must be loved *before* it is loveable. There is the terrible allegory of the 'Sleeping Beauty', which tells how the human creature was blessed with all birthday gifts, yet cursed with death; and how death also may perhaps be softened to a sleep. But I am not concerned with any of the separate statutes of elfland, but with the whole spirit of its law, which I learnt before I could speak, and shall retain when I cannot write. I am concerned with a certain way of looking at life, which was created in me by the fairy tales, but has since been meekly ratified by the mere facts.

It might be stated this way. There are certain sequences or developments (cases of one thing following another), which are, in the true sense of the word, reasonable. They are, in the true sense of the word, necessary. Such are mathematical and merely logical sequences. We in fairyland (who are the most reasonable of all creatures) admit that reason and that necessity. For instance, if the Ugly Sisters are older than Cinderella, it is (in an iron and awful sense) *necessary* that Cinderella is younger than the Ugly Sisters. There is no getting out of it. Haeckel may talk as much fatalism about that fact as he pleases: it really must be. If Jack is the son of a miller, a miller is the father of Jack. Cold reason decrees it from her awful throne: and we in fairyland submit. If the three brothers all ride horses, there are six animals and eighteen legs involved: that is true rationalism, and fairyland is full of it. But as I put my head over the hedge of the elves and began to take notice of the natural world, I observed an extraordinary thing. I observed that learned men in spectacles were talking of the actual things that happened – dawn and death and so on – as if *they* were rational and inevitable. They talked as if the fact that trees bear fruit were just as *necessary* as the fact that two and one trees make three. But it is not. There is an enormous difference by the test of fairyland; which is the test of the imagination. You cannot *imagine* two and one not making three. But you can easily imagine trees not growing fruit; you can imagine them growing golden candlesticks or tigers hanging on by the tail. These men in spectacles spoke much of a man named Newton, who was hit by an apple, and who discovered a law. But they could not be got to see the distinction between a true law, a law of reason, and the mere fact of apples falling. If the apple hit Newton's nose, Newton's nose hit the apple. That is a true necessity: because we cannot conceive the one occurring without the other. But we can quite well conceive the apple not falling on his nose; we can fancy it flying ardently through the air to hit some other nose, of which it had a more definite dislike. We have always in our fairy tales kept this sharp distinction between the science of mental relations, in which there really are laws, and the science of physical facts, in which there are no laws, but only weird repetitions. We believe in bodily miracles, but not in mental impossibilities. We believe that a beanstalk climbed up to Heaven; but that does not at all confuse our convictions on the philosophical question of how many beans make five.

Here is the peculiar perfection of tone and truth in the nursery tales. The man of science says, 'Cut the stalk, and the apple will fall'; but he says it calmly, as if the one idea really led up to the other. The witch in the fairy tale says, 'Blow the horn, and the ogre's castle will fall'; but she does not say it as if it were something in which the effect obviously arose out of the cause. Doubtless she has given the advice to many champions, and has seen many castles fall, but she does not lose either her wonder or her reason. She does not muddle her head until it imagines a necessary mental connection between a horn and a falling tower. But the scientific men do muddle their heads, until they imagine a necessary mental connection between an apple leaving the tree and an apple reaching the ground. They do really talk as if they had found not only a set of marvellous facts, but a truth connecting those facts. They do talk as if the connection of two strange things physically connected them philosophically. They feel that because one incomprehensible thing constantly follows another incomprehensible thing the two together somehow make up a comprehensible thing. Two black riddles make a white answer.

In fairyland we avoid the word 'law'; but in the land of science they are singularly fond of it. Thus they will call some interesting conjecture about how forgotten folks pronounced the alphabet,

Grimm's Law. But Grimm's Law is far less intellectual than Grimm's Fairy Tales. The tales are, at any rate, certainly tales; while the law is not a law. A law implies that we know the nature of the generalization and enactment; not merely that we have noticed some of the effects. If there is a law that pick-pockets shall go to prison, it implies that there is an imaginable mental connection between the idea of prison and the idea of picking pockets. And we know what the idea is. We can say why we take liberty from a man who takes liberties. But we cannot say why an egg can turn into a chicken any more than we can say why a bear could turn into a fairy prince. As *ideas*, the egg and the chicken are further off each other than the bear and the prince; for no egg in itself suggests a chicken, whereas some princes do suggest bears. Granted, then, that certain transformations do happen, it is essential that we should regard them in the philosophic manner of fairy tales, not in the unphilosophic manner of science and the 'Laws of Nature'. When we are asked why eggs turn to birds or fruits fall in autumn, we must answer exactly as the fairy godmother would answer if Cinderella asked her why mice turned to horses or her clothes fell from her at twelve o'clock. We must answer that it is *magic*. It is not a 'law', for we do not understand its general formula. It is not a necessity, for though we can count on it happening practically, we have no right to say that it must always happen. It is no argument for unalterable law (as Huxley fancied) that we count on the ordinary course of things. We do not count on it; we bet on it. We risk the remote possibility of a miracle as we do that of a poisoned pancake or a world-destroying comet. We leave it out of account, not because it is a miracle, and therefore an impossibility, but because it is a miracle, and therefore an exception. All the terms used in the science books, 'law', 'necessity', 'order', 'tendency', and so on, are really unintellectual, because they assume an inner synthesis which we do not possess. The only words that ever satisfied me as describing Nature are the terms used in the fairy books, 'charm', 'spell', 'enchantment'. They express the arbitrariness of the fact and its mystery. A tree grows fruit because it is a *magic* tree. Water runs downhill because it is bewitched. The sun shines because it is bewitched.

I deny altogether that this is fantastic or even mystical. We may have some mysticism later on; but this fairy-tale language about things is simply rational and agnostic. It is the only way I can express in words my clear and definite perception that one thing is quite distinct from another; that there is no logical connection between flying and laying eggs. It is the man who talks about 'a law' that he has never seen who is the mystic. Nay, the ordinary scientific man is strictly a sentimentalist. He is a sentimentalist in this essential sense, that he is soaked and swept away by mere associations. He has so often seen birds fly and lay eggs that he feels as if there must be some dreamy, tender connection between the two ideas, whereas there is none. A forlorn lover might be unable to dissociate the moon from lost love; so the materialist is unable to dissociate the moon from the tide. In both cases there is no connection, except that one has seen them together. A sentimentalist might shed tears at the smell of apple-blossom, because, by a dark association of his own, it reminded him of his boyhood. So the materialist professor (though he conceals his tears) is yet a sentimentalist, because, by a dark association of his own, apple-blossoms remind him of apples. But the cool rationalist from fairyland does not see why, in the abstract, the apple tree should not grow crimson tulips; it sometimes does in his country.

This elementary wonder, however, is not a mere fancy derived from the fairy tales; on the contrary, all the fire of the fairy tales is derived from this. Just as we all like love tales because there is an instinct of sex, we all like astonishing tales because they touch the nerve of the ancient instinct of astonishment. This is proved by the fact that when we are very young children we do not need fairy tales: we only need tales. Mere life is interesting enough. A child of seven is excited by being told that Tommy opened a door and saw a dragon. But a child of three is excited by being told that Tommy opened a door. Boys like romantic tales; but babies like realistic tales – because they find them romantic. In fact, a baby is about the only person, I should think, to whom a modern realistic novel could be read without boring him. This proves that even nursery tales only echo an almost pre-natal leap of interest and amazement. These tales say that apples were golden only to refresh the forgotten moment when we found that they were green.

They make rivers run with wine only to make us remember, for one wild moment, that they run with water. I have said that this is wholly reasonable and even agnostic. And, indeed, on this point I am all for the higher agnosticism; its better name is Ignorance. We have all read in scientific books, and, indeed, in all romances, the story of the man who has forgotten his name. This man walks about the streets and can see and appreciate everything; only he cannot remember who he is. Well, every man is that man in the story. Every man has forgotten who he is. One may understand the cosmos, but never the ego; the self is more distant than any star. Thou shalt love the Lord thy God; but thou shalt not know thyself. We are all under the same mental calamity; we have all forgotten our names. We have all forgotten what we really are. All that we call common sense and rationality and practicality and positivism only means that for certain dead levels of our life we forget that we have forgotten. All that we call spirit and art and ecstasy only means that for one awful instant we remember that we forget.

But though (like the man without memory in the novel) we walk the streets with a sort of half-witted admiration, still it is admiration. It is admiration in English and not only admiration in Latin. The wonder has a positive element of praise. This is the next milestone to be definitely marked on our road through fairyland. I shall speak in the next chapter about optimists and pessimists in their intellectual aspect, so far as they have one. Here I am only trying to describe the enormous emotions which cannot be described. And the strongest emotion was that life was as precious as it was puzzling. It was an ecstasy because it was an adventure; it was an adventure because it was an opportunity. The goodness of the fairy tale was not affected by the fact that there might be more dragons than princesses; it was good to be in a fairy tale. The test of all happiness is gratitude; and I felt grateful, though I hardly knew to whom. Children are grateful when Santa Claus puts in their stockings gifts of toys or sweets. Could I not be grateful to Santa Claus when he put in my stockings the gift of two miraculous legs? We thank people for birthday presents of cigars and slippers. Can I thank no one for the birthday present of birth?

There were, then, these two first feelings, indefensible and indisputable. The world was a shock, but it was not merely shocking; existence was a surprise, but it was a pleasant surprise. In fact, all my first views were exactly uttered in a riddle that stuck in my brain from boyhood. The question was, 'What did the first frog say?' And the answer was, 'Lord, how you made me jump!' That says succinctly all that I am saying. God made the frog jump; but the frog prefers jumping. But when these things are settled there enters the second great principle of the fairy philosophy.

Any one can see it who will simply read *Grimm's Fairy Tales* or the fine collections of Mr. Andrew Lang. For the pleasure of pedantry I will call it the Doctrine of Conditional Joy. Touchstone talked of much virtue in an 'if'; according to elfin ethics all virtue is in an 'if'. The note of the fairy utterance always is, 'You may live in a palace of gold and sapphire, *if* you do not say the word "cow"'; or 'You may live happily with the King's daughter, *if* you do not show her an onion.' The vision always hangs upon a veto. All the dizzy and colossal things conceded depend upon one small thing withheld. All the wild and whirling things that are let loose depend upon one thing that is forbidden. Mr. W. B. Yeats, in his exquisite and piercing elfin poetry, describes the elves as lawless; they plunge in innocent anarchy on the unbridled horses of the air —

> Ride on the crest of the dishevelled tide,
> And dance upon the mountains like a flame.

It is a dreadful thing to say that Mr. W. B. Yeats does not understand fairyland. But I do say it. He is an ironical Irishman, full of intellectual reactions. He is not stupid enough to understand fairyland. Fairies prefer people of the yokel type like myself; people who gape and grin and do as they are told. Mr. Yeats reads into elfland all the righteous insurrection of his own race. But the lawlessness of Ireland is a Christian lawlessness, founded on reason and justice. The Fenian is rebelling against something he understands only too well; but the true citizen of fairyland is obeying something that he does not understand at all. In the fairy tale an incomprehensible happiness rests upon an incomprehensible condition. A box is opened, and all evils fly out. A word is forgotten, and cities perish. A lamp is lit, and love flies away. A flower is plucked, and human lives are forfeited. An apple is eaten, and the hope of God is gone.

This is the tone of fairy tales, and it is certainly not lawlessness or even liberty, though men under a mean modern tyranny may think it liberty by comparison. People out of Portland Gaol might think Fleet Street free; but closer study will prove that both fairies and journalists are the slaves of duty. Fairy godmothers seem at least as strict as other godmothers. Cinderella received a coach out of Wonderland and a coachman out of nowhere, but she received a command – which might have come out of Brixton – that she should be back by twelve. Also, she had a glass slipper; and it cannot be a coincidence that glass is so common a substance in folk-lore. This princess lives in a glass castle, that princess on a glass hill; this one sees all things in a mirror; they may all live in glass houses if they will not throw stones. For this thin glitter of glass everywhere is the expression of the fact that the happiness is bright but brittle, like the substance most easily smashed by a housemaid or a cat. And this fairy-tale sentiment also sank into me and became my sentiment towards the whole world. I felt and feel that life itself is as bright as the diamond, but as brittle as the window-pane; and when the heavens were compared to the terrible crystal I can remember a shudder. I was afraid that God would drop the cosmos with a crash.

Remember, however, that to be breakable is not the same as to be perishable. Strike a glass, and it will not endure an instant; simply do not strike it, and it will endure a thousand years. Such, it seemed, was the joy of man, either in elfland or on earth; the happiness depended on *not doing something* which you could at any moment do and which, very often, it was not obvious why you should not do. Now, the point here is that to *me* this did not seem unjust. If the miller's third son said to the fairy, 'Explain why I must not stand on my head in the fairy palace,' the other might fairly reply, 'Well, if it comes to that, explain the fairy palace.' If Cinderella says, 'How is it that I must leave the ball at twelve?' her godmother might answer, 'How is it that you are going there till twelve?' If I leave a man in my will ten talking elephants and a hundred winged horses, he cannot complain if the conditions partake of the slight eccentricity of the gift. He must not look a winged horse in the mouth. And it seemed to me that existence was itself so very eccentric a legacy that I could not complain of not understanding the limitations of the vision when I did not understand the vision they limited. The frame was no stranger than the picture. The veto might well be as wild as the vision; it might be as startling as the sun, as elusive as the waters, as fantastic and terrible as the towering trees.

For this reason (we may call it the fairy godmother philosophy) I never could join the young men of my time in feeling what they called the general sentiment of *revolt*. I should have resisted, let us hope, any rules that were evil, and with these and their definition I shall deal in another chapter. But I did not feel disposed to resist any rule merely because it was mysterious. Estates are sometimes held by foolish forms, the breaking of a stick or the payment of a peppercorn: I was willing to hold the huge estate of earth and heaven by any such feudal fantasy. It could not well be wilder than the fact that I was allowed to hold it at all. At this stage I give only one ethical instance to show my meaning. I could never mix in the common murmur of that rising generation against monogamy, because no restriction on sex seemed so odd and unexpected as sex itself. To be allowed, like Endymion, to make love to the moon and then to complain that Jupiter kept his own moons in a harem seemed to me (bred on fairy tales like Endymion's) a vulgar anti-climax. Keeping to one woman is a small price for so much as seeing one woman. To complain that I could only be married once was like complaining that I had only been born once. It was incommensurate with the terrible excitement of which one was talking. It showed, not an exaggerated sensibility to sex, but a curious insensibility to it. A man is a fool who complains that he cannot enter Eden by five gates at once. Polygamy is a lack of the realization of sex; it is like a man plucking five pears in mere absence of mind. The aesthetes touched the last insane limits of language in their eulogy on lovely things. The thistledown made them weep; a burnished beetle brought them to their knees. Yet their emotion never impressed me for an instant, for this reason, that it never occurred to them to pay for their pleasure in any sort of symbolic sacrifice. Men (I felt) might fast forty days for the sake of hearing a blackbird sing. Men might go through fire to find a cowslip. Yet these lovers of beauty could not even keep sober for the blackbird. They would not go through common Christian marriage by way of recompense to the cowslip. Surely one might pay for extraordinary joy in ordinary morals. Oscar Wilde said that sunsets were not valued because we could not pay for sunsets. But Oscar Wilde was wrong; we can pay for sunsets. We can pay for them by not being Oscar Wilde.

Well, I left the fairy tales lying on the floor of the nursery, and I have not found any books so sensible since. I left the nurse guardian of tradition and democracy, and I have not found any modern type so sanely radical or so sanely conservative. But the matter for important comment was here: that when I first went out into the mental atmosphere of the modern world, I found that the modern world was positively opposed on two points to my nurse and to the nursery tales. It has taken me a long time to find out that the modern world is wrong and my nurse was right. The really curious thing was this: that modern thought contradicted this basic creed of my boyhood on its two most essential doctrines. I have explained that the fairy tales founded in me two convictions; first, that this world is a wild and startling place, which might have been quite different, but which is quite delightful; second, that before this wildness and delight one may well be modest and submit to the queerest limitations of so queer a kindness. But I found the whole modern world running like a high tide against both my tendernesses; and the shock of that collision created two sudden and spontaneous sentiments, which I have had ever since and which, crude as they were, have since hardened into convictions.

First, I found the whole modern world talking scientific fatalism; saying that everything is as it must always have been, being unfolded without fault from the beginning. The leaf on the tree is green because it could never have been anything else. Now, the fairy-tale philosopher is glad that the leaf is green precisely because it might have been scarlet. He feels as if it had turned green an instant before he looked at it. He is pleased that snow is white on the strictly reasonable ground that it might have been black. Every colour has in it a bold quality as of choice; the red of garden roses is not only decisive but dramatic, like suddenly spilt blood. He feels that something has been *done*. But the great determinists of the nineteenth century were strongly against this native feeling that something had happened an instant before. In fact, according to them, nothing ever really had happened since the beginning of the world. Nothing ever had happened since existence had happened; and even about the date of that they were not very sure.

The modern world as I found it was solid for modern Calvinism, for the necessity of things being as they are. But when I came to ask them I found they had really no proof of this unavoidable repetition in things except the fact that the things were repeated. Now, the mere repetition made the things to me rather more weird than more rational. It was as if, having seen a curiously shaped nose in the street and dismissed it as an accident, I had then seen six other noses of the same astonishing shape. I should have fancied for a moment that it must be some local secret society. So one elephant having a trunk was odd; but all elephants having trunks looked like a plot. I speak here only of an emotion, and of an emotion at once stubborn and subtle. But the repetition in Nature seemed sometimes to be an excited repetition, like that of an angry schoolmaster saying the same thing over and over again. The grass seemed signalling to me with all its fingers at once; the crowded stars seemed bent upon being understood. The sun would make me see him if he rose a thousand times. The recurrences of the universe rose to the maddening rhythm of an incantation, and I began to see an idea.

All the towering materialism which dominates the modern mind rests ultimately upon one assumption; a false assumption. It is supposed that if a thing goes on repeating itself it is probably dead; a piece of clockwork. People feel that if the universe was personal it would vary; if the sun were alive it would dance. This is a fallacy even in relation to known fact. For the variation in human affairs is generally brought into them, not by life, but by death; by the dying down or breaking off of their strength or desire. A man varies his movements because of some slight element of failure or fatigue. He gets into an omnibus because he is tired of walking; or he walks because he is tired of sitting still. But if his life and joy were so gigantic that he never tired of going to Islington, he might go to Islington as regularly as the Thames goes to Sheerness. The very speed and ecstasy of his life would have the stillness of death.

The sun rises every morning. I do not rise every morning; but the variation is due not to my activity, but to my inaction. Now, to put the matter in a popular phrase, it might be true that the sun rises regularly because he never gets tired of rising. His routine might be due, not to a lifelessness, but to a rush of life. The thing I mean can be seen, for instance, in children, when they find some game or joke that they specially enjoy. A child kicks his legs rhythmically through excess, not absence, of life. Because children have abounding vitality, because they are in spirit fierce and free, therefore they want things repeated and unchanged. They always say, 'Do it again'; and the grown-up person does it again until he is nearly dead. For grown-up people are not strong enough to exult in monotony. But perhaps God is strong enough to exult in monotony. It is possible that God says every morning, 'Do it again' to the sun; and every evening, 'Do it again' to the moon. It may not be automatic necessity that makes all daisies alike; it may be that God makes every daisy separately, but has never got tired of making them. It may be that He has the eternal appetite of infancy; for we have sinned and grown old, and our Father is younger than we. The repetition in Nature may not be a mere recurrence; it may be a theatrical *encore*. Heaven may *encore* the bird who laid an egg. If the human being conceives and brings forth a human child instead of bringing forth a fish, or a bat, or a griffin, the reason may not be that we are fixed in an animal fate without life or purpose. It may be that our little tragedy has touched the gods, that they admire it from their starry galleries, and that at the end of every human drama man is called again and again before the curtain. Repetition may go on for millions of years, by mere choice, and at any instant it may stop. Man may stand on the earth generation after generation, and yet each birth be his positively last appearance.

This was my first conviction; made by the shock of my childish emotions meeting the modern creed in mid-career. I had always vaguely felt facts to be miracles in the sense that they are wonderful: now I began to think them miracles in the stricter sense that they were *wilful*. I mean that they were, or might be, repeated exercises of some will. In short, I had always believed that the world involved magic: now I thought that perhaps it involved a magician. And this pointed a profound emotion always present and sub-conscious; that this world of ours has some purpose; and if there is a purpose, there is a person. I had always felt life first as a story: and if there is a story there is a story-teller.

But modern thought also hit my second human tradition. It went against the fairy feeling about strict limits and conditions. The one thing it loved to talk about was expansion and largeness. Herbert Spencer would have been greatly annoyed if any one had called him an imperialist, and therefore it is highly regrettable that nobody did. But he was an imperialist of the lowest type. He popularized this contemptible notion that the size of the solar system ought to over-awe the spiritual dogma of man. Why should a man surrender his dignity to the solar system any more than to a whale? If mere size proves that man is not the image of God, then a whale may be the image of God; a somewhat formless image; what one might call an impressionist portrait. It is quite futile to argue that man is small compared to the cosmos; for man was always small compared to the nearest tree. But Herbert Spencer, in his headlong imperialism, would insist that we had in some way been conquered and annexed by the astronomical universe. He spoke about men and their ideals exactly as the most insolent Unionist talks about the Irish and their ideals. He turned mankind into a small nationality. And his evil influence can be seen even in the most spirited and honourable of later scientific authors; notably in the early romances of Mr. H. G. Wells. Many moralists have in an exaggerated way represented the earth as wicked. But Mr. Wells and his school made the heavens wicked. We should lift up our eyes to the stars from whence would come our ruin.

But the expansion of which I speak was much more evil than all this. I have remarked that the materialist, like the madman, is in prison; in the prison of one thought. These people seemed to think it singularly inspiring to keep on saying that the prison was very large. The size of this scientific universe gave one no novelty, no relief. The cosmos went on for ever, but not in its wildest constellation could there be anything really interesting; anything, for instance, such as forgiveness or free will. The grandeur or infinity of the secret of its cosmos added nothing to it. It was like telling a prisoner in Reading Gaol that he would be glad to hear that the gaol now covered half the county. The warder would have nothing to show the man except more and more long corridors of stone lit by ghastly lights and empty of all that is human. So these expanders of the universe had nothing to show us except more and more infinite corridors of space lit by ghastly suns and empty of all that is divine.

In fairyland there had been a real law; a law that could be broken, for the definition of a law is something that can be broken. But the machinery of this cosmic prison was something that could not be broken; for we ourselves were only a part of its machinery. We were either unable to do things or we were destined to do them. The idea of the mystical condition quite disappeared; one can neither have the firmness of keeping laws nor the fun of breaking them. The largeness of this universe had nothing of that freshness and airy outbreak which we have praised in the universe of the poet. This modern universe is literally an empire; that is, it is vast, but it is not free. One went into larger and larger windowless rooms, rooms big with Babylonian perspective; but one never found the smallest window or a whisper of outer air.

Their infernal parallels seemed to expand with distance; but for me all good things come to a point, swords for instance. So finding the boast of the big cosmos so unsatisfactory to my emotions I began to argue about it a little; and I soon found that the whole attitude was even shallower than could have been expected. According to these people the cosmos was one thing since it had one unbroken rule. Only (they would say) while it is one thing it is also the only thing there is. Why, then, should one worry particularly to call it large? There is nothing to compare it with. It would be just as sensible to call it small. A man may say, 'I like this vast cosmos, with its throng of stars and its crowd of varied creatures.' But if it comes to that why should not a man say, 'I like this cosy little cosmos, with its decent number of stars and as neat a provision of live stock as I wish to see'? One is as good as the other; they are both mere sentiments. It is mere sentiment to rejoice that the sun is larger than the earth; it is quite as sane a sentiment to rejoice that the sun is no larger than it is. A man chooses to have an emotion about the largeness of the world; why should he not choose to have an emotion about its smallness?

It happened that I had that emotion. When one is fond of anything one addresses it by diminutives, even if it is an elephant or a lifeguardsman. The reason is, that anything, however huge, that can be conceived of as complete, can be conceived of as small. If military moustaches did not suggest a sword or tusks a tail, then the object would be vast because it would be immeasurable. But the moment you can imagine a guardsman you can imagine a small guardsman. The moment you really see an elephant you can call it 'Tiny'. If you can make a statue of a thing you can make a statuette of it. These people professed that the universe was one coherent thing; but they were not fond of the universe. But I was frightfully fond of the universe and wanted to address it by a diminutive. I often did so; and it never seemed to mind. Actually and in truth I did feel that these dim dogmas of vitality were better expressed by calling the world small than by calling it large. For about infinity there was a sort of carelessness which was the reverse of the fierce and pious care which I felt touching the pricelessness and the peril of life. They showed only a dreary waste; but I felt a sort of sacred thrift. For economy is far more romantic than extravagance. To them stars were an unending income of halfpence; but I felt about the golden sun and the silver moon as a schoolboy feels if he has one sovereign and one shilling.

These subconscious convictions are best hit off by the colour and tone of certain tales. Thus I have said that stories of magic alone can express my sense that life is not only a pleasure but a kind of eccentric privilege. I may express this other feeling of cosmic cosiness by allusion to another book always read in boyhood, *Robinson Crusoe*, which I read about this time, and which owes its eternal vivacity to the fact that it celebrates the poetry of limits, nay, even the wild romance of prudence. Crusoe is a man on a small rock with a few comforts just snatched from the sea: the best thing in the book is simply the list of things saved from the wreck. The greatest of poems is an inventory. Every kitchen tool becomes ideal because Crusoe might have dropped it in the sea. It is a good exercise, in empty or ugly hours of the day, to look at anything, the coal-scuttle or the book-case, and think how happy one could be to have brought it out of the sinking ship on to the solitary island. But it is a better exercise still to remember how all things have had this hair-breadth escape: everything has been saved from a wreck. Every man has had one horrible adventure: as a hidden untimely birth he had not been, as infants that never see the light. Men spoke much in my boyhood of restricted or ruined men of genius: and it was common to say that many a man was a Great Might-Have-Been. To me it is a more solid and startling fact that any man in the street is a Great Might-Not-Have-Been.

But I really felt (the fancy may seem foolish) as if all the order and number of things were the romantic remnant of Crusoe's ship. That there are two sexes and one sun, was like the fact that there were two guns and one axe. It was poignantly urgent that none should be lost; but somehow, it was rather fun that none could be added. The trees and the planets seemed like things saved from the wreck: and when I saw the Matterhorn I was glad that it had not been overlooked in the confusion. I felt economical about the stars as if they were sapphires (they are called so in Milton's Eden): I hoarded the hills. For the universe is a single jewel, and while it is a natural cant to talk of a jewel as peerless and priceless, of this jewel it is literally true. This cosmos is indeed without peer and without price: for there cannot be another one.

Thus ends, in unavoidable inadequacy, the attempt to utter the unutterable things. These are my ultimate attitudes towards life; the soils for the seeds of doctrine. These in some dark way I thought before I could write, and felt before I could think: that we may proceed more easily afterwards, I will roughly recapitulate them now. I felt in my bones; first, that this world does not explain itself. It may be a miracle with a supernatural explanation; it may be a conjuring trick, with a natural explanation. But the explanation of the conjuring trick, if it is to satisfy me, will have to be better than the natural explanations I have heard. The thing is magic, true or false. Second, I came to feel as if magic must have a meaning, and meaning must have someone to mean it. There was something personal in the world, as in a work of art; whatever it meant it meant violently. Third, I thought this purpose beautiful in its old design, in spite of its defects, such as dragons. Fourth, that the proper form of thanks to it is some form of humility and restraint: we should thank God for beer and Burgundy by not drinking too much of them. We owed, also, an obedience to whatever made us.

And last, and strangest, there had come into my mind a vague and vast impression that in some way all good was a remnant to be stored and held sacred out of some primordial ruin. Man had saved his good as Crusoe saved his goods: he had saved them from a wreck. All this I felt and the age gave me no encouragement to feel it. And all this time I had not even thought of Christian theology.

Chapter VI
The Paradoxes of Christianity

The real trouble with this world of ours is not that it is an unreasonable world, nor even that it is a reasonable one. The commonest kind of trouble is that it is nearly reasonable, but not quite. Life is not an illogicality; yet it is a trap for logicians. It looks just a little more mathematical and regular than it is; its exactitude is obvious, but its inexactitude is hidden; its wildness lies in wait. I give one coarse instance of what I mean. Suppose some mathematical creature from the moon were to reckon up the human body; he would at once see that the essential thing about it was that it was duplicate. A man is two men, he on the right exactly resembling him on the left. Having noted that there was an arm on the right and one on the left, a leg on the right and one on the left, he might go further and still find on each side the same number of fingers, the same number of toes, twin eyes, twin ears, twin nostrils, and even twin lobes of the brain. At last he would take it as a law; and then, where he found a heart on one side, would deduce that there was another heart on the other. And just then, where he most felt he was right, he would be wrong.

It is this silent swerving from accuracy by an inch that is the uncanny element in everything. It seems a sort of secret treason in the universe. An apple or an orange is round enough to get itself called round, and yet is not round after all. The earth itself is shaped like an orange in order to lure some simple astronomer into calling it a globe. A blade of grass is called after the blade of a sword, because it comes to a point; but it doesn't. Everywhere in things there is this element of the quiet and incalculable. It escapes the rationalists, but it never escapes till the last moment. From the grand curve of our earth it could easily be inferred that every inch of it was thus curved. It would seem rational that as a man has a brain on both sides, he should have a heart on both sides. Yet scientific men are still organizing expeditions to find the North Pole, because they are so fond of flat country. Scientific men are also still organizing expeditions to find a man's heart; and when they try to find it, they generally get on the wrong side of him.

Now, actual insight or inspiration is best tested by whether it guesses these hidden malformations or surprises. If our mathematician from the moon saw the two arms and the two ears, he might deduce the two shoulder-blades and the two halves of the brain. But if he guessed that the man's heart was in the right place, then I should call him something more than a mathematician. Now, this is exactly the claim which I have since come to propound for Christianity. Not merely that it deduces logical truths, but that when it suddenly becomes illogical, it has found, so to speak, an illogical truth. It not only goes right about things, but it goes wrong (if one may say so) exactly where the things go wrong. Its plan suits the secret irregularities, and expects the unexpected. It is simple about the simple truth; but it is stubborn about the subtle truth. It will admit that a man has two hands, it will not admit (though all the Modernists wail to it) the obvious deduction that he has two hearts. It is my only purpose in this chapter to point this out; to show that whenever we feel there is something odd in Christian theology, we shall generally find that there is something odd in the truth.

I have alluded to an unmeaning phrase to the effect that such and such a creed cannot be believed in our age. Of course, anything can be believed in any age. But, oddly enough, there really is a sense in which a creed, if it is believed at all, can be believed more fixedly in a complex society than in a simple one. If a man finds Christianity true in Birmingham, he has actually clearer reasons for faith than if he had found it true in Mercia. For the more complicated seems the coincidence, the less it can be a coincidence. If snowflakes fell in the shape, say, of the heart of Midlothian, it might be an accident. But if snowflakes fell in the exact shape of the maze at

Hampton Court, I think one might call it a miracle. It is exactly as of such a miracle that I have since come to feel of the philosophy of Christianity. The complication of our modern world proves the truth of the creed more perfectly than any of the plain problems of the ages of faith. It was in Notting Hill and Battersea that I began to see that Christianity was true. This is why the faith has that elaboration of doctrines and details which so much distresses those who admire Christianity without believing in it. When once one believes in a creed, one is proud of its complexity, as scientists are proud of the complexity of science. It shows how rich it is in discoveries. If it is right at all, it is a compliment to say that it's elaborately right. A stick might fit a hole or a stone a hollow by accident. But a key and a lock are both complex. And if a key fits a lock, you know it is the right key.

But this involved accuracy of the thing makes it very difficult to do what I now have to do, to describe this accumulation of truth. It is very hard for a man to defend anything of which he is entirely convinced. It is comparatively easy when he is only partially convinced. He is partially convinced because he has found this or that proof of the thing, and he can expound it. But a man is not really convinced of a philosophic theory when he finds that something proves it. He is only really convinced when he finds that everything proves it. And the more converging reasons he finds pointing to this conviction, the more bewildered he is if asked suddenly to sum them up. Thus, if one asked an ordinary intelligent man, on the spur of the moment, 'Why do you prefer civilization to savagery?' he would look wildly round at object after object, and would only be able to answer vaguely, 'Why, there is that bookcase . . . and the coals in the coal-scuttle . . . and pianos . . . and policemen.' The whole case for civilization is that the case for it is complex. It has done so many things. But that very multiplicity of proof which ought to make reply overwhelming makes reply impossible.

There is, therefore, about all complete conviction a kind of huge helplessness. The belief is so big that it takes a long time to get it into action. And this hesitation chiefly arises, oddly enough, from an indifference about where one should begin. All roads lead to Rome; which is one reason why many people never get there. In the case of this defence of the Christian conviction I confess that I would as soon begin the argument with one thing as another; I would begin it with a turnip or a taximeter cab. But if I am to be at all careful about making my meaning clear, it will, I think, be wiser to continue the current arguments of the last chapter, which was concerned to urge the first of these mystical coincidences, or rather ratifications. All I had hitherto heard of Christian theology had alienated me from it. I was a pagan at the age of twelve, and a complete agnostic by the age of sixteen; and I cannot understand anyone passing the age of seventeen without having asked himself so simple a question. I did, indeed, retain a cloudy reverence for a cosmic deity and a great historical interest in the Founder of Christianity. But I certainly regarded Him as a man; though perhaps I thought that, even in that point, He had an advantage over some of His modern critics. I read the scientific and sceptical literature of my time – all of it, at least, that I could find written in English and lying about; and I read nothing else; I mean I read nothing else on any other note of philosophy. The penny dreadfuls which I also read were indeed in a healthy and heroic tradition of Christianity; but I did not know this at the time. I never read a line of Christian apologetics. I read as little as I can of them now. It was Huxley and Herbert Spencer and Bradlaugh who brought me back to orthodox theology. They sowed in my mind my first wild doubts of doubt. Our grandmothers were quite right when they said that Tom Paine and the free-thinkers unsettled the mind. They do. They unsettled mine horribly. The rationalist made me question whether reason was of any use whatever; and when I had finished Herbert Spencer I had got as far as doubting (for the first time) whether evolution had occurred at all. As I laid down the last of Colonel Ingersoll's atheistic lectures the dreadful thought broke across my mind, 'Almost thou persuadest me to be a Christian.' I was in a desperate way.

This odd effect of the great agnostics in arousing doubts deeper than their own might be illustrated in many ways. I take only one. As I read and re-read all the non-Christian or anti-Christian accounts of the faith, from Huxley to Bradlaugh, a slow and awful impression grew gradually but graphically upon my mind – the impression that Christianity must be a most extraordinary thing.

For not only (as I understood) had Christianity the most flaming vices, but it had apparently a mystical talent for combining vices which seemed inconsistent with each other. It was attacked on all sides and for all contradictory reasons. No sooner had one rationalist demonstrated that it was too far to the East than another demonstrated with equal clearness that it was much too far to the West. No sooner had my indignation died down at its angular and aggressive squareness than I was called up again to notice and condemn its enervating and sensual roundness. In case any reader has not come across the thing I mean, I will give such instances as I remember at random of this self-contradiction in the sceptical attack. I give four or five of them; there are fifty more.

Thus, for instance, I was much moved by the eloquent attack on Christianity as a thing of inhuman gloom; for I thought (and still think) sincere pessimism the unpardonable sin. Insincere pessimism is a social accomplishment, rather agreeable than otherwise; and fortunately nearly all pessimism is insincere. But if Christianity was, as these people said, a thing purely pessimistic and opposed to life, then I was quite prepared to blow up St. Paul's Cathedral. But the extraordinary thing is this. They did prove to me in Chapter I (to my complete satisfaction) that Christianity was too pessimistic; and then, in Chapter II, they began to prove to me that it was a great deal too optimistic. One accusation against Christianity was that it prevented men, by morbid tears and terrors, from seeking joy and liberty in the bosom of Nature. But another accusation was that it comforted men with a fictitious providence, and put them in a pink-and-white nursery. One great agnostic asked why Nature was not beautiful enough, and why it was hard to be free. Another great agnostic objected that Christian optimism, 'the garment of make-believe woven by pious hands', hid from us the fact that Nature was ugly, and that it was impossible to be free. One rationalist had hardly done calling Christianity a nightmare before another began to call it a fool's paradise. This puzzled me; the charges seemed inconsistent. Christianity could not at once be the black mask on a white world, and also the white mask on a black world. The state of the Christian could not be at once so comfortable that he was a coward to cling to it, and so uncomfortable that he was a fool to stand it. If it falsified human vision it must falsify it one way or another; it could not wear both green and rose-coloured spectacles. I rolled on my tongue with a terrible joy, as did all young men of that time, the taunts which Swinburne hurled at the dreariness of the creed —

Thou hast conquered, O pale Galilaean, the world has grown gray with Thy breath.

But when I read the same poet's accounts of paganism (as in 'Atalanta'), I gathered that the world was, if possible, more gray before the Galilaean breathed on it than afterwards. The poet maintained, indeed, in the abstract, that life itself was pitch dark. And yet, somehow, Christianity had darkened it. The very man who denounced Christianity for pessimism was himself a pessimist. I thought there must be something wrong. And it did for one wild moment cross my mind that, perhaps, those might not be the very best judges of the relation of religion to happiness who, by their own account, had neither one nor the other.

It must be understood that I did not conclude hastily that the accusations were false or the accusers fools. I simply deduced that Christianity must be something even weirder and wickeder than they made out. A thing might have these two opposite vices; but it must be a rather queer thing if it did. A man might be too fat in one place and too thin in another; but he would be an odd shape. At this point my thoughts were only of the odd shape of the Christian religion; I did not allege any odd shape in the rationalistic mind.

Here is another case of the same kind. I felt that a strong case against Christianity lay in the charge that there is something timid, monkish, and unmanly about all that is called 'Christian', especially in its attitude towards resistance and fighting. The great sceptics of the nineteenth century were largely virile. Bradlaugh in an expansive way, Huxley in a reticent way, were decidedly men. In comparison, it did seem tenable that there was something weak and over patient about Christian counsels. The Gospel paradox about the other cheek, the fact that priests never fought, a hundred things made plausible the accusation that Christianity was an attempt to make a man too like a sheep. I read it and believed it, and if I had read nothing different, I should have gone on believing it.

But I read something very different. I turned the next page in my agnostic manual, and my brain turned upside down. Now I found that I was to hate Christianity not for fighting too little, but for fighting too much. Christianity, it seemed, was the mother of wars. Christianity had deluged the world with blood. I had got thoroughly angry with the Christian, because he never was angry. And now I was told to be angry with him because his anger had been the most huge and horrible thing in human history; because his anger had soaked the earth and smoked to the sun. The very people who reproached Christianity with the meekness and non-resistance of the monasteries were the very people who reproached it also with the violence and valour of the Crusades. It was the fault of poor old Christianity (somehow or other) both that Edward the Confessor did not fight and that Richard Cœur de Lion did. The Quakers (we were told) were the only characteristic Christians; and yet the massacres of Cromwell and Alva were characteristic Christian crimes. What could it all mean? What was this Christianity which always forbade war and always produced wars? What could be the nature of the thing which one could abuse first because it would not fight, and second because it was always fighting? In what world of riddles was born this monstrous murder and this monstrous meekness? The shape of Christianity grew a queerer shape every instant.

I take a third case; the strangest of all, because it involves the one real objection to the faith. The one real objection to the Christian religion is simply that it is one religion. The world is a big place, full of very different kinds of people. Christianity (it may reasonably be said) is one thing confined to one kind of people; it began in Palestine, it has practically stopped with Europe. I was duly impressed with this argument in my youth, and I was much drawn towards the doctrine often preached in Ethical Societies – I mean the doctrine that there is one great unconscious church of all humanity founded on the omnipresence of the human conscience. Creeds, it was said, divided men; but at least morals united them. The soul might seek the strangest and most remote lands and ages and still find essential ethical common sense. It might find Confucius under Eastern trees, and he would be writing 'Thou shalt not steal.' It might decipher the darkest hieroglyphic on the most primeval desert, and the meaning when deciphered would be 'Little boys should tell the truth.' I believed this doctrine of the brotherhood of all men in the possession of a moral sense, and I believe it still – with other things. And I was thoroughly annoyed with Christianity for suggesting (as I supposed) that whole ages and empires of men had utterly escaped this light of justice and reason. But then I found an astonishing thing. I found that the very people who said that mankind was one church from Plato to Emerson were the very people who said that morality had changed altogether, and that what was right in one age was wrong in another. If I asked, say, for an altar, I was told that we needed none, for men our brothers gave us clear oracles and one creed in their universal customs and ideals. But if I mildly pointed out that one of men's universal customs was to have an altar, then my agnostic teachers turned clean round and told me that men had always been in darkness and the superstitions of savages. I found it was their daily taunt against Christianity that it was the light of one people and had left all others to die in the dark. But I also found that it was their special boast for themselves that science and progress were the discovery of one people, and that all other peoples had died in the dark. Their chief insult to Christianity was actually their chief compliment to themselves, and there seemed to be a strange unfairness about all their relative insistence on the two things. When considering some pagan or agnostic, we were to remember that all men had one religion; when considering some mystic or spiritualist, we were only to consider what absurd religions some men had. We could trust the ethics of Epictetus, because ethics had never changed. We must not trust the ethics of Bossuet, because ethics had changed. They changed in two hundred years, but not in two thousand.

This began to be alarming. It looked not so much as if Christianity was bad enough to include any vices, but rather as if any stick was good enough to beat Christianity with. What again could this astonishing thing be like which people were so anxious to contradict, that in doing so they did not mind contradicting themselves? I saw the same thing on every side. I can give no further space to this discussion of it in detail; but lest any one supposes that I have unfairly selected three accidental cases I will run briefly through a few others. Thus, certain sceptics wrote that the great crime of Christianity had been its attack on the family; it had dragged women to the loneliness and contemplation of the cloister, away from their homes and their children. But, then, other sceptics (slightly more advanced) said that the great crime of Christianity was forcing the family and marriage upon us; that it doomed women to the drudgery of their homes and children, and forbade them loneliness and contemplation. The charge was actually reversed. Or, again, certain phrases in the Epistles or the Marriage Service, were said by the anti-Christians to show contempt for woman's intellect. But I found that the anti-Christians themselves had a contempt for woman's intellect; for it was their great sneer at the Church on the Continent that 'only women' went to it. Or again, Christianity was reproached with its naked and hungry habits; with its sackcloth and dried peas. But the next minute Christianity was being reproached with its pomp and its ritualism; its shrines of porphyry and its robes of gold. It was abused for being too plain and for being too coloured. Again Christianity had always been accused of restraining sexuality too much, when Bradlaugh the Malthusian discovered that it restrained it too little. It is often accused in the same breath of prim respectability and of religious extravagance. Between the covers of the same atheistic pamphlet I have found the faith rebuked for its disunion, 'One thinks one thing, and one another', and rebuked also for its union, 'It is difference of opinion that prevents the world from going to the dogs.' In the same conversation a free-thinker, a friend of mine, blamed Christianity for despising Jews, and then despised it himself for being Jewish.

I wished to be quite fair then, and I wish to be quite fair now; and I did not conclude that the attack on Christianity was all wrong. I only concluded that if Christianity was wrong, it was very wrong indeed. Such hostile horrors might be combined in one thing, but that thing must be very strange and solitary. There are men who are misers, and also spendthrifts; but they are rare. There are men sensual and also ascetic; but they are rare. But if this mass of mad contradictions really existed, quakerish and bloodthirsty, too gorgeous and too thread-bare, austere, yet pandering preposterously to the lust of the eye, the enemy of women and their foolish refuge, a solemn pessimist and a silly optimist, if this evil existed, then there was in this evil something quite supreme and unique. For I found in my rationalist teachers no explanation of such exceptional corruption. Christianity (theoretically speaking) was in their eyes only one of the ordinary myths and errors of mortals. *They* gave me no key to this twisted and unnatural badness. Such a paradox of evil rose to the stature of the supernatural. It was, indeed, almost as supernatural as the infallibility of the Pope. An historic institution, which never went right, is really quite as much of a miracle as an institution that cannot go wrong. The only explanation which immediately occurred to my mind was that Christianity did not come from heaven, but from hell. Really, if Jesus of Nazareth was not Christ, He must have been Antichrist.

And then in a quiet hour a strange thought struck me like a still thunderbolt. There had suddenly come into my mind another explanation. Suppose we heard an unknown man spoken of by many men. Suppose we were puzzled to hear that some men said he was too tall and some too short; some objected to his fatness, some lamented his leanness; some thought him too dark, and some too fair. One explanation (as has been already admitted) would be that he might be an odd shape. But there is another explanation. He might be the right shape. Outrageously tall men might feel him to be short. Very short men might feel him to be tall. Old bucks who are growing stout might consider him insufficiently filled out; old beaux who were growing thin might feel that he expanded beyond the narrow lines of elegance. Perhaps Swedes (who have pale hair like tow) called him a dark man, while negroes considered him distinctly blonde. Perhaps (in short) this extraordinary thing is really the ordinary thing; at least the normal thing, the centre. Perhaps, after all, it is Christianity that is sane and all its critics that are mad – in various ways. I tested this idea by asking myself whether there was about any of the accusers anything morbid that might explain the accusation. I was startled to find that this key fitted a lock. For instance, it was certainly odd that the modern world charged Christianity at once with bodily austerity and with artistic pomp. But then it was also odd, very odd, that the modern world itself combined extreme bodily luxury with an extreme absence of artistic pomp. The modern man thought Becket's robes too rich and his meals too poor. But then the modern man was really exceptional in history; no man before ever ate such elaborate dinners in such ugly clothes. The modern man found the church too simple exactly where modern life is too complex; he found the church too gorgeous exactly where modern life is too dingy. The man who disliked the plain fasts and feasts was mad on *entrées*. The man who disliked vestments wore a pair of preposterous trousers. And surely if there was any insanity involved in the matter at all it was in the trousers, not in the simply falling robe. If there was any insanity at all, it was in the extravagant *entrées*, not in the bread and wine.

I went over all the cases, and I found the key fitted so far. The fact that Swinburne was irritated at the unhappiness of Christians and yet more irritated at their happiness was easily explained. It was no longer a complication of diseases in Christianity, but a complication of diseases in Swinburne. The restraints of Christians saddened him simply because he was more hedonist than a healthy man should be. The faith of Christians angered him because he was more pessimist than a healthy man should be. In the same way the Malthusians by instinct attacked Christianity; not because there is anything especially anti-Malthusian about Christianity, but because there is something a little anti-human about Malthusianism.

Nevertheless it could not, I felt, be quite true that Christianity was merely sensible and stood in the middle. There was really an element in it of emphasis and even frenzy which had justified the secularists in their superficial criticism. It might be wise, I began more and more to think that it was wise, but it was not merely worldly wise; it was not merely temperate and respectable. Its fierce crusaders and meek saints might balance each other; still, the crusaders were very fierce and the saints were very meek, meek beyond all decency. Now, it was just at this point of the speculation that I remembered my thoughts about the martyr and the suicide. In that matter there had been this combination between two almost insane positions which yet somehow amounted to sanity. This was just such another contradiction; and this I had already found to be true. This was exactly one of the paradoxes in which sceptics found the creed wrong; and in this I had found it right. Madly as Christians might love the martyr or hate the suicide, they never felt these passions more madly than I had felt them long before I dreamed of Christianity. Then the most difficult and interesting part of the mental process opened, and I began to trace this idea darkly through all the enormous thoughts of our theology. The idea was that which I had outlined touching the optimist and the pessimist; that we want not an amalgam or compromise, but both things at the top of their energy; love and wrath both burning. Here I shall only trace it in relation to ethics. But I need not remind the reader that the idea of this combination is indeed central in orthodox theology. For orthodox theology has specially insisted that Christ was not a being apart from God and man, like an elf, nor yet a being half human and half not, like a centaur, but both things at once and both things thoroughly, very man and very God. Now let me trace this notion as I found it.

All sane men can see that sanity is some kind of equilibrium; that one may be mad and eat too much, or mad and eat too little. Some moderns have indeed appeared with vague versions of progress and evolution which seeks to destroy the μέσον or balance of Aristotle. They seem to suggest that we are meant to starve progressively, or to go on eating larger and larger breakfasts every morning for ever. But the great truism of the μέσον remains for all thinking men, and these people have not upset any balance except their own. But granted that we have all to keep a balance, the real interest comes in with the question of how that balance can be kept. That was the problem which Paganism tried to solve: that was the problem which I think Christianity solved and solved in a very strange way.

Paganism declared that virtue was in a balance; Christianity declared it was in a conflict: the collision of two passions apparently opposite. Of course they were not really inconsistent; but they were such that it was hard to hold simultaneously. Let us follow for a moment the clue of the martyr and the suicide; and take the case of courage. No quality has ever so much addled the brains and tangled the definitions of merely rational sages. Courage is almost a contradiction in terms. It means a strong desire to live taking the form of a readiness to die. 'He that will lose his life, the same shall save it', is not a piece of mysticism for saints and heroes. It is a piece of everyday advice for sailors or mountaineers. It might be printed in an Alpine guide or a drill book. This paradox is the whole principle of courage; even of quite earthly or quite brutal courage. A man cut off by the sea may save his life if he will risk it on the precipice. He can only get away from death by continually stepping within an inch of it. A soldier surrounded by enemies, if he is to cut his way out, needs to combine a strong desire for living with a strange carelessness about dying. He must not merely cling to life, for then he will be a coward, and will not escape. He must not merely wait for death, for then he will be a suicide, and will not escape. He must seek his life in a spirit of furious indifference to it; he must desire life like water and yet drink death like wine. No philosopher, I fancy, has ever expressed this romantic riddle with adequate lucidity, and I certainly have not done so. But Christianity has done more: it has marked the limits of it in the awful graves of the suicide and the hero, showing the distance between him who dies for the sake of living and him who dies for the sake of dying. And it has held up ever since above the European lances the banner of the mystery of chivalry: the Christian courage, which is a disdain of death; not the Chinese courage, which is a disdain of life.

And now I began to find that this duplex passion was the Christian key to ethics everywhere. Everywhere the creed made a moderation out of the still crash of two impetuous emotions. Take, for instance, the matter of modesty, of the balance between mere pride and mere prostration. The average pagan, like the average agnostic, would merely say that he was content with himself, but not insolently self-satisfied, that there were many better and many worse, that his deserts were limited, but he would see that he got them. In short, he would walk with his head in the air; but not necessarily with his nose in the air. This is a manly and rational position, but it is open to the objection we noted against the compromise between optimism and pessimism – the 'resignation' of Matthew Arnold. Being a mixture of two things, it is a dilution of two things; neither is present in its full strength or contributes its full colour. This proper pride does not lift the heart like the tongue of trumpets; you cannot go clad in crimson and gold for this. On the other hand, this mild rationalist modesty does not cleanse the soul with fire and make it clear like crystal; it does not (like a strict and searching humility) make a man as a little child, who can sit at the feet of the grass. It does not make him look up and see marvels; for Alice must grow small if she is to be Alice in Wonderland. Thus it loses both the poetry of being proud and the poetry of being humble. Christianity sought by this same strange expedient to save both of them.

It separated the two ideas and then exaggerated them both. In one way Man was to be haughtier than he had ever been before; in another way he was to be humbler than he had ever been before. In so far as I am Man I am the chief of creatures. In so far as I am *a* man I am the chief of sinners. All humility that had meant pessimism, that had meant man taking a vague or mean view of his whole destiny – all that was to go. We were to hear no more the wail of Ecclesiastes that humanity had no pre-eminence over the brute, or the awful cry of Homer that Man was only the saddest of all the beasts of the field. Man was a statue of God walking about the garden. Man had pre-eminence over all the brutes; Man was only sad because he was not a beast, but a broken god. The Greek had spoken of men creeping on the earth, as if clinging to it. Now Man was to tread on the earth as if to subdue it. Christianity thus held a thought of the dignity of Man that could only be expressed in crowns rayed like the sun and fans of peacock plumage. Yet at the same time it could hold a thought about the abject smallness of Man that could only be expressed in fasting and fantastic submission, in the grey ashes of St. Dominic and the white snows of St. Bernard. When one came to think of *one's self*, there was vista and void enough for any amount of bleak abnegation and bitter truth. There the realistic gentleman could let himself go – as long as he let himself go at himself. There was an open playground for the happy pessimist. Let him say anything against himself short of blaspheming the original aim of his being; let him call himself a fool and even a damned fool (though that is Calvinistic); but he must not say that fools are not worth saving. He must not say that a man, *quâ* man, can be valueless. Here again, in short, Christianity got over the difficulty of combining furious opposites, by keeping them both, and keeping them both furious. The Church was positive on both points. One can hardly think too little of one's self. One can hardly think too much of one's soul.

Take another case: the complicated question of charity, which some highly uncharitable idealists seem to think quite easy. Charity is a paradox, like modesty and courage. Stated baldly, charity certainly means one of two things – pardoning unpardonable acts, or loving unlovable people. But if we ask ourselves (as we did in the case of pride) what a sensible pagan would feel about such a subject, we shall probably be beginning at the bottom of it. A sensible pagan would say that there were some people one could forgive, and some one couldn't: a slave who stole wine could be laughed at; a slave who betrayed his benefactor could be killed, and cursed even after he was killed. In so far as the act was pardonable, the man was pardonable. That again is rational, and even refreshing; but it is a dilution. It leaves no place for a pure horror of injustice, such as that which is a great beauty in the innocent. And it leaves no place for a mere tenderness for men as men, such as is the whole fascination of the charitable. Christianity came in here as before. It came in startlingly with a sword, and clove one thing from another. It divided the crime from the criminal. The criminal we must forgive unto seventy times seven. The crime we must not forgive at all. It was not enough that slaves who stole wine inspired partly anger and partly kindness. We must be much more angry with theft than before, and yet much kinder to thieves than before. There was room for wrath and love to run wild. And the more I considered Christianity, the more I found that while it had established a rule and order, the chief aim of that order was to give room for good things to run wild.

Mental and emotional liberty are not so simple as they look. Really they require almost as careful a balance of laws and conditions as do social and political liberty. The ordinary aesthetic anarchist who sets out to feel everything freely gets knotted at last in a paradox that prevents him feeling at all. He breaks away from home limits to follow poetry. But in ceasing to feel home limits he has ceased to feel the *Odyssey*. He is free from national prejudices and outside patriotism. But being outside patriotism he is outside *Henry V*. Such a literary man is simply outside all literature: he is more of a prisoner than any bigot. For if there is a wall between you and the world, it makes little difference whether you describe yourself as locked in or as locked out. What we want is not the universality that is outside all normal sentiments; we want the universality that is inside all normal sentiments. It is all the difference between being free from them, as a man is free from a prison, and being free of them as a man is free of a city. I am free from Windsor Castle (that is, I am not forcibly detained there), but I am by no means free of that building. How can man be approximately free of fine emotions, able to swing them in a clear space without breakage or wrong? *This* was the achievement of this Christian paradox of the parallel passions. Granted the primary dogma of the war between divine and diabolic, the revolt and ruin of the world, their optimism and pessimism, as pure poetry, could be loosened like cataracts.

St. Francis, in praising all good, could be a more shouting optimist than Walt Whitman. St. Jerome, in denouncing all evil, could paint the world blacker than Schopenhauer. Both passions were free because both were kept in their place. The optimist could pour out all the praise he liked on the gay music of the march, the golden trumpets, and the purple banners going into battle. But he must not call the fight needless. The pessimist might draw as darkly as he chose the sickening marches or the sanguine wounds. But he must not call the fight hopeless. So it was with all the other moral problems, with pride, with protest, and with compassion. By defining its main doctrine, the Church not only kept seemingly inconsistent things side by side, but, what was more, allowed them to break out in a sort of artistic violence otherwise possible only to anarchists. Meekness grew more dramatic than madness. Historic Christianity rose into a high and strange *coup de théatre* of morality – things that are to virtue what the crimes of Nero are to vice. The spirits of indignation and of charity took terrible and attractive forms, ranging from that monkish fierceness that scourged like a dog the first and greatest of the Plantagenets, to the sublime pity of St. Catherine, who, in the official shambles, kissed the bloody head of the criminal. Poetry could be acted as well as composed. This heroic and monumental manner in ethics has entirely vanished with supernatural religion. They, being humble, could parade themselves; but we are too proud to be prominent. Our ethical teachers write reasonably for prison reform; but we are not likely to see Mr. Cadbury, or any eminent philanthropist, go into Reading Gaol and embrace the strangled corpse before it is cast into the quicklime. Our ethical teachers write mildly against the power of millionaires; but we are not likely to see Mr. Rockefeller, or any modern tyrant, publicly whipped in Westminster Abbey.

Thus, the double charges of the secularists, though throwing nothing but darkness and confusion on themselves, throw a real light on the faith. It *is* true that the historic Church has at once emphasized celibacy and emphasized the family; has at once (if one may put it so) been fiercely for having children and fiercely for not having children. It has kept them side by side like two strong colours, red and white, like the red and white upon the shield of St. George. It has always had a healthy hatred of pink. It hates that combination of two colours which is the feeble expedient of the philosophers. It hates that evolution of black into white which is tantamount to a dirty grey. In fact, the whole theory of the Church on virginity might be symbolized in the statement that white is a colour: not merely the absence of a colour. All that I am urging here can be expressed by saying that Christianity sought in most of these cases to keep two colours co-existent but pure. It is not a mixture like russet or purple; it is rather like a shot silk, for a shot silk is always at right angles, and is in the pattern of the cross.

So it is also, of course, with the contradictory charges of the anti-Christians about submission and slaughter. It *is* true that the Church told some men to fight and others not to fight; and it *is* true that those who fought were like thunderbolts and those who did not fight were like statues. All this simply means that the Church preferred to use its Supermen and to use its Tolstoyans. There must be *some* good in the life of battle, for so many good men have enjoyed being soldiers. There must be *some* good in the idea of non-resistance, for so many good men seem to enjoy being Quakers. All that the Church did (so far as that goes) was to prevent either of these good things from ousting the other. They existed side by side. The Tolstoyans, having all the scruples of monks, simply became monks. The Quakers became a club instead of becoming a sect. Monks said all that Tolstoy says; they poured out lucid lamentations about the cruelty of battles and the vanity of revenge. But the Tolstoyans are not quite right enough to run the whole world; and in the ages of faith they were not allowed to run it. The world did not lose the last charge of Sir James Douglas or the banner of Joan the Maid. And sometimes this pure gentleness and this pure fierceness met and justified their juncture; the paradox of all the prophets was fulfilled, and, in the soul of St. Louis, the lion lay down with the lamb. But remember that this text is too lightly interpreted. It is constantly assured, especially in our Tolstoyan tendencies, that when the lion lies down with the lamb the lion becomes lamb-like. But that is brutal annexation and imperialism on the part of the lamb. That is simply the lamb absorbing the lion instead of the lion eating the lamb. The real problem is – can the lion lie down with the lamb and still retain his royal ferocity? *That* is the problem the Church attempted; *that* is the miracle she achieved.

This is what I have called guessing the hidden eccentricities of life. This is knowing that a man's heart is to the left and not in the middle. This is knowing not only that the earth is round, but knowing exactly where it is flat. Christian doctrine detected the oddities of life. It not only discovered the law, but it foresaw the exceptions. Those underrate Christianity who say that it discovered mercy; anyone might discover mercy. In fact everyone did. But to discover a plan for being merciful and also severe – *that* was to anticipate a strange need of human nature. For no one wants to be forgiven for a big sin as if it were a little one. Anyone might say that we should be neither quite miserable nor quite happy. But to find out how far one *may* be quite miserable without making it impossible to be quite happy – that was a discovery in psychology. Anyone might say, 'Neither swagger nor grovel'; and it would have been a limit. But to say, 'Here you can swagger and there you can grovel' – that was an emancipation.

This was the big fact about Christian ethics; the discovery of the new balance. Paganism had been like a pillar of marble, upright because proportioned with symmetry. Christianity was like a huge and ragged and romantic rock, which, though it sways on its pedestal at a touch, yet, because its exaggerated excrescences exactly balance each other, is enthroned there for a thousand years. In a Gothic cathedral the columns were all different, but they were all necessary. Every support seemed an accidental and fantastic support; every buttress was a flying buttress. So in Christendom apparent accidents balanced. Becket wore a hair shirt under his gold and crimson, and there is much to be said for the combination; for Becket got the benefit of the hair shirt while the people in the street got the benefit of the crimson and gold. It is at least better than the manner of the modern millionaire, who has the black and the drab outwardly for others, and the gold next his heart. But the balance was not always in one man's body as in Becket's; the balance was often distributed over the whole body of Christendom. Because a man prayed and fasted on the northern snows, flowers could be flung at his festival in the southern cities; and because fanatics drank water on the sands of Syria, men could still drink cider in the orchards of England. This is what makes Christendom at once so much more perplexing and so much more interesting than the Pagan empire; just as Amiens Cathedral is not better but more interesting than the Parthenon. If anyone wants a modern proof of all this, let him consider the curious fact that, under Christianity, Europe (while remaining a unity) has broken up into individual nations. Patriotism is a perfect example of this deliberate balancing of one emphasis against another emphasis. The instinct of the Pagan empire would have said, 'You shall all be Roman citizens, and grow alike; let the German grow less slow and reverent; the Frenchman less experimental and swift.' But the instinct of Christian Europe says, 'Let the German remain slow and reverent, that the Frenchman may the more safely be swift and experimental. We will make an equipoise out of these excesses. The absurdity called Germany shall correct the insanity called France.'

Last and most important, it is exactly this which explains what is so inexplicable to all the modern critics of the history of Christianity. I mean the monstrous wars about small points of theology, the earthquakes of emotion about a gesture or a word. It was only a matter of an inch; but an inch is everything when you are balancing. The Church could not afford to swerve a hair's breadth on some things if she was to continue her great and daring experiment of the irregular equilibrium. Once let one idea become less powerful and some other idea would become too powerful. It was no flock of sheep the Christian shepherd was leading, but a herd of bulls and tigers, of terrible ideals and devouring doctrines, each one of them strong enough to turn to a false religion and lay waste the world. Remember that the Church went in specifically for dangerous ideas; she was a lion tamer. The idea of birth through a Holy Spirit, of the death of a divine being, of the forgiveness of sins, or the fulfilment of prophecies, are ideas which, anyone can see, need but a touch to turn them into something blasphemous or ferocious. The smallest link was let drop by the artificers of the Mediterranean, and the lion of ancestral pessimism burst his chain in the forgotten forests of the north. Of these theological equalizations I have to speak afterwards. Here it is enough to notice that if some small mistake were made in doctrine, huge blunders might be made in human happiness. A sentence phrased wrong about the nature of symbolism would have broken all the best statues in Europe. A slip in the definitions might stop all the dances; might wither all the Christmas trees or break all the Easter eggs. Doctrines had to be defined within strict limits, even in order that man might enjoy general human liberties. The Church had to be careful, if only that the world might be careless.

This is the thrilling romance of Orthodoxy. People have fallen into a foolish habit of speaking of orthodoxy as something heavy, humdrum, and safe. There never was anything so perilous or so exciting as orthodoxy. It was sanity: and to be sane is more dramatic than to be mad. It was the equilibrium of a man behind madly rushing horses, seeming to stoop this way and to sway that, yet in every attitude having the grace of statuary and the accuracy of arithmetic. The Church in its early days went fierce and fast with any warhorse; yet it is utterly unhistoric to say that she merely went mad along one idea, like a vulgar fanaticism. She swerved to left and right, so as exactly to avoid enormous obstacles. She left on one hand the huge bulk of Arianism, buttressed by all the worldly powers to make Christianity too worldly. The next instant she was swerving to avoid an orientalism, which would have made it too unworldly. The orthodox Church never took the tame course or accepted the conventions; the orthodox Church was never respectable. It would have been easier to have accepted the earthly power of the Arians. It would have been easy, in the Calvinistic seventeenth century, to fall into the bottomless pit of predestination. It is easy to be a madman: it is easy to be a heretic. It is always easy to let the age have its head; the difficult thing is to keep one's own. It is always easy to be a Modernist; as it is easy to be a snob. To have fallen into any of those open traps of error and exaggeration which fashion after fashion and sect after sect set along the historic path of Christendom – that would indeed have been simple. It is always simple to fall; there are an infinity of angles at which one falls, only one at which one stands. To have fallen into any one of the fads from Gnosticism to Christian Science would indeed have been obvious and tame. But to have avoided them all has been one whirling adventure; and in my vision the heavenly chariot flies thundering through the ages, the dull heresies sprawling and prostrate, the wild truth reeling but erect.

The Everlasting Man

Man and Mythologies

What are here called the Gods might almost alternatively be called the Day-Dreams. To compare them to dreams is not to deny that dreams can come true. To compare them to travellers' tales is not to deny that they may be true tales, or at least truthful tales. In truth they are the sort of tales the traveller tells to himself. All this mythological business belongs to the poetical part of men. It seems strangely forgotten nowadays that a myth is a work of imagination and therefore a work of art. It needs a poet to make it. It needs a poet to criticize it. There are more poets than non-poets in the world, as is proved by the popular origin of such legends. But for some reason I have never heard explained, it is only the minority of unpoetical people who are allowed to write critical studies of these popular poems. We do not submit a sonnet to a mathematician or a song to a calculating boy; but we do indulge the equally fantastic idea that folklore can be treated as a science. Unless these things are appreciated artistically they are not appreciated at all. When the professor is told by the barbarian that once there was nothing except a great feathered serpent, unless the learned man feels a thrill and a half temptation to wish it were true, he is no judge of such things at all. When he is assured, on the best Red Indian authority, that a primitive hero carried the sun and moon and stars in a box, unless he claps his hands and almost kicks his legs as a child would at such a charming fancy, he knows nothing about the matter. This test is not nonsensical; primitive children and barbaric children do laugh and kick like other children; and we must have a certain simplicity to repicture the childhood of the world. When Hiawatha was told by his nurse that a warrior threw his grandmother up to the moon, he laughed like any English child told by his nurse that a cow jumped over the moon. The child sees the joke as well as most men, and better than some scientific men. But the ultimate test even of the fantastic is the appropriateness of the inappropriate. And the test must appear merely arbitrary because it is merely artistic. If any student tells me that the infant Hiawatha only laughed out of respect for the tribal custom of sacrificing the aged to economical housekeeping, I say he did not. If any scholar tells me that the cow jumped over the moon only because a heifer was sacrificed to Diana, I answer that it did not. It happened because it is obviously the right thing for a cow to jump over the moon. Mythology is a lost art, one of the few arts that really are lost; but it is an art. The horned moon and the horned mooncalf make a harmonious and almost a quiet pattern. And throwing your grandmother into the sky is not good behaviour; but it is perfectly good taste.

Thus scientists seldom understand, as artists understand, that one branch of the beautiful is the ugly. They seldom allow for the legitimate liberty of the grotesque. And they will dismiss a savage myth as merely coarse and clumsy and an evidence of degradation, because it has not all the beauty of the herald Mercury new lighted on a heaven-kissing hill; when it really has the beauty of the Mock Turtle or the Mad Hatter. It is the supreme proof of a man being prosaic that he always insists on poetry being poetical. Sometimes the humour is in the very subject as well as the style of the fable. The Australian aborigines, regarded as the rudest of savages, have a story about a giant frog who had swallowed the sea and all the waters of the world; and who was only forced to spill them by being made to laugh. All the animals with all their antics passed before him and, like Queen Victoria, he was not amused. He collapsed at last before an eel who stood delicately balanced on the tip of its tail, doubtless with a rather desperate dignity. Any amount of fine fantastic literature might be made out of that fable. There is philosophy in that vision of the dry world before the beatific Deluge of laughter. There is imagination in the mountainous monster erupting like an aqueous volcano; there is plenty of fun in the thought of his goggling visage as the pelican or the penguin passed by. Anyhow the frog laughed; but the folklore student remains grave.

Moreover, even where the fables are inferior as art, they cannot be properly judged by science; still less properly judged as science. Some myths are very crude and queer like the early drawings of the children; but the child is trying to draw. It is none the less an error to treat his drawing as if it were a diagram, or intended to be a diagram. The student cannot make a scientific statement about the savage, because the savage is not making a scientific statement about the world. He is saying something quite different; what might be called the gossip of the gods. We may say, if we like, that it is believed before there is time to examine it. It would be truer to say it is accepted before there is time to believe it.

I confess I doubt the whole theory of the dissemination of myths or (as it commonly is) of one myth. It is true that something in our nature and conditions makes many stories similar; but each of them may be original. One man does not borrow the story from the other man, though he may tell it from the same motive as the other man. It would be easy to apply the whole argument about legend to literature; and turn it into a vulgar monomania of plagiarism. I would undertake to trace a notion like that of the Golden Bough through individual modern novels as easily as through communal and antiquated myths. I would undertake to find something like a bunch of flowers figuring again and again from the fatal bouquet of Becky Sharpe to the spray of roses sent by the Princess of Ruritania. But though these flowers may spring from the same soil, it is not the same faded flower that is flung from hand to hand. Those flowers are always fresh.

The true origin of all the myths has been discovered much too often. There are too many keys to mythology, as there are too many cryptograms in Shakespeare. Everything is phallic; everything is totemistic; everything is seed-time and harvest; everything is ghosts and grave-offerings; everything is the golden bough of sacrifice; everything is the sun and moon; everything is everything. Every folklore student who knew a little more than his own monomania, every man of wider reading and critical culture like Andrew Lang, has practically confessed that the bewilderment of these things left his brain spinning. Yet the whole trouble comes from a man trying to look at these stories from the outside, as if they were scientific objects. He has only to look at them from the inside, and ask himself how he would begin a story. A story may start with anything and go anywhere. It may start with a bird without the bird being a totem; it may start with the sun without being a solar myth. It is said there are only ten plots in the world; and there will certainly be common and recurrent elements. Set ten thousand children talking at once, and telling tarradiddles about what they did in the wood; and it will not be hard to find parallels suggesting sun-worship or animal-worship. Some of the stories may be pretty and some silly and some perhaps dirty; but they can only be judged as stories. In the modern dialect, they can only be judged aesthetically. It is strange that aesthetics, or mere feeling, which is now allowed to usurp where it has no rights at all, to wreck reason with pragmatism and morals with anarchy, is apparently not allowed to give a purely aesthetic judgment on what is obviously a purely aesthetic question. We may be fanciful about everything except fairy tales.

Now the first fact is that the most simple people have the most subtle ideas. Everybody ought to know that, for everybody has been a child. Ignorant as a child is, he knows more than he can say and feels not only atmospheres but fine shades. And in this matter there are several fine shades. Nobody understands it who has not had what can only be called the ache of the artist to find some sense and some story in the beautiful things he sees; his hunger for secrets and his anger at any tower or tree escaping with its tale untold. He feels that nothing is perfect unless it is personal. Without that the blind unconscious beauty of the world stands in its garden like a headless statue. One need only be a very minor poet to have wrestled with the tower or the tree until it spoke like a titan or a dryad. It is often said that pagan mythology was a personification of the powers of Nature. The phrase is true in a sense, but it is very unsatisfactory; because it implies that the forces are abstractions and the personification is artificial. Myths are not allegories. Natural powers are not in this case abstractions. It is not as if there were a God of Gravitation. There may be a genius of the waterfall; but not of mere falling, even less than of mere water. The impersonation is not of something impersonal. The point is that the personality perfects the water with significance. Father Christmas is not an allegory of snow and holly; he is not merely the stuff called snow afterwards artificially given a human form, like a snowman. He is something that gives a new meaning to the white world and the evergreens; so that snow itself seems to be warm rather than cold. The test, therefore, is purely imaginative. But imaginative does not mean imaginary. It does not follow that it is all what the moderns call subjective, when they mean false. Every true artist does feel, consciously or unconsciously, that he is touching transcendental truths; that his images are shadows of things seen through the veil. In other words, the natural mystic does know that there is something *there*; something behind the clouds or within the trees; but he believes that the pursuit of beauty is the way to find it; that imagination is a sort of incantation that can call it up.

Now we do not comprehend this process in ourselves, far less in our most remote fellow-creatures. And the danger of these things being classified is that they may seem to be comprehended. A really fine work of folklore, like *The Golden Bough*, will leave too many readers with the idea, for instance, that this or that story of a giant's or wizard's heart in a casket or a cave only 'means' some stupid and static superstition called 'the external soul'. But we do not know what these things mean, simply because we do not know what we ourselves mean when we are moved by them. Suppose somebody in a story says 'Pluck this flower and a princess will die in a castle beyond the sea', we do not know why something stirs in the subconsciousness, or why what is impossible seems also inevitable. Suppose we read 'And in the hour when the king extinguished the candle his ships were wrecked far away on the coast of the Hebrides.' We do not know why the imagination has accepted that image before the reason can reject it; or why such correspondences seem really to correspond to something in the soul. Very deep things in our nature, some dim sense of the dependence of great things upon small, some dark suggestion that the things nearest to us stretch far beyond our power, some sacramental feeling of the magic in material substances, and many more emotions past finding out, are in an idea like that of the external soul. The power even in the myths of savages is like the power in the metaphors of poets. The soul of such a metaphor is often very emphatically an external soul. The best critics have remarked that in the best poets the simile is often a picture that seems quite separate from the text. It is as irrelevant as the remote castle to the flower or the Hebridean coast to the candle. Shelley compares the skylark to a young woman in a turret, to a rose embedded in thick foliage, to a series of things that seem to be about as unlike a skylark in the sky as anything we can imagine. I suppose the most potent piece of pure magic in English literature is the much-quoted passage in Keats's 'Nightingale' about the casements opening on the perilous foam. And nobody notices that the image seems to come from nowhere; that it appears abruptly after some almost equally irrelevant remarks about Ruth; and that it has nothing in the world to do with the subject of the poem. If there is one place in the world where nobody could reasonably expect to find a nightingale, it is on a window-sill at the seaside. But it is only in the same sense that nobody would expect to find a giant's heart in a casket under the sea. Now, it would be very dangerous to classify the metaphors of the poets. When Shelley says that the cloud will rise 'like a child from the womb, like a ghost from the tomb', it would be quite possible to call the first a case of the coarse primitive birth-myth and the second a survival of the ghost-worship which became ancestor-worship. But it is the wrong way of dealing with a cloud; and is liable to leave the learned in the condition of Polonius, only too ready to think it like a weasel, or very like a whale.

Two facts follow from this psychology of day-dreams, which must be kept in mind throughout their development in mythologies and even religions. First, these imaginative impressions are often strictly local. So far from being abstractions, turned into allegories, they are often images almost concentrated into idols. The poet feels the mystery of a particular forest; not of the science of afforestation or the department of woods and forests. He worships the peak of a particular mountain, not the abstract idea of altitude. So we find the god is not merely water but often one special river; he may be the sea because the sea is single like a stream; the river that runs round the world. Ultimately doubtless many deities are enlarged into elements; but they are something more than omnipresent. Apollo does not merely dwell wherever the sun shines; his home is on the rock of Delphi. Diana is great enough to be in three places at once, earth and heaven and hell, but greater is Diana of the Ephesians. This localized feeling has its lowest form in the mere fetish or talisman, such as millionaires put in their motor-cars. But it can also harden into something like a high and serious religion, where it is connected with high and serious duties; into the gods of the city or even the gods of the hearth.

The second consequence is this: that in these pagan cults there is every shade of sincerity – and insincerity. In what sense exactly did an Athenian really think he had to sacrifice to Pallas Athene? What scholar is really certain of the answer? In what sense did Dr. Johnson really think that he had to touch all the posts in the street or that he had to collect orange-peel? In what sense does a child really think that he ought to step on every alternate paving-stone? Two things are at least fairly clear. First, in simpler and less self-conscious times these forms could become more solid without really becoming more serious. Day-dreams could be acted in broad daylight, with more liberty of artistic expression; but still perhaps with something of the light step of the somnambulist. Wrap Dr. Johnson in an antique mantle, crown him (by his kind permission) with a garland, and he will move in state under those ancient skies of morning; touching a series of sacred posts carved with the heads of the strange terminal gods, that stand at the limits of the land and of the life of man. Make the child free of the marbles and mosaics of some classical temple, to play on a whole floor inlaid with squares of black and white; and he will willingly make this fulfilment of his idle and drifting day-dream the clear field for a grave and graceful dance. But the posts and the paving-stones are little more and little less real than they are under modern limits. They are not really much more serious for being taken seriously. They have the sort of sincerity that they always had; the sincerity of art as a symbol that expresses very real spiritualities under the surface of life. But they are only sincere in the same sense as art; not sincere in the same sense as morality. The eccentric's collection of orange-peel may turn to oranges in a Mediterranean festival or to golden apples in a Mediterranean myth. But they are never on the same plane with the difference between giving the orange to a blind beggar and carefully placing the orange-peel so that the beggar may fall and break his leg. Between these two things there is a difference of kind and not of degree. The child does not think it wrong to step on the paving-stone as he thinks it wrong to step on a dog's tail. And it is very certain that whatever jest or sentiment or fancy first set Johnson touching the wooden posts, he never touched wood with any of the feeling with which he stretched out his hands to the timber of that terrible tree, which was the death of God and the life of man.

As already noted, this does not mean that there was no reality or even no religious sentiment in such a mood. As a matter of fact the Catholic Church has taken over with uproarious success the whole of this popular business of giving people local legends and lighter ceremonial movements. In so far as all this sort of paganism was innocent and in touch with nature, there is no reason why it should not be patronized by patron saints as much as by pagan gods. And in any case there are degrees of seriousness in the most natural make-believe. There is all the difference between fancying there are fairies in the wood, which often only means fancying a certain wood as fit for fairies, and really frightening ourselves until we will walk a mile rather than pass a house we have told ourselves is haunted. Behind all these things is the fact that beauty and terror are very real things and related to a real spiritual world; and to touch them at all, even in doubt or fancy, is to stir the deep things of the soul. We all understand that and the pagans understood it. The point is that paganism did not really stir the soul except with these doubts and fancies; with the consequence that we today can have little beyond doubts and fancies about paganism. All the best critics agree that all the greatest poets, in pagan Hellas for example, had an attitude towards their gods which is quite queer and puzzling to men in the Christian era. There seems to be an admitted conflict between the god and the man; but everybody seems to be doubtful about which is the hero and which is the villain. This doubt does not merely apply to a doubter like Euripides in the *Bacchae*; it applies to a moderate conservative like Sophocles in the *Antigone*; or even to a regular Tory and reactionary like Aristophanes in the *Frogs*. Sometimes it would seem that the Greeks believed above all things in reverence, only they had nobody to revere. But the point of the puzzle is this: that all this vagueness and variation arise from the fact of the whole thing being in fancy and in dreaming; and that there are no rules of architecture for a castle in the clouds.

This is the mighty and branching tree called mythology which ramifies round the whole world, whose remote branches under separate skies bear like coloured birds the costly idols of Asia and the half-baked fetishes of Africa and the fairy kings and princesses of the folk-tales of the forests, and buried amid vines and olives the Lares of the Latins, and carried on the clouds of Olympus the buoyant supremacy of the gods of Greece. These are the myths: and he who has no sympathy with myths has no sympathy with men. But he who has most sympathy with myths will most fully realize that they are not and never were a religion, in the sense that Christianity or even Islam is a religion. They satisfy some of the needs satisfied by a religion; and notably the need for doing certain things at certain dates; the need of the twin ideas of festivity and formality. But though they provide a man with a calendar, they do not provide him with a creed. A man did not stand up and say 'I believe in Jupiter and Juno and Neptune', etc., as he stands up and says 'I believe in God the Father Almighty' and the rest of the Apostles' Creed. Many believed in some and not in others, or more in some and less in others, or only in a very vague poetical sense in any. There was no moment when they were all collected into an orthodox order which men would fight and be tortured to keep intact. Still less did anybody ever say in that fashion: 'I believe in Odin and Thor and Freya', for outside Olympus even the Olympian order grows cloudy and chaotic. It seems clear to me that Thor was not a god at all but a hero. Nothing resembling a religion would picture anybody resembling a god as groping like a pigmy in a great cavern, that turned out to be the glove of a giant. That is the glorious ignorance called adventure. Thor may have been a great adventurer; but to call him a god is like trying to compare Jehovah with Jack and the Beanstalk. Odin seems to have been a real barbarian chief, possibly of the Dark Ages after Christianity. Polytheism fades away at its fringes into fairy tales or barbaric memories; it is not a thing like monotheism as held by serious monotheists. Again it does satisfy the need to cry out on some uplifted name or some notable memory in moments that are themselves noble and uplifted; such as the birth of a child or the saving of a city. But the name was so used by many to whom it was only a name. Finally it did satisfy, or rather it partially satisfied, a thing very deep in humanity indeed; the idea of surrendering something as the portion of the unknown powers; of pouring out wine upon the ground, of throwing a ring into the sea; in a word, of sacrifice. It is the wise and worthy idea of not taking our advantage to the full; of putting something in the other balance to ballast our dubious pride, of paying tithes to nature for our land. This deep truth of the danger of insolence, or being too big for our boots, runs through all the great Greek tragedies and makes them great. But it runs side by side with an almost cryptic agnosticism about the real nature of the gods to be propitiated. Where that gesture of surrender is most magnificent, as among the great Greeks, there is really much more idea that the man will be the better for losing the ox than that the god will be the better for getting it. It is said that in its grosser forms there are often actions grotesquely suggestive of the god really eating the sacrifice. But this fact is falsified by the error that I put first in this note on mythology. It is misunderstanding the psychology of day-dreams. A child pretending there is a goblin in a hollow tree will do a crude and material thing, like leaving a piece of cake for him. A poet might do a more dignified and elegant thing, like bringing to the god fruits as well as flowers. But the degree of *seriousness* in both acts may be the same or it may vary in almost any degree. The crude fancy is no more a creed than the ideal fancy is a creed. Certainly the pagan does not disbelieve like an atheist, any more than he believes like a Christian. He feels the presence of powers about which he guesses and invents. St. Paul said that the Greeks had one altar to an unknown god. But in truth all their gods were unknown gods. And the real break in history did come when St. Paul declared to them whom they had ignorantly worshipped.

The substance of all such paganism may be summarized thus. It is an attempt to reach the divine reality through the imagination alone; in its own field reason does not restrain it at all. It is vital to the view of all history that reason is something separate from religion even in the most rational of these civilizations. It is only as an afterthought, when such cults are decadent or on the defensive, that a few Neo-Platonists or a few Brahmins are found trying to rationalize them, and even then only by trying to allegorize them. But in reality the rivers of mythology and philosophy run parallel and do not mingle till they meet in the sea of Christendom. Simple secularists still talk as if the Church had introduced a sort of schism between reason and religion. The truth is that the Church was actually the first thing that ever tried to combine reason and religion. There had never before been any such union of the priests and the philosophers. Mythology, then, sought God through the imagination; or sought truth by means of beauty, in the sense in which beauty includes much of the most grotesque ugliness. But the imagination has its own laws and therefore its own triumphs, which neither logicians nor men of science can understand. It remained true to that imaginative instinct through a thousand extravagances, through every crude cosmic pantomime of a pig eating the moon or the world being cut out of a cow, through all the dizzy convolutions and mystic malformations of Asiatic art, through all the stark and staring rigidity of Egyptian and Assyrian portraiture, through every kind of cracked mirror of mad art that seemed to deform the world and displace the sky, it remained true to something about which there can be no argument; something that makes it possible for some artist of some school to stand suddenly still before that particular deformity and say, 'My dream has come true.' Therefore do we all in fact feel that pagan or primitive myths are infinitely suggestive, so long as we are wise enough not to inquire what they suggest. Therefore we all feel what is meant by Prometheus stealing fire from heaven, until some prig of a pessimist or progressive person explains what it means. Therefore we all know the meaning of Jack and the Beanstalk, until we are told. In this sense it is true that it is the ignorant who accept myths, but only because it is the ignorant who appreciate poems. Imagination has its own laws and triumphs; and a tremendous power began to clothe its images, whether images in the mind or in the mud, whether in the bamboo of the South Sea Islands or the marble of the mountains of Hellas. But there was always a trouble in the triumph, which in these pages I have tried to analyze in vain; but perhaps I might in conclusion state it thus.

The crux and crisis is that man found it natural to worship; even natural to worship unnatural things. The posture of the idol might be stiff and strange; but the gesture of the worshipper was generous and beautiful. He not only felt freer when he bent; he actually felt taller when he bowed. Henceforth anything that took away the gesture of worship would stunt and even maim him for ever. Henceforth being merely secular would be a servitude and an inhibition. If man cannot pray he is gagged; if he cannot kneel he is in irons. We therefore feel throughout the whole of paganism a curious double feeling of trust and distrust. When the man makes the gesture of salutation and of sacrifice, when he pours out the libation or lifts up the sword, he knows he is doing a worthy and a virile thing. He knows he is doing one of the things for which a man was made. His imaginative experiment is therefore justified. But precisely because it began with imagination, there is to the end something of mockery in it, and especially in the object of it. This mockery, in the more intense moments of the intellect, becomes the almost intolerable irony of Greek tragedy. There seems a disproportion between the priest and the altar or between the altar and the god. The priest seems more solemn and almost more sacred than the god. All the order of the temple is solid and sane and satisfactory to certain parts of our nature; except the very centre of it, which seems strangely mutable and dubious, like a dancing flame. It is the first thought round which the whole has been built; and the first thought is still a fancy and almost a frivolity. In that strange place of meeting, the man seems more statuesque than the statue. He himself can stand for ever in the noble and natural attitude of the statue of the Praying Boy. But whatever name be written on the pedestal, whether Zeus or Ammon or Apollo, the god whom he worships is Proteus.

The Praying Boy may be said to express a need rather than to satisfy a need. It is by a normal and necessary action that his hands are lifted; but it is no less a parable that his hands are empty. About the nature of that need there will be more to say; but at this point it may be said that perhaps after all this true instinct, that prayer and sacrifice are a liberty and an enlargement, refers back to that vast and half-forgotten conception of universal fatherhood, which we have already seen everywhere fading from the morning sky. This is true; and yet it is not all the truth. There remains an indestructible instinct, in the poet as represented by the pagan, that he is not entirely wrong in localizing his god. It is something in the soul of poetry if not of piety. And the greatest of poets, when he defined the poet, did not say that he gave us the universe or the absolute or the infinite; but, in his own larger language, a local habitation and a name. No poet is merely a pantheist; those who are counted most pantheistic, like Shelley, start with some local and particular image as the pagans did. After all, Shelley wrote of the skylark because it was a skylark. You could not issue an imperial or international translation of it for use in South Africa, in which it was changed to an ostrich. So the mythological imagination moves as it were in circles, hovering either to find a place or to return to it. In a word, mythology is a *search*; it is something that combines a recurrent desire with a recurrent doubt, mixing a most hungry sincerity in the idea of seeking for a place with a most dark and deep and mysterious levity about all the places found. So far could the lonely imagination lead, and we must turn later to the lonely reason. Nowhere along this road did the two ever travel together.

That is where all these things differed from religion or the reality in which these different dimensions met in a sort of solid. They differed from the reality not in what they looked like but in what they were. A picture may look like a landscape; it may look in every detail exactly like a landscape. The only detail in which it differs is that it is not a landscape. The difference is only that which divides a portrait of Queen Elizabeth from Queen Elizabeth. Only in this mythical and mystical world the portrait could exist before the person; and the portrait was therefore more vague and doubtful. But anybody who has felt and fed on the atmosphere of these myths will know what I mean when I say that in one sense they did not really profess to be realities. The pagans had dreams about realities; and they would have been the first to admit, in their own words, that some came through the gate of ivory and others through the gate of horn. The dreams do indeed tend to be very vivid dreams when they touch on those tender or tragic things, which can really make a sleeper awaken with the sense that his heart has been broken in his sleep. They tend continually to hover over certain passionate themes of meeting and parting, of a life that ends in death or a death that is the beginning of life. Demeter wanders over a stricken world looking for a stolen child; Isis stretches out her arms over the earth in vain to gather the limbs of Osiris; and there is lamentation upon the hills for Atys and through the woods for Adonis. There mingles with all such mourning the mystical and profound sense that death can be a deliverer and an appeasement; that such death gives us a divine blood for a renovating river and that all good is found in gathering the broken body of the god. We may truly call these foreshadowings; so long as we remember that foreshadowings are shadows. And the metaphor of a shadow happens to hit very exactly the truth that is very vital here. For a shadow is a shape; a thing which produces shape but not texture. These things were something *like* the real thing; and to say that they were like is to say that they were different. Saying something is like a dog is another way of saying it is not a dog; and it is in this sense of identity that a myth is not a man. Nobody really thought of Isis as a human being; nobody really thought of Demeter as a historical character; nobody thought of Adonis as the founder of a Church. There was no idea that any one of them had changed the world; but rather that their recurrent death and life bore the sad and beautiful burden of the changelessness of the world. Not one of them was a revolution, save in the sense of the revolution of the sun and the moon. Their whole meaning is missed if we do not see that they mean the shadows that we are and the shadows that we pursue. In certain sacrificial and communal aspects they naturally suggest what sort of a god might satisfy men; but they do not profess to be satisfied. Any one who says they do is a bad judge of poetry.

Those who talk about Pagan Christs have less sympathy with Paganism than with Christianity. Those who call these cults 'religions', and 'compare' them with the certitude and challenge of the Church have much less appreciation than we have of what made heathenism human, or of why classic literature is still something that hangs in the air like a song. It is no very human tenderness for the hungry to prove that hunger is the same as food. It is no very genial understanding of youth to argue that hope destroys the need for happiness. And it is utterly unreal to argue that these images in the mind, admired entirely in the abstract, were even in the same world with a living man and a living polity that were worshipped because they were concrete. We might as well say that a boy playing at robbers is the same as a man in his first day in the trenches; or that a boy's first fancies about 'the not impossible she' are the same as the sacrament of marriage. They are fundamentally different exactly where they are superficially similar; we might almost say they are not the same even when they are the same. They are only different because one is real and the other is not. I do not mean merely that I myself believe that one is true and the other is not. I mean that one was never meant to be true in the same sense as the other. The sense in which it was meant to be true I have tried to suggest vaguely here, but it is undoubtedly very subtle and almost indescribable. It is so subtle that the students who profess to put it up as a rival to our religion miss the whole meaning and purport of their own study. We know better than the scholars, even those of us who are no scholars, what was in that hollow cry that went forth over the dead Adonis and why the Great Mother had a daughter wedded to death. We have entered more deeply than they into the Eleusinian Mysteries and have passed a higher grade, where gate within gate guarded the wisdom of Orpheus. We know the meaning of all the myths. We know the last secret revealed to the perfect initiate. And it is not the voice of a priest or a prophet saying, 'These things are.' It is the voice of a dreamer and an idealist crying, 'Why cannot these things be?'

The Riddles of the Gospel

To understand the nature of this chapter, it is necessary to recur to the nature of this book. The argument which is meant to be the backbone of the book is of the kind called the *reductio ad absurdum*. It suggests that the results of assuming the rationalist thesis are more irrational than ours; but to prove it we must assume that thesis. Thus in the first section I often treated man as merely an animal, to show that the effect was more impossible than if he were treated as an angel. In the sense in which it was necessary to treat man merely as an animal, it is necessary to treat Christ merely as a man. I have to suspend my own beliefs, which are much more positive; and assume this limitation even in order to remove it. I must try to imagine what would happen to a man who did really read the story of Christ as the story of a man; and even of a man of whom he had never heard before. And I wish to point out that a really impartial reading of that kind would lead, if not immediately to belief, at least to a bewilderment of which there is really no solution except in belief. In this chapter, for this reason, I shall bring in nothing of the spirit of my own creed: I shall exclude the very style of diction, and even of lettering, which I should think fitting in speaking in my own person. I am speaking as an imaginary heathen human being, honestly staring at the Gospel story for the first time.

Now it is not at all easy to regard the New Testament as a New Testament. It is not at all easy to realize the good news as new. Both for good and evil familiarity fills us with assumptions and associations; and no man of our civilization, whatever he thinks of our religion, can really read the thing as if he had never heard of it before. Of course it is in any case utterly unhistorical to talk as if the New Testament were a neatly bound book that had fallen from heaven. It is simply the selection made by the authority of the Church from a mass of early Christian literature. But apart from any such question, there is a psychological difficulty in feeling the New Testament as new. There is a psychological difficulty in seeing those well-known words simply as they stand and without going beyond what they intrinsically stand for. And this difficulty must indeed be very great; for the result of it is very curious. The result of it is that most modern critics and most current criticism, even popular criticism, makes a comment that is the exact reverse of the truth. It is so completely the reverse of the truth that one could almost suspect that they had never read the New Testament at all.

We have all heard people say a hundred times over, for they seem never to tire of saying it, that the Jesus of the New Testament is indeed a most merciful and humane lover of humanity, but that the Church has hidden this human character in repellent dogmas and stiffened it with ecclesiastical terrors till it has taken on an inhuman character. This is, I venture to repeat, very nearly the reverse of the truth. The truth is that it is the image of Christ in the churches that is almost entirely mild and merciful. It is the image of Christ in the Gospels that is a good many other things as well. The figure in the Gospels does indeed utter in words of almost heart-breaking beauty his pity for our broken hearts. But they are very far from being the only sort of words that he utters. Nevertheless they are almost the only kind of words that the Church in its popular imagery ever represents him as uttering. That popular imagery is inspired by a perfectly sound popular instinct. The mass of the poor are broken, and the mass of the people are poor, and for the mass of mankind the main thing is to carry the conviction of the incredible compassion of God. But nobody with his eyes open can doubt that it is chiefly this idea of compassion that the popular machinery of the Church does seek to carry. The popular imagery carries a great deal to excess the sentiment of 'Gentle Jesus, meek and mild.' It is the first thing that the outsider feels and criticizes in a Pietà or a shrine of the Sacred Heart. As I say, while the art may be insufficient, I am not sure that the instinct is unsound. In any case there is something appalling, something that makes the blood run cold, in the idea of having a statue of Christ in wrath. There is something insupportable even to the imagination in the idea of turning the corner of a street or coming out into the spaces of a market-place to meet the petrifying petrifaction of *that* figure as it turned upon a generation of vipers, or that face as it looked at the face of a hypocrite. The Church can reasonably be justified therefore if she turns the most merciful face or aspect towards men; but it is certainly the most merciful aspect that she does turn. And the point is here that it is very much more specially and exclusively merciful than any impression that could be formed by a man merely reading the New Testament for the first time. A man simply taking the words of the story as they stand would form quite another impression; an impression full of mystery and possibly of inconsistency; but certainly not merely an impression of mildness. It would be intensely interesting; but part of the interest would consist in its leaving a good deal to be guessed at or explained. It is full of sudden gestures evidently significant except that we hardly know what they signify; of enigmatic silences; of ironical replies. The outbreaks of wrath, like storms above our atmosphere, do not seem to break out exactly where we should expect them, but to follow some higher weather-chart of their own. The Peter whom popular Church teaching presents is very rightly the Peter to whom Christ said in forgiveness, 'Feed my lambs.' He is not the Peter upon whom Christ turned as if he were the devil, crying in that obscure wrath, 'Get thee behind me, Satan.' Christ lamented with nothing but love and pity over Jerusalem which was to murder him. We do not know what strange spiritual atmosphere or spiritual insight led Him to sink Bethsaida lower in the pit than Sodom. I am putting aside for the moment all questions of doctrinal inferences or expositions, orthodox or otherwise; I am simply imagining the effect on a man's mind if he did really do what these critics are always talking about doing; if he did really read the New Testament without reference to orthodoxy ᵃnd even without reference to doctrine. He would find a number of things which fit in far less with the current unorthodoxy than they do with the current orthodoxy. He would find, for instance, that if there are any descriptions that deserved to be called realistic, they are precisely the descriptions of the supernatural. If there is one aspect of the New Testament Jesus in which He may be said to present himself eminently as a practical person, it is in the aspect of an exorcist. There is nothing meek and mild, there is nothing even in the ordinary sense mystical, about the tone of the voice that says 'Hold thy peace and come out of him.' It is much more like the tone of a very business-like lion-tamer or a strong-minded doctor dealing with a homicidal maniac. But this is only a side issue for the sake of illustration; I am not now raising these controversies; but considering the case of the imaginary man from the moon to whom the New Testament is new.

Now the first thing to note is that if we take it merely as a human story, it is in some ways a very strange story. I do not refer here to its tremendous and tragic culmination or to any implications involving triumph in that tragedy. I do not refer to what is commonly called the miraculous element; for on that point philosophies vary and modern philosophies very decidedly waver. Indeed the educated Englishman of today may be said to have passed from an old fashion, in which he would not believe in any miracles unless they were ancient, and adopted a new fashion in which he will not believe in any miracles unless they are modern. He used to hold that miraculous cures stopped with the first Christians and is now inclined to suspect that they began with the first Christian Scientists. But I refer here rather specially to unmiraculous and even to unnoticed and inconspicuous parts of the story. There are a great many things about it which nobody would have invented, for they are things that nobody has ever made any particular use of; things which if they were remarked at all have remained rather as puzzles. For instance, there is that long stretch of silence in the life of Christ up to the age of thirty. It is of all silences the most immense and imaginatively impressive. But it is not the sort of thing that anybody is particularly likely to invent in order to prove something; and nobody so far as I know has ever tried to prove anything in particular from it. It is impressive, but it is only impressive as a fact; there is nothing particularly popular or obvious about it as a fable. The ordinary trend of hero-worship and myth-making is much more likely to say the precise opposite. It is much more likely to say (as I believe some of the gospels rejected by the Church do say) that Jesus displayed a divine precocity and began His mission at a miraculously early age. And there is indeed something strange in the thought that He who of all humanity needed least preparation seems to have had most. Whether it was some mode of the divine humility, or some truth of which we see the shadow in the longer domestic tutelage of the higher creatures of the earth, I do not propose to speculate; I mention it simply as an example of the sort of thing that does in any case give rise to speculations, quite apart from recognized religious speculations. Now the whole story is full of these things. It is not by any means, as baldly presented in print, a story that it is easy to get to the bottom of. It is anything but what these people talk of as a simple Gospel. Relatively speaking, it is the Gospel that has the mysticism and the Church that has the rationalism. As I should put it, of course, it is the Gospel that is the riddle and the Church that is the answer. But whatever be the answer, the Gospel as it stands is almost a book of riddles.

First, a man reading the Gospel sayings would not find platitudes. If he had read even in the most respectful spirit the majority of ancient philosophers and of modern moralists, he would appreciate the unique importance of saying that he did not find platitudes. It is more than can be said even of Plato. It is much more than can be said of Epictetus or Seneca or Marcus Aurelius or Apollonius of Tyana. And it is immeasurably more than can be said of most of the agnostic moralists and the preachers of the ethical societies, with their songs of service and their religion of brotherhood. The morality of most moralists, ancient and modern, has been one solid and polished cataract of platitudes flowing for ever and ever. That would certainly not be the impression of the imaginary independent outsider studying the New Testament. He would be conscious of nothing so commonplace and in a sense of nothing so continuous as that stream. He would find a number of strange claims that might sound like the claim to be the brother of the sun and moon; a number of very startling pieces of advice; a number of stunning rebukes; a number of strangely beautiful stories. He would see some very gigantesque figures of speech about the impossibility of threading a needle with a camel or the possibility of throwing a mountain into the sea. He would see a number of very daring simplifications of the difficulties of life; like the advice to shine upon everybody indifferently as does the sunshine or not to worry about the future any more than the birds. He would find on the other hand some passages of almost impenetrable darkness, so far as he is concerned, such as the moral of the parable of the Unjust Steward. Some of these things might strike him as fables and some as truths; but none as truisms. For instance, he would not find the ordinary platitudes in favour of peace. He would find several paradoxes in favour of peace. He would find several ideals of non-resistance, which taken as they stand would be rather too pacific for any pacifist. He would be told in one passage to treat a robber *not* with passive resistance, but rather with positive and enthusiastic encouragement, if the terms be taken literally; heaping up gifts upon the man who had stolen goods. But he would not find a word of all that obvious rhetoric against war which has filled countless books and odes and orations; not a word about the wickedness of war, the wastefulness of war, the appalling scale of the slaughter in war and all the rest of the familiar frenzy; indeed not a word about war at all. There is nothing that throws any particular light on Christ's attitude towards organized warfare, except that He seems to have been rather fond of Roman soldiers. Indeed it is another perplexity, speaking from the same external and human standpoint, that He seems to have got on much better with Romans than He did with Jews. But the question here is a certain tone to be appreciated by merely reading a certain text; and we might give any number of instances of it.

The statement that the meek shall inherit the earth is very far from being a meek statement. I mean it is not meek in the ordinary sense of mild and moderate and inoffensive. To justify it, it would be necessary to go very deep into history and anticipate things undreamed of then and by many unrealized even now; such as the way in which the mystical monks reclaimed the lands which the practical kings had lost. If it was a truth at all, it was because it was a prophecy. But certainly it was not a truth in the sense of a truism. The blessing upon the meek would seem to be a very violent statement; in the sense of doing violence to reason and probability. And with this we come to another important stage in the speculation. As a prophecy it really was fulfilled; but it was only fulfilled long afterwards. The monasteries were the most practical and prosperous estates and experiments in reconstruction after the barbaric deluge; the meek did really inherit the earth. But nobody could have known anything of the sort at the time – unless indeed there was one who knew. Something of the same thing may be said about the incident of Martha and Mary; which has been interpreted in retrospect and from the inside by the mystics of the Christian contemplative life. But it was not at all an obvious view of it; and most moralists, ancient and modern, could be trusted to make a rush for the obvious. What torrents of effortless eloquence would have flowed from them to swell any slight superiority on the part of Martha; what splendid sermons about the Joy of Service and the Gospel of Work and the World Left Better Than We Found It, and generally all the ten thousand platitudes that can be uttered in favour of taking trouble – by people who need take no trouble to utter them. If in Mary the mystic and child of love Christ was guarding the seed of something more subtle, who was likely to understand it at the time? Nobody else could have seen Clare and Catherine and Teresa shining above the little roof at Bethany. It is so in another way with that magnificent menace about bringing into the world a sword to sunder and divide. Nobody could have guessed then either how it could be fulfilled or how it could be justified. Indeed some freethinkers are still so simple as to fall into the trap and be shocked at a phrase so deliberately defiant. They actually complain of the paradox for not being a platitude.

But the point here is that if we *could* read the Gospel reports as things as new as newspaper reports, they would puzzle us and perhaps terrify us much *more* than the same things as developed by historical Christianity. For instance; Christ after a clear allusion to the eunuchs of eastern courts, said there would be eunuchs of the kingdom of heaven. If this does not mean the voluntary enthusiasm of virginity, it could only be made to mean something much more unnatural or uncouth. It is the historical religion that humanizes it for us by experience of Franciscans or of Sisters of Mercy. The mere statement standing by itself might very well suggest a rather dehumanized atmosphere; the sinister and inhuman silence of the Asiatic harem and divan. This is but one instance out of scores; but the moral is that the Christ of the Gospel might actually seem more strange and terrible than the Christ of the Church.

I am dwelling on the dark or dazzling or defiant or mysterious side of the Gospel words, not because they had not obviously a more obvious and popular side, but because this is the answer to a common criticism on a vital point. The freethinker frequently says that Jesus of Nazareth was a man of his time, even if He was in advance of His time; and that we cannot accept His ethics as final for humanity. The freethinker then goes on to criticize his ethics, saying plausibly enough that men cannot turn the other cheek, or that they must take thought for the morrow, or that the self-denial is too ascetic or the monogamy too severe. But the Zealots and the Legionaries did not turn the other cheek any more than we do, if so much. The Jewish traders and Roman tax-gatherers took thought for the morrow as much as we, if not more. We cannot pretend to be abandoning the morality of the past for one more suited to the present. It is certainly not the morality of another age, but it might be of another world.

In short, we can say that these ideals are impossible in themselves. Exactly what we cannot say is that they are impossible for us. They are rather notably marked by a mysticism which, if it be a sort of madness, would always have struck the same sort of people as mad. Take, for instance, the case of marriage and the relations of the sexes. It might very well have been true that a Galilean teacher taught things natural to a Galilean environment; but it is not. It might rationally be expected that a man in the time of Tiberius would have advanced a view conditioned by the time of Tiberius; but he did not. What he advanced was something quite different; something very difficult; but something no more difficult now than it was then. When, for instance, Mahomet made his polygamous compromise we may reasonably say that it was conditioned by a polygamous society. When he allowed a man four wives he was really doing something suited to the circumstances, which might have been less suited to other circumstances. Nobody will pretend that the four wives were like the four winds, something seemingly a part of the order of nature; nobody will say that the figure four was written for ever in stars upon the sky. But neither will anyone say that the figure four is an inconceivable ideal; that it is beyond the power of the mind of man to count up to four; or to count the number of his wives and see whether it amounts to four. It is a practical compromise carrying with it the character of a particular society. If Mahomet had been born in Acton in the nineteenth century, we may well doubt whether he would instantly have filled that suburb with harems of four wives apiece. As he was born in Arabia in the sixth century, he did in his conjugal arrangements suggest the conditions of Arabia in the sixth century. But Christ in his view of marriage does not in the least suggest the conditions of Palestine in the first century. He does not suggest anything at all, except the sacramental view of marriage as developed long afterwards by the Catholic Church. It was quite as difficult for people then as for people now. It was much more puzzling to people then than to people now. Jews and Romans and Greeks did not believe, and did not even understand enough to disbelieve, the mystical idea that the man and the woman had become one sacramental substance. We may think it an incredible or impossible ideal; but we cannot think it any more incredible or impossible than they would have thought it. In other words, whatever else is true, it is not true that the controversy has been altered by time. Whatever else is true, it is emphatically not true that the ideas of Jesus of Nazareth were suitable to His time, but are no longer suitable to our time. Exactly how suitable they were to His time is perhaps suggested in the end of His story.

The same truth might be stated in another way by saying that if the story be regarded as merely human and historical, it is extraordinary how very little there is in the recorded words of Christ that ties Him at all to His own time. I do not mean the details of a period, which even a man of the period knows to be passing. I mean the fundamentals which even the wisest man often vaguely assumes to be eternal. For instance, Aristotle was perhaps the wisest and most wide-minded man who ever lived. He founded himself entirely upon fundamentals, which have been generally found to remain rational and solid through all social and historical changes. Still, he lived in a world in which it was thought as natural to have slaves as to have children. And therefore he did permit himself a serious recognition of a difference between slaves and free men. Christ as much as Aristotle lived in a world that took slavery for granted. He did not particularly denounce slavery. He started a movement that could exist in a world with slavery. But He started a movement that could exist in a world without slavery. He never used a phrase that made His philosophy depend even upon the very existence of the social order in which He lived. He spoke as one conscious that everything was ephemeral, including the things that Aristotle thought eternal. By that time the Roman Empire had come to be merely the *orbis terrarum*, another name for the world. But He never made his morality dependent on the existence of the Roman Empire or even on the existence of the world. 'Heaven and earth shall pass away; but my words shall not pass away.'

The truth is that when critics have spoken of the local limitations of the Galilean, it has always been a case of the local limitations of the critics. He did undoubtedly believe in certain things that one particular modern sect of materialists do not believe. But they were not things particularly peculiar to His time. It would be nearer the truth to say that the denial of them is quite peculiar to our time. Doubtless it would be nearer still to the truth to say merely that a certain solemn social importance, in the minority disbelieving them, is peculiar to our time. He believed, for instance, in evil spirits or in the psychic healing of bodily ills; but not because He was a Galilean born under Augustus. It is absurd to say that a man believed things because he was a Galilean under Augustus when he might have believed the same things if he had been an Egyptian under Tuten-kamen or an Indian under Gengis Khan. But with this general question of the philosophy of diabolism or of divine miracles I deal elsewhere. It is enough to say that the materialists have to prove the impossibility of miracles against the testimony of all mankind, not against the prejudices of provincials in North Palestine under the first Roman Emperors. What they have to prove, for the present argument, is the presence in the Gospels of those particular prejudices of those particular provincials. And, humanly speaking, it is astonishing how little they can produce even to make a beginning of proving it.

So it is in this case of the sacrament of marriage. We may not believe in sacraments, as we may not believe in spirits, but it is quite clear that Christ believed in this sacrament in His own way and not in any current or contemporary way. He certainly did not get His argument against divorce from the Mosaic law or the Roman law or the habits of the Palestinian people. It would appear to His critics then exactly what it appears to His critics now; an arbitrary and transcendental dogma coming from nowhere save in the sense that it came from Him. I am not at all concerned here to defend that dogma; the point here is that it is just as easy to defend it now as it was to defend it then. It is an ideal altogether outside time; difficult at any period; impossible at no period. In other words, if anyone says it is what might be expected of a man walking about in that place at that period, we can quite fairly answer that it is much *more* like what might be the mysterious utterance of a being beyond man, if he walked alive among men.

I maintain therefore that a man reading the New Testament frankly and freshly would *not* get the impression of what is now often meant by a human Christ. The merely human Christ is a made-up figure, a piece of artificial selection, like the merely evolutionary man. Moreover there have been too many of these human Christs found in the same story, just as there have been too many keys to mythology found in the same stories. Three or four separate schools of rationalism have worked over the ground and produced three or four equally rational explanations of His life. The first rational explanation of His life was that He never lived. And this in turn gave an opportunity for three or four different explanations; as that He was a sun-myth or a corn-myth, or any other kind of myth that is also a monomania. Then the idea that He was a divine being who did not exist gave place to the idea that He was a human being who did exist. In my youth it was the fashion to say that He was merely an ethical teacher in the manner of the Essenes, who had apparently nothing very much to say that Hillel or a hundred other Jews might not have said; as that it is a kindly thing to be kind and an assistance to purification to be pure. Then somebody said He was a madman with a Messianic delusion. Then others said He was indeed an original teacher because He cared about nothing but Socialism; or (as others said) about nothing but Pacifism. Then a more grimly scientific character appeared who said that Jesus would never have been heard of at all except for His prophecies of the end of the world. He was important merely as a Millennarian like Dr. Cumming; and created a provincial scare by announcing the exact date of the crack of doom. Among other variants on the same theme was the theory that He was a spiritual healer and nothing else; a view implied by Christian Science, which has really to expound a Christianity without the Crucifixion in order to explain the curing of Peter's wife's mother or the daughter of a centurion. There is another theory that concentrates entirely on the business of diabolism and what it would call the contemporary superstition about demoniacs; as if Christ, like a young deacon taking his first orders, had got as far as exorcism and never got any further. Now each of these explanations in itself seems to me singularly inadequate; but taken together they do suggest something of the very mystery which they miss. There must surely have been something not only mysterious but many-sided about Christ if so many smaller Christs can be carved out of Him. If the Christian Scientist is satisfied with Him as a spiritual healer and the Christian Socialist is satisfied with Him as a social reformer, so satisfied that they do not even expect Him to be anything else, it looks as if He really covered rather more ground than they could be expected to expect. And it does seem to suggest that there might be more than they fancy in these other mysterious attributes of casting out devils or prophesying doom.

Above all, would not such a new reader of the New Testament stumble over something that would startle him much more than it startles us? I have here more than once attempted the rather impossible task of reversing time and the historic method; and in fancy looking forward to the facts, instead of backward through the memories. So I have imagined the monster that man might have seemed at first to the mere nature around him. We should have a worse shock if we really imagined the nature of Christ named for the first time. What should we feel at the first whisper of a certain suggestion about a certain man? Certainly it is not for us to blame anybody who should find that first wild whisper merely impious and insane. On the contrary, stumbling on that rock of scandal is the first step. Stark staring incredulity is a far more loyal tribute to that truth than a modernist metaphysic that would make it out merely a matter of degree. It were better to rend our robes with a great cry against blasphemy, like Caiaphas in the judgment, or to lay hold of the man as a maniac possessed of devils like the kinsmen and the crowd, rather than to stand stupidly debating fine shades of pantheism in the presence of so catastrophic a claim. There is more of the wisdom that is one with surprise in any simple person, full of the sensitiveness of simplicity, who should expect the grass to wither and the birds to drop dead out of the air, when a strolling carpenter's apprentice said calmly and almost carelessly, like one looking over his shoulder: 'Before Abraham was, I am.'

THE BIOGRAPHIES

CHESTERTON wrote full-length studies of a great number (and a surprising variety) of writers including Blake, Chaucer, Dickens, Browning, Aquinas, St. Francis, Stevenson and Cobbett. He also wrote a study of the painter G. F. Watts which, apart from some painterly touches in his fiction, is almost the only legacy which survives from his art school training. The Watts biography is little read today, but it brought to Chesterton the offer of the Chair of English Literature at Birmingham University. It is fruitless, but perhaps fascinating, to speculate upon what might have happened to his career had he accepted it.

It is a matter of tradition rather than definition that these works are called biographies; the biographical element in them is the least important and, in modern terms, the most sketchy. But Chesterton's biographies had a rather different purpose from most modern examples of the genre. In spirit they are much closer to the earliest examples of the genre: more like Aubrey and Izaak Walton than like today's researchers and card-indexers. Chesterton was trying to analyze and understand the *spirit* of his subject rather than map his physical course through life.

Dylan Thomas in his *Conversation About Christmas* remembers being given a book that 'told me everything about the wasp, except why'. And it is that kind of *why* that Chesterton is addressing in his studies of writers. They may be called biographies, but they are much more works of appreciation and criticism than of day-to-day activity. You will not discover from *Charles Dickens* any details of what went wrong with his marriage, but you will find out what it meant for his delineation of character that he was expected to put on performances to amuse his father. The Browning biography begins with Browning and not with his grandfather's baptism.

It is necessary to go back and ask the very elementary question of what a biography is for. The modern appetite is for facts, for anything that is susceptible of confirmation. There is nothing wrong with that. It may be of interest to know that such and such a poet left his job as an insurance agent on 23rd November 1951 and wrote forty-two articles for the *London Magazine*; that he had a dislike for coloured shirts and celery soup and wrote only in yellow notebooks obtained in Hungary. But woe betide the biographer if someone in Weston-super-Mare can show that he wrote only forty-one articles or that six pages of his third novel were written in a Boots Scribbling Diary. Because the trouble is that for minds that enjoy or need that kind of information, one slip is enough to invalidate the whole book. *Radio Times* once printed a letter from someone who complained that the whole of the film *Far from the Madding Crowd* had been 'totally ruined' (this is not an exaggeration) by the fact that for a few seconds in one shot a black-and-white cow had been glimpsed. The Friesian cow had not been introduced to Britain until etc. etc. The rest of the complaint may be imagined very easily. Now, Hardy is a particularly difficult author to capture on screen and, despite a casting that looked at first sight very unlikely to succeed, it is, in spirit, one of the very best films of a novel – any novel, not just Hardy – that has ever been made. To make such a criticism of it, even if the criticism is literally true, is to miss the point.

Chesterton can never be accused of missing the point. Whatever else is wrong about his biographies, the whole picture is definitely hanging straight. He himself was not ashamed to admit to the odd Friesian cow, as it were, but the heart of his argument was definitely in the right place. Much biography today is, in the end, unsatisfactory; especially biography which deals with a writer. The reason for this is that we have met the writer first of all by way of the works, through the imagination; and the imagination of a good writer is much more impressive and indeed much more important than a list of what he read and how many hours a day were spent at the typewriter, and for whose bed he left that typewriter. If, however, the biographer can understand the way a writer's imagination works, what nourished it, what constrained it and how it differs from other imaginations, then the biographical details will become part of our original vision and appreciation. We will not suffer the disappointment that biographies can sometimes bring for we shall have been told what we needed to hear. It is all a matter of what is relevant and what is irrelevant. And, of course, what is relevant to the merely nosey or prurient reader will probably be quite beside the point for the reader who really wants to understand what it is that turns a person into a writer and then steers their imagination through their experiences.

I can see, in a vague sense and certainly in the sense that anybody else can see, that Dickens is a particularly *English* writer. But that sense for me is focused when I read in Chesterton of Dickens's travels:

> In the sunlight of the southern world, he was still dreaming
> of the firelight of the north. Among the palaces and the white
> campanili, he shut his eyes to see Marylebone and dreamed
> a lovely dream about chimney-pots.

Now I understand why he did not write of Italy; Italy merely showed him a contrast with the London he loved and understood. Just as Dvorak in his Ninth Symphony wrote most poignantly about his native land when he was thousands of miles away from it, so Dickens worked on 'The Chimes', one of his most English of stories, lamplight, fog, snow and all, when he was in Italy. I do not need to know how many collar-studs he owned and whether he was good at finding them.

This is not to say that the best modern criticism has not gone much more deeply into Dickens or any of the other authors Chesterton wrote about, and revealed more things and deeper things. What Chesterton was supreme at doing, and what is largely now left undone, is to reveal the essential. He is the Father Brown of literature: just as Father Brown could find out the truth because he was capable of a kind of spiritual identification with a murderer, so Chesterton himself plays something of the same trick with the subjects of his biographies.

As a writer himself he understood that there is something in all of us which corresponds to a landscape in which we like to move. It could be called a mindset, but the image of a landscape is much closer to what we actually feel about it. When we talk about a writer's *world* we are being less metaphorical than perhaps we think. This is the aspect of a writer that Chesterton could grasp so securely and could communicate to the rest of us.

In case it should be thought that this is somehow a lesser quality than finding out and revealing new facts, we should turn from Dickens to St. Thomas Aquinas and hear what the greatest of all the historians of medieval thought, Etienne Gilson, had to say about Chesterton's book on Aquinas:

> I consider it as being without comparison the best book ever written on St. Thomas. Nothing short of genius can account for such an achievement. Everybody will no doubt admit that it is a 'clever' book, but few readers who have spent twenty or thirty years in studying St. Thomas Aquinas, and who, perhaps, have themselves published two or three volumes on the subject, can fail to perceive that the so-called 'wit' of Chesterton has put their scholarship to shame. He has guessed all that they tried to demonstrate, and he has said all that which they were more or less clumsily attempting to express in academic formulas.

In an introduction to *The Old Curiosity Shop*, Chesterton lays out his own stall as a critic:

> Criticism does not exist to say about authors the things that they knew themselves. It exists to say the things about them which they did not know themselves. If a critic says that the *Iliad* has a pagan rather than a Christian pity, or that it is full of pictures made by one epithet, of course he does not mean that Homer could have said that. If Homer could have said that the critic would leave Homer to say it. The function of criticism, if it has a legitimate function at all, can only be one function – that of dealing with the subconscious part of the author's mind which only the critic can express, and not with the conscious part of the author's mind, which the author himself can express. Either criticism is no good at all (a very defensible position) or else criticism means saying about an author the very things that would have made him jump out of his boots.

In his enthusiasm, in his unbounded delight in writers for being what they are and not what what we mistake them for or would like them to be, Chesterton has been considered old-fashioned. But then, the concept 'old-fashioned' is itself a result of fashion.

It may be true that there has not been any age that has not been in danger of losing its soul. But it is equally true that each age has needed its prophets, its spokesmen, and these have more often been found in the ranks of the poets and the writers than among politicians and the acknowledged legislators. Often the things Chesterton says seem so obvious once he has said them that we can all too easily dismiss him as unoriginal. But then, the very word *original* is linguistically paradoxical in true Chestertonian style. Truth is bound to be unoriginal in that it is not new, and original, by definition, since it is *of our origins*. He would have been delighted to be accused of unoriginality; and by it to have counterweighted all the brash, tired, specious and short-lived originality that is so prized by the twentieth century.

St. Thomas Aquinas

The Permanent Philosophy

It is a pity that the word Anthropology has been degraded to the study of Anthropoids. It is now incurably associated with squabbles between prehistoric professors (in more senses than one) about whether a chip of stone is the tooth of a man or an ape; sometimes settled as in that famous case, when it was found to be the tooth of a pig. It is very right that there should be a purely physical science of such things; but the name commonly used might well, by analogy, have been dedicated to things not only wider and deeper, but rather more relevant. Just as, in America, the new Humanists have pointed out to the old Humanitarians that their humanitarianism has been largely concentrated on things that are *not* specially human, such as physical conditions, appetites, economic needs, environment and so on – so in practice those who are called Anthropologists have to narrow their minds to the materialistic things that are *not* notably anthropic. They have to hunt through history and pre-history something which emphatically is not *Homo Sapiens*, but is always in fact regarded as *Simius Insipiens*. *Homo Sapiens* can only be considered in relation to *Sapientia*; and only a book like that of St. Thomas is really devoted to the intrinsic idea of *Sapientia*. In short, there ought to be a real study called Anthropology corresponding to Theology. In this sense St. Thomas Aquinas, perhaps more than he is anything else, is a great Anthropologist.

I apologize for the opening words of this chapter to all those excellent and eminent men of science, who are engaged in the real study of humanity in its relation to biology. But I rather fancy that they will be the last to deny that there has been a somewhat disproportionate disposition, in popular science, to turn the study of human beings into the study of savages. And savagery is not history: it is either the beginning of history or the end of it. I suspect that the greatest scientists would agree that only too many professors have thus been lost in the bush or the jungle; professors who wanted to study anthropology and never got any further than anthropophagy. But I have a particular reason for prefacing this suggestion of a higher anthropology by an apology to any genuine biologists who might seem to be included, but are certainly not included, in a protest against cheap popular science. For the first thing to be said about St. Thomas as an Anthropologist, is that he is really remarkably like the best sort of modern biological Anthropologists; of the sort who would call themselves Agnostics. This fact is so sharp and decisive a turning point in history, that the history really needs to be recalled and recorded.

St. Thomas Aquinas closely resembles the great Professor Huxley, the Agnostic who invented the word Agnosticism. He is like him in his way of starting the argument, and he is unlike everybody else, before and after, until the Huxleyan age. He adopts almost literally the Huxleyan definition of the Agnostic method: 'To follow reason as far as it will go'; the only question is – where does it go? He lays down the almost startlingly modern or materialist statement: 'Everything that is in the intellect has been in the senses.' This is where he began, as much as any modern man of science, nay, as much as any modern materialist who can now hardly be called a man of science; at the very opposite end of inquiry from that of the mere mystic. The Platonists, or at least the Neo-Platonists, all tended to the view that the mind was lit entirely from within; St. Thomas insisted that it was lit by five windows, that we call the windows of the senses. But he wanted the light from without to shine on what was within. He wanted to study the nature of Man, and not merely of such moss and mushrooms as he might see through the window, and which he valued as the first enlightening experience of Man. And starting from this point, he proceeds to climb the House of Man, step by step and storey by storey, until he has come out on the highest tower and beheld the largest vision.

In other words, he is an Anthropologist, with a complete theory of Man, right or wrong. Now the modern Anthropologists, who called themselves Agnostics, completely failed to be Anthropologists at all. Under their limitations, they could not get a complete theory of Man, let alone a complete theory of Nature. They began by ruling out something which they called the Unknowable. The incomprehensibility was almost comprehensible, if we could really understand the Unknowable in the sense of the Ultimate. But it rapidly became apparent that all sorts of things were Unknowable, which were exactly the things that a man has got to know. It is necessary to know whether he is responsible or irresponsible, perfect or imperfect, perfectible or unperfectible, mortal or immortal, doomed or free: not in order to understand God, but in order to understand Man. Nothing that leaves these things under a cloud of religious doubt can possibly pretend to be a Science of Man; it shrinks from anthropology as completely as from theology. Has a man free will; or is his sense of choice an illusion? Has he a conscience, or has his conscience any authority; or is it only the prejudice of the tribal past? Is there any real hope of settling these things by human reason; and has *that* any authority? Is he to regard death as final; and is he to regard miraculous help as possible? Now it is all nonsense to say that these are unknowable in any remote sense, like the distinction between the Cherubim and the Seraphim, or the Procession of the Holy Ghost. The Schoolmen may have shot too far beyond our limits in pursuing the Cherubim and Seraphim. But in asking whether a man can choose or whether a man will die, they were asking ordinary questions in natural history; like whether a cat can scratch or whether a dog can smell. Nothing calling itself a complete Science of Man can shirk them. And the great Agnostics did shirk them. They may have said they had no scientific evidence; in that case they failed to produce even a scientific hypothesis. What they generally did produce was a wildly unscientific contradiction. Most Monist moralists simply said that Man has no choice; but he must think and act heroically as if he had. Huxley made morality, and even Victorian morality, in the exact sense, supernatural. He said it had arbitrary rights above Nature; a sort of theology without theism.

I do not know for certain why St. Thomas was called the Angelic Doctor: whether it was that he had an angelic temper, or the intellectualism of an Angel; or whether there was a later legend that he concentrated on Angels – especially on the points of needles. If so, I do not quite understand how this idea arose; history has many examples of an irritating habit of labelling somebody in connection with something, as if he never did anything else. Who was it who began the inane habit of referring to Dr. Johnson as 'our lexicographer'; as if he never did anything but write a dictionary? Why do most people insist on meeting the large and far-reaching mind of Pascal at its very narrowest point; the point at which it was sharpened into a spike by the spite of the Jansenists against the Jesuits? It is just possible, for all I know, that this labelling of Aquinas as a specialist was an obscure depreciation of him as a universalist. For that is a very common trick for the belittling of literary or scientific men. St. Thomas must have made a certain number of enemies, though he hardly ever treated them as enemies. Unfortunately, good temper is sometimes more irritating than bad temper. And he had, after all, done a great deal of damage, as many medieval men would have thought; and, what is more curious, a good deal of damage to both sides. He had been a revolutionist against Augustine and a traditionalist against Averrhoes. He might appear to some to have tried to wreck that ancient beauty of the City of God, which bore some resemblance to the Republic of Plato. He might appear to others to have inflicted a blow on the advancing and levelling forces of Islam, as dramatic as that of Godfrey storming Jerusalem. It is possible that these enemies, by way of damning with faint praise, talked about his very respectable little work on Angels; as a man might say that Darwin was really reliable when writing on coral insects, or that some of Milton's Latin poems were very creditable indeed. But this is only a conjecture, and many other conjectures are possible. And I am disposed to think that St. Thomas really was rather specially interested in the nature of Angels, for the same reason that made him even more interested in the nature of men. It was a part of that strong personal interest in things subordinate and semi-dependent, which runs through his whole system; a hierarchy of higher and lower liberties. He was interested in the problem of the Angel, as he was interested in the problem of the Man, because it was a problem; and especially because it was a problem of an intermediate creature. I do not pretend to deal here with this mysterious quality, as he conceives it to exist in that inscrutable intellectual being, who is less than God but more than Man. But it was this quality of a link in the chain, or a rung in the ladder, which mainly concerned the theologian in developing his own particular theory of degrees. Above all, it is this which chiefly moves him when he finds so fascinating the central mystery of Man. And for him the point is always that Man is not a balloon going up into the sky, nor a mole burrowing merely in the earth; but rather a thing like a tree, whose roots are fed from the earth, while its highest branches seem to rise almost to the stars.

I have pointed out that mere modern free-thought has left everything in a fog, including itself. The assertion that thought is free led first to the denial that will is free; but even about that there was no real determination among the Determinists. In practice, they told men that they must treat their will as free though it was not free. In other words, Man must live a double life; which is exactly the old heresy of Siger of Brabant about the Double Mind. In other words, the nineteenth century left everything in chaos; and the importance of Thomism to the twentieth century is that it may give us back a cosmos. We can give here only the rudest sketch of how Aquinas, like the Agnostics, beginning in the cosmic cellars, yet climbed to the cosmic towers.

Without pretending to span within such limits the essential Thomist idea, I may be allowed to throw out a sort of rough version of the fundamental question, which I think I have known myself, consciously or unconsciously, since my childhood. When a child looks out of the nursery window and sees anything, say the green lawn of the garden, what does he actually know; or does he know anything? There are all sorts of nursery games of negative philosophy played round this question. A brilliant Victorian scientist delighted in declaring that the child does not see any grass at all; but only a sort of green mist reflected in a tiny mirror of the human eye. This piece of rationalism has always struck me as almost insanely irrational. If he is not sure of the existence of the grass, which he sees through the glass of a window, how on earth can he be sure of the existence of the retina, which he sees through the glass of a microscope? If sight deceives, why can it not go on deceiving? Men of another school answer that grass is a mere green impression on the mind; and that the child can be sure of nothing except the mind. They declare that he can only be conscious of his own consciousness;

which happens to be the one thing that we know the child is not conscious of at all. In that sense, it would be far truer to say that there is grass and no child, than to say that there is a conscious child but no grass. St. Thomas Aquinas, suddenly intervening in this nursery quarrel, says emphatically that the child is aware of *Ens*. Long before he knows that grass is grass, or self is self, he knows that something is something. Perhaps it would be best to say very emphatically (with a blow on the table), 'There *is* an Is.' That is as much monkish credulity as St. Thomas asks of us at the start. Very few unbelievers start by asking us to believe so little. And yet, upon this sharp pin-point of reality, he rears by long logical processes that have never really been successfully overthrown, the whole cosmic system of Christendom.

Thus, Aquinas insists very profoundly, but very practically, that there *instantly* enters, with this idea of affirmation, the idea of contradiction. It is instantly apparent, even to the child, that there cannot be both affirmation and contradiction. Whatever you call the thing he sees, a lawn or a mirage or a sensation or a state of consciousness, when he sees it, he knows it is not true that he does not see it. Or whatever you call what he is supposed to be doing, seeing or dreaming or being conscious of an impression, he knows that if he is doing it, it is a lie to say he is not doing it. Therefore there has already entered *something* beyond even the first fact of being; there follows it like its shadow the first fundamental creed or commandment; that a thing cannot be and not be. Henceforth, in common or popular language, there is a false and true. I say in popular language, because Aquinas is nowhere more subtle than in pointing out that being is not strictly the same as truth; seeing truth must mean the appreciation of being by some mind capable of appreciating it. But in a general sense there has entered that primeval world of pure actuality, the division and dilemma that brings the ultimate sort of war into the world; the everlasting duel between Yes and No. This is the dilemma that many sceptics have darkened the universe and dissolved the mind, solely in order to escape. They are those who maintain that there is something that is both Yes and No. I do not know whether they pronounce it Yo.

The next step following on this acceptance of actuality or

certainty, or whatever we call it in popular language, is much more difficult to explain in that language. But it represents exactly the point at which nearly all other systems go wrong; and in taking the third step abandon the first. Aquinas has affirmed that our first sense of fact is a fact; and he cannot go back on it without falsehood. But when we come to look at the fact or facts, as we know them, we observe that they have a rather queer character, which has made many moderns grow strangely and restlessly sceptical about them. For instance, they are largely in a state of change, from being one thing to being another; or their qualities are relative to other things; or they appear to move incessantly; or they appear to vanish entirely. At this point, as I say, many sages lose hold of the first principle of reality, which they would concede at first; and fall back on saying that there is nothing except change; or nothing except comparison; or nothing except flux; or in effect that there is nothing at all. Aquinas turns the whole argument the other way, keeping in line with his first realization of reality. There is no doubt about the being of being, even if it does sometimes look like becoming; that is because what we see is not the fullness of being; or (to continue a sort of colloquial slang) we never see being being as much as it can. Ice is melted into cold water and cold water is heated into hot water; it cannot be all three at once. But this does not make water unreal or even relative; it only means that its being is limited to being one thing at a time. But the fullness of being is everything that it can be; and without it the lesser or approximate forms of being cannot be explained as anything; unless they are explained away as nothing.

This crude outline can only at the best be historical rather than philosophical. It is impossible to compress into it the metaphysical proofs of such an idea; especially in the medieval metaphysical language. But this distinction in philosophy is tremendous as a turning-point in history. Most thinkers, on realizing the apparent mutability of being, have really forgotten their own realization of the being, and believed only in the mutability. They cannot even say that a thing changes into another thing; for them there is no instant in the process at which it is a thing at all. It is only a change. It would be more logical to call it nothing changing into nothing, than to say (on these principles) that there ever was or will be a moment when the thing is itself. St. Thomas maintains that the ordinary thing at any moment is something; but it is not everything that it could be. There is a fullness of being, in which it could be everything that it can be. Thus, while most sages come at last to nothing but naked change, he comes to the ultimate thing that is unchangeable, because it is all the other things at once. While they describe a change which is really a change in nothing, he describes a changelessness which includes the changes of everything. Things change because they are not complete; but their reality can only be explained as part of something that is complete. It is God.

Historically, at least, it was round this sharp and crooked corner that all the sophists have followed each other, while the great Schoolman went up the high road of experience and expansion; to the beholding of cities; to the building of cities. They all failed at this early stage because, in the words of the old game, they took away the number they first thought of. The recognition of something, of a thing or things, is the first act of the intellect. But because the examination of a thing shows it is not a fixed or final thing, they inferred that there is nothing fixed or final. Thus, in various ways, they all began to see a thing as something thinner than a thing; a wave; a weakness; an abstract instability. St. Thomas, to use the same rude figure, saw a thing that was thicker than a thing; that was even more solid than the solid but secondary facts he had started by admitting as facts. Since we know them to be real, any elusive or bewildering element in their reality cannot really be unreality; and must be merely their relation to the real reality. A hundred human philosophies, ranging over the earth from Nominalism to Nirvana and Maya, from formless Evolutionism to mindless Quietism, all come from this first break in the Thomist chain; the notion that, because what we see does not satisfy us, or explain itself, it is not even what we see. That cosmos is a contradiction in terms and strangles itself; but Thomism cuts itself free. The defect we see, in what is, is simply that it is not all that is. God is more actual even than Man; more actual even than Matter; for God with all His powers at every instant is immortally in action.

A cosmic comedy of a very curious sort occurred recently; involving the views of very brilliant men, such as Mr. Bernard

Shaw and the Dean of St. Paul's. Briefly, free-thinkers of many sorts had often said they had no need of a Creation, because the cosmos had always existed and always would exist. Mr. Bernard Shaw said he had become an atheist because the universe had gone on making itself from the beginning, or without a beginning; Dean Inge later displayed consternation at the very idea that the universe could have an end. Most modern Christians, living by tradition where medieval Christians could live by logic or reason, vaguely felt that it was a dreadful idea to deprive them of the Day of Judgment. Most modern agnostics (who are delighted to have their ideas called dreadful) cried out all the more, with one accord, that the self-producing, self-existent, truly scientific universe had never needed to have a beginning and could not come to an end. At this very instant, quite suddenly, like the look-out man on a ship who shouts a warning about a rock, the *real* man of science, the expert who was examining the facts, announced in a loud voice that the universe *was* coming to an end. He had not been listening, of course, to the talk of the amateurs; he had been actually examining the texture of matter; and he said it was disintegrating; the world was apparently blowing itself up by a gradual explosion called energy; the whole business would certainly have an end and had presumably had a beginning. This was very shocking indeed; not to the orthodox, but rather specially to the unorthodox, who are rather more easily shocked. Dean Inge, who had been lecturing the orthodox for years on their stern duty of accepting all scientific discoveries, positively wailed aloud over this truly tactless scientific discovery; and practically implored the scientific discoverers to go away and discover something different. It seems almost incredible; but it is a fact that he asked what God would have to amuse Him, if the universe ceased. That is a measure of how much the modern mind needs Thomas Aquinas. But even without Aquinas, I can hardly conceive any educated man, let alone such a learned man, believing in God at all without assuming that God contains in Himself every perfection including eternal joy; and does not require the solar system to entertain Him like a circus.

To step out of these presumptions, prejudices and private disappointments, into the world of St. Thomas, is like escaping from a scuffle in a dark room into the broad daylight. St.

Thomas says, quite straightforwardly, that he himself believes this world has a beginning and end; because such seems to be the teaching of the Church; the validity of which mystical message to mankind he defends elsewhere with dozens of quite different arguments. Anyhow, the Church said the world would end, and apparently the Church was right; always supposing (as we are always supposed to suppose) that the latest men of science are right. But Aquinas says he sees no particular reason, in reason, why this world should not be a world without end; or even without beginning. And he is quite certain that, if it were entirely without end or beginning, there would still be exactly the same logical need of a Creator. Anybody who does not see that, he gently implies, does not really understand what is meant by a Creator.

For what St. Thomas means is not a medieval picture of an old king; but this second step in the great argument about *Ens* or Being; the second point which is so desperately difficult to put correctly in popular language. That is why I have introduced it here in the particular form of the argument that there must be a Creator even if there is no Day of Creation. Looking at Being as it is now, as the baby looks at the grass, we see a second thing about it; in quite popular language, it *looks* secondary and dependent. Existence exists; but it is not sufficiently self-existent; and would never become so merely by going on existing. The same primary sense which tells us it is Being, tells us that it is not perfect Being; not merely imperfect in the popular controversial sense of containing sin or sorrow; but imperfect as Being; less actual than the actuality it implies. For instance, its Being is often only Becoming; beginning to Be or ceasing to Be; it implies a more constant or complete thing of which it gives in itself no example. That is the meaning of that basic medieval phrase, 'Everything that is moving is moved by another'; which, in the clear subtlety of St. Thomas, means inexpressibly more than the mere Deistic 'somebody wound up the clock' with which it is probably often confounded. Anyone who thinks deeply will see that motion has about it an essential incompleteness, which approximates to something more complete. The actual argument is rather technical; and concerns the fact that potentiality does not explain itself;

moreover, in any case unfolding must be of something folded. Suffice it to say that the mere modern evolutionists, who would ignore the argument, do not do so because they have discovered any flaw in the argument; for they have never discovered the argument itself. They do so because they are too shallow to see the flaw in their own argument; for the weakness of their thesis is covered by fashionable phraseology, as the strength of the old thesis is covered by old-fashioned phraseology. But, for those who really think, there is always something really unthinkable about the whole evolutionary cosmos, as they conceive it; because it is something coming out of nothing; an ever-increasing flood of water pouring out of an empty jug. Those who can simply accept that, without even seeing the difficulty, are not likely to go so deep as Aquinas and see the solution of his difficulty. In a word, the world does not explain itself, and cannot do so merely by continuing to expand itself. But anyhow it is absurd for the Evolutionist to complain that it is unthinkable for an admittedly unthinkable God to make everything out of nothing; and then pretend that it is *more* thinkable that nothing should turn itself into everything.

We have seen that most philosophers simply fail to philosophize about things because they change; they also fail to philosophize about things because they differ. We have no space to follow St. Thomas through all these negative heresies; but a word must be said about Nominalism, or the doubt founded on the things that differ. Everyone knows that the Nominalist declared that things differ too much to be really classified; so that they are only labelled. Aquinas was a firm but moderate Realist, and therefore held that there really are general qualities; as that human beings are human, and other paradoxes. To be an extreme Realist would have taken him too near to being a Platonist. He recognized that individuality is real, but said that it coexists with a common character making some generalization possible; in fact, as in most things, he said exactly what all common sense would say, if no intelligent heretics had ever disturbed it. Nevertheless, they still continue to disturb it. I remember when Mr. H. G. Wells had an alarming fit of Nominalist philosophy, and poured forth book after book to argue that everything is unique and untypical; as that a man is so much an individual that he is not even a man. It is a quaint and almost comic fact, that this chaotic negation especially attracts those who are always complaining of social chaos, and who propose to replace it by the most sweeping social regulations. It is the very men, who say that nothing can be classified, who say that everything must be codified. Thus Mr. Bernard Shaw said that the only golden rule is that there is no golden rule. He prefers an iron rule; as in Russia.

But this is only a small inconsistency in some moderns as individuals. There is a much deeper inconsistency in them as theorists in relation to the general theory called Creative Evolution. They seem to imagine that they avoid the metaphysical doubt about mere change by assuming (it is not very clear why) that the change will always be for the better. But the mathematical difficulty of finding a corner in a curve is not altered by turning the chart upside down, and saying that a downward curve is now an upward curve. The point is that there is no point in the curve; no place at which we have a logical right to say that the curve has reached its climax, or revealed its origin, or come to its end. It makes no difference that they choose to be cheerful about it, and say, 'It is enough that there is always a beyond': instead of lamenting, like the more realistic poets of the past, over the tragedy of mere Mutability. It is not enough that there is always a beyond; because it might be beyond bearing. Indeed the only defence of this view is that sheer boredom is such an agony, that any movement is a relief. But the truth is that they have never read St. Thomas; or they would find, with no little terror, that they really agree with him. What they really mean is that change is not mere change, but is the unfolding of something; and if it is thus unfolded, though the unfolding takes twelve million years, it must be there already. In other words, they agree with Aquinas that there is everywhere potentiality that has not reached its end in act. But if it is a definite potentiality, and if it can only end in a definite act, why then there is a Great Being, in whom all potentialities already exist as a plan of action. In other words, it is impossible even to say that the change is for the better, unless the best exists somewhere, both before and after the change. Otherwise it is indeed mere change; as the blankest sceptics or the blackest pessimists would see it. Suppose two entirely new paths open before the progress of Creative Evolution. How is the evolutionist to know which Beyond is the better; unless he accepts from the past and present some standard of the best? By their superficial theory everything can change; everything can improve, even the nature of improvement. But in their submerged common sense, they do not really think that an ideal of kindness could change to an ideal of cruelty. It is typical of them that they will sometimes rather timidly use the word Purpose; but blush at the very mention of the word Person.

St. Thomas is the very reverse of anthropomorphic, in spite of his shrewdness as an anthropologist. Some theologians have even claimed that he is too much of an agnostic; and has left the nature of God too much of an intellectual abstraction. But we do not need even St. Thomas, we do not need anything but our own common sense, to tell us that if there has been from the beginning anything that can possibly be called a Purpose, it must reside in something that has the essential elements of a Person. There cannot be an intention hovering in the air all by itself, any more than a memory that nobody remembers or a joke that nobody has made. The only chance for those supporting such suggestions is to take refuge in blank and bottomless irrationality; and even then it is impossible to prove that anybody has any right to be unreasonable, if St. Thomas has no right to be reasonable.

In a sketch that aims only at the baldest simplification, this does seem to me the simplest truth about St. Thomas the philosopher. He is one, so to speak, who is faithful to his first love; and it is love at first sight. I mean that he immediately recognized a real quality in things; and afterwards resisted all the disintegrating doubts arising from the nature of those things. That is why I emphasize, even in the first few pages, the fact that there is a sort of purely Christian humility and fidelity underlying his philosophic realism. St. Thomas could as truly say, of having seen merely a stick or a stone, what St. Paul said of having seen the rending of the secret heavens, 'I was not disobedient to the heavenly vision.' For though the stick or the stone is an earthly vision, it is through them that St. Thomas finds his way to heaven; and the point is that he is obedient to the vision; he does not go back on it. Nearly all the other sages who have led or misled mankind do, on one excuse or another, go back on it. They dissolve the stick or the stone in chemical solutions of scepticism; either in the medium of mere time and change; or in the difficulties of classification of unique units; or in the difficulty of recognizing variety while admitting unity. The first of these three is called debate about flux and formless transition; the second is the debate about Nominalism and Realism, or the existence of general ideas; the third is called the ancient metaphysical riddle of the One and the Many. But they can all be reduced under a rough image to this same statement about St. Thomas. He is still true to the first truth and refusing the first treason. He will not deny what he has seen, though it be a secondary and diverse reality. He will not take away the numbers he first thought of, though there may be quite a number of them.

He has seen grass; and will not say he has not seen grass, because it today is and tomorrow is cast into the oven. That is the substance of all scepticism about change, transition, transformism and the rest. He will not say that there is no grass but only growth. If grass grows and withers, it can only mean that it is part of a greater thing, which is even more real; not that the grass is less real than it looks. St. Thomas has a really logical right to say, in the words of the modern mystic, A. E.: 'I begin by the grass to be bound again to the Lord.'

He has seen grass and grain; and he will not say that they do not differ, because there is something common to grass and grain. Nor will he say that, because there is something common to grass and grain, they do not really differ. He will not say, with the extreme Nominalists, that because grain can be differentiated into all sorts of fruitage, or grass trodden into mire with any kind of weed, therefore there can be no *classification* to distinguish weeds from slime or to draw a fine distinction between cattle-food and cattle. He will not say with the extreme Platonists, on the other hand, that he saw the perfect fruit in his own head by shutting his eyes, *before* he saw any difference between grain and grass. He saw one thing and then another thing, and then a common quality; but he does not really pretend that he saw the quality before the thing.

He has seen grass and gravel; that is to say, he has seen things really different; things not classified together like grass and grain. The first flash of fact shows us a world of really strange things; not merely strange to us, but strange to each other. The separate things need have nothing in common except Being. Everything is Being; but it is not true that everything is Unity. It is here, as I have said, that St. Thomas does definitely, one might say defiantly, part company with the Pantheist and the Monist. All things are; but among the things that are is the thing called difference, quite as much as the thing called similarity. And here again we begin to be bound again to the Lord, not only by the universality of grass, but by the incompatibility of grass and gravel. For this world of different and varied beings is especially the world of the Christian Creator; the world of created things, like things made by an artist; as compared with the world that is only one thing, with a sort of shimmering and shifting veil of misleading change, which is the conception of so many of the ancient religions of Asia and the modern sophistries of Germany. In the face of these, St. Thomas still stands stubborn in the same obstinate objective fidelity. He has seen grass and gravel; and he is not disobedient to the heavenly vision.

To sum up; the reality of things, the mutability of things, the diversity of things, and all other such things that can be attributed to things, is followed carefully by the medieval philosopher, without losing touch with the original point of the reality. There is no space in this book to specify the thousand steps of thought, by which he shows that he is right. But the point is that, even apart from being right, he is real. He is a realist in a rather curious sense of his own, which is a third thing, distinct from the almost contrary medieval and modern meanings of the word. Even the doubts and difficulties about reality have driven him to believe in more reality rather than less. The *deceitfulness* of things which has had so sad an effect on so many sages, has almost a contrary effect on this sage. If things deceive us, it is by being more real than they seem. As ends in themselves they always deceive us; but as things tending to a greater end, they are even more real than we think them. If they seem to have a relative unreality (so to speak) it is because they are potential and not actual; they are unfulfilled, like packets of seeds or boxes of fireworks. They have it in them to be more real than they are. And there is an upper world of what the Schoolman called Fruition, or Fulfilment, in which all this relative relativity becomes actuality; in which the trees burst into flower or the rockets into flame. . . .

Charles Dickens

The Dickens Period

Much of our modern difficulty, in religion and other things, arises merely from this; that we confuse the word 'indefinable' with the word 'vague'. If someone speaks of a spiritual fact as 'indefinable' we promptly picture something misty, a cloud with indeterminate edges. But this is an error even in commonplace logic. The thing that cannot be defined is the first thing; the primary fact. It is our arms and legs, our pots and pans, that are indefinable. The indefinable is the indisputable. The man next door is indefinable, because he is too actual to be defined. And there are some to whom spiritual things have the same fierce and practical proximity; some to whom God is too actual to be defined.

But there is a third class of primary terms. There are popular expressions which everyone uses and no one can explain; which the wise man will accept and reverence, as he reverences desire or darkness or any elemental thing. The prigs of the debating club will demand that he should define his terms. And, being a wise man, he will flatly refuse. This first inexplicable term is the most important term of all. The word that has no definition is the word that has no substitute. If a man falls back again and again on some such word as 'vulgar' or 'manly', do not suppose that the word means nothing because he cannot say what it means. If he could say what the word means he would say what it means instead of saying the word. When the Game Chicken (that fine thinker) kept on saying to Mr. Toots, 'It's mean. That's what it is – it's mean', he was using language in the wisest possible way. For what else could he say? There is no word for mean except mean. A man must be very mean himself before he comes to defining meanness. Precisely because the word is indefinable, the word is indispensable.

In everyday talk, or in any of our journals, we may find the loose but important phrase, 'Why have we no great men today? Why have we no great men like Thackeray, or Carlyle, or Dickens?' Do not let us dismiss this expression, because it appears loose or arbitrary. 'Great' does mean something, and the test of its actuality is to be found by noting how instinctively and decisively we do apply it to some men and not to others; above all, how instinctively and decisively we do apply it to four or five men in the Victorian era, four or five men of whom Dickens was not the least. The term is found to fit a definite thing. Dickens was what it means. Even the fastidious and unhappy who cannot read his books without a continuous critical exasperation, would use the word of him without stopping to think. They feel that Dickens is a great writer even if he is not a good writer. He is treated as a classic; that is, as a king who may now be deserted, but who cannot now be dethroned. The atmosphere of this word clings to him; and the curious thing is that we cannot get it to cling to any of the men of our own generation. 'Great' is the first adjective which the most supercilious modern critic would apply to Dickens. And 'great' is the last adjective the most supercilious critic would apply to himself. We dare not claim to be great men, even when we claim to be superior to them.

Is there, then, any vital meaning in this idea of 'greatness' or in our laments over its absence in our own time? Some people say, indeed, that this sense of mass is but a mirage of distance, and that men always think dead men great and live men small. They seem to think that the law of perspective in the mental world is the precise opposite to the law of perspective in the physical world. They think that figures grow larger as they walk away. But this theory cannot be made to correspond with the facts. We do not lack great men in our own day because we decline to look for them in our own day; on the contrary, we are looking for them all day long. We are not, as a matter of fact, mere examples of those who stone the prophets and leave it to their posterity to build their sepulchres. If the world would only produce our perfect prophet, solemn, searching, universal, nothing would give us keener pleasure than to build his sepulchre. In our eagerness we might even bury him alive. Nor is it true that the great men of the Victorian era were not called great in their own time. By many they were called great from the first. Charlotte Brontë held this heroic language about Thackeray. Ruskin held it about Carlyle. A definite school regarded Dickens as a great man from the first days of his fame: Dickens certainly belonged to this school.

In reply to this question, 'Why have we no great men today?'

many modern explanations are offered. Advertisements, cigarette smoking, the decay of religion, the decay of agriculture, too much humanitarianism, too little humanitarianism, the fact that people are educated insufficiently, the fact that they are educated at all, all these are reasons given. If I give my own explanation, it is not for its intrinsic value; it is because my answer to the question, 'Why have we no great men?' is a short way of stating the deepest and most catastrophic difference between the age in which we live and the early nineteenth century; the age under the shadow of the French Revolution, the age in which Dickens was born.

The soundest of the Dickens critics, a man of genius, Mr. George Gissing, opens his criticism by remarking that the world in which Dickens grew up was a hard and cruel world. He notes its gross feeding, its fierce sports, its fighting and foul humour, and all this he summarizes in the words hard and cruel. It is curious how different are the impressions of men. To me this old English world seems infinitely less hard and cruel than the world described in Gissing's own novels. Coarse external customs are merely relative, and easily assimilated. A man soon learnt to harden his hands and harden his head. Faced with the world of Gissing, he can do little but harden his heart. But the fundamental difference between the beginning of the nineteenth century and the end of it is a difference simple but enormous. The first period was full of evil things, but it was full of hope. The second period, *fin de siècle*, was even full (in some sense) of good things. But it was occupied in asking what was the good of good things. Joy itself became joyless; and the fighting of Cobbett was happier than the feasting of Walter Pater. The men of Cobbett's day were sturdy enough to endure and inflict brutality; but they were also sturdy enough to alter it. This 'hard and cruel' age was, after all, the age of reform. The gibbet stood up black above them; but it was black against the dawn.

This dawn, against which the gibbet and all the old cruelties stood out so black and clear, was the developing idea of liberalism, the French Revolution. It was a clear and a happy philosophy. And only against such philosophies do evils appear evident at all. The optimist is a better reformer than the pessimist; and the man who believes life to be excellent is the man who alters it most. It seems a paradox, yet the reason of it is very plain. The pessimist can be enraged at evil. But only the optimist can be surprised at it. From the reformer is required a simplicity of surprise. He must have the faculty of a violent and virgin astonishment. It is not enough that he should think injustice distressing; he must think injustice *absurd*, an anomaly in existence, a matter less for tears than for a shattering laughter. On the other hand, the pessimists at the end of the century could hardly curse even the blackest thing; for they could hardly see it against its black and eternal background. Nothing was bad, because everything was bad. Life in prison was infamous – like life anywhere else. The fires of persecution were vile – like the stars. We perpetually find this paradox of a contented discontent. Dr. Johnson takes too sad a view of humanity, but he is also too satisfied a Conservative. Rousseau takes too rosy a view of humanity, but he causes a revolution. Swift is angry, but a Tory. Shelley is happy, and a rebel. Dickens, the optimist, satirizes the Fleet, and the Fleet is gone. Gissing, the pessimist, satirizes Suburbia, and Suburbia remains.

Mr. Gissing's error, then, about the early Dickens period we may put thus: in calling it hard and cruel he omits the wind of hope and humanity that was blowing through it. It may have been full of inhuman institutions, but it was full of humanitarian people. And this humanitarianism was very much the better (in my view) because it was a rough and even rowdy humanitarianism. It was free from all the faults that cling to the name. It was, if you will, a coarse humanitarianism. It was a shouting, fighting, drinking philanthropy – a noble thing. But, in any case, this atmosphere was the atmosphere of the Revolution; and its main idea was the idea of human equality. I am not concerned here to defend the egalitarian idea against the solemn and babyish attacks made upon it by the rich and learned of today. I am merely concerned to state one of its practical consequences. One of the actual and certain consequences of the idea that all men are equal is immediately to produce very great men. I would say superior men, only that the hero thinks of himself as great, but not as superior. This has been hidden from us of late by a foolish worship of sinister and exceptional men, men without comradeship, or any infectious virtue. This type of Caesar does exist. There is a great man who makes every man feel small. But the real great man is the man who makes every man feel great.

The spirit of the early century produced great men, because it believed that men were great. It made strong men by encouraging weak men. Its education, its public habits, its rhetoric, were all addressed towards encouraging the greatness in everybody. And by encouraging the greatness in everybody, it naturally encouraged superlative greatness in some. Superiority came out of the high rapture of equality. It is precisely in this sort of passionate unconsciousness and bewildering community of thought that men do become more than themselves. No man by taking thought can add one cubit to his stature; but a man may add many cubits to his stature by not taking thought. The best men of the Revolution were simply common men at their best. This is why our age can never understand Napoleon. Because he was something great and triumphant, we suppose that he must have been something extraordinary, something inhuman. Some say he was the Devil; some say he was the Superman. Was he a very, very bad man? Was he a good man with some greater moral code? We strive in vain to invent the mysteries behind that immortal mask of brass. The modern world with all its subtleness will never guess his strange secret; for his strange secret was that he was very like other people.

And almost without exception all the great men have come out of this atmosphere of equality. Great men may make despotisms; but democracies make great men. The other main factory of heroes besides a revolution is a religion. And a religion again, is a thing which, by its nature, does not think of men as more or less valuable, but of men as all intensely and painfully valuable, a democracy of eternal danger. For religion all men are equal, as all pennies are equal, because the only value in any of them is that they bear the image of the King. This fact has been quite insufficiently observed in the study of religious heroes. Piety produces intellectual greatness precisely because piety in itself is quite indifferent to intellectual greatness. The strength of Cromwell was that he cared for religion. But the strength of religion was that it did not care for Cromwell; did not care for him, that is, any more than for anybody else. He and his footman were equally welcomed to warm places in the hospitality of hell. It has often been said, very truly, that religion is the thing that makes the ordinary man feel extraordinary; it is an equally important truth that religion is the thing that makes the extraordinary man feel ordinary.

Carlyle killed the heroes; there have been none since his time. He killed the heroic (which he sincerely loved) by forcing upon each man this question: 'Am I strong or weak?' To which the answer from any honest man whatever (yes, from Caesar or Bismarck) would certainly be 'weak'. He asked for candidates for a definite aristocracy, for men who should hold themselves consciously above their fellows. He advertised for them, so to speak; he promised them glory; he promised them omnipotence. They have not appeared yet. They never will. For the real heroes of whom he wrote had appeared out of an ecstasy of the ordinary. I have already instanced such a case as Cromwell. But there is no need to go through all the great men of Carlyle. Carlyle himself was as great as any of them; and if ever there was a typical child of the French Revolution, it was he. He began with the wildest hopes from the Reform Bill, and although he soured afterwards, he had been made and moulded by those hopes. He was disappointed with Equality; but Equality was not disappointed with him. Equality is justified of all her children.

But we, in the post-Carlylean period, have become fastidious about great men. Every man examines himself, every man examines his neighbours, to see whether they or he quite come up to the exact line of greatness. The answer is, naturally, 'No'. And many a man calls himself contentedly 'a minor poet' who would then have been inspired to be a major prophet. We are hard to please and of little faith. We can hardly believe that there is such a thing as a great man. They could hardly believe there was such a thing as a small one. But we are always praying that our eyes may behold greatness, instead of praying that our heart may be filled with it. Thus, for instance, the Liberal party (to which I belong) was, in its period of exile, always saying, 'O for a Gladstone!' and such things. We were always asking that it might be strengthened from above, instead of ourselves strengthening it from below, with our hope and our anger and our youth. Every man was waiting for a leader. Every man ought to be waiting for a chance to lead. If a god does come upon the earth, he will descend at the sight of the brave. Our prostrations and litanies are of no avail; our new moons and our sabbaths are an abomination. The great man will come when all of us are feeling great, not when all of us are feeling small. He will ride in at some splendid moment when we all feel that we could do without him.

We are then able to answer in some manner the question, 'Why have we no great men?' We have no great men chiefly because we are always looking for them. We are connoisseurs of greatness, and connoisseurs can never be great; we are fastidious, that is, we are small. When Diogenes went about with a lantern looking for an honest man, I am afraid he had very little time to be honest himself. And when anybody goes about on his hands and knees looking for a great man to worship, he is making sure that one man at any rate shall not be great. Now, the error of Diogenes is evident. The error of Diogenes lay in the fact that he omitted to notice that every man is both an honest man and a dishonest man. Diogenes looked for his honest man inside every crypt and cavern; but he never thought of looking inside the thief. And that is where the Founder of Christianity found the honest man; He found him on a gibbet and promised him Paradise. Just as Christianity looked for the honest man inside the thief, democracy looked for the wise man inside the fool. It encouraged the fool to be wise. We can call this thing sometimes optimism, sometimes equality; the nearest name for it is encouragement. It had its exaggerations – failure to understand original sin, notions that education would make all men good, the childlike yet pedantic philosophies of human perfectibility. But the whole was full of a faith in the infinity of human souls, which is in itself not only Christian but orthodox; and this we have lost amid the limitations of a pessimistic science. Christianity said that any man could be a saint if he chose; democracy, that any man could be a citizen if he chose. The note of the last few decades in art and ethics has been that a man is stamped with an irrevocable psychology, and is cramped for perpetuity in the prison of his skull. It was a world that expected everything of everybody. It was a world that encouraged anybody to be anything. And in England and literature its living expression was Dickens.

We shall consider Dickens in many other capacities, but let us put this one first. He was the voice in England of this humane intoxication and expansion, this encouraging of anybody to be anything. His best books are a carnival of liberty, and there is more of the real spirit of the French Revolution in *Nicholas Nickleby* than in *The Tale of Two Cities*. His work has the great glory of the Revolution, the bidding of every man to be himself; it has also the revolutionary deficiency; it seems to think that this mere emancipation is enough. No man *encouraged* his characters so much as Dickens. 'I am a fond father,' he says, 'to every child of my fancy.' He was not only a fond father, he was an over-indulgent father. The children of his fancy are spoilt children. They shake the house like heavy and shouting schoolboys; they smash the story to pieces like so much furniture. When we moderns write stories our characters are better controlled. But, alas! our characters are rather easier to control. We are in no danger from the gigantic gambols of creatures like Mantalini and Micawber. We are in no danger of giving our readers too much Weller or Wegg. We have not got it to give. When we experience the ungovernable sense of life which goes along with the old Dickens sense of liberty, we experience the best of the revolution. We are filled with the first of all democratic doctrines, that all men are interesting; Dickens tried to make some of his people appear dull people but he could not keep them dull. He could not make a monotonous man. The bores in his books are brighter than the wits in other books.

I have put this position first for a defined reason. It is useless for us to attempt to imagine Dickens and his life unless we are able at least to imagine this old atmosphere of a democratic optimism – a confidence in common men. Dickens depends upon such a comprehension in a rather unusual manner, a manner worth explanation, or at least remark.

The disadvantage under which Dickens has fallen, both as an artist and a moralist, is very plain. His misfortune is that neither of the two last movements in literary criticism has done him any good. He has suffered alike from his enemies, and from the enemies of his enemies. The facts to which I refer are familiar. When the world first awoke from the mere hypnotism of Dickens, from the direct tyranny of his temperament, there was, of course, a reaction. At the head of it came the Realists, with their documents, like Miss Flite. They declared that scenes and types in Dickens were wholly impossible (in which they were perfectly right), and on this rather paradoxical ground objected to them as literature. They were not 'like life', and there, they thought, was an end of the matter. The Realist for a time prevailed. But Realists did not enjoy their victory (if they enjoyed anything) very long. A more symbolic school of criticism soon arose. Men saw that it was necessary to give a much deeper and more delicate meaning to the expression 'like life'. Streets are not life, cities and civilizations are not life, faces even and voices are not life itself. Life is within, and no man hath seen it at any time. As for our meals, and our manners, and our daily dress, these are things exactly like sonnets; they are random symbols of the soul. One man tries to express himself in books, another in boots; both probably fail. Our solid houses and square meals are in the strict sense fiction. They are things made up to typify our thoughts. The coat a man wears may be wholly fictitious; the movement of his hands may be quite unlike life.

This much the intelligence of men soon perceived. And by this much Dickens's fame should have greatly profited. For Dickens is 'like life' in the truer sense, in the sense that he is akin to the living principle in us and in the universe; he is like life, at least in this detail, that he is alive. His art is like life, because, like life, it cares for nothing outside itself, and goes on its way rejoicing. Both produce monsters with a kind of carelessness, like enormous by-products; life producing the rhinoceros, and art Mr. Bunsby. Art indeed copies life in not copying life, for life copies nothing. Dickens's art is like life because, like life, it is irresponsible, because, like life, it is incredible.

Yet the return of this realization has not greatly profited Dickens, the return of romance has been almost useless to this great romantic. He has gained as little from the fall of the Realists as from their triumph; there has been a revolution, there has been a counter-revolution, there has been no restoration. And the reason of this brings us back to that atmosphere of popular optimism of which I spoke. And the shortest way of expressing the more recent neglect of Dickens is to say that for our time and taste he exaggerates the wrong thing.

Exaggeration is the definition of art. That Dickens and the Moderns understood. Art is, in its inmost nature, fantastic. Time brings queer revenges, and while the Realists were yet living, the art of Dickens was justified by Aubrey Beardsley. But men like Aubrey Beardsley were allowed to be fantastic, because the mood which they overstrained and overstated was a mood which their period understood. Dickens overstrains and overstates a mood our period does not understand. The truth he exaggerates is exactly this old Revolution sense of infinite opportunity and boisterous brotherhood. And we resent his undue sense of it, because we ourselves have not even a due sense of it. We feel troubled with too much where we have too little; we wish he would keep it within bounds. For we are all exact and scientific on the subjects we do not care about. We all immediately detect exaggeration in an exposition of Mormonism or a patriotic speech from Paraguay. We all require sobriety on the subject of the sea-serpent. But the moment we begin to believe a thing ourselves, that moment we begin easily to overstate it; and the moment our souls become serious, our words become a little wild. And certain Moderns are thus placed towards exaggeration. They permit any writer to emphasize doubts for instance, for doubts are their religion, but they permit no man to emphasize dogmas. If a man be the mildest Christian, they smell 'cant'; but he can be a ravaging windmill of pessimism, and they call it 'temperament'. If a moralist paints a wild picture of immorality, they doubt its truth, they say that devils are not so black as they are painted. But if a pessimist paints a wild picture of melancholy, they accept the whole horrible psychology, and they never ask if devils are as blue as they are painted.

It is evident, in short, why even those who admire exaggeration do not admire Dickens. He is exaggerating the wrong thing. They know what it is to feel a sadness so strange and deep that only impossible characters can express it: they do not know what it is to feel a joy so vital and violent that only impossible characters can express that. They know that the soul can be so sad as to dream naturally of the blue faces of the corpses of Baudelaire: they do not know that the soul can be so cheerful as to dream naturally of the blue face of Major Bagstock. They know that there is a point of depression at which one believes in Tintagiles: they do not know that there is a point of exhilaration at which one believes in Mr. Wegg. To them the impossibilities of Dickens seem much more impossible than they really are, because they are already attuned to the opposite impossibilities of Maeterlinck. For every mood there is an appropriate impossibility – a decent and tactful impossibility – fitted to the frame of mind. Every train of thought may end in an ecstasy, and all roads lead to Elfland. But few now walk far enough along the street of Dickens to find the place where the cockney villas grow so comic that they become poetical. People do not know how far mere good spirits will go. For instance, we never think (as the old folk-lore did) of good spirits reaching to the spiritual world. We see this in the complete absence from modern, popular supernaturalism of the old popular mirth. We hear plenty today of the wisdom of the spiritual world; but we do not hear, as our fathers did, of the folly of the spiritual world, of the tricks of the gods, and the jokes of the patron saints. Our popular tales tell us of a man who is so wise that he touches the supernatural, like Dr. Nikola; but they never tell us (like the popular tales of the past) of a man who was so silly that he touched the supernatural, like Bottom the Weaver. We do not understand the dark and transcendental sympathy between fairies and fools. We understand a devout occultism, an evil occultism, a tragic occultism, but a farcical occultism is beyond us. Yet a farcical occultism is the very essence of *The Midsummer Night's Dream*. It is also the right and credible essence of *The Christmas Carol*. Whether we understand it depends upon whether we can understand that exhilaration is not a physical accident, but a mystical fact; that exhilaration can be infinite, like sorrow; that a joke can be so big that it breaks the roof of the stars. By simply going on being absurd, a thing can become godlike; there is but one step from the ridiculous to the sublime.

Dickens was great because he was immoderately possessed with all this; if we are to understand him at all we must also be moderately possessed with it. We must understand this old limitless hilarity and human confidence, at least enough to be able to endure it when it is pushed a great deal too far. For Dickens did push it too far; he did push the hilarity to the point of incredible character-drawing; he did push the human confidence to the point of an unconvincing sentimentalism. You can trace, if you will, the revolutionary joy till it reaches the incredible Sapsea epitaph; you can trace the revolutionary hope till it reaches the repentance of Dombey. There is plenty to carp at in this man if you are inclined to carp; you may easily find him vulgar if you cannot see that he is divine; and if you cannot laugh with Dickens, undoubtedly you can laugh at him.

I believe myself that this braver world of his will certainly return; for I believe that it is bound up with the realities, like morning and the spring. But for those who beyond remedy regard it as an error, I put this appeal before any other observations on Dickens. First let us sympathize, if only for an instant, with the hopes of the Dickens period, with that cheerful trouble of change. If democracy has disappointed you, do not think of it as a burst bubble, but at least as a broken heart, an old love-affair. Do not sneer at the time when the creed of humanity was on its honeymoon; treat it with the dreadful reverence that is due to youth. For you, perhaps, a drearier philosophy has covered and eclipsed the earth. The fierce poet of the Middle Ages wrote, 'Abandon hope, all ye who enter here', over the gates of the lower world. The emancipated poets of today have written it over the gates of this world. But if we are to understand the story which follows, we must erase that apocalyptic writing, if only for an hour. We must recreate the faith of our fathers, if only as an artistic atmosphere. If, then, you are a pessimist, in reading this story, forgo for a little the pleasures of pessimism. Dream for one mad moment that the grass is green. Unlearn that sinister learning that you think so clear; deny that deadly knowledge that you think you know. Surrender the very flower of your culture; give up the very jewel of your pride; abandon hopelessness, all ye who enter here.

The Great Dickens Characters

All criticism tends too much to become criticism of criticism; and the reason is very evident. It is that criticism of creation is so very staggering a thing. We see this in the difficulty of criticizing any artistic creation. We see it again in the difficulty of criticizing that creation which is spelt with a capital C. The pessimists who attack the universe are always under this disadvantage. They have an exhilarating consciousness that they could make the sun and moon better; but they also have the depressing consciousness that they could not make the sun and moon at all. A man looking at a hippopotamus may sometimes be tempted to regard a hippopotamus as an enormous mistake; but he is also bound to confess that a fortunate inferiority prevents him personally from making such mistakes. It is neither a blasphemy nor an exaggeration to say that we feel something of the same difficulty in judging of the very creative element in human literature. And this is the first and last dignity of Dickens; that he was a creator. He did not point out things, he made them. We may disapprove of Mr. Guppy, but we recognize him as a creation flung down like a miracle out of an upper sphere; we can pull him to pieces, but we could not have put him together. We can destroy Mrs. Gamp in our wrath, but we could not have made her in our joy. Under this disadvantage any book about Dickens must definitely labour. Real primary creation (such as the sun or the birth of a child) calls forth not criticism, not appreciation, but a kind of incoherent gratitude. This is why most hymns about God are bad; and this is why most eulogies on Dickens are bad. The eulogists of the divine and of the human creator are alike inclined to appear sentimentalists because they are talking about something as very real. In the same way love-letters always sound florid and artificial because they are about something real.

Any chapter such as this chapter must therefore in a sense be inadequate. There is no way of dealing properly with the ultimate greatness of Dickens, except by offering sacrifice to him as a god; and this is opposed to the etiquette of our time. But something can perhaps be done in the way of suggesting what was the quality of this creation. But even in considering its quality we ought to remember that quality is not the whole question. One of the godlike things about Dickens is his quantity, his quantity as such, the enormous output, the incredible fecundity of his invention. I have said a moment ago that not one of us could have invented Mr. Guppy. But even if we could have stolen Mr. Guppy from

Dickens we have still to confront the fact that Dickens would have been able to invent another quite inconceivable character to take his place. Perhaps we could have created Mr. Guppy; but the effort would certainly have exhausted us; we should be ever afterwards wheeled about in a bath-chair at Bournemouth.

Nevertheless there is something that is worth saying about the quality of Dickens. At the very beginning of this review I remarked that the reader must be in a mood, at least, of democracy. To some it may have sounded irrelevant: but the Revolution was as much behind all the books of the nineteenth century as the Catholic religion (let us say) was behind all the colours and carving of the Middle Ages. Another great name of the nineteenth century will afford an evidence of this; and will also bring us most sharply to the problem of the literary quality of Dickens.

Of all these nineteenth-century writers there is none, in the noblest sense, more democratic than Walter Scott. As this may be disputed, and as it is relevant, I will expand the remark. There are two rooted spiritual realities out of which grow all kinds of democratic conception or sentiment of human equality. There are two things in which all men are manifestly and unmistakably equal. They are not equally clever or equally muscular or equally fat, as the sages of the modern reaction (with piercing insight) perceive. But this is a spiritual certainty, that all men are tragic. And this, again, is an equally sublime spiritual certainty, that all men are comic. No special and private sorrow can be so dreadful as the fact of having to die. And no freak or deformity can be so funny as the mere fact of having two legs. Every man is important if he loses his life; and every man is funny if he loses his hat, and has to run after it. And the universal test everywhere of whether a thing is popular, of the people, is whether it employs vigorously these extremes of the tragic and the comic. Shelley, for instance, was an aristocrat, if ever there was one in this world. He was a Republican, but he was not a democrat: in his poetry there is every perfect quality except this pungent and popular stab. For the tragic and the comic you must go, say, to Burns, a poor man. And all over the world, the folk literature, the popular literature, is the same. It consists of very dignified sorrow and very undignified fun. Its sad tales are of broken hearts; its happy tales are of broken heads.

These, I say, are two roots of democratic reality. But they have in more civilized literature, a more civilized embodiment of form. In literature such as that of the nineteenth century the two elements appear somewhat thus. Tragedy becomes a profound sense of human dignity. The other and jollier element becomes a delighted sense of human variety. The first supports equality by saying that all men are equally sublime. The second supports equality by observing that all men are equally interesting.

In this democratic aspect of the interest and variety of all men, there is, of course, no democrat so great as Dickens. But in the other matter, in the idea of the dignity of all men, I repeat that there is no democrat so great as Scott. This fact, which is the moral and enduring magnificence of Scott, has been astonishingly overlooked. His rich and dramatic effects are gained in almost every case by some grotesque or beggarly figure rising into a human pride and rhetoric. The common man, in the sense of the paltry man, becomes the common man in the sense of the universal man. He declares his humanity. For the meanest of all the modernities has been the notion that the heroic is an oddity or variation, and that the things that unite us are merely flat or foul. The common things are terrible and startling, death, for instance, and first love: the things that are common are the things that are not commonplace. Into such high and central passions the comic Scott character will suddenly rise. Remember the firm and almost stately answer of the preposterous Nicol Jarvie when Helen Macgregor seeks to browbeat him into condoning lawlessness and breaking his bourgeois decency. That speech is a great monument of the middle class. Molière made M. Jourdain talk prose; but Scott made him talk poetry. Think of the rising and rousing voice of the dull and gluttonous Athelstane when he answers and overwhelms De Bracy. Think of the proud appeal of the old beggar in the *Antiquary* when he rebukes the duellists. Scott was fond of describing kings in disguise. But all his characters are kings in disguise. He was, with all his errors, profoundly possessed with the old religious conception, the only possible democratic basis, the idea that man himself is a king in disguise.

In all this Scott, though a Royalist and a Tory, had in the strangest way, the heart of the Revolution. For instance, he

regarded rhetoric, the art of the orator, as the immediate weapon
of the oppressed. All his poor men make grand speeches, as they
did in the Jacobin Club, which Scott would have so much detested.
And it is odd to reflect that he was, as an author, giving free speech
to fictitious rebels while he was, as a stupid politician, denying it
to real ones. But the point for us here is this: that all this popular
sympathy of his rests on the graver basis, on the dark dignity of
man. 'Can you find no way?' asks Sir Arthur Wardour of the beggar
when they are cut off by the tide. 'I'll give you a farm . . . I'll make
you rich.' . . . 'Our riches will soon be equal,' says the beggar, and
looks out across the advancing sea.

Now, I have dwelt on this strong point of Scott because it is the
best illustration of the one weak point of Dickens. Dickens had
little or none of this sense of the concealed sublimity of every
separate man. Dickens's sense of democracy was entirely of the
other kind; it rested on the other of the two supports of which
I have spoken. It rested on the sense that all men were wildly
interesting and wildly varied. When a Dickens character becomes
excited he becomes more and more himself. He does not, like the
Scott beggar, turn more and more into man. As he rises he grows
more and more into a gargoyle or grotesque. He does not, like
the fine speaker in Scott, grow more classical as he grows more
passionate, more universal as he grows more intense. The thing can
only be illustrated by a special case. Dickens did more than once, of
course, make one of his quaint or humble characters assert himself
in a serious crisis or defy the powerful. There is, for instance, the
quite admirable scene in which Susan Nipper (one of the greatest
of Dickens's achievements) faces and rebukes Mr. Dombey. But
it is still true (and quite appropriate in its own place and manner)
that Susan Nipper remains a purely comic character throughout her
speech, and even grows more comic as she goes on. She is more
serious than usual in her meaning, but not more serious in her
style. Dickens keeps the natural diction of Nipper, but makes her
grow more Nipperish as she grows more warm. But Scott keeps the
natural diction of Baillie Jarvie, but insensibly sobers and uplifts
the style until it reaches a plain and appropriate eloquence. This
plain and appropriate eloquence was (except in a few places at
the end of *Pickwick*) almost unknown to Dickens. Whenever he

made comic characters talk sentiment comically, as in the instance of Susan, it was a success, but an avowedly extravagant success. Whenever he made comic characters talk sentiment seriously it was an extravagant failure. Humour was his medium; his only way of approaching emotion. Wherever you do not get humour, you get unconscious humour. . . .

On the Alleged Optimism of Dickens

In one of the plays of the decadent period, an intellectual expressed the atmosphere of his epoch by referring to Dickens as 'a vulgar optimist'. I have in a previous chapter suggested something of the real strangeness of such a term. After all, the main matter of astonishment (or rather of admiration) is that optimism should be vulgar. In a world in which physical distress is almost the common lot, we actually complain that happiness is too common. In a world in which the majority is physically miserable we actually complain of the sameness of praise; we are bored with the abundance of approval. When we consider what the conditions of the vulgar really are, it is difficult to imagine a stranger or more splendid tribute to humanity than such a phrase as vulgar optimism. It is as if one spoke of 'vulgar martyrdom' or 'common crucifixion'.

First, however, let it be said frankly that there is a foundation for the charge against Dickens which is implied in the phrase about vulgar optimism. It does not concern itself with Dickens's confidence in the value of existence and the intrinsic victory of virtue; that is not optimism but religion. It is not concerned with his habit of making bright occasions bright, and happy stories happy; that is not optimism, but literature. Nor is it concerned even with his peculiar genius for the description of an almost bloated joviality; that is not optimism, it is simply Dickens. With all these higher variations of optimism I deal elsewhere. But over and above all these there is a real sense in which Dickens laid himself open to the accusation of a vulgar optimism, and I desire to put the admission of this first, before the discussion that follows. Dickens did have a disposition to make his characters at all costs happy, or, to speak more strictly, he had a disposition to make them comfortable rather than happy. He had a sort of literary hospitality; he too often treated his characters as if they were his guests. From a host is always expected, and always ought to be expected as long as human civilization is healthy, a strictly physical benevolence, if you will, a kind of coarse benevolence. Food and fire and such things should always be the symbols of the man entertaining men; because they are things which all men beyond question have in common. But something more than this is needed from a man who is imagining and making men, the artist, the man who is not receiving men, but rather sending them forth.

As I shall remark in a moment in the matter of the Dickens villains, it is not true that he made every one thus at home. But he did do it to a certain wide class of incongruous characters, he did it to all who had been in any way unfortunate. It had needed its origin (a very beautiful origin) in his realization of how much a little pleasure was to such people. He knew well that the greatest happiness that has been known since Eden is the happiness of the unhappy. So far he is admirable. And as long as he was describing the ecstasy of the poor, the borderland between pain and pleasure, he was at his highest. Nothing that has ever been written about human delights, no Earthly Paradise, no Utopia has ever come so near the quick nerve of happiness as his descriptions of the rare extravagances of the poor; such an admirable description, for instance, as that of Kit Nubbles taking his family to the theatre. For he seizes on the real source of the whole pleasure; a holy fear. Kit tells the waiter to bring the beer. And the waiter, instead of saying, 'Did you address that language to me,' said, 'Pot of beer, sir; yes, sir.' That internal and quivering humility of Kit is the only way to enjoy life or banquets; and the fear of the waiter is the beginning of dining. People in this mood 'take their pleasures sadly'; which is the only way of taking them at all.

So far Dickens is supremely right. As long as he was dealing with such penury and such festivity his touch was almost invariably sure. But when he came to more difficult cases, to people who for one reason or another could not be cured with one good dinner, he did develop this other evil, this genuinely vulgar optimism of which I speak. And the mark of it is this: that he gave the characters a comfort that had no especial connection with themselves; he threw comfort at them like alms. There are cases at the end of his stories in which his kindness to his characters is a careless and insolent kindness. He loses his real charity and adopts the charity of the Charity Organization Society; the charity that is not kind, the charity that is puffed up, and that does behave itself unseemly. At the end of some of his stories he deals out his characters a kind of outdoor relief.

I will give two instances. The whole meaning of the character of Mr. Micawber is that a man can be always almost rich by constantly expecting riches. The lesson is a really important one in our sweeping modern sociology. We talk of the man whose life is a failure; but Micawber's life never is a failure, because it is always a crisis. We think constantly of the man who if he looked back would see that his existence was unsuccessful; but Micawber never does look back; he always looks forward, because the bailiff is coming tomorrow. You cannot say he is defeated, for his absurd battle never ends; he cannot despair of life, for he is so much occupied in living. All this is of immense importance in the understanding of the poor; it is worth all the slum novelists that ever insulted democracy. But how did it happen that the man who created this Micawber could pension him off at the end of the story and make him a successful colonial mayor? Micawber never did succeed, never ought to succeed; his kingdom is not of this world. But this is an excellent instance of Dickens's disposition to make his characters grossly and incongruously comfortable. There is another instance in the same book. Dora, the first wife of David Copperfield, is a very genuine and amusing figure; she has certainly far more force of character than Agnes. She represents the infinite and divine irrationality of the human heart. What possessed Dickens to make her such a dehumanized prig as to recommend her husband to marry another woman? One could easily respect a husband who after time and development made such a marriage, but surely not a wife who desired it. If Dora had died hating Agnes we should know that everything was right, and that God would reconcile the irreconcilable. When Dora dies recommending Agnes we know that everything is wrong, at least if hypocrisy and artificiality and moral vulgarity are wrong. There, again, Dickens yields to a mere desire to give comfort. He wishes to pile up pillows round Dora; and he smothers her with them, like Othello.

This is the real vulgar optimism of Dickens: it does exist; and I have deliberately put it first. Let us admit that Dickens's mind was far too much filled with pictures of satisfaction and cosiness and repose. Let us admit that he thought principally of the pleasures of the oppressed classes; let us admit that it hardly cost him any artistic pang to make out human beings as much happier than they are. Let us admit all this, and a curious fact remains.

For it was this too easily contented Dickens, this man with cushions at his back and (it sometimes seems) cotton wool in his ears; it was this happy dreamer, this vulgar optimist who alone of modern writers did really destroy some of the wrongs he hated and bring about some of the reforms he desired. Dickens did help to pull down the debtors' prisons; and if he was too much of an optimist he was quite enough of a destroyer. Dickens did drive Squeers out of his Yorkshire den; and if Dickens was too contented, it was more than Squeers was. Dickens did leave his mark on parochialism, on nursing, on funerals, on public executions, on workhouses, on the Court of Chancery. These things were altered; they are different. It may be that such reforms are not adequate remedies; that is another question altogether. The next sociologists may think these old Radical reforms quite narrow or accidental. But such as they were, the old Radicals got them done; and the new sociologists cannot get anything done at all. And in the practical doing of them Dickens played a solid and quite demonstrable part; that is the plain matter that concerns us here. If Dickens was an optimist he was an uncommonly active and useful kind of optimist. If Dickens was a sentimentalist he was a very practical sentimentalist.

And the reason of this is one that goes deep into Dickens's social reform, and like every other real and desirable thing, involves a kind of mystical contradiction. If we are to save the oppressed, we must have two apparently antagonistic emotions in us at the same time. We must think the oppressed man intensely miserable, and at the same time intensely attractive and important. We must insist with violence upon his degradation; we must insist with the same violence upon his dignity. For if we relax by one inch the one assertion, men will say he does not need saving. And if we relax by one inch the other assertion, men will say he is not worth saving. The optimists will say that reform is needless. The pessimists will say that reform is hopeless. We must apply both simultaneously to the same oppressed man; we must say that he is a worm and a god; and we must thus lay ourselves open to the accusation (or the compliment) of transcendentalism. This is, indeed, the strongest argument for the religious conception of life. If the dignity of man is an earthly dignity we shall be tempted to deny his earthly degradation. If it is a heavenly dignity we can admit the earthly degradation with all the candour of Zola. If we are idealists about the other world we can be realists about this world. But that is not here the point. What is quite evident is that if a logical praise of the poor man is pushed too far, and if a logical distress about him is pushed too far, either will involve wreckage to the central paradox of reform. If the poor man is made too admirable he ceases to be pitiable; if the poor man is made too pitiable he becomes merely contemptible. There is a school of smug optimists who will deny that he is a poor man. There is a school of scientific pessimists who will deny that he is a man.

Out of this perennial contradiction arises the fact that there are always two types of the reformer. The first we may call for convenience the pessimistic, the second the optimistic reformer. One dwells upon the fact that souls are being lost; the other dwells upon the fact that they are worth saving. Both, of course, are (so far as that is concerned) quite right, but they naturally tend to a difference of method, and sometimes to a difference of perception. The pessimistic reformer points out the good elements that oppression has destroyed; the optimistic reformer, with an even fiercer joy, points out the good elements that it has not destroyed. It is the case for the first reformer that slavery has made men slavish. It is the case for the second reformer that slavery has not made men slavish. The first describes how bad men are under bad conditions. The second describes how good men are under bad conditions. Of the first class of writers, for instance, is Gorky. Of the second class of writers is Dickens.

But here we must register a real and somewhat startling fact. In the face of all apparent probability, it is certainly true that the optimistic reformer reforms much more completely than the pessimistic reformer. People produce violent changes by being contented, by being far too contented. The man who said that 'revolutions are not made with rose-water' was obviously inexperienced in practical human affairs. Men like Rousseau and Shelley do make revolutions, and do make them with rose-water; that is, with a too rosy and sentimental view of human goodness. Figures that come before and create convulsion and change (for instance, the central figure of the New Testament) always have the air of walking in an unnatural sweetness and calm. They give us their peace ultimately in blood and battle and division; not as the world giveth give they unto us.

Nor is the real reason of the triumph of the too-contented reformer particularly difficult to define. He triumphs because he keeps alive in the human soul an invincible sense of the thing being worth doing, of the war being worth winning, of the people being worth their deliverance. I remember that Mr. William Archer, some time ago, published in one of his interesting series of interviews, an interview with Mr. Thomas Hardy. That powerful writer was represented as saying, in the course of the conversation, that he did not wish at the particular moment to define his opinion with regard to the ultimate problem of whether life itself was worth living. There are, he said, hundreds of remediable evils in this world. When we have remedied all these (such was his argument), it will be time enough to ask whether existence itself under its best possible conditions is valuable or desirable. Here we have presented, with a considerable element of what can only be called unconscious humour, the plain reason of the failure of the pessimist as a reformer. Mr. Hardy is asking us, I will not say to buy a pig in a poke; he is asking us to buy a poke on the remote chance of there being a pig in it. When we have for some few frantic centuries tortured ourselves to save mankind, it will then be 'time enough' to discuss whether they can possibly be saved. When, in the case of infant mortality, for example, we have exhausted ourselves with the earth-shaking efforts required to save the life of every individual baby, it will then be time enough to consider whether every individual baby would not have been happier dead. We are to remove mountains and bring the millennium, because then we can have a quiet moment to discuss whether the millennium is at all desirable. Here we have the low-water mark of the impotence of the sad reformer. And here we have the reason of the paradoxical triumph of the happy one. His triumph is a religious triumph; it rests upon his perpetual assertion of the value of the human soul and of human daily life. It rests upon his assertion that human life is enjoyable because it is human. And he will never admit, like so many compassionate pessimists, that human life ever ceases to be human. He does not merely pity the lowness of men; he feels an insult to their elevation. Brute pity should be given only to brutes. Cruelty to animals is cruelty and a vile thing; but cruelty to a man is not cruelty, it is treason. Tyranny over a man is not tyranny, it is rebellion, for man is royal. Now, the practical weakness of the vast mass of modern pity for the poor and the oppressed is precisely that it is merely pity; the pity is pitiful, but not respectful. Men feel that the cruelty to the poor is a kind of cruelty to animals. They never feel that it is justice to equals; nay, it is treachery to comrades. This dark scientific pity, this brutal pity, has an elemental sincerity of its own; but it is entirely useless for all ends of social reform. Democracy swept Europe with the sabre when it was founded upon the Rights of Man. It has done literally nothing at all since it has been founded only upon the wrongs of man. Or, more strictly speaking, its recent failure has been due to its not admitting the existence of any rights, or wrongs, or indeed of any humanity. Evolution (the sinister enemy of revolution) does not especially deny the existence of God; what it does deny is the existence of man. And all the despair about the poor, and the cold and repugnant pity for them, has been largely due to the vague sense that they have literally relapsed into the state of the lower animals.

A writer sufficiently typical of recent revolutionism – Gorky – has called one of his books by the eerie and effective title *Creatures that once were Men*. That title explains the whole failure of the Russian revolution. And the reason why the English writers, such as Dickens, did with all their limitations achieve so many of the actual things at which they aimed was that they could not possibly have put such a title upon a human book. Dickens really helped the unfortunate in the matters to which he set himself. And the reason is that across all his books and sketches about the unfortunate might be written the common title, 'Creatures that Still are Men'.

There does exist, then, this strange optimistic reformer; the man whose work begins with approval and ends with earthquake. Jesus Christ was destined to found a faith which made the rich poorer and the poor rich; but even when He was going to enrich them, He began with the phrase, 'Blessed are the poor.' The Gissings and the Gorkys say, as an universal literary motto, 'Cursed are the poor.' Among a million who have faintly followed Christ in this divine contradiction, Dickens stands out especially. He said, in all his reforming utterances, 'Cure poverty'; but he said in all his actual descriptions, 'Blessed are the poor.' He described their happiness, and men rushed to remove their sorrow. He described them as human, and men resented the insults to their humanity. It is not difficult to see why, as I said at an earlier stage of this book, Dickens's denunciations have had so much more practical an effect than the denunciations of such a man as Gissing. Both agreed that the souls of the people were in a kind of prison. But Gissing said that the prison was full of dead souls. Dickens said that the prison was full of living souls. And the fiery cavalcade of rescuers felt that they had not come too late.

Of this general fact about Dickens's descriptions of poverty there will not, I suppose, be any serious dispute. The dispute will only be about the truth of those descriptions. It is clear that whereas Gissing would say, 'See how their poverty depresses the Smiths or the Browns', Dickens says, 'See how little, after all, their poverty can depress the Cratchits.' No one will deny that he made a special feature of the poor. We will come to the discussion of the veracity of these scenes in a moment. It is here sufficient to register in conclusion of our examination of the reforming optimist, that Dickens certainly was such an optimist, and that he made it his business to insist upon what happiness there is in the lives of the unhappy. His poor man is always a Mark Tapley, a man the optimism of whose spirit increases if anything with the pessimism of his experience. It can also be registered as a fact equally solid and quite equally demonstrable that this optimistic Dickens did effect great reforms.

The reforms in which Dickens was instrumental were indeed, from the point of view of our sweeping social panaceas, special and limited. But perhaps, for that reason especially, they afford a compact and concrete instance of the psychological paradox of which we speak. Dickens did definitely destroy – or at the very least help to destroy – certain institutions: he destroyed those institutions simply by describing them. But the crux and peculiarity of the whole matter is this, that, in a sense, it can really be said that he described these things too optimistically. In a real sense, he described Dotheboys Hall as a better place than it is. In a real sense, he made out the workhouse as a pleasanter place than it can ever be. For the chief glory of Dickens is that he made these places interesting; and the chief infamy of England is that it has made these places dull. Dullness was the thing that Dickens's genius could never succeed in describing, his vitality was so violent that he could not introduce into his books the genuine impression even of a moment of monotony. If there is anywhere in his novels an instant of silence, we only hear more clearly the hero whispering with the heroine, the villain sharpening his dagger, or the creaking of the machinery that is to give out the god from the machine. He could splendidly describe gloomy places, but he could not describe dreary places. He could describe miserable marriages, but not monotonous marriages. It must have been genuinely entertaining to be married to Mr. Quilp. This sense of a still incessant excitement he spreads over every inch of his story, and over every dark tract of his landscape. His idea of a desolate place is a place where anything can happen, he has no idea of that desolate place where nothing can happen. This is a good thing for his soul, for the place where nothing can happen is hell. But still, it might reasonably be maintained by the modern mind that he is hampered in describing human evil and sorrow by this inability to imagine tedium, this dullness in the matter of dullness. For, after all, it is certainly true that the worst part of the lot of the unfortunate is the fact that they have long spaces in which to review the irrevocability of their doom. It is certainly true that the worst days of the oppressed man are the nine days out of ten in which he is not oppressed. This sense of sickness and sameness Dickens did certainly fail or refuse to give. When we read such a description as that excellent one – in detail – of Dotheboys Hall, we feel that, while everything else is accurate, the author does, in the words of the excellent Captain Nares in Stevenson's *Wrecker*, 'draw the dreariness rather mild'. The boys at Dotheboys were, perhaps, less bullied, but they were certainly more bored. For, indeed, how could anyone be bored with the society of so sumptuous a creature as Mr. Squeers? Who would not put up with a few illogical floggings in order to enjoy the conversation of a man who could say, 'She's a rum 'un is Natur' . . . Natur' is more easier conceived than described.' The same principle applies to the workhouse in *Oliver Twist*. We feel vaguely that neither Oliver nor anyone else could be entirely unhappy in the presence of the purple personality of Mr. Bumble. The one thing he did not describe in any of the abuses he denounced was the soul-destroying potency of routine. He made out the bad school, the bad parochial system, the bad debtor's prison as very much jollier and more exciting than they may really have been. In a sense, then, he flattered them; but he destroyed them with the flattery. By making Mrs. Gamp delightful he made her impossible. He gave every one an interest in Mr. Bumble's existence; and by the same act gave every one an interest in his destruction. It would be difficult to find a stronger instance of the utility and energy of the method which we have, for the sake of argument, called the method of the optimistic reformer. As long as low Yorkshire schools were entirely colourless and dreary, they continued quietly tolerated by the public and quietly intolerable to the victims. So long as Squeers was dull as well as cruel he was permitted; the moment he became amusing as well as cruel he was destroyed. As long as Bumble was merely inhuman he was allowed. When he became human, humanity wiped him right out. For in order to do these great acts of justice we must always realize not only the humanity of the oppressed, but even the humanity of the oppressor. The satirist had, in a sense, to create the images in the mind before, as an iconoclast, he could destroy them. Dickens had to make Squeers live before he could make him die.

In connection with the accusation of vulgar optimism, which I have taken as a text for this chapter, there is another somewhat odd thing to notice. Nobody in the world was ever less optimistic than Dickens in his treatment of evil or the evil man. When I say optimist in this matter I mean optimism, in the modern sense, of an attempt to whitewash evil. Nobody ever made less attempt to whitewash evil than Dickens. Nobody black was ever less white than Dickens's black. He painted his villains and lost characters more black than they really are. He crowds his stories with a kind of villain rare in modern fiction – the villain really without any 'redeeming point'. There is no redeeming point in Squeers, or in Monks, or in Ralph Nickleby, or in Bill Sikes, or in Quilp, or in Brass, or in Mr. Chester, or in Mr. Pecksniff, or in Jonas Chuzzlewit, or in Carker, or in Uriah Heep, or in Blandois, or in a hundred more. So far as the balance of good and evil in human characters is concerned, Dickens certainly could not be called a vulgar optimist. His emphasis on evil was melodramatic. He might be called a vulgar pessimist.

Some will dismiss this lurid villainy as a detail of his artificial romance. I am not inclined to do so. He inherited, undoubtedly, this unqualified villain as he inherited so many other things, from the whole history of European literature. But he breathed into the blackguard a peculiar and vigorous life of his own. He did not show any tendency to modify his blackguardism in accordance with the increasing considerateness of the age; he did not seem to wish to make his villain less villainous; he did not wish to imitate the analysis of George Eliot, or the reverent scepticism of Thackeray. And all this works back, I think, to a real thing in him, that he wished to have an obstreperous and incalculable enemy. He wished to keep alive the idea of combat, which means, of necessity, a combat against something individual and alive. I do not know whether, in the kindly rationalism of his epoch, he kept any belief in a personal devil in his theology, but he certainly created a personal devil in every one of his books.

A good example of my meaning can be found, for instance, in such a character as Quilp. Dickens may, for all I know, have had originally some idea of describing Quilp as the bitter and unhappy cripple, a deformity whose mind is stunted along with his body. But if he had such an idea, he soon abandoned it. Quilp is not in the least unhappy. His whole picturesqueness consists in the fact that he has a kind of hellish happiness, an atrocious hilarity that makes him go bounding about like an indiarubber ball. Quilp is not in the least bitter; he has an unaffected gaiety, an expansiveness, an universality. He desires to hurt people in the same hearty way that a good-natured man desires to help them. He likes to poison people with the same kind of clamorous camaraderie with which an honest man like to stand them drink. Quilp is not in the least stunted in mind; he is not in reality even stunted in body – his body, that is, does not in any way fall short of what he wants it to do. His smallness gives him rather the promptitude of a bird or the precipitance of a bullet. In a word, Quilp is precisely the devil of the Middle Ages; he belongs to that amazingly healthy period when even lost spirits were hilarious.

This heartiness and vivacity in the villains of Dickens is worthy of note because it is directly connected with his own cheerfulness. This is a truth little understood in our time, but it is a very essential one. If optimism means a general approval, it is certainly true that the more a man becomes an optimist the more he becomes a melancholy man. If he manages to praise everything, his praise will develop an alarming resemblance to a polite boredom. He will say that the marsh is as good as the garden; he will mean that the garden is as dull as the marsh. He may force himself to say that emptiness is good, but he will hardly prevent himself from asking what is the good of such good. This optimism does exist – this optimism which is more hopeless than pessimism – this optimism which is the very heart of hell.

Against such an aching vacuum of joyless approval there is only one antidote – a sudden and pugnacious belief in positive evil. This world can be made beautiful again by beholding it as a battlefield. When we have defined and isolated the evil thing, the colours come back into everything else. When evil things have become evil, good things, in a blazing apocalypse, become good. There are some men who are dreary because they do not believe in God; but there are many others who are dreary because they do not believe in the devil. The grass grows green again when we believe in the devil, the roses grow red again when we believe in the devil.

No man was more filled with the sense of this bellicose basis of all cheerfulness than Dickens. He knew very well the essential truth, that the true optimist can only continue an optimist so long as he is discontented. For the full value of this life can only be got by fighting; the violent take it by storm. And if we have accepted everything, we have missed something – war. This life of ours is a very enjoyable fight, but a very miserable truce. And it appears strange to me that so few critics of Dickens or of other romantic writers have noticed this philosophical meaning in the undiluted villain. The villain is not in the story to be a character; he is there to be a danger – a ceaseless, ruthless, and uncompromising menace, like that of wild beasts or the sea. For the full satisfaction of the sense of combat, which everywhere and always involves a sense of equality, it is necessary to make the evil thing a man; but it is not always necessary, it is not even always artistic, to make him a mixed and probable man. In any tale, the tone of which is at all symbolic, he may quite legitimately be made an aboriginal and infernal energy. He must be a man only in the sense that he must have a wit and will to be matched with the wit and will of the man chiefly fighting. The evil may be inhuman, but it must not be impersonal, which is almost exactly the position occupied by Satan in the theological scheme.

But when all is said, as I have remarked before, the chief fountain in Dickens of what I have called cheerfulness, and some prefer to call optimism, is something deeper than a verbal philosophy. It is, after all, an incomparable hunger and pleasure for the vitality and the variety, for the infinite eccentricity of existence. And this word 'eccentricity' brings us, perhaps, nearer to the matter than any other. It is, perhaps, the strongest mark of the divinity of man that he talks of this world as 'a strange world', though he has seen no other. We feel that all there is is eccentric, though we do not know what is the centre. This sentiment of the grotesqueness of the universe ran through Dickens's brain and body like the mad blood of the elves. He saw all his streets in fantastic perspectives, he saw all his cockney villas as top heavy and wild, he saw every man's nose twice as big as it was, and every man's eyes like saucers. And this was the basis of his gaiety – the only real basis of any philosophical gaiety. This world is not to be justified as it is justified by the mechanical optimists; it is not to be justified as the best of all possible worlds. Its merit is not that it is orderly and explicable; its merit is that it is wild and utterly unexplained. Its merit is precisely that none of us could have conceived such a thing, that we should have rejected the bare idea of it as miracle and unreason. It is the best of all impossible worlds.

Notes

1. Coren, Michael, *Gilbert: The Man Who Was G. K. Chesterton*, p. 135.
2. Chesterton, G. K., *Autobiography*, Chapter 1.
3. Coren, op. cit., pp. 34–35.
4. The full text appears in Appendix B of Maisie Ward's *Gilbert Keith Chesterton*.
5. Quoted in Maisie Ward, op. cit., p. 90.
6. Coren, op. cit., p. 119.
7. Letter from Edward Macdonald, quoted in Maisie Ward, op. cit., p. 163.
8. Chesterton, G. K., 'Mr. McCabe and a Divine Frivolity', From *Heretics*.
9. Chesterton, G. K., *Orthodoxy*, Chapter VII, 'The Eternal Revolution'.
10. Chesterton, G. K., *The Superstition of Divorce*.
11. Chesterton, G. K., *The Man Who Was Thursday*.
12. Chesterton, G. K., *Charles Dickens*.
13. Chesterton, G. K., *The Everlasting Man*.
14. Chesterton, G. K., *Heretics*.
15. Chesterton, G. K., *St. Thomas Aquinas*, Chapter 1, 'On Two Friars'.
16. Chesterton, G. K., *Autobiography*, Chapter XVI, 'The God with the Golden Key'.
17. Ibid.
18. Ward, Maisie, op. cit., p. 244.
19. Lewis, C. S., *The Screwtape Letters*, Letter XXV.
20. Chesterton, G. K., *Orthodoxy*, Chapter VIII, 'The Romance of Orthodoxy'.

A Chesterton Chronology

Year	Life	Work	Contemporary Publications and Events
1874	Chesterton born, 29th May.		Disraeli becomes Prime Minister. Lawn tennis invented. Bruckner: 4th Symphony. Hardy: *Far from the Madding Crowd*.
1881	Family moves to Warwick Gardens.		Gladstone in second year of second ministry. Natural History Museum opens. Panama Canal begun. James: *Portrait of a Lady*. Stevenson: *Virginibus Puerisque*. Wilde: Poems.
1887	Attends St. Paul's School.		Queen Victoria's Golden Jubilee. Parnell involved in Phoenix Park murders. Conan Doyle: *A Study in Scarlet*. Zola: *La Terre*. Browning: *Parleyings with Certain People*.
1892	Attends Slade School and University College, London.		Shaw: *Widowers' Houses*. Yeats: *The Countess Cathleen*. Kipling: *Barrack-Room Ballads*.
1895	Employment with Redway and then T. Fisher Unwin.		Jameson Raid. Cinematograph patented. Röntgen experiments with X-Rays. Wilde imprisoned. Wells: *The Time Machine*. Hardy: *Jude the Obscure*. Kipling: *The Second Jungle Book*.

1900	Meets Hilaire Belloc.	*Greybeards at Play.* *'The Wild Knight' and other poems.*	Relief of Mafeking. First Zeppelin made. Labour Party initiated. Freud: *The Interpretation of Dreams.* Elgar: *The Dream of Gerontius.* Conrad: *Lord Jim.* Shaw: *Captain Brassbound's Conversion.*
1901	Marries Frances Blogg. Moves to Overstrand Mansions. Begins association with *Daily News* and *The Defendant.*		Death of Queen Victoria. Accession of Edward VII. Roosevelt becomes President of USA. Marconi transmits morse signals across the Atlantic. First electric tram in London. Mann: *Buddenbrooks.* Yeats: *Poems.*
1902		*Twelve Types.*	Boer War ends. Caruso makes first record. Potter: *Peter Rabbit.* Nesbit: *Five Children and It.* Masefield: *Salt-Water Ballads.* Belloc: *The Path to Rome.*
1903		*Robert Browning.* *Varied Types.*	Women's Social and Political Union demands votes for women. Ford Motor Co. founded. Wright brothers fly 852 feet. British speed limit increased to 20 mph. Butler: *The Way of All Flesh.* James: *The Ambassadors.* Synge: *In the Shadow of the Glen.*
1904		*G. F. Watts.* *The Napoleon of Notting Hill.*	Outbreak of Russo-Japanese War. Royce produces his first car. A. C. Bradley: *Shakespearean Tragedy.* Barrie: *Peter Pan.* Rolfe: *Hadrian VII.* Chekhov: *The Cherry Orchard.*
1905	Begins to write for the *Illustrated London News.*	*The Club of Queer Trades.* *Heretics.*	Motorbuses first used in London. Forster: *Where Angels Fear to Tread.* London: *White Fang.* Conan Doyle: *The Return of Sherlock Holmes.* Shaw: *Major Barbara; Man and Superman.*

1906	Meets George Bernard Shaw in Rodin's Paris studio. This is probably but not demonstrably their first meeting.	*Charles Dickens.*	Simplon Tunnel opened. Launching of HMS *Dreadnought*. Fowler: *The King's English*. Nesbit: *The Railway Children*. de la Mare: *Poems*.
1908		*The Man Who Was Thursday*. *All Things Considered*. *Orthodoxy*.	Asquith becomes Prime Minister. First Boy Scout Troop set up by Baden-Powell. Bennett: *The Old Wives' Tale*. Grahame: *The Wind in the Willows*. Yeats: *Collected Works*.
1909	Moves to Overroads, Beaconsfield.	*George Bernard Shaw*. *Tremendous Trifles*.	Old age pensions for over-70s. Bleriot makes first cross-Channel flight. Selfridges opens. Pound: *Exultations*; *Personae*. Buchan: *Prester John*. Meredith: *Last Poems*.
1910		*The Ball and the Cross*. *What's Wrong with the World*. *Alarms and Discursions*. *William Blake*. *Five Types*.	Death of Edward VII. Accession of George V. Dominion of S. Africa formed. Crippen arrested by means of a radio message to ship. Noyes: *Collected Poems*. Forster: *Howards End*. Belloc: *Verses*. Shaw: *Misalliance*.
1911	Begins to contribute to *Eye Witness* (later, the *New Witness*).	*A Chesterton Calendar*. *Appreciations and Criticisms of the Works of Charles Dickens*. *The Innocence of Father Brown*. *The Ballad of the White Horse*.	National Insurance Act. Germans send gunboat to Agadir and cause international incident. Amundsen reaches South Pole. Italians in Libya use aircraft for first time in war. Brooke: *Poems*. Lawrence: *The White Peacock*. Beerbohm: *Zuleika Dobson*. Pound: *Canzoni*.

1912		*Manalive.* *A Miscellany of Men.*	War in the Balkans. Scott's expedition reaches South Pole. Sinking of the *Titanic*. Jung: *The Psychology of the* *Unconscious.* Mann: *Death in Venice.* Belloc: *The Servile State.*
1913	Involvement in Marconi Scandal along with brother, Cecil.	*The Victorian Age in* *Literature.* *Magic.*	Suffragette killed by King's horse at Derby. Panama Canal completed. First woman magistrate in Britain. Stravinsky: *The Rite of Spring.* Alain-Fournier: *Le Grand* *Meaulnes.* Bentley: *Trent's Last Case.* Shaw: *Androcles and the Lion.* Frost: *A Boy's Will.*
1914	Falls ill and loses consciousness for three months.	*The Flying Inn.* *The Wisdom of* *Father Brown.* *The Barbarism* *of Berlin.*	Outbreak of First World War. Home Rule Act for Ireland. First Zeppelin raid. Saki: *Beasts and Superbeasts.* Shaw: *Pygmalion.* Hardy: *Satires of Circumstance.*
1915	Recovers from his illness.	*Letters to an Old* *Garibaldian.* *Poems.* *Wine, Water and* *Song* (rep. from *The* *Flying Inn*). *The Crimes of England.*	Battles of Ypres, Neuve Chapelle and Loos. Gallipoli landings. Nurse Cavell executed by Germans. Sinking of *Lusitania*. Lawrence's *The Rainbow* deemed obscene. Buchan: *The Thirty-Nine Steps.* Woolf: *The Journey Out.* Ford: *The Good Soldier.* E. Sitwell: *The Mother and* *Other Poems.*
1916	Replaces Cecil as editor of *New Witness*.		Battles of Verdun and Somme. Compulsory military service introduced. Holst: *The Planets.* Joyce: *A Portrait of the Artist as* *a Young Man.* W. H. Davies: *Collected Poems.* Flecker: *Collected Poems.*

1917		*Lord Kitchener.* *A Short History* *of England.*	Germany tries to cut off Britain with submarine warfare. USA enters war. Balfour announces intent of establishing Jewish homeland in Palestine. Douglas: *South Wind*. Eliot: *Prufrock and Other* *Observations*. E. Thomas: *Poems*. Kipling: *The Years Between*.
1918	Cecil Chesterton dies. Gilbert visits Ireland.		Kaiser abdicates. Armistice signed. Parliamentary Reform Act gives vote to men over 21, women over 30. School leaving age raised to 14. Bartok: *Duke Bluebeard's Castle*. Strachey: *Eminent Victorians*. Hopkins: (d. 1889) *Poems* (ed. Bridges). Sassoon: *Counter-Attack and* *Other Poems*.
1919	Visits Palestine.	*Irish Impressions.*	League of Nations established. Mussolini founds Fascist party. Hitler founds National Socialist German Workers' Party. Bauhaus formed. Elgar: *Cello Concerto*. Ashford: *The Young Visiters*. Hardy: *Collected Poems*. Firbank: *Valmouth*.
1920	Lecture tour to the United States.	*The Superstition* *of Divorce.* *The Uses of Diversity.* *The New Jerusalem.*	Anglican Church disestablished in Wales. American women given the vote. Prohibition starts in USA. Women allowed to take degrees at Oxford University. Christie: *The Mysterious* *Affair at Styles*. Mansfield: *Bliss and* *Other Stories*. Wells: *The Outline of History*. Owen: (d. 1918) *Poems*.

1922	Received into the Catholic Church.	*Eugenics and Other Evils.* *What I Saw in America.* *The Ballad of St. Barbara and Other Verses.* *The Man Who Knew Too Much.*	Bonar Law becomes Prime Minister. Mussolini becomes premier of Italy. BBC starts radio broadcasts. Tutankhamun's tomb discovered. Vaughan Williams: 3rd Symphony. Cummings: *The Enormous Room.* Eliot: *The Waste Land.* E. Sitwell: *Facade.* Joyce: *Ulysses.*
1923		*Fancies versus Fads.* *St. Francis of Assisi.*	Russian Civil War ends with formation of USSR. Hitler's putsch in Munich fails. End of Ottoman Empire with republic formed under Mustapha Kemal. Huxley: *Antic Hay.* Shaw: *St. Joan.* Stevens: *The Harmonium.*
1925	Editor of *GK's Weekly* until his death.	*Tales of the Longbow.* *The Everlasting Man.* *William Cobbett.*	First Surrealist exhibition in Paris. The Charleston and Louis Armstrong are popular. Coward: *Hay Fever.* Fitzgerald: *The Great Gatsby.* Woolf: *Mrs. Dalloway.* Hugh MacDiarmid: *Sangschaw.* Muir: *First Poems.*
1926	Beginning of the Distributist League.	*The Incredulity of Father Brown.* *The Outline of Sanity.* *The Queen of Seven Swords.* *The Catholic Church and Conversion.*	The General Strike. Adoption of children legalized in England. USA build first liquid fuel rocket. Hemingway: *The Sun Also Rises.* O'Casey: *The Plough and the Stars.* Milne: *Winnie-the-Pooh.* Travers: *Rookery Nook.*

1927	Makes visit to Poland.	*The Return of Don Quixote.* *Collected Poems.* *The Secret of Father Brown.* *The Judgment of Dr. Johnson.* *Robert Louis Stevenson.* *Gloria in Profundis* (Ariel poem).	Trotsky expelled from Communist Party. Lindbergh makes first flight across Atlantic. First 'talkie' film: *The Jazz Singer.* Williamson: *Tarka the Otter.* Marquis: *archy and mehitabel.* Woolf: *To the Lighthouse.* Lowes: *The Road to Xanadu.*
1928	Broadcast debate with George Bernard Shaw.	*Generally Speaking.*	Women over 21 given vote in Britain. Fleming discovers properties of penicillin. Foam rubber developed. BBC transmits television stills. Blunden: *Undertones of War.* Huxley: *Point Counter Point.* Lawrence: *Lady Chatterley's Lover.* Waugh: *Decline and Fall.*
1929	Visits Rome.	*The Poet and the Lunatics.* *The Thing.* *GKC as MC.* *The Turkey and the Turk.* *Ubi Ecclesia* (Ariel poem). *The Father Brown Stories* (omnibus volume).	Collapse of New York Stock Exchange brings in the Depression. Cocteau: *Les Enfants Terribles.* Green: *Living.* Graves: *Goodbye to All That.* Hemingway: *A Farewell to Arms.* Shaw: *The Apple Cart.*
1930	Second lecture tour of the United States.	*Four Faultless Felons.* *The Resurrection of Rome.* *Come to Think of it.* *The Grave of Arthur* (Ariel poem).	Nazis elected to Reichstag. Ghandi defies British Government. Destruction of Airship R101. Stravinsky: Symphony of Psalms. Ransome: *Swallows and Amazons.* Maugham: *Cakes and Ale.* Auden: *Poems.*
1931	Continues US tour.	*All Is Grist.*	Britain in financial crisis. Gold standard abandoned. MacDonald forms National Government. Electric razor invented. Woolf: *The Waves.* O'Neill: *Mourning Becomes Electra.* Binyon: *Collected Poems.*

1932	Begins regular BBC broadcasts.	*Chaucer.* *Sidelights on New London and Newer York.*	Stalin begins purges. First motorway built from Bonn to Cologne. Gibbons: *Cold Comfort Farm.* Leavis: *New Bearings in English Poetry.* Greene: *Stamboul Train.* Huxley: *Brave New World.*
1933		*All I Survey.* *St. Thomas Aquinas.*	Hitler appointed Chancellor. Concentration camps started. Prohibition repealed in USA. Invention of polythene. Stein: *The Autobiography of Alice B. Toklas.* Orwell: *Down and Out in Paris and London.* de la Mare: *The Fleeting and other Poems.* Lorca: *Blood Wedding.*
1934	Visits Rome and Sicily.	*Avowals and Denials.*	Night of the Long Knives. Mao Tse-Tung starts 'Long March' across China. Bonnie and Clyde ambushed. Hilton: *Goodbye, Mr. Chips.* Sayers: *The Nine Taylors.* Waugh: *A Handful of Dust.* Dylan Thomas: *Eighteen Poems.*
1935		*The Scandal of Father Brown.* *The Well and the Shallows.*	Baldwin PM for third time. Italy invades Abyssinia. In Britain, Hore-Belisha introduces pedestrian crossings and increases speed limit to 30 mph. First Penguin Books issued, price sixpence. Eliot: *Murder in the Cathedral.* MacNeice: *Poems.*
1936	Dies at Beaconsfield.	*As I Was Saying.*	Death of George V and accession of Edward VIII. Edward abdicates. Accession of George VI. Start of Spanish Civil War. C. S. Lewis: *The Allegory of Love.* Smith: *Novel on Yellow Paper.*

Posthumous Publications

Autobiography
The Paradoxes of Mr. Pond
The Coloured Lands
The End of the Armistice
The Common Man
A Handful of Authors
The Glass Walking Stick
Lunacy and Letters
Where All Roads Lead
The Spice of Life
Chesterton on Shakespeare